KT-166-261

FINLAND'S LAKELAND

TAMPERE

HELSINKI

TURKU

SOUTHERN FINLAND

STOCKHOLM

AROUND STOCKHOLM

CENTRAL SWEDEN

DALARNA

SWEDEN'S GREAT LAKES

GÖTEBORG

SOUTHERN SWEDEN

BORNHOLM

THE HEART OF NORWAY

OSLO

OSLO AND ITS FJORDS

SWEDEN'S WEST COAST

COPENHAGEN

ZEALAND

FUNEN

JUTLAND

BERGEN

SOUTHERN NORWAY

INSIGHT GUIDES
SCANDINAVIA

Contents

THE BEST OF SCANDINAVIA: TOP ATTRACTIONS

Whether you want to see the Northern Lights, take a Finnish sauna, go island-hopping off the coast of Denmark, explore Norway's fjords or see brown bears in Sweden, we'll point you in the right direction.

△ **Vigeland Sculpture Park, Oslo**. An open-air sculpture park filled with huge, arresting figures, many writhing and tumbling, in Vigeland's fantastic vision of humanity. A favourite with Oslo inhabitants. See page 179.

△ **Fjords**. Norway's breathtaking fjords are an experience not to be missed. The Hurtigruten coastal steamships make 34 ports of call, heading way up north from Bergen to the North Cape and Kirkenes. See page 214.

▽ **Stockholm**. Europe's first Green Capital floats on 14 islands; visit Gamla Stan, a medieval maze of alleyways and enchanting architecture. See page 239.

△ **Orsa Björnpark, Sweden**. Old honeypaws, the King of the Forest, is a shy creature in the wild: this park offers a great chance to see brown bears and their cubs up close. See page 275.

△ **Bohuslän Coast**. Sun-worshippers flock to the sandy beaches of Bohuslän in summer, or take to sailing boats and kayaks to explore thousands of offshore islands, skerries, rocks and reefs. See page 265.

▷ **Turku**. Finland's oldest city and medievawl capital, the "cradle of Finnish culture" brims with history and vitality. See page 323.

◁ **Åland Islands**. Explore this lush collection of islands off the west coast of Finland by bike. See page 321.

△ **Bergen**. Norway's most beautiful city sits on a craggy shoreline surrounded by hills, and makes an ideal base for a fjord holiday. A highlight of any visit is a summer concert at Troldhaugen, the former villa of composer Edvard Grieg. See page 199.

▽ **Icefjord, Disko Bay, Greenland**. Countless icebergs calve from Greenland's most productive glacier and float out to sea in a glinting parade at this Unesco World Heritage site, near Ilulissat. See page 156.

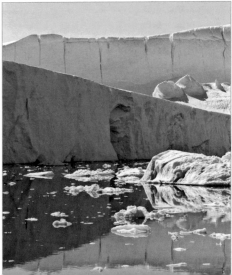

△ **Helsinki**. Discover great works by the masters of Finnish art at the Ateneum, one among many great museums in the capital, then head for the galleries and boutiques of the design district. See page 301.

◁ **Medieval Trondheim**. Norway's ancient capital and its third-largest city is steeped in history and atmosphere. See page 217.

△ **Bornholm**. A well-kept Danish secret, the island of Bornholm is the sunniest place in Scandinavia. Hire a bicycle and explore its rugged coastline and unique medieval round churches. See page 136.

△ **Porvoo**. An elegant Finnish town, with a gorgeous riverside setting and a rich cultural heritage. In winter, with its low wooden houses set against the snow, their chimneys expelling smoke, exudes a fairytale atmosphere. See page 318.

△ **Inlandsbanan**. This historic railway runs from Sweden's heartland right into the Arctic Circle, stopping at tiny stations for meals, and to shoo reindeer off the tracks. See page 278.

◁ **Frederiksborg Slot, Hillerød**. Scandinavia's largest Renaissance castle, built across three islands in the middle of a lake, comes straight from the pages of a children's storybook. See page 134.

△ **Northern Lights**. The eerie aurora borealis billows like smoke and streaks like silent fireworks across the winter skies in Greenland and Arctic Scandinavia. Experience them in Tromsø, "Gateway to the Arctic", and Norway's far north. See page 22.

△ **Bog bodies, Jutland**. Denmark's peaty soil has preserved some of Europe's most remarkable archaeological finds, like the 2,000-year-old bodies of Tollund Man and Graballe Man, now in Silkeborg and Moesgaard museums. See page 149.

△ **Kungsleden Trail**. Sweden's most famous long-distance walking path wends its way through the mountains of Lapland, through dark forests and broad green valleys scattered with Alpine flowers. See pages 75 and 385.

△ **Viking Ship Museum, Roskilde**. State-of-the-art ships and superb seafaring knowledge swept the Vikings to success: this excellent museum contains five original Viking vessels, and lets visitors row a reconstruction around the fjord. See page 134.

△ **Visby, Gotland**. Turreted walls encircle this medieval Hanseatic trading town, full of crooked houses, cobbled streets and rose-covered ruins. In August, troubadours and jousting knights bring the past to life during the Medeltidsveckan festival. See page 259.

THE BEST OF SCANDINAVIA: EDITOR'S CHOICE

Stunning scenic journeys, the best museums, festivals, family fun and unique attractions... here, at a glance, are our recommendations for a memorable visit to Scandinavia, plus some money-saving tips.

OUTDOOR ADVENTURES

Husky safaris, reindeer-sledging and snowmobiling (Finland). Explore Lapland's icy wastes in classic fashion, driven along by a team of huskies or reindeer, or hop on a skidoo. See page 345.

Cycling (Denmark). Flat countryside and fabulous bike paths make Denmark a cycling dream. Try Bornholm island for a taste of two-wheeled freedom. See page 139.

Cross-country skiing (Oslo, Norway). The Oslomarka area has an incredible 2,500km (1,500 miles) of cross-country skiing trails. See page 175.

Sailing (Sweden). Experience the joy of sailing the Stockholm archipelago on a full-day sailing adventure in a historic schooner or a modern luxury yacht. See page 252.

Bear-watching (Finland). Get up close and be mesmerised by Finland's brown bears in their natural habitat. See page 343.

Hiking (Norway). Scandinavia offers plenty of exceptional hiking, but there's something magical about the vast Jotunheimen National Park as well as the Hordaland area, with its impressive Trolltunga rock formation. See page 207.

The railway from Myrdal to Flåm winds through magnificent mountain scenery.

BEST JOURNEYS

Hurtigruten (Norway). The world-famous postal boat sails up Norway's fjord-lined coast, stopping in at 34 picturesque ports along its 12-day route. See page 214.

Göta Kanal (Sweden). Cross the country in the most leisurely manner possible, along Sweden's 19th-century engineering masterpiece, the Göta Kanal. See page 271.

Karelia (Finland). Pull on your walking boots and launch yourself into the wilderness – the region's 1,000km (620-mile) of trails take in four stunning national parks. See page 74.

King's Trail (Sweden). Suitable to all levels, this 150km (93-mile) historic walking trail affords superb mountain views. See page 385.

Flåmsbana (Norway). The mountain railway journey from Myrdal to Flåm packs the most dramatic scenery – ravines, rivers and toppling waterfalls – into its 20km (12-mile) route. This is part of the "Norway in a Nutshell" trip that adopts a variety of forms of transport to experience Norway's exhilarating natural beauty. See page 210.

Snowmobiling through Lapland's snowy terrain.

BEST MUSEUMS

Vasa Museum carvings.

Vasa Museum (Stockholm, Sweden). Carvings of cherubs and mermaids festoon this spectacular 17th-century warship. See page 243.

Viking Ship Museum (Oslo, Norway). On display are splendid Viking longships unearthed in southern Norway. See page 181.

Skansen (Stockholm, Sweden). Over 150 traditional Swedish buildings at the world's oldest open-air museum. See page 242.

Louisiana (Humlebæk, Denmark). This huge modern-art gallery contains an impressive collection, including works by Giacometti and Andy Warhol. See page 133.

Alvar Aalto Museum (Jyväskylä, Finland). Discover Finland's best-loved designer and architect. See page 331.

National Gallery (Oslo, Norway). Among the paintings here is Edvard Munch's *The Scream*. See page 178.

ARoS Århus Art Museum (Århus, Denmark). An overview of Danish contemporary art with extraordinary views from a rainbow glass walkway. See page 147.

Museum of Prehistory (Moesgård, Denmark). Visit the 2,000-year-old Grauballe Man in a sleek brand new exhibition house with a sloping grass rooftop that visitors can stroll onto. See page 149.

Sami woman, Finnmark, Norway.

ONLY IN SCANDINAVIA

Sami culture. The nomadic Sami still base their calendar and culture around ancient reindeer-herding traditions. See page 78.

Lumilinna (Kemi, Finland). Each year, the marvellous Snow Castle is fashioned from blocks of snow and ice. See page 339.

Scandinavian style. From Saab cars, IKEA furniture and Arne Jacobsen chairs to Marimekko textiles, the success of Nordic design is a global phenomenon. See page 83.

Baltic skerries

(Sweden). Navigate through waters loaded with 24,000 islands and islets of the Stockholm archipelago – charter a sailing boat or hop on a ferry. See page 252.

Father Christmas. Several places in Scandinavia claim Santa Claus as their own. Joulupukin Pajakylä in Lapland allegedly has the real thing. See page 347.

Stave churches (Norway). Two of the most striking of these ancient wooden churches are at Urnes and the Heddal in Telemark. See pages 210 and 191.

FINEST FOOD TRADITIONS

Crayfish parties. In July and August, crayfish parties are the speciality to celebrate the long days in Finland and Sweden.

Artistic sandwiches. *Smørrebrød* in Denmark, *smörgåsbord* in Sweden and *voileipäpöytä* in Finland – all wonderfully pretty hot-and-cold buffet dishes.

Pickled herring. An acquired taste, but one that will always bring

back fond memories of Scandinavia.

Cloudberries. Picked and devoured in Scandinavian forests in late summer and early autumn.

New Nordic cuisine. The rise of this type of food, led by Copenhagen's pioneering restaurant, Noma, has put Scandinavia's capitals firmly on the culinary map.

New Nordic cuisine has taken the world by storm.

SCANDINAVIA FOR FAMILIES

Legoland (Billund, Denmark). Win eternal admiration by taking your children to Legoland, with waterpark, rides and the marvellous Miniland, created from 20 million bricks. See page 150.

Tivoli (Copenhagen, Denmark). Utterly delightful theme park and gardens, right in the heart of the capital city. Fountains and fairground rides as well as jugglers and acrobats make this a fun family day out for everyone. See page 116.

Moomin World (Finland). A theme park for smaller children based on the Moomin books by Tove Jansson. The blue-coloured Moomin House is the main attraction. See page 402.

Glasriket (Småland, Sweden). For something a little different, let your children paint, engrave and even blow their own glass at a traditional glassworks. See page 258.

Egeskov Slot (Funen, Denmark). One of Denmark's most famous historic sights. This well-preserved fairytale castle has a gardenful of endearing attractions, including one of the world's biggest permanent mazes. See page 143.

Norwegian Museum of Cultural History (Oslo, Norway). The Folk Museum on Bygdøy peninsula offers something for children of all ages. Horse and wagon rides, livestock, folk dancing and music and a playground, all in a charming historic setting. See page 181.

The Blue Planet (Copenhagen, Denmark). Scandinavia's biggest state-of-the-art aquarium opened in 2013 with a spectacular shark tunnel. See page 118.

Midsummer bonfire at Frederiksborg, Denmark.

BEST FESTIVALS

Midsummer. Celebrated with bonfires, parties and great gusto across Scandinavia on the nearest weekend to 23 June.

Savolinna Opera Festival (Finland). International artists perform at Olavinlinna castle, on Lake Pihlajavesi, in July at Finland's most famous cultural festival.

Holmenkollen Ski Festival (Norway). Oslo's Holmenkollen ski jump is the focus of this traditional sports event, held annually in March.

Horsens Middle Ages Festival (Denmark). Medieval history is brought to life in late August at this lively festival, with music, dancing and theatrical performances.

Dalhalla Summer Music (Sweden). There's something to appeal to everyone at this cavernous open-air arena, set in the depths of an abandoned limestone quarry near Rättvik. Its summer-long music programme encompasses opera, jazz, pop and rock.

Roskilde (Denmark). Northern Europe's largest annual music festival, held over four days in early July, features world-famous rock and pop bands.

Bergen International Festival (Norway). Norway's answer to the Edinburgh festival; from late May to early June artists and musicians flock to Bergen from all over the world to perform in this, the loveliest of Norway's cities. Ibsen and Grieg are, of course, focal points.

All aboard the Legoland train, in Billund, East Jutland, Denmark.

BEST IN SCANDINAVIAN DESIGN

Oslo Opera House (Norway). This striking building in white granite and glass sitting on the Bjørvika waterfront is one of Oslo's top attractions. Other landmark constructions in the area include the Barcode and the Akrobaten bridge. See page 176.

Carl Larsson's house (Sundborn, Sweden). The artist's beautiful riverside cottage is a humbling example of love, family life and Swedish design working in perfect harmony. See page 274.

Finnish Jugendstil (Finland). The National Romantics used art and architecture to express independence from Russian rule: you can admire their beautiful Art Nouveau buildings in Helsinki's Katajanokka area. See page 308.

Designmuseum Danmark (Copenhagen, Denmark). Ceramics, furniture, textiles, prints and posters – the best in Danish design is here. See page 121.

Lysøen (Norway). The residence of violin virtuoso Ole Bull, on an island outside Bergen, is a daring blend of styles that never fails to wow visitors. See page 203.

Dramatic Preikestolen.

NATURAL WONDERS

Stockholm archipelago (Sweden). Right on the city's doorstep lie 24,000 islets and skerries, a sight that gave author August Strindberg "goose pimples of sheer delight". See page 249.

Preikestolen (Norway). Featured in every tourist brochure on Norway, majestic Pulpit Rock has unbeatable fjord views. See page 191.

Jostedalsbreen Glacier (Sognefjord, Norway). Europe's largest glacier. See page 210.

Lake Päijänne (Finland). 33,000 islands are yours to explore in Finland's Lakeland. See page 329.

Cliffs of Møn (Denmark). Hunt for fossils along the edges of Denmark's most famous landscape, the shining white chalk cliffs of Møn. See page 135.

Ruska (Lapland). The dazzling electric colours of nature as seen during *Ruska* (Indian summer) in late August in Lapland. See page 345.

Oslo Opera House sits dramatically on the waterfront.

MONEY-SAVING TIPS

Tourist Cards. All of Scandinavia's capitals (and some larger cities such as Göteborg) offer 24- 48- and 72-hour tourist cards, which are well worth the money as the price includes admission to many museums, galleries and tourist attractions, and usually free access to public transport or car-parking.

Hostels. Youth hostels in Scandinavia are well worth considering: they tend to be good value, family-orientated and have excellent facilities. Bring your own sheets and towels to save on rental costs.

City Bikes. Getting around Scandinavian cities by bicycle is generally a liberating experience. Borrow public bicycles in Norway (Oslo, Drammen and Trondheim), Sweden (Stockholm) and Denmark (Copenhagen) and explore further afield.

Food. Self-service buffet breakfasts in hostels and hotels are a great boon to the thrifty traveller. Fill up in the morning; at lunchtime snack on sandwiches or look for the daily special on restaurant menus; many places do "early bird" evening deals, usually between 5.30pm and 7pm.

Nature. Wild, empty space is Scandinavia's greatest treasure. Get back to nature with a tent and immerse yourself in solitude.

Free Festivals. Check what's on and when. Many Scandinavian festivals have free as well as ticketed events: for example, at the Copenhagen Jazz Festival in July, the city streets become a venue.

Karelian forest, Finland.

Reindeer herd in Finnmark,
Norway.

NORTHERLY NEIGHBOURS

At the top of the map, but no longer aloof, the Scandinavian countries are Europe's best-kept secret.

Bronze-Age rock carvings at Tanumshede, Sweden.

To fly over Scandinavia is to discover a vast, sparsely inhabited, natural landscape of sparkling fjords and rocky mountains, glassy lakes and rushing rivers, dense forests and frozen tundra, extending from temperate Denmark far north to the land of the Sami and including Greenland and the Faroe Islands.

Norway, Denmark, Sweden and Finland are among Europe's most ancient civilisations. Early Norse traders ventured deep into Asia, leaving graphic runic graffiti in their wake, and later, the infamous Vikings pillaged round the coasts of Ireland, Britain and France, establishing a network of Norse kingdoms. They were followed by kings, queens and tsars who schemed and battled. Borders shifted, unions came and went, and by the start of the 20th century four distinct nations emerged, growing into today's modern, highly individualistic countries.

The Nordic reputation for cool reserve has had its day, and visitors receive a warm welcome. But cool design remains: everything from bottle openers to new buildings has the stamp of chic Scandinavian understatement. Copenhagen, Oslo, Stockholm and Helsinki are vibrant capitals with some of the most inspirational museums and art collections in Europe, and Århus was deservedly chosen as a European Capital of Culture in 2017.

Colourful Nyhavn, Copenhagen.

An inherent love of nature is deeply rooted within the national psyches. At the slightest excuse Scandinavians will take to the outdoors, on bicycles along Denmark's winding lanes, skiing on floodlit trails around Oslo, escaping to red-painted waterside cottages in Sweden, or plunging from sauna to ice pool in Finland. Arrive in any of the Scandinavian countries in Midsummer and you'll find the locals dancing and feasting around maypoles and bonfires.

Transport and communications are excellent: roads join southerly Denmark with the North Cape, railways penetrate Lapland, ferries ply the fjords and link remote islands, and planes cut journey times. Far from being an isolated northern region, Scandinavia is just a short step from its European neighbours.

A howling husky in Lapland.

A WILD LAND

Scandinavia's countryside is cherished by its green-minded inhabitants, a spiritual retreat full of lush berries and wild animals.

Stretching from mainland Europe to the North Pole's back yard, Scandinavia's vast territory covers all manner of environments. From well-groomed Danish farmland to Norway's wild and breathtaking fjords; from Sweden's great lakes and islands to bear-filled Finnish forests; from white-sand beaches full of sunbathers to empty oceans drifting with icebergs – there's a Scandinavian habitat to suit every mood.

Country retreats

Scandinavians, many only a few generations away from rural life, have a deep-rooted love of nature. With thousands of square miles of pristine countryside, and an enshrined legal freedom to roam through it at will, it's no wonder that they head for the hills at every opportunity. In Norway, Sweden and Finland, the family *hytte*, *stuga* or *mökki* is not just a holiday cottage, but a place for spiritual rejuvenation.

Berry-picking is a common summer pastime – crowberries, bilberries, lingonberries and precious Arctic brambles and cloudberries appear on kitchen tables, supplemented in autumn by earthy mushrooms.

Scandinavians have always integrated home and landscape, from wood-built cottages to turf-roofed houses. Modern architecture uses glass to bring nature inside, and the simple lines of Scandinavian design often echo the curves of a lakeshore, or the pale slant of winter sunlight.

Scandinavian landscapes

Finland was flattened during the Ice Age. As the earth warmed, the melting icesheet left behind low rounded hills and tens of thousands of lakes – an angler's delight and perfect

Wind farms are sprouting throughout the Finnish countryside.

for wild swimmers. "Finland" and "forests" go together like coffee and cake – trees cover 86 percent of the land, and although much of the timber is felled for export, the forests are managed as naturally as possible.

Denmark's countryside was also compressed – Møllehøj in East Jutland is its zenith, a vertiginous 170 metres (560ft) above sea level. Free from trees, 40 percent of Denmark is rich arable farmland, glowing with blossom in spring, and golden harvest fields in late summer. With more than 7,400 km (4,600 miles) of coastline, no point in the country is more than a 45-minute drive from the sea. North Zealand and Jutland are frilled by sandy beaches, which draw countless summer visitors, as do the wonderful 70-million-year-old chalk cliffs at Møns Klint.

Sweden's south, too, is characterised by mild, fertile farmland. But Skåne's rolling fields soon give way to vast lakes and heavy woods. In Dalarna, Lake Siljan was formed not by glacial retreat, but by the catastrophic impact of a 2.5km (1.5-mile) wide meteorite. In the northwest of Sweden, the land rises, Alpine peaks shrug off their tree cover, and huge boulders, glaciers and rushing rivers dominate the scenery.

Composer Edvard Grieg acknowledged a hint of the "trollish" in some of his music, a

north you go, the more days of midnight sun there are – in Svalbard, it shines for a steady 126 days. The phenomenon is caused by the tilt of the earth as it orbits the sun. This lopsided angle ensures that the North Pole always

The Arctic skies contain other odd light displays besides the aurora borealis. Sundogs, ice pillars, arcs and coronas often appear in high-latitude skies, as ice crystals in the atmosphere cause the sun's light to refract.

Mushroom-picking is a favourite pastime.

Bears roam the northeast of Finland.

sound that summons up Norway's mountains, fjords and valleys. Whereas the Ice Age levelled much of Finland, Sweden and Denmark, in Norway the Scandinavian Mountains run like a rocky spine over 46 percent of the country, from south to northern tip. Glaciers scored great grooved valleys into the rock, which filled with water and became Norway's amazing fjords when the ice retreated.

Midnight sun

Like Scandinavians, the sun in summer shows no inclination to sleep. From within the Arctic Circle, it appears to observers that the "midnight sun" never sets, but simply travels around the horizon in a circle. The further

faces sunwards in summer… and sits in darkness all winter long.

Northern Lights

As summer ebbs away, the gloom is relieved by the bewitching greens, purples, pinks and reds of the aurora borealis, or Northern Lights, which flicker and pulse across the winter sky. Many a high-latitude tale was born while watching the display: the lights were the Sami, out looking for reindeer, or sparks crackling from a fox's fur as it ran across the sky, or even the spirits of the restless dead.

The scientific explanation is no less astonishing. The lights are caused by streams of charged particles – "solar wind" – that flare into space from our sun. When the wind comes into contact with the earth's magnetic field, it is drawn towards the poles where its electrical charge agitates particles of oxygen and nitrogen in the atmosphere, making them glow. Solar activity follows an 11-year cycle, due to peak in 2022. The light displays during this period will be even more spectacular, and witnessed in areas that don't usual experience these mesmeric light displays. In March 2015, the Faroe Islands experienced an even more unusual spectacle – a full solar eclipse.

Environmental challenges

Scandinavia is blessed with vast uninhabited landscapes, and a small, environmentally-aware population who recycle, have a passion for bicycles and public transport, and see their countryside as a national asset that must be protected. Their environmental record puts the rest of Europe to shame. Stockholm was designated Europe's first Green Capital in 2010, while Copenhagen held this title in 2014. Sweden and Finland plan to be carbon-neutral by 2050, Norway by 2030, and Denmark by 2025. Wind supplies 40 percent of Denmark's electricity, while the largest number of environmentally-friendly electric vehicles per capita in the world is to be found in Norway.

There are some headaches. Nitrogen run-off from Sweden's southern farmland contributes to Baltic Sea pollution; in Denmark, overfishing is a serious concern; and in Finland's forests, fertiliser use causes water pollution. The demands of a greedy 21st century are seen most clearly in Greenland, whose melting icecaps and stranded polar bears are shorthand for global warming. Denmark and Norway have no nuclear power stations. Sweden is reassessing its own following the failure of Japan's Fukushima nuclear plant in 2011. Finland meanwhile will start operating its fifth reactor in 2015, and by 2025, it is thought that 60 percent of the country's electricity will be produced in nuclear power plants.

Finland's forests contain almost 2.2 billion sq metres (23.6 billion sq ft) of timber – enough to build a 1-metre (3ft) wide, 15-storey-high stockade around the entire planet.

Northern Lights.

SCANDINAVIAN WILDLIFE

Finland, Norway and Sweden contain an exciting array of big beasts, with the brown bear the undisputed King of the Forest. Finland's national animal once had dozens of euphemistic names, such as "forest grandfather" and "honey-eater", as it was taboo to speak the true name of such a fearsome creature. Orsa Björnpark, in Dalarna, central Sweden, is Europe's biggest bear park; and wild bear-watching tours operate on the Finland–Russia border (see page 343).

Lynx live in all three countries, although their nocturnal habits mean that they are rarely seen by visitors. The wolverine, actually part of the weasel family, is the most secretive of all Scandinavia's predators – numbers are still unknown. Wolves are fighting their way back from extinction across the region. Knobbly-kneed elk can grow to 2 metres (6.5ft) tall, and have a dangerous habit of lolloping in front of moving cars. Visitors to the far north will see reindeer, traditionally herded by the Sami. The sharp-eyed might spot lemming and foxes and, in northern Finland, the intriguing Siberian flying squirrel.

Denmark has no big forest predators, but it is good for birdlife, particularly aquatic varieties. Greenland's shores contain (rare) polar bears, lemming, Arctic foxes and hares, reindeer and musk oxen. Anyone taking a boat trip will appreciate the abundant marine life, including millions of seals, 15 whale species and walruses.

DECISIVE DATES

Early History: 10,000 BC–AD 800

From 10,000 BC

Hunter-gatherer tribes follow the melting ice northwards, establishing settlements in southern Scandinavia.

1500 BC

Trade routes are forged through the rivers of Eastern Europe to the Danube.

c.500 BC–AD 800

Iron Age Grauballe Man and Tollund Man are buried in peat bogs in Denmark.

c.AD 100

The historian Tacitus mentions the Fenni (the Sami of Finland) in his *Germania* and describes the Sveas who inhabit what is now central Sweden.

c.AD 400

Suomalaiset (Baltic Finns) settle in Finland. Sweden's influence over its "eastern province" begins.

The Viking Age

800–1060

Vikings earn a reputation as sea warriors. Swedish Vikings (Varangians) soon control trade routes to Byzantium.

830

A Benedictine monk, Ansgar (801–65), lands on Björkö in Sweden and founds a church.

861

Vikings sack Paris.

866

Vikings raid and plunder, eventually controlling most of England and Normandy.

940–95

Harald Bluetooth brings Christianity to Denmark; Olav Tryggvason uses force in his attempts to convert the Norwegian Vikings.

1001

Leifur Eiríksson discovers Vinland (America).

1050

Harald Hardrada of Norway founds Oslo.

1066

Defeat in England brings the Viking Age to an end.

Middle Ages c.1100–1500

1070

Building of Nidaros Cathedral begins in Norway.

1155

King Erik of Sweden launches a crusade into Finland; further Swedish invasions take place in 1239 and 1293.

1319–43

Inter-Scandinavian royal marriages produce a joint Norwegian–Swedish monarchy.

1362

Finland becomes a province of Sweden.

1397

The Kalmar Union unites the kingdoms of Norway, Denmark and Sweden.

1417

Eric VII of Denmark makes Copenhagen his capital and builds a palace at Helsingør.

Wars and Reformation

1520

Kristian II of Denmark invades Sweden and massacres the nobility in the "Stockholm Bloodbath". Gustav Vasa drives him out and the Kalmar Union is disbanded.

1523

In Sweden, Gustav Vasa ascends the throne, marking the start of the Vasa dynasty (1523–1720), which also holds power in Finland.

1530

The Reformation; the Lutheran faith is introduced.

A Sami family at the turn of the 19th century.

1536
Norway ceases to be an independent kingdom as the Danes take control.

1548
Mikael Agricola's translation of the Bible forms the basis of the Finnish literary language.

1588–1648
Denmark flourishes under Kristian IV (1577–1648).

1625–57
The Thirty Years War launched by the Danish king, Kristian IV, to check Swedish expansion ends in defeat for Denmark.

1714–41
Russia and Sweden battle over Finland. Under the Treaty of Turku (1743) Russia moves its border westwards.

Nineteenth Century

1801–14
During the Napoleonic Wars, English fleets twice bombard Copenhagen. Denmark sides with Napoleon and suffers defeat; Norway is ceded to Sweden.

1807–1905
Tsar Alexander I occupies Finland in 1807. In 1899 the composer Jean Sibelius writes his patriotic *Finlandia*, and Finnish resistance grows.

1812
Tsar Alexander makes Helsinki Finland's capital.

1815–1907
In Sweden, Jean-Baptiste Bernadotte, French marshal of Napoleon, succeeds to the throne as Karl XIV Johan (1818–44). The great exodus to the United States takes place.

1864
Denmark and Prussia at war. Denmark loses Schleswig—Holstein.

Modern Times

1905
Referendum in Norway leads to the end of the union with Sweden. The Danish prince Håkon VII is King of Norway.

1906
Finnish women become the first in Europe to win the vote.

1917–19
Finland declares its independence from the Soviet Union, but is plunged into civil war.

1919
The Republic of Finland is born under its first president, K.J. Ståhlberg.

1930s
Sweden and Denmark establish welfare states.

1939–48
Winter War between Finland and the Soviet Union: Finland is forced to cede land and war reparations are severe. Sweden remains neutral in World Wars I and II. Norway proclaims neutrality in World War II, but is attacked by the Germans, who also occupy Denmark.

1949
Denmark becomes a founding member of NATO.

1960s
Norway begins oil exploration.

1986
Olof Palme, Swedish prime minister and international peacemaker, is assassinated.

Tarja Halonen, Finland's first female president.

1973
Denmark joins the EEC (EU).

1995
Finland and Sweden join the EU. Norway votes against joining (1972 and 1994).

2000
Øresund bridge opens between Denmark and Sweden.

2006
Finland's first female president, Tarja Halonen, re-elected.

2011
A bomb in Oslo and shooting on Utøya island kill 76 people. The gunman, a right-wing Christian extremist, accuses Norway's Labour government of failing on immigration.

2014
Anti-immigrant sentiment is growing across all Scandinavian countries, with right-wing parties winning a substantial number of votes in European Parliament elections.

2015
A young radical Islamist goes on a killing spree in central Copenhagen, leaving two people dead and five injured at a synagogue and a café in Copenhagen.

BEGINNINGS

As the ice floes retreated, so the hunter-gatherers moved north, colonising the Nordic lands and giving rise to the Viking Age.

For 1.6 million years, Scandinavia languished under an ice-sheet that oozed out of the Jostedalsbreen in Norway, stretched as far as the British Isles and Moscow, and was 3,000 metres (9,800ft) thick. When eventually it melted, nomadic hunters and gatherers went after the plants and animals that surfaced in its wake. Some 12,000 years ago, the peninsula celebrated its final liberation from the crushing weight of the ice by rising like bread in an oven. Unleavened Denmark, however, remained barely above sea level, the land bridge with Norway and Sweden broken.

The first inhabitants

Some of the earliest arrivals in this re-sculptured land brought with them tame dogs, knew how to make leather boats, and kept a well-stocked armoury of bows, arrows, harpoons and spears. Not much else is known about them, so a case has been made for recognising the nomadic Sami as Scandinavia's quasi-aboriginals. Other schools of thought put them down as comparatively recent arrivals from Siberia.

As for the Finns, the second group of somewhat exceptional Scandinavians, a 19th-century scholar, M.A. Castren, suggested that they and anyone else speaking a Finno-Ugric language, which includes Hungarians, Estonians and the Sami, hailed from Outer Mongolia and could therefore claim kinship with the likes of Genghis Khan. An increasing number of Finns see themselves as indigenous Baltic folk who drifted into their present location between the Bronze Age and the start of the great European migration in the 5th century AD.

Tollund Man.

The origins of today's Swedes, Norwegians and Danes are also something of a mystery. In the Mesolithic era, shifting tribes of hunter-gatherers lived along the coasts of southern Scandinavia, making seasonal trips inland to hunt boar and deer in the rich forests that covered the region at the time. These inhabitants constituted one of the last major hunter-gatherer complexes in Stone Age Europe, and it was always assumed that they evolved into today's Scandinavians.

However, in 2009 genetics research conducted at Uppsala University discovered that these hunter-gatherers are not related to modern Scandinavians – in fact, they seem to have vanished entirely from the region around 4,000 years ago. The theory now is that a new influx of people must have settled at the end of the Stone Age – but who they were, nobody knows.

Bronze Age artwork

As there were still no written records in Scandinavia by the Nordic Bronze Age (1800–500 BC), we can only guess at the religion, law, language and culture of the mysterious new settlers. But they have left tantalising glimpses of their lives. Swords, shields, jewellery and musical instruments have been

men into trousers instead of belted cloaks. The beginning of the Iron Age in Scandinavia appears to have been filled with great social change and deep unrest – quantities of swords and other items have been found in peat bogs, presumed to have been sacrificed

> To facilitate carving in wood or stone, the runic alphabet consisted of permutations of straight lines. It was used initially only for names and invocations against evil spirits.

Bronze Age sun chariot, National Museum of Denmark, Copenhagen.

found across Scandinavia. The Trundholm sun chariot appears to be a religious artefact, showing a horse pulling the sun across the sky; and the well-preserved body of the Egtved Girl, found in southern Jutland, gives us a close-up view of a 3,500-year-old person and her possessions. Bronze Age rock carvings, such as those at Tanumshede in Sweden, reveal a well-appointed world of horse-drawn carts, ships with curious beaks at either end, weapons and a religion devoted to the worship of the sun and fertility.

Travellers' tales

In 500 BC, a drastic turn in the weather killed off livestock, wrecked agriculture and forced

by their desperate owners. Humans, too, have been unearthed from the depths of Denmark's bogs – Tollund Man, Grauballe Man and Elling Woman were all killed and cast into the peaty waters during these troubled centuries.

In the meantime, sun-drenched Athenians were building the Parthenon and, like most Europeans, had no idea whatsoever of Scandinavia until the voyager Pytheas of Marseilles returned a little before 300 BC with tales of a land north of Britain where it was light enough, even at midnight, to pick lice out of a shirt. The local population were barbarians who lived on millet, herbs, roots and fruit because, he noticed, they had hardly any domestic animals, and threshing generally had to be done indoors. Nevertheless, grain fermented with honey produced a giddying drink they enjoyed.

Four centuries later, the Roman historian Tacitus reported significant improvements. The Suiones (Uppland Swedes) had developed a healthy respect for wealth, recognised a king "with an unchallengeable right to obedience", and built powerful sailing ships "unusual in that there is a prow at each end". Augustus and Nero sent expeditions to find out more, and Roman contact may have inspired the Scandinavians to produce their own runic alphabet.

design appeared off the coast of Dorset, southwest England, and the local magistrate ambled down to welcome them. Heavily armed warriors leapt ashore and subjected the hapless man to a fate known as "kissing the thin lips of the axe". As his head rolled, they filled their ships with whatever caught their fancy, including a number of attractive natives, and were gone. The bemused *Anglo-Saxon Chronicle* could only say that they were apparently "Northmen from Hordaland" (Norwegians from the Bergen area). They, however, called themselves Vikings.

Weather vane from a Viking ship.

Jordanes, the 6th-century historian of the Goths, was the first to identify "Dani" among the local tribes, said to be taller than Germans and ferocious fighters. Procopius, the Byzantine historian, singled out the Sami as people who had neither crops nor wine and wore animal skins held together with sinews. Sami babies, he said, did not touch milk. Put into skin cradles and left dangling from trees while their mothers worked, they tucked into bone marrow. Procopius also described hunters on skis and an excessive enthusiasm for human sacrifice.

Raiding parties

In 789, however, the Scandinavians spoke up for themselves. Three ships of unfamiliar

VIKING SHIP DESIGN

A Viking's ticket to foreign parts was the latest evolution of the ship design first shown in Bronze Age rock carvings. The prows at either end were the extremities of a keel made out of a single oak. It could twist like a tree in the wind, hence its great strength. A fighting ship of the type found at Gokstad in Norway was 25 metres (82ft) long, 6 metres (19ft) wide, and carried a crew of 70. Clinker-built, caulked with tarred animal hair or wool, it had a hinged steering oar that swung out of the way so the ships could be aimed at a beach at full speed. An important innovation was the use of sail. Viking ships could cross the North Sea to England in 72 hours.

The Vikings returned four years later. As committed pagans, the raiders were unaffected by the sanctity of Christian monasteries stuffed with valuables. Beginning with Lindisfarne in Northumbria, they murdered monks and ransacked coastal monasteries all around the British Isles, repeating the performance every summer.

Around the same time, Swedish counterparts capitalised on the almost uninterrupted navigable grid of lakes and rivers between the Gulf of Finland and the Caspian and Black seas. At the far end lay Constantinople, the richest city

The Gokstad ship in the Viking Ship Museum, Oslo.

on earth and an inexhaustible market for northern products like amber, furs, weapons and European slaves. The Arab traveller and diplomat Ibn Fadlan was impressed by the Swedes' appearance – "perfect physical specimens, tall as date palms, blond and ruddy" – but had reservations about their insistence on exercising seigneurial rights over the merchandise in public and en masse. "A man will have sexual intercourse with slave girls while his companions look on," he said.

On a third contemporary front, Charlemagne's crusade against the heathen Saxons of northwest Germany brought him into contact with their Danish neighbours on the other side of the Eider, whose look he liked even less. As

the Danes felt exactly the same way about him and his Franks, they built the Danevirke wall across the Jutland peninsula to keep them at bay and secure the border town of Hedeby. Thus were sown the seeds of the Schleswig-

> Vikings weren't always victorious. A raid on Córdoba failed, and the emir sent a gift of 200 Vikings' heads to his Moroccan ally. Some of the vanquished Vikings converted to Islam and opened a successful cheese farm in Isla Menor!

Holstein imbroglio, a territorial dispute of such complexity that even 1,000 years later anyone dragged into it, according to 19th-century British prime minister Lord Palmerston, was in danger of going mad or dying.

Al-Tartushi, another Arab traveller, went to see Hedeby, "a large town at the farthest end of the world ocean." The carcasses of sacrificed animals swung from poles, but the main food was fish "as there is so much of it". Both men and women used eye make-up, he said (not that anyone else ever noticed), and women could unilaterally divorce their husbands whenever they felt like it.

Taken together, these developments across three fronts signalled the start of the "Viking Age" in which they went abroad to conquer most of the British Isles, carve a Norman province out of France, invade Germany, Spain and Italy, settle Iceland and Greenland, discover America, terrorise the Mediterranean, dominate the Baltic region, Poland, Russia and Ukraine, fight for and against Byzantium, attack the Muslim Caliphate in Baghdad, and contribute to the liberation of Jerusalem. Meanwhile, the pack of warring chieftainships and petty kingdoms at home was being shuffled and cut down to form the separate states that exist today.

Trade with Byzantium

Muslim conquests in Europe disrupted traditional trade, encouraging the Swedes to open up alternative routes through Russia. Apparently the Slavs then begged them to take charge of their territory. "Our land is large and fruitful but it lacks order," the message allegedly read. "Come over and rule us." By 900, Swedish influence radiated throughout Eastern Europe from their strongholds at Novgorod and Kiev. The Swedes were soon assimilated under the weight of Slavic numbers, but they left an indelible mark in the name by which they were locally known, Rus.

Polygamy and primogeniture also shaped the Viking Age. Only a tiny proportion of Scandinavia was actually habitable, and farmland could only be subdivided so many times. The whole of a patrimony generally went to the eldest son, or rather the eldest surviving son, so Swedish kings with 40 women in their harem, or Norwegian earls with a dozen sons by various wives

Denmark, his first foray in 844 opened with a rebuff at La Coruña on Spain's Atlantic coast, improved with the sacking of Lisbon, Cádiz and Seville, and ended with the loss of two ships crammed with gold, silver and prisoners to the Moors.

Terrorising the Mediterranean

Back again in 859 with a fleet of 62 red-sailed ships, Hasting negotiated the Straits of Gibraltar, sacked Algeciras, spent a week in Morocco rounding up "blue men" for subsequent sale in Ireland and then wintered on La Camar-

Ancient rock carvings of longboats in Østfold, Norway.

In Arthurian romances the Vikings were described as being "wild and savage and had not in them the love of God nor their neighbours".

gue in the Rhône Delta, "causing great annoyance and detriment to the inhabitants". Come spring, he was ready for Italy. After looting Pisa, he turned south and came across a city of such marbled magnificence that it could only be Rome.

Hasting dispatched messengers who related that their leader was dying, and his last wish was to be given a Christian burial in hallowed ground. Permission granted, the gates admitted a coffin followed by a long procession of mournful Vikings. As the local bishop was praying over the coffin it flew open and out leapt Hasting himself. The startled bishop was run through with Hasting's sword, and the mourners went off to reduce the city to ashes. Only

and concubines, were sure recipes for orgiastic fratricide. Harald Fairhair's ascendancy, c.890, went a long way towards defining Norway, but as he stripped and disbanded numerous lesser dynasties, their scions were compelled to try their luck abroad.

To begin with, Viking enterprise abroad was a matter of independent initiative, as epitomised by a certain Hasting. Born in then did Hasting learn that he had destroyed Luna, not Rome, and felt so cheated that he ordered the massacre of all male prisoners. His next port of call was Alexandria in Egypt. The campaign closed in 862 with an overland march to sack Pamplona.

England under attack

Three years later, in 865, Hasting appeared at the mouth of the Thames with a new fleet of 80 ships just as "a big heathen horde", according to the *Anglo-Saxon Chronicle*, arrived elsewhere in England under Ivar the Boneless. Their imme-

The Vikings on their way to invade England.

diate mission was to avenge a private grievance, the cruel death of their father Ragnar in a pit full of snakes, but with Hasting's fleet and other Danish private armies dotted around the country, the show took on the appearance of a concerted Danish conquest. The outcome was a Danish kingdom in England and the imposition of a stiff tax, Danegeld.

Ironically, Harald Bluetooth of Denmark (*c.*910–85) was in turn obliged to prostrate himself. His *bête noire* was the crusading Holy Roman Emperor Otto I, a German, who could be appeased only by Harald's submission to Christian baptism. Most of Europe had been Christian for five centuries or more, but Scandinavia was not inclined to abandon

paganism. Harald's son and successor, Swein Forkbeard, brushed aside his father's baptism as an aberration. The Norwegian king Olav Tryggvason (*c.*965–1000), a hell-raising pirate from the age of 12, was supposedly convinced by a wise hermit in the Scillies in England, but the methods he then employed to convert his subjects were pure Viking. Sweden remained true to paganism by turning Christian missionaries into martyrs. Sacrifices in the golden temple at Uppsala continued into the late 11th century.

Norman conquest

In France, Vikings who sailed up the Seine and attacked Paris were given 3,000kg (3 tons) of silver by Charles the Bald of France to go away, while his successor Charles the Simple ceded an entire province to Rolf (or "Rollo") the Ganger, a Viking too big to ride any horse. The province became the Duchy of Normandy, and within two centuries it was the springboard for the 1066 Norman conquest of Anglo-Danish England. But if the conquest was a great triumph for Norman arms, it also accelerated the end of the Viking Age.

Harald Hardrada of Norway (1015–66), the "Thunderbolt of the North", had tried to preempt William's seizure of England with an invasion of his own, and it was not long before Danish and Norwegian forces attempted to unseat William. But England under the Normans was a tough nut to crack; Normandy itself was no longer open to disgruntled Scandinavians, and Iceland was full. Greenland was the next possibility, and it was from here that Leifur Eiríksson set sail to see if he could find something better in the unknown world to the west. He returned with tales of Vinland, a land of warm sunshine, trees, grass and, as the name implied, grapes. His brother Thorvaldur followed his directions, and on landing in Vinland walked straight into an Indian arrow. The next assessment of the land's potential was by a fearsome woman, Freydís, who murdered most of her party en route. She was not over-impressed: the future America, she thought, was not more than "all right".

Grauballe Man was discovered in a Danish peat bog in 1952. The victim, in his mid-30s, had eaten a meal of wheat porridge before his throat was slashed and his body dumped. Estimated time of death: 300 BC.

MEDIEVAL THUGS OR MERCHANT TRADERS?

The Vikings plundered their way into the annals of Scandinavian history. But archaeology reveals there's more to these raiders than meets the eye.

At first glance the Viking legacy appears to be little more than an impressive catalogue of violence and piracy. Archaeological finds have, however, shed light not only on the way the Vikings lived (everything from the food they ate to the clothing they wore) but also on their burial traditions. Today, the Vikings are recognised for their skills as craftsmen, traders and, of course, sailors.

The Viking longship, essential for both raiding and trading, was also used to bury kings and chieftains. Superb examples can be seen at the Viking ship museums in Roskilde, Denmark, and Oslo, Norway, where textiles, household utensils and other artefacts excavated from the burial mounds around the Oslo Fjord are also on display. In Denmark, Funen's Ladby Ship Museum houses a magnificent burial ship with a dragon's head and tail.

Sites and open-air museums such as those at Birka outside Stockholm, and Denmark's Fyrkat and Trelleborg, offer a unique look into the daily lives of the Vikings. Other places of interest include the burial ground at Lindholm Høje, Jutland, and Jelling in Zealand, with its runes and burial mounds, often referred to as Denmark's "birth certificate".

Open-air museums offer activities and re-enactments, giving visitors a chance to relive the Viking experience at first hand.

The Vikings would commemorate an event or a death on runestones like this one at Lovo Church, Kalmar Lan, Sweden.

Only a handful of Viking helmets have been found, but many carvings show warriors with helmets.

11th-century Viking arm ring.

THE VIKING SILK ROUTE

This bishop's crosier from Ireland, pictured above, was found at the site of Sweden's first Viking town, Birka. Situated 30km (19 miles) west of Stockholm, Birka was founded towards the end of the 8th century.

Archaeological excavations have revealed trade networks stretching east to Byzantium and as far as China. The finds, which include silks from the Far East, Arabic coins and glass beads from the Arabic Caliphate, have challenged the belief that the Viking Age was all murder and mayhem. They point instead to a burgeoning, prosperous society made up of merchants, traders and farmers.

Birka was the first town in Sweden to come into contact with Christianity. But the town was never evangelised, and in some graves Thor's hammer was found alongside a crucifix.

The museum at Birka is open between mid-May and mid-September. Boats leave from outside Stockholm City Hall, at Stadshusbron.

Coins entered the region as a result of trading contacts both with Western Europe and the Islamic world. They were valued for their weight and purity, as it was the metal itself which was important, not the coins.

A pair of harness mounts from Gotland, known as Odin's Birds, with exaggerated beak and talons.

The Oseberg ship in Oslo's Viking Ship Museum is thought to be the tomb of a queen buried in 834 with her maidservant and most valued possessions.

WAR AND PEACE

From the end of the Viking Age to the dawn of the
20th century, kings battled for supremacy, land
changed hands and unions were made and broken.

As the Viking Age drew to a close in the 11th century, the kings of Norway, Sweden and Denmark – "all handsome and big men, of noble looks and well spoken" – met at Konghelle on the Göta River in 1098 to acknowledge one another's legitimacy and to adopt a common policy on robbery and theft, ever the crimes of greatest concern. To seal the pact, King Magnus of Norway – known as "Barelegs" since returning from Scotland sporting a kilt – married Inge of Sweden's daughter Margaret, hence "The Peace Maiden".

Five years later, however, Magnus fulfilled one of his own favourite sayings – "a king stands for his country's honour and glory, not for a long life" – by being killed in action in Ireland. Norway was carved up among his three young sons, undoing the single Norwegian kingdom hammered together by Harald Fairhair, and the prospect of smooth Scandinavian coexistence.

Kristian II of Denmark (1513–23).

Converting the heathens

Denmark's particular difficulty was not fragmentation but a succession of kings so ineffectual (e.g. "Harald the Hen") that several were simply taken out to sea and drowned. In Sweden, the throne bobbed between two dynasties who routinely murdered the opposing incumbent. Next to these goings-on, the princes of the new power in the land, the Church, looked purposeful. As comfortable in the saddle as the pulpit, Bishop Absalon of Roskilde (1128–1201) personally sorted out "the heathen Wend", a tribe of defiant Baltic pagans whose headquarters were on Rügen island. Smashing the four-headed god Svantevit, he offered everyone the choice of embracing Christ or dying immediately. The island became part of his booming diocese.

THE GREAT EXODUS

The 19th century witnessed a mass exodus of Scandinavians in search of a better life in the New World. "Potatoes, peace and vaccination" were blamed for a population explosion at home which contributed to an outflow of 750,000 Norwegian and one million Swedish emigrants – a quarter of the Swedish population.

The new settlers sent back glowing accounts of their lives in America, and money to support those left behind. These signs of prosperity and other factors such as The United States Homestead Act of 1862, which promised land almost free to settlers willing to travel west, encouraged others to follow.

With bishops like Absalon around, ambitious kings were obliged to demonstrate their religious credentials by "taking the Cross" and joining a crusade. Sigurd of Norway, one of Barelegs' sons, went to the Holy Land. Valdemar I (1131–82), a more dashing king than Denmark had seen for some time, fought 28 battles against assorted heathens. His successor Valdemar II concentrated on Estonians, and in spite of a fleet of 1,000 ships was only rescued from one certain defeat by the miraculous apparition of a red-and-white banner in the heavens. It became Denmark's national flag.

Like the Church, German and Dutch Hansa traders recognised the chaotic absence of government as an excellent opportunity. Scandinavia had an abundance of fish but a shortage of grain. By tying up the markets in both commodities, and the shipping in between, the

> The oldest national flag in the world is a source of pride among Danes. It must never touch the ground and only a pennant version may be flown at night.

The Swedish army is defeated by Peter the Great of Russia at the battle of Poltava, 1709.

Sweden annexes Finland

Erik I of Sweden did his crusader service among the Finns during the 12th century, marking the start of Sweden's 700-year annexation of Finland and Erik's climb to the status of his country's patron saint. But aggrandisement was all too easily reversed, as occurred in Denmark on Valdemar II's exit. "The crown fell off the head of the Danes," a chronicle wailed, "and they became the laughing stock for all their neighbours through civil wars and mutual destruction."

In Sweden, the saintly Erik I was murdered by the son of the king he had removed, Sverker, leaving Erik's son in no doubt about what was expected of him. He did not disappoint.

Hansa had a goose of pure gold, and it gave them a network of strategic ports and market towns across the continent. But if Scandinavia was sapped by an extortionate exchange rate between fish and grain, it was then poleaxed by the Black Death in 1349. With the population of Norway, for example, cut by more than half, economics reverted to the Stone Age.

One interlude in the slow reconstruction process was the arrival of shoals of herring so dense that fish could be caught with bare hands. Fishing vessels raced from all over Europe until some 40,000 were crammed into the Sound, temporarily loosening the Hansa's grip on the market. The 14th-century king Valdemar IV of Denmark launched a snap invasion of the Hansa's base at Visby in Gotland and, flushed with success, assumed the title of "King of the Goths". The Hansa were not amused. Throwing the resources of their 77 towns and cities into a military alliance with Sweden, they bounced Valdemar off his Danish throne and invited applications. Margrethe, the young wife of King Håkon VI of Norway, proposed their son Oluf. He was five years old.

A scheming queen

Margrethe, who had married in 1363 at the age of 10 and given birth to Oluf at 17, knew what she was doing. With Denmark under Oluf's little belt and the Norwegian crown bound to follow in due course, she encouraged him to think of himself as "the true heir to Sweden" as well, a presumption that infuriated Albrecht, the reigning king of Sweden.

Nevertheless, Margrethe had to think again when Oluf died at 17. While personally keeping the Danish throne warm, she persuaded the Norwegian nobility to recognise her grandnephew Erik of Pomerania as Oluf's successor. Erik, too, was five at this turning point in his career. Margrethe went behind Albrecht's back to offer the Swedish nobles perpetual rights to their property and privileges in exchange for their support against him. Albrecht could take no more. Raising an army of German mercenaries, he demanded satisfaction at Falköping. A chronicler was surprised by the outcome: "God gave an unexpected victory into the hands of a woman."

Margrethe's grand scheme was at last realised at Kalmar in 1397 when Erik, now 14, donned

> *Gustav Vasa, the enigmatic king portrayed on the Swedish 1,000-krona note, is credited with founding the Swedish state. He's a folkloric hero, yet his brutal behaviour led to armed rebellions in Småland and Dalarna.*

the three crowns of Norway, Denmark and Sweden. "Rash, violent and obstinate", he faced the tall order of running an empire from the Arctic Circle (including Swedish Finland) to the Eider, and west to Greenland, with no money or support from the wary nobility. Margrethe had her hands full nursing the damage caused by Erik's railings against these constraints, and she was

addressing the aftermath of a war with Holstein when she collapsed. The Danish nobility wondered aloud whether their interests might be better served by Erik's nephew, Christopher of Bavaria, and the talk in Sweden was of a separate constitution and a fresh crowned head. Meanwhile, Erik retired to Visborg Castle in Gotland and applied himself, privately and very profitably, to the business of piracy.

Stockholm Bloodbath

After more than one trial separation Denmark and Sweden were together again under the

Queen Margrethe's sarcophagus in Roskilde Cathedral.

Danish king Kristian II (1481–1559). Anti-Danish feeling was growing apace in Sweden when the Swedish assembly voted to burn the fortress of the Archbishop of Sweden, a pro-Dane, Gustav Trolle. In the event Trolle was merely imprisoned, but in 1520 the Papal Court excommunicated the Swedish regent, Sten Sture the Younger, for this act. Kristian II had the justification he sought for invading Sweden. He invited Sweden's leading nobles to a feast in Stockholm at which he chopped off the heads of 82 of Sweden's finest. This "Stockholm Bloodbath" provoked a rebellion. Kristian was driven out of Sweden and Gustav Vasa, a nobleman whose family had been victims in the massacre, seized power. Thus began a Swedish dynasty of exceptional distinction and durability.

Hounded out of Denmark, Kristian II sought refuge in the Netherlands. Norway's clergy, staunchly loyal to Rome, made him an offer of the Norwegian throne, which provoked violent intervention by Danish and Hanseatic forces with far-reaching consequences. Kristian spent the rest of his life in Sonderborg Castle, while the Norwegian Church was purged of Roman Catholics to make it Lutheran, and the Norwegian monarchy was abolished. Norway was thereafter a mere province of Denmark. The tripartite Kalmar Union was dead.

Battle on ice

A larger-than-life character, Kristian IV (1577–1648) was on the Danish throne for 52 years, building palaces and towns, turning Copenhagen into an important European capital, trebling the size of the navy, and sending explorers to investigate the possibility of a northwest passage to Asia. He took an avuncular interest in Norway, renaming Oslo after himself ("Kristiania"), but never managed to achieve friendly

The Swedish royal palace of Drottningholm, designed in the 17th century by Tessin the Elder.

LINNAEUS, THE PLANTSMAN

Carl Linnaeus (also known as von Linné; 1707–1778), the Swedish naturalist who devised the modern classification system for plants and animals, was one of the great scientists of 18th-century Scandinavia. He studied medicine at the University of Lund and botany at Uppsala. He travelled widely and was a leading figure in the founding of the Swedish Academy of Science. As chair of botany, dietetics and *materia medica* at Uppsala, he pursued his research into nomenclature. His publications include *Systema Naturae* (1735), *Philosophia Botanica* (1750) and *Species Plantarum* (1753). His house and garden in Uppsala can be visited.

relations with Sweden, and the two countries inevitably entered the Thirty Years War on opposite sides.

The battling continued, but it was the Swedish King Karl X Gustav who seized an opportunity when the Sound (Øresund) froze over during the winter of 1657. Two cavalry squadrons crossed the ice and a resounding victory cost Denmark all its territory on the Swedish side of the Sound.

The warrior king

In Karl XII (1682–1718), Sweden seemed to acquire a reincarnation of the Vikings who fought and caroused their way across Russia. Taking over the mantle of the traditional

Germanic *Drang nach Osten* (drive to the east), he collided with Peter the Great of Russia.

The Russians eventually got the better of a titanic struggle, putting Karl in the impossible position of trying to rule Sweden from his bolthole in Turkey. Finally, he rode home with two companions, a journey of 2,100km (1,300 miles), only to find that in his absence Sweden had been stripped of all his recent gains. His plan to put matters right began and ended with a siege of Frederiksten in southern Norway. The bullet through his head may have been fired by a genuine enemy sniper or

decriminalisation of fornication and adultery, and the abolition of capital punishment for all but the most unspeakable crimes. He could not have envisaged, as he extended his stately role to touch on the void in Queen Caroline Matilde's conjugal life, that he

> Sweden typically bribed North African pirates not to attack their ships, but to plunder those of the Norwegians who insisted on sailing under their own colours.

Conversation at Drottningholm, 1779.

a contracted assassin, but in any case Sweden decided to give absolutism a rest and explore constitutional government.

Denmark's first taste of quasi-constitutional government was deferred until the 1770s and even then only materialised in strange circumstances. Kristian VII's increasingly erratic behaviour clearly needed medical attention, a task entrusted to a German doctor, Johann Friederich Struensee. The patient was off his head, Struensee decided, so the best he could do was to run the country himself. And so he did.

In little more than a year, Struensee drew up 1,069 bills introducing freedom of speech and the press, a national budget, the

would be dragged out of bed at dawn and charged with just such a crime, one that still carried the supreme penalty. Locked up in Kronborg Castle at Helsingør, his partner in crime was rescued from her fate by an English warship sent by George III, himself showing signs of instability but her brother nonetheless.

The same navy was again under the guns of Kronborg Castle at the outbreak of the Napoleonic War in the early 19th century, in this instance because Denmark had sided with Russia, at that stage Napoleon's ally. While Britain bombarded Copenhagen, Tsar Alexander I occupied Finland, bringing the ages-old Swedish rule initiated by St Erik to a close.

Russia wins Finland

Russia later changed sides and was sitting with the victors when reparations were decided after the Battle of Waterloo (1815). Russia was allowed to keep Finland; Norway was detached from Denmark and handed to Sweden, albeit not as a colony but as a supposed equal in a union under a common crown.

The king in question was a curious choice: Jean-Baptiste Bernadotte was French and not only a former general of the French Revolution but a key member of Napoleon's staff. If taking the name Karl Johan was meant to help him to

Alfred Nobel (1833–96), Swedish chemist, inventor of dynamite and founder of the Nobel Prizes.

blend into his new surroundings, this was offset by his refusal to speak anything but French.

Thus reorganised, the Scandinavian states stepped into the frenzy of romantic nationalism that swept across Europe and inspired phenomenal scientific progress and a flowering of the arts. In these respects Scandinavia did its bit and more. Sweden was especially strong in the sciences; consider, for one, Linnaeus, the naturalist and Alfred Nobel, the chemist, engineer and inventor of dynamite. Denmark's most notable contributions were the writer Hans Christian Andersen (see page 145) and the philosopher Søren Kierkegaard. Norway offered Edvard Grieg (composer), Henrik Ibsen

(dramatist) and Edvard Munch (painter), and Finland (pre-Sibelius) contributed the *Kalevala*, an epic which Elias Lönnrot compiled from old ballads and songs to reinvent his country's hitherto elusive past.

Language became a vexing issue in both Finland and Norway. Mikael Agricola, the Bishop of Turku, had produced a Finnish translation of the Bible as early as 1642, and although Finnish had always been spoken by the majority of the population, it had no official status. The Russians even banned books written in Finnish. In Norway, Old Norse had gone to Iceland with the Viking settlers, while the language in Norway itself had been affected by Danish connections. Pure Danish was used for official business, in literature and by the educated classes. In the 19th century Norwegian nationalists wanted to revert to untainted Norwegian. They concocted a cocktail from Norway's surviving rural dialects called "New Norwegian".

Friends and foes

One 19th-century development was that Swedish, Danish and Norwegian (but not yet Finnish) historians could at last get together for a chat without coming to blows, and in this spirit Swedish and Danish university students took advantage of the atrocious winter of 1838, when the Sound again froze over, to walk across the ice, meet in the middle and improvise odes to Scandinavian solidarity.

If this was reminiscent of Magnus Barelegs and company at Konghelle, the dream was again upset by events in Norway, where the union with Sweden was in trouble. Norway strengthened its border fortifications, and Sweden had its army on alert before a compromise was worked out. The union dissolved in 1905, following a plebiscite that voted overwhelmingly in favour of Norwegian independence. Norway opted for a monarchy rather than a republic, and went shopping for a new king. Scandinavia braced itself for the 20th century.

When Alfred Nobel's brother Ludvig died in 1888, a French newspaper accidentally printed Alfred's obituary, condemning him for his killer invention dynamite. Historians speculate that Alfred rewrote his will, bequeathing his fortune to establish the Nobel Prizes.

THE MODERN AGE

Two world wars took their toll on the Nordic
countries, but by the end of the 20th century they
had emerged as sophisticated economic powers.

The 20th century dawned with not only the union of Sweden and Norway on the rocks but also the special relationship between Finland and Russia. A new tsar, the ill-fated Nicholas II, did not share his predecessors' fond view of Finland as a separate grand duchy. So while breakaway Norway recruited Håkon VII, né Prince Carl of Denmark, as its first independent king for 600 years, Finland was delivered into the hands of Nikolai Ivanovich Bobrikov, a hard-boiled martinet whose previous assignment had been to knock some sense into Russia's wayward Baltic provinces.

King Håkon accepted the job only after a plebiscite indicated that three-quarters of the Norwegian population wanted him. Bobrikov did not bother with such trifles. Having abolished the Finns' exemption from service in the Russian imperial forces, he was systematically shredding their freedom of speech and other rights when he was met on the staircase to the Senate by Eugen Schauman, a civil servant. Schauman put three bullets into the brute before turning the revolver on himself.

Evacuated Finnish family, 1939.

The onset of World War I

Fortunately for Finland, the tsar was too involved in war with Japan and later in the St Petersburg uprising to avenge Bobrikov's murder. Every one of 40 previous wars with Russia had gone badly for the Finns, but they were always ready to try again. The first whiff of World War I saw volunteers flocking to Germany to join a special "Jagar battalion" which duly entered the field against Russia alongside Kaiser Wilhelm's forces.

For their part, the three kings of Scandinavia met at Malmö in Sweden in December 1914 and declared their neutrality. However, putting the proclamation into practice was not so easy. After centuries of anguish over Schleswig-Holstein, Denmark was not Germany's greatest admirer, but it was in no position to defy the Kaiser's orders to mine Danish sea-lanes against the British navy. Conversely, Norway received a warning from Britain that selling fish, iron pyrites or copper to Germany would not be tolerated, and Sweden was blockaded, eventually suffering acute food shortages, for trading too eagerly with Wilhelm. The worst blow, though, was Germany's declaration of unrestricted submarine warfare in 1916. Hundreds of Scandinavian ships and crews commandeered by Britain went to the bottom, with heavy losses.

On Russia's withdrawal from the war after the Bolshevik revolution in 1917, Lenin appealed directly to sympathisers in Scandinavia, particularly Finland. The Finnish Red Guard, about 30,000 strong, accordingly seized government offices in Helsinki and proclaimed a Socialist Workers' Republic. The government's response was to raise a White Guard, including the Jagar battalion, Swedish volunteers and 12,000 German troops, under the command of General Baron Gustaf Mannerheim, a former White Russian cavalry officer. The revolution lasted less than four months, but there were

World War II poster published during the German occupation of Norway, 1941.

24,000 casualties and a comparable number of Red sympathisers were subsequently executed or left to die in internment camps.

The inter-war years

Consideration was then given to turning Finland into a kingdom with one of Kaiser Wilhelm's sons on the throne, but Germany's defeat in the war turned opinion in favour of a republic under the presidency of Kaarlo Juho Ståhlberg, a local professor of law. The Soviet Union raised no objection to Finland's independence and signed the Treaty of Tartu to that effect, but Finland's fanatical Christian fundamentalists, the Lapua pietists, were

determined to clear the nest of vipers. Suspected Communists were kidnapped, beaten and dumped at the Soviet border. The pietists forced the government to ban Communism completely and were arming themselves for a full-scale coup d'état when the army decided enough was enough.

Sweden sailed through the post-war years on a wave of international demand for Swedish steel and ball bearings, Ericsson telephones and Electrolux vacuum cleaners. While also doing well, Norway and Denmark clashed over Greenland and the Arctic islands of Svalbard (Spitzbergen) and Jan Mayen, which raised issues rooted in Viking times. Asked to arbitrate, the international court at The Hague gave Greenland to Denmark, the islands to Norway.

Scandinavia emerged from the second crisis of the inter-war years, the Great Depression, with improved political systems. Small parties with narrow interests – farmers' parties being a prime example – were forced to remove their blinkers and join broader coalitions, the front runners generally calling themselves "Social Democrats".

World War II

As the storm clouds of World War II gathered, Hitler's rise was especially worrying to Denmark because Germany had never formally agreed to the Schleswig-Holstein border after World War I. Accepting his surprising offer of a non-aggression pact, Denmark nevertheless joined Sweden and Norway in another declaration of neutrality.

Finland was again a special case. When Hitler invaded Poland, Stalin assumed Russia would be next and seized a strip of Finnish territory to strengthen the defences around Leningrad. The 1939 Nazi–Soviet pact removed this threat, but at the same time it allowed Stalin a free hand in Finland, and he ordered an invasion at the end of November that year. Marshal Mannerheim, now in his seventies, came out of retirement to lead Finland in what came to be known as the Winter War.

Finland's wars with Russia

The Finns were outnumbered three to one on the ground, and faced an air force of around 2,500 aircraft – almost 30 times larger than their own. But near-invisible in their white uniforms against driving snow, Finnish troops went into action on skis, employing guerrilla tactics against Russian tanks in temperatures as low as minus 40°C (-40°F). Surprise attacks against frozen, demoralised Soviet troops resulted in some surprising victories: the battle of Suomussalmi is still a textbook example of how small, strategic-ally used forces can defeat a much larger foe. But the odds, ultimately, were against the Finns. Surrender came after 105 days, when around a tenth of the country, including the Karelian Isthmus, was ceded to Stalin.

When the Nazi–Soviet pact collapsed in 1941, Germany invaded Russia, and the Finns saw their chance to recover their recent losses, entering into battle against Russia yet again. This round of hostilities lasted until September 1944; Finland did not regain its territories, and was thereafter stigmatised as one of Hitler's allies, although it had never signed a formal military alliance with Germany.

Invasion of Denmark

The German invasion of Denmark and Norway began on 9 April 1940. Some troops crossed the Jutland border into Denmark, others emerged from hiding in German merchant ships in

German aircraft on Finland's tundra, 1941.

THE DEMON DRINK

Stringent laws on the purchase of alcohol in Norway and Sweden have been somewhat at odds with the figure these countries have wanted to cut in the modern world. The time-honoured yearning for drink can be blamed on long winter nights, but ancient Scandinavians also drank like fish because their food was preserved with lashings of salt. King Sverre of Norway experimented with prohibition as early as the 12th century. In 1775, however, King Gustav III of Sweden turned the distillation and sale of spirits into a royal monopoly and encouraged his subjects to drink because he needed the money. Against this backdrop, 20th-century prohibitionists had problems. The conundrum in Norway was that France, Spain and Portugal, major consumers of Norwegian fish, had always bartered with wine or brandy. The issue of prohibition led to the downfall of three successive governments in the early 20th century.

Sweden, however, put its faith in the "Bratt Liquor Control System", a certain Dr Ivan Bratt having worked out exactly how much alcohol an individual could consume according to age, physique and other considerations, with the result that it was almost impossible for a married woman to qualify for a single drink in any circumstances. Today, as in Gustav III's time, the sale of wines and spirits in both countries, as well as in Finland, is a state monopoly.

Copenhagen harbour, and paratroops landed at key points around the country. The Danish army was in barracks, the navy was too surprised to fire a single shot, and the air force was destroyed on the ground. If nothing else, the Royal Life Guards at Amalienborg Palace in Copenhagen prevented the Germans from capturing King Kristian X just long enough for him to order a surrender.

Denmark remained in theory a sovereign state under German protection, but when the king ignored Hitler's effusive greetings on his birthday in 1942, the pretence was dropped. A

The great long-distance runner Paavo Nurmi lights the Olympic flame at the 1952 Helsinki Games.

new government was expected to jump at Hitler's whim, but it refused to sanction death sentences on members of the increasingly active Resistance movement and made arrangements to smuggle Denmark's endangered Jews to safety in Sweden.

Norway is overrun

In Norway's case, gunners in an old fortress on Oslo Fjord had the satisfaction of sinking the German cruiser *Blücher* on the first day of the invasion, killing around 830 of those on board. While Hitler's local stooge, Vidkun Quisling, the leader of the Fascist National Unity Party, proclaimed himself prime minister, King

Håkon and most members of the government escaped to Tromsø in northern Norway and remained there while a combined force of British, French, Polish and Norwegian units recaptured the iron-ore port of Narvik. The sudden collapse of France, however, created a greater demand for the expeditionary force elsewhere. The Allies withdrew, and the king and his entourage were evacuated to England.

Neutral throughout the war, Sweden took in 300,000 refugees. The Swedish Red Cross, led by Count Folke Bernadotte, a nephew of the king, secured the release of 30,000 prisoners of various nationalities from German concentration camps, and the diplomat Raoul Wallenberg played "Schindler" to Jews in Hungary. But it was also the case that German troops and materials were given permission to cross Sweden on their way to Norway in 1940 and thereafter when they went on leave. Moreover, Sweden supplied iron ore critical to the German war machine. These are matters which Norwegians to this day cannot easily forget.

Peacetime recovery

The last stage of the war, with German forces scorching the earth in their retreat from the advancing Soviets, hurt northern Norway but was utterly devastating in Finland. The latter, then, could hardly have been in a worse position to meet Soviet demands for US$600 million in reparations – around half of Finland's annual GDP at the time. Barred by its 1948 treaty with Moscow from accepting Marshall aid, Finland nevertheless beat the 10-year deadline by creating a diversified industrial economy from scratch. Shipbuilding, oil refineries, textiles – the USSR provided a bottomless market for these new industries, and paid for its goods in dirt-cheap oil. Ironically, war reparations transformed Finland into a modern industrial nation – albeit one over which the USSR held great sway.

Recovery from the war in Denmark and Norway was set in motion by the Marshall Plan (1947–51). Neutral Sweden also accepted Marshall aid, and all four Scandinavian countries were caught up in the wave of economic growth that swept through post-war Europe. The comprehensive "cradle-to-grave" welfare systems came into full being during the 1950s and 1960s. To begin with at least, Scandinavians were happy to live with the high taxes needed to cover their cost, if only because memories of bitterly hard times without a social safety net were still so fresh.

Sweden's international reputation, somewhat damaged by its questionable war role, was given a boost by the selection of diplomat Dag Hammarskjöld as Secretary-General of the UN in 1953. He threw himself into the role, enhancing the reputation of the UN and acting as peace-broker in international disputes from China to Palestine to the Suez Canal. In 1961, Hammarskjöld was killed in a plane crash;

Measured against population, the prize in Norway was much bigger and triggered lavish expenditure on road tunnels and other infrastructure investments. By the 1990s, Norway had paid off its entire foreign debt; and in 1995, it began to stash away the cash for a rainy day, creating a sovereign wealth fund with the surplus petroleum money. Oslo began its transformation from quiet town to Europe's fastest-growing city: within 40 years, oil money had created a futuristic harbourside, new financial district and world-class buildings like the Opera House.

Olof Palme, prime minister of Sweden, assassinated in 1986.

Dag Hammarskjöld, Secretary-General of the UN.

he became the first person to be awarded the Nobel Peace Prize posthumously.

The new oil-rich nations...

During the late 1960s and early 1970s, the economies of Norway and Denmark were given another welcome leg-up – they struck oil. Denmark had become adept at exploiting niche markets (think Lego, Bang & Olufsen, Carlsberg, and selling streaky bacon to Britain), but this was the first time the country had enjoyed the luxury of natural resources since the 14th-century herring shoals. Ironically, Denmark's North Sea windfall arrived in the middle of its first experiments with wind farms.

UNDERCOVER OPERATIONS

The Resistance movement in Denmark and Norway was crucial in undermining the German campaign during World War II. Anders Lassen epitomised the 20,000-strong Danish Resistance. By the time he died aged 24, he had fought in France, Greece, the Balkans and Italy. His commanding officer said, "Anders caused more discomfort to the enemy over five years of war than any other man of his rank and age." Other heroes included the Norwegians who knocked out the heavy water plant at Rjukan. Two museums, Frihedsmuseet, Copenhagen, and Norges Hjemmefrontmuseum, Oslo, document the movement's history.

The Royal Line

Monarchy is alive and well in Scandinavia. Sweden, Norway and Denmark all have royal figureheads. Only Finland is a republic.

Monarchy could hardly be more entrenched than in Denmark. Queen Margrethe II is the 53rd in an unbroken line of sovereigns spanning more than 1,000 years. Sweden, too, has had more than 60

King Harald of Norway and King Carl Gustav of Sweden.

kings since 980. The present King Carl Gustaf may be "XVI", but his direct line begins with Jean-Baptiste Bernadotte, the French marshal who became heir apparent in 1810 and Sweden's king in 1818. Norway's royal line ceased when Norway became a Danish province and the monarchy was only restored, after a referendum, following the dissolution in 1905 of the subsequent union with Sweden. The present king, Harald V, is the third of the modern line, the "V" notwithstanding. Finland also considered a monarchy on breaking away from Russia, but chose to become a republic instead.

Nevertheless, not a little craft has gone into keeping the Scandinavian monarchies in good health. When Carl XVI Gustaf ascended the Swedish throne in 1973, the Constitution began with: "The King

alone shall govern the realm..." Lest he got the wrong impression, this was hastily changed to: "All public power in Sweden emanates from the people..." The king decided his own official motto ought to be: "For Sweden – in Keeping with the Times". This was the cue for changing the rules of succession so that they no longer discriminated against daughters. Consequently, next in line is Crown Princess Victoria rather than her younger brother. Second in line of succession is now Princess Estelle, whom Princess Victoria gave birth to in 2012, following her 2010 wedding that drew crowds of half a million onto Stockholm's streets. In 2013, the youngest of the king's children, Princess Madeleine, got married and, as of early 2015, is expecting her second child. Yet the Swedish royal family has also experienced some lows. In 2011, revelations about Queen Silvia's father's Nazi connections came hot on the heels of a best-selling biography about the king, which contained details of his wild sex life.

Carl Gustaf is also not averse to tearing around in a Ferrari, and was reported to the police in Denmark for doing an alleged 250kph (155mph) on the Copenhagen expressway. In contrast, King Harald loves boats, representing Norway at the Olympic Games, and winning the European Championship in 2005 – right after a heart bypass. Unlike his Swedish counterpart, Harald would not be seen dead in a Ferrari. He uses public transport. Queen Sonja is the daughter of an Oslo shopkeeper and their children went to state schools. Fittingly, the Crown Prince found himself a bachelor flat in an unfashionable part of Oslo, but let the side down, as it were, by sharing it with a waitress, and her three-year-old son by a man who was in prison for drug offences; they are now married and have two children of their own.

If conscientious exercises in non-charisma go down well in Norway, Queen Margrethe could not hope to do the same in Denmark. She has been showered with academic honours from the likes of Cambridge, Oxford and the London School of Economics. While trying unsuccessfully to hide her distinguished output as a painter, writer and designer behind a string of aliases, she has at least persuaded her friends to call her Daisy. Crown Prince Frederik, her heir, is not much better at disguise. Dressing down for a night on the town, he turned out so scruffy that the bar refused to let him in. As a trained soldier, no mean dancer and the leader of a husky-drawn expedition across Greenland, Frederik's status as a dashing bachelor ended in marriage to Australian Mary Donaldson, with whom he now has four children.

...and their oil-free neighbours

Deprived of any share of the North Sea bonanza, Sweden's "Middle Way", a compromise between capitalism and socialism, showed signs of turning into a cul-de-sac. Industry had long been pampered with low taxes while individual taxpayers were bled white, but it still complained loudly about its employees' national insurance contributions, shorter working weeks and longer holidays. By the 1990s, just as Norway was becoming rich as Croesus, recession hit Sweden hard. Swedes were astonished and dismayed when Saab was swallowed by General Motors, Volvo by Ford, and a regiment of other prestigious companies decamped abroad. The government introduced austerity measures, designed to stave off the worst; but interest rates rocketed. Huge public expenditure cuts followed, and in 1994 the Swedish people voted to throw in their lot with the European Union.

Finland too fell into a deep recession, exacerbated by the collapse of the USSR in 1991. Finland gained greater political freedom with the fall of its neighbour, but at the same time the Finnish economy was left floundering – seeking stability, it too joined the EU. But the country went on to experience its second economic miracle since World War II, when amongst other things Nokia recognised the potential of the mobile phone and Porsche decided to build its new Boxster model in Finland.

Assassination shockwaves

Despite Scandinavia's economic ups and downs, an underlying sense of social wellbeing had always prevailed. This was shattered on 28 February 1986, when Sweden's prime minister, Olof Palme, was assassinated in central Stockholm as he and his wife walked home from the cinema. Shock and incredulity swept across Scandinavia – increasing when the police failed to find either the murderer or his gun. Palme was a politician of international standing, with strong socialist views that he did not hesitate to express. Conspiracy theories abound, with the KGB, the CIA and the Yugoslavian UDBA variously blamed, but a satisfactory explanation for the assassination has never been found.

Scandinavia was further stunned in 2003 when history appeared to repeat itself. The popular Swedish Minister for Foreign Affairs Anna Lindh, widely tipped to be the next prime minister, was knifed while shopping in central Stockholm, and subsequently died of her wounds. Mijailo Mijailović was eventually convicted of her killing: he blamed "voices in his head".

Immigration tensions

From the 1950s onwards, Scandinavia began to receive its first immigrants – "guest workers" from Turkey and the former Yugoslavia, and political refugees from Hungary and the former Czechoslovakia. Initially immigrants received a warm welcome, but the growing

Anna Lindh, Minister for Foreign Affairs, was also killed.

number of foreigners, particularly from Muslim countries, has led to a steady rise in the popularity of mainstream right-wing, anti-immigration political parties across Scandinavia. The past 20 years have also seen an increase in activity by the extreme right wing, apprehensive over jobs and the perceived threat to traditional Nordic culture.

The debate over Muslim immigration and integration reached a head when in 2005 Danish newspaper *Jyllands-Posten* published cartoons, some of them depicting the Prophet Muhammad, as a way of stimulating debate on the place of Islam within Western democracies. Their publication caused widespread offence across the Muslim world. Ten years later the

French weekly *Charlie Hebdo*'s controversial Muhammad cartoons sparked attacks in which 12 people were killed in Paris. Due to security concerns, *Jyllands-Posten* was the only major Danish newspaper that did not reprint the original pictures.

Norwegian massacre

Nothing, though, could have prepared the Scandinavian countries for what happened in Norway on 22 July 2011, when Anders Behring Breivik exploded a car bomb near government buildings in Oslo, killing eight

Bridge to the future

The new millennium brought change for one of Scandinavia's oldest schisms. The Øresund road and rail bridge rejoined Denmark and Sweden in 2000, a connection broken by the cataclysmic convulsion at the end of the Ice Age.

At this time of global economic malaise, Scandinavian economies have remained quite strong, and there are plenty of ambitious projects in the works. Denmark and Germany are forging closer links with a 32 billion-kroner undersea tunnel across the Fehmarn Strait, due to be completed in 2021. In Sweden, the

Allure of the Seas, the world's largest cruise ship, with its sister ship, Oasis of the Seas.

people, then travelled to the nearby island of Utøya and gunned down 68 young people attending a Labour Party youth rally. Breivik claimed he had carried out the killings to precipitate a revolution against Islam and multi-culturalism.

The massacres led to much soul-searching across the region, shaking as they did the traditional image of the Scandinavian countries as places of tolerance, liberalism and hospitality. In 2012, Breivik was sentenced to 21 years in prison. Anti-immigrant sentiment across Scandinavian countries has been growing steadily, with a rising support for the right-wing populist parties, as shown in the 2014 European Parliament election.

Hallandsås railway tunnel will open in 2016, part of a larger project to create super-efficient train links between Norway, Sweden and Germany. Finland, on the other hand, hasn't been so lucky and has been experiencing the most dramatic lows with Nokia devoured by Microsoft in 2014 and its big trading partner Russia suffering a severe economic downturn. Norway insulated itself from economic pain by using its sovereign wealth fund to buy cheap shares – in 2014, the fund topped 5.5 trillion kroner (over US$710 billion). Norway has the highest GDP per person and the lowest working hours in Scandinavia, pointing to a level of individual wealth and leisure that the rest of us can only dream of.

Øresund road and rail bridge, completed in 2000.

Fishing is a way of life in Scandinavia.

THE DANES

They're generally warm, witty and welcoming.
But they can also be cool and reserved. It depends
where you meet them.

Danes have two reputations in the world, one at home and another abroad. Outside their homeland, Danes are known as warm, curious, friendly, funny, charming. In their modest way, Danish travellers bring on laughs and a sense of pure enjoyment for life. They try not to act too offended when, outside Europe, people ask: "Is Denmark the capital of Sweden?" or "What language do you speak – Dutch?" A short, firm geography lesson is given on the spot, but modesty usually prevents the Dane from pointing out that Denmark is the oldest monarchy in the world, dating from AD 935.

At home, Danes are seen by foreign visitors as distant, sombre, even cold. They keep to themselves. Danes blame this image on the wet, cool climate. "Not much of our social life happens on the pavements or out in front of the home," says Frans Kjær Nielsen, a teacher. "We spend much of our time indoors with our families and friends."

Eating alfresco in Copenhagen.

Cosiness prevails

Inside this thin barrier of social contact, Denmark is one of the warmest countries in the world. People are genuine. They speak their minds. They thrive on making life cosy, relaxing and enjoyable – from festive occasions to mundane coffee breaks. This is what Danish *hygge* is all about. *Hygge* (pronounced *whoo-guh*) stands for any and every sense of cosiness, and it is found everywhere in Denmark. A good meal has *hygge*, a house can have *hygge*, a story, a walk in the woods, a meeting at a café, even a person can have *hygge*. Parties for weddings, birthdays, anniversaries and the like have *hygge* at their core. Tables are decorated with flowers and candles and creatively folded napkins. A three-course meal is usually interspersed with songs

and speeches, which end in a collective "Hurrah!" Wine flows freely. As the Danish poet and troubadour Benny Andersen wrote in a song well known among Danes: "One must keep the mood wet. I'm drunk and I'm feeling great."

Six hours into such a celebration and filled with spirits, a partygoer has a chance to get up from the table, dance a bit, then fetch some coffee and cookies and sit down again. Later, the hosts serve the final course, called "get out food", and guests gradually take the hint.

Hygge was born, no doubt, indoors during the grey winter months. From November to February, Danes go to work in darkness and return home in darkness. Warm candlelight fills flats, homes and offices in natural defence.

During *Jul* (Christmas), live candles decorate Christmas trees indoors, around which families join hands and sing carols. Local ferries light up the black water with strings of white lights. On New Year's Eve, the Queen gives her annual talk to the nation on television, and fireworks spark and pop, lighting up the midnight sky.

A whiff of spring

By February, winter seems to drag on for ever. In his essay, *Oh! To be Danish*, the author Klaus Rifbjerg writes of this time: "Sure, it can be

July, nearly the whole country goes on holiday for three weeks. Barbecues are lit and bathing suits donned.

By late summer, farmers' tractors haul grain and hay, holding up traffic. Towns hold harvest festivals, children start school and families

> More than 100 dialects are spoken in Denmark. Some vary greatly. People in south Jutland are hardly understood by the residents of Copenhagen.

Copenhagen has over 300km (186 miles) of cycling routes.

grim, and now and then we might want to turn our collar up and jump in the river. But then the light suddenly changes and there's a melody in the air, a whiff of spring to come, the smell of the sea and a blackbird singing on a rooftop."

Fields of fluorescent yellow winter rape blossom in May, and the days grow longer. In spring and summer, urban Danes cycle out to their garden houses on the edge of town, and rural Danes collect dead branches and greenery into huge piles on the beaches and in the countryside. On the evening of 23 June, Midsummer's Eve, those piles of wood are topped with an effigy of a witch and set on fire to drive bad spirits from the land. In

hunt for mushrooms and berries in the forests. People complain about the diminishing light and increasing rain, and soon temperatures can drop so low the sea freezes solid. So, the Danes light a candle, make some *hygge* with hot cocoa and buns, and look forward to *Jul* again.

A sense of Danish togetherness can be felt in society as well, starting with the generous welfare system. Social benefits are high, workers' unions are strong, and the cooperative spirit prevails. Only four out of 100 Danes do not belong to an association. "We have a joke that if two Danes sit together for five minutes, they will start an association," says Frans Kjær Nielsen.

Danish challenges

But this idyllic-sounding vision of cosiness and cooperation does have its darker side. During the 1980s, a wave of refugees shook up the homogeneity of this little Scandinavian country – threatening, perhaps, that all-important feeling of *hygge*. Denmark was unprepared, and immigration became a huge and emotive domestic issue – and it still is.

Being a Dane today therefore involves a great deal of soul-searching on the subjects of tolerance, integration and immigration. The country came under intense criticism

proud of their welfare safety net, and are happy to pay high taxes to support it, but the system's costs and benefits are another of the country's major preoccupations. The system is very supportive of women, and maternity and paternity leave is generous. Once all-important, the family is on the retreat now, though. Over 42 percent of marriages end in divorce, half of the children are born out of wedlock, and the birth rate is on a steady decline. And despite having the highest rate of cancer in the world they are still scoring highly on international happiness surveys.

Drinks on the waterfront.

in 2005, after the newspaper *Jyllands-Posten* published cartoons that caused offence across the Islamic world. Danes were polarised. While some still cleaved to their belief in an egalitarian society for all, others turned to the far-right, anti-immigration Danish People's Party to represent their hardening attitudes. With nearly 27 percent of votes, the party won the European Parliament election in 2014. Since 1984 the number of non-Western immigrants has risen more than five-fold; they now make up over 11 percent of the population.

Although economic inequality has been increasing, Denmark still has one of the strongest economies in Europe. Danes are

EQUALITY FOR ALL

Denmark is an egalitarian society with a high standard of living where, as the Danes themselves say, "Few have too much and fewer have too little." The welfare system gives everyone the same opportunities: free health service, education, support for the elderly and handicapped, unemployment benefits, pensions and more. The system carries a price: goods and services are taxed at 25 percent, and 50–70 percent of income is taxed.

Welfare equality carries through to social mores. Everyone is on first-name terms, the formal address, *De*, being reserved mainly for the Queen. Dress is casual and a tie in the workplace is rare.

THE NORWEGIANS

Forget the stereotypical image of a cool
Scandinavian: visitors to Norway can be assured
of a warm and friendly welcome.

Some say that Norwegians can be cool almost to the point of rudeness when you first meet them. Thomas Hylland Eriksen, Professor of Social Anthropology at the University of Oslo, wants to set that stereotype straight. "Norwegians have a general reputation for being slightly aloof and difficult to approach. While there may be some truth to this, due to late urbanisation and the persistence of rural values, one cannot generalise." It's equally true to say that once you've overcome that initial distance and a Norwegian has got to know you, their warmth and hospitality are unmistakable.

The Norwegian character is complex and sometimes contradictory. Norwegians may be slow in offering their opinions, but when they do their views are forthright. They pride themselves on their internationalism (rather than nationalism), yet can be incredibly inward-looking. They have strong cultural and economic links with the rest of Europe but stubbornly insist on staying outside the European Union. And the enthusiasm of so many Norwegians to participate in commercial whaling often seems to have less to do with its value as an industry, and more to do

National pride at the Holmenkollen ski jump.

> Norwegian women have fought for equality for over a century – and appear to be winning. Women are particularly well represented in the political sphere, making up 40 percent of MPs and exactly half of the cabinet, itself headed by PM Erna Solberg.

with a hatred of being told what to do by the international community.

The rugged landscapes, which centuries ago created Norway's geographical isolation, have taught Norwegians to be fiercely independent and self-reliant. This independence was reinforced by the discovery of oil in the 1960s. A strong, stable economy and comprehensive social security system have created a comfortable standard of living and cohesive society, where people feel protected if things go wrong. Norwegians have been known to grumble about bad roads and expensive gasoline, but they feel quite secure in their country, where democratic values are upheld and there is little, if any, corruption.

Immigration challenges

Historically, Norway is one of the oldest nations in Europe, if not the oldest. Its people can trace an unbroken line of descent from those who inhabited the area in prehistoric times. During the Viking era, Norway controlled an enormous territory from Russia to the British Isles, and the common European tongue was Old Norse. Yet today's Norway was reconstituted as late as 1905 when the union with Sweden was finally dissolved. The dominance of Old Norse may have gone, but today's Norwegians have regained their pride.

World War II, and the Nazi occupation, was a massive shock to the Norwegian psyche. There's still a deep-felt anger against the supposedly neutral Swedes for permitting the transit of German troops into Norway. After the war,

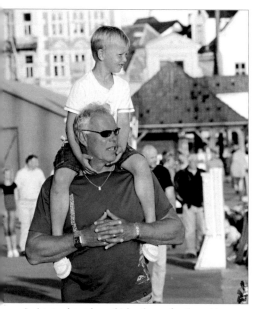

Society tends to place a high value on family and long-term friends.

the Norwegians realised with some reluctance that strategically they had no choice but to seek the protection of others. So they signed up to NATO, not least as protection against Russia, another unreliable neighbour in the north. But they turned their backs on the European Union. The importance of fishing and farming and the security of the oil revenues meant that economically they preferred to go it alone.

It's too easy, however, to equate this self-reliance with xenophobia. Norwegians don't fear or dislike foreigners, although like their Scandic neighbours, they have experienced an influx of immigrants in recent years. Unfortunately this has given fuel to far-right politicians eager to

exploit people's fears of an invading "otherness". In 2013, the centre-right bloc led by the Conservative Party won the election and formed a ruling coalition with the populist Progress Party. In spite of immigration concerns and far-right rhetoric, Norway is one of the most stable of European countries, and its economy has been outperforming the rest of Europe's since the 2008 economic crisis. Thanks to the country's oil wealth, Norway runs the largest sovereign wealth fund (SWF) in the world, held for the benefit of the whole nation. As of 2014, the SWF exceeds 5.5 trillion kroner, and new oil and gas exploration in the Arctic regions look set to fill the piggy bank to bursting.

Home comforts

Hospitality is second nature to a Norwegian, whether he or she lives in Oslo or in the remotest corner of Finnmark. If you're planning to visit people at home be prepared – there's lots of coffee to be drunk and cake to be eaten. Schnapps is also something that gets poured generously. The food will be plentiful and wholesome; your host will expect nothing in return except some appreciative comments about the welcome and any traditional dishes being served.

Thanks to all that oil, and a very generous social security system, there is relatively little poverty in Norway. But nor are they at all ostentatious about their wealth and, especially in rural areas, life can still be very simple.

Small-town life

The more enigmatic aspects of the Norwegian character – including the Nordic gloom that can descend after a drink too many – have been famously scrutinised by Henrik Ibsen. He was brought up in small communities and, during a long exile, turned his critical eye on the experience. One of the themes running through Ibsen's work is the double-edged nature of life in such a community: mutual support in adversity weighed against a suffocating lack of privacy at other times.

The lesser-known, Danish/Norwegian Aksel Sandemose wrote "Ten Commandments for Village Life" in a fictional novel about a town called Jante, the essence being humility bordering on self-abasement. They included: "You must not think that you are worth anything; you must not think that you are better than anyone else; you must not think yourself capable of anything worthwhile; and you must not think that you are in any way exceptional." Scandinavians today are still guided by this fictional Jante law (*janteloven*).

> Although Norway's economy thrives on oil, the country actually boasts the largest number of electric cars per capita in the world. In 2014, one in every 100 passenger vehicles on Norwegian roads was a plug-in electric.

realised it was taking national pride too far to deny the pre-eminence of English. Indeed, many an urbanite will claim it's much easier to understand a foreigner speaking English than one of their compatriots speaking a regional dialect.

Worlds apart

Norway's geography and its sparse population (5 million people) have entrenched cultural and economic fragmentation too. Rural lives depended on agriculture, and the land was too poor to support more than a family or two in a single valley. Separated from their neighbours

Paraglider flying the national flag.

Land of many dialects

Norway's rural nature has compounded one of its thorniest problems – language. The issue has split the country for over a century. Throwing off the Danish-dominated *bokmål* (book language) was crucial to the independence activists of the 19th century. Unfortunately there was no Norwegian alternative on offer, just a variety of often very divergent dialects. Various attempts were made to bring these together into a truly national language known as *nynorsk* (new Norwegian), but these were never more than a partial success, and even now there are huge regional variations in the spoken tongue.

Most Norwegians speak English extremely well and are more than happy to do so. They

by mountains, which were easier to cross in winter on skis than in summer on foot, they effectively lived in worlds apart. Families managed on their own, a resourcefulness which still runs in the blood.

Whether it's the outdoor life or all the fish in the diet, Norwegians enjoy amazing longevity. They manage to look remarkably healthy all their lives, and the octogenarian grandmother whizzing by on skis is not entirely a myth.

The Swedish king who reluctantly oversaw Norway's independence predicted that bureaucratic incompetence would soon have Norwegians begging to return to the fold. That, of course, never happened, and modern Norway is a strong, successful socialist state.

THE SWEDES

Beneath the cool, sophisticated exterior, the Swede
harbours a deep and heartfelt passion for nature,
tradition and schnapps.

Swedes have a reputation for being dry, sombre and painfully serious. It is true that the average Swede is quite quiet and reserved, and that instant gushing friendliness is not commonly witnessed. But contrary to popular opinion, Swedes do have a sense of humour – one that is as elusive as Garbo and as fleeting as a Swedish summer. Swedes may seem calm and collected on the outside, but they're every bit as prone to ribald fits of laughter as the next person, even if they do recover their solemn faces much more quickly. So remember that appearances can be deceptive: underneath that composed exterior, you'll usually find a warm, friendly individual. And once a Swede has decided to let their guard down and befriend you, they will be a friend for life.

Blond and blue-eyed?

When it comes to Sweden, popular misconceptions are rife. Think "Swede", and an image of a blue-eyed blond, no doubt sitting at the wheel of a Volvo, may well spring to mind. But only a proportion of native Swedes fit the old stereo-type: Sweden today is a country of growing cultural and social diversity. In 2015, over 1.3 million of Sweden's 9.6 million inhabitants were born abroad, the majority in Finland, Iraq, Poland and the former Yugoslavia.

However, Sweden's traditionally tolerant outlook has been called into question recently. The high standard of living, strong economy and cradle-to-grave welfare system enjoyed by Swedes has come under increasing pressure ever since the 2008 financial crash. Far-right groups who place the blame on immigrants have made political headway: in the 2010 elections, the anti-immigration Sweden Democrats won parliamentary representation for the first time,

A traditional summer farm in Dalarna.

receiving nearly 6 percent of the vote. Four years later, they polled nearly 13 percent of the vote and won 49 of the 349 parliamentary seats, thus becoming Sweden's third-largest party.

Children of nature

It's no exaggeration to say that Swedes are potty about nature. It's somehow a part of the Swedish soul. They are quick to wax lyrical about the grassy plains of Skåne, expound the virtues of lakeside Dalarna and remind you that theirs is the only true wilderness left in all Europe. Ask any Swede to recount tales of their childhood and they'll dreamily recall summers spent in the country with a noticeable softening of facial expression and a faraway look in their eye.

Nowadays the little red cottage is Sweden's most enduring image, and there's nothing Swedes like better than to take off to their *stuga*, where they can kick off their shoes, swim naked and bond with nature.

Life in Sweden is intrinsically linked to the changing seasons. Swedish winters are famous for their darkness, longevity and Arctic temperatures. But Swedes have learnt how to make the most of it, and winter sports are popular with Swedes of all ages. They eagerly await the spring and the return of sunlight with all the excited anticipation of children at Christmas. Like

law. The new goal is to make Sweden carbon-neutral by 2050 and have fossil-fuel-free transport by 2030.

Cosmopolitan citizens of the world

Despite such closeness to the countryside, Sweden is no nation of bumpkins. Its people are a true blend of the provincial *and* the cosmopolitan, every bit at home in the concrete jungle as going barefoot at their place in the country – 85 percent of the country's inhabitants live in an urban area.

Holiday-makers build rafts on the Klarälven River, Varmland.

Fiskebäckskil on the west coast.

hibernating animals re-emerging after winter, sun-starved Swedes are wont to stand on street corners, at crossings, in traffic lights, and any other spot with a south-facing aspect, soaking up the first warming rays of spring.

This deep-rooted love of nature means that environmental concerns are a high priority in Sweden. Yet the country plans to wean itself off oil by 2020 has never been made into a

> Friendships are often sealed over schnapps. Delicately flavoured with fruits or spices, schnapps is a perennial favourite and every Swede can name his or her tipple.

Swedes have a reputation for forward thinking, with Sweden deemed to be Europe's most innovative country; in the 2014 Bloomberg's Global Innovation Index Sweden ranked second, outrun only by South Korea. Biotechnology and pharmaceuticals are a major export, and IT companies thrive: one of Skype's two co-founders is Swedish, and the online music service Spotify is a Swedish creation.

Swedes also have a strong international perspective, and many of Sweden's most (in)famous people (Dag Hammarskjöld; Olof Palme; Dr Hans Blix, who led the search for weapons of mass destruction in Iraq in 2003) have loomed large on the world stage.

National pride

Swedes have a high opinion of their country and like nothing more than to talk about Sweden itself. This is not to say that Swedes are braggarts: a more humble, self-deprecating tribe you'd be hard pushed to find. But their modesty is merely a thin veil, and all young Swedes are well versed in the achievements of their countrymen, be it Alfred Nobel or August Strindberg. And perhaps this universal satisfaction is not so misplaced: after all, in recent times the rest of the world has come to appreciate various Swedish exports. IKEA sells Swedish homeware in 46 countries, and it is said that one in 10 Europeans was conceived in an IKEA bed! Culturally, Stieg Larsson's thrillers *The Girl with the Dragon Tattoo*, *The Girl Who Played with Fire* and *The Girl Who Kicked the Hornets' Nest* have sold over 75 million copies since the first book was published posthumously in 2005. And at a time when TV series are becoming more popular than movies, both Sweden and Denmark have successfully exported "Nordic Noir" to the rest of Europe, with hits like *The Killing*, *Borgen*, *The Bridge*, *Arne Dahl* and *Wallander*.

Cosmopolitan Stockholm.

WINING AND DINING

"Ska vi fika?" ("Shall we have a coffee break?") is a question that induces a warm glow in every Swedish heart; and the answer is always *"Ja!"*. Coffee is vital to Sweden's wellbeing – only Finland consumes more. A snug place in which to drink it is vital, as is a piece of cake, usually a cinnamon bun *(kanelbullar)*.

Coffee is one thing, alcohol another. An unyielding state monopoly and steep prices create a faint sense of prohibition. On Friday evenings, stoical Swedes queue at the state's Systembolaget off licences to buy wine or a six-pack. Customs laws changed in 2003, allowing Swedes to bring quantities of alcohol from the EU into the country; but cautious Sweden still sees more harm than good in deregulating alcohol sales. Yet when the chance to indulge presents itself, Swedes love celebrations… as long as all is done with regard to etiquette. Punctuality is a must, and toasts are made according to strict rules. Impeccable manners only seem to loosen at a crayfish feast, when Swedes will merrily rip off claws with their hands and clash beer glasses in true Viking fashion.

In line with the new Nordic cuisine revolution that has swept across Scandinavia recently, Stockholm has seen a restaurant boom. Cosy bistros and sophisticated restaurants (six with Michelin stars) have sprung up everywhere, placing the city firmly on the gastronomic map.

THE FINNS

Cool, but not humourless, the innovative Finns have fought hard to preserve their identity and move with the times.

Finns are sometimes mistakenly described as being cold, but their demeanour can better be described as calm, modest, even a bit shy. Geographical isolation has created a hardy, self-reliant people who don't feel the need to be overly garrulous. Finns will weigh their words carefully; silences are considered a natural part of conversation, and empty small talk is, frankly, a puzzle. One Finnish proverb advises, "Take a man by his words, take a bull by its horns."

With such respect for speech, it's no surprise that Finns embraced the mobile phone so readily... particularly as it combines communication with an ideal shield from excessive intimacy. Finnish passions find their release not in conversation, but in poetry and music, athletics, football, ice hockey and, oddly, the tango. Practised with Argentinian fervour, the dance has become a national symbol, and festivals and contests are held all over the country.

Generations old and new.

ROMANY GYPSIES

One of the oldest groups in Finland who are not ethnic Finns are the Romany gypsies, whose womenfolk are instantly recognisable by their elaborate embroidered lace blouses and voluminous skirts. Although today most speak only Finnish, few have intermarried, so their dark good looks stand out against fairer Finns.

Most gypsies are no longer nomadic and live instead in houses and flats. Some families still tend to wander, especially in autumn, from one market place to another. Little horse-trading is done these days, however, and the gypsies' appearance at these fairs is little more than a vestige of nostalgia.

Nordic links

The "typical Finn", should such a person exist, has a genetic combination that is 75 percent identical to that of other Scandinavians, but 25 percent derives from tribes that probably migrated to Finland from east of the Ural Mountains. This more oriental strain accounts for physical traits that set Finns apart from their Nordic neighbours – finely pronounced cheekbones and quite small, slatey-grey or blue eyes. Laplanders tend to be smaller in stature and more sturdily built. Karelians are stockier and slightly smaller than people from originating from the west coast, whose ancestors merged with the gargantuan Vikings.

Nature is sacred

All Finns, no matter what their genetic makeup, are heavily influenced by their land of lakes and forests. More than 400,000 Finns own a plot of forest, and everyone has the right to roam. Nature is regarded as near-sacred, a place full of mystery as well as one of renewal. The country shuts down for at least a month after Midsummer, when the Finns take to their summer cabins en masse. Fishing, swimming, berry-picking and a host of other outdoor pursuits fill the warm days; most cabins have a sauna, and steam-basking

Identity and immigration

In the past, Finland has focused much of its energy on the struggle to keep its identity, defending its language against the Russian regime more than 100 years ago and being long dominated by Sweden. In recent years, however, there has been a broadening of interest in the outside world. Many younger Finns go on to study, work and travel abroad, and Finnish businesses have made serious investments in nearby Estonia over the last 15 years.

Helsinki itself has taken on a more mul-

With the first sign of summer, cafés spill out onto Helsinki's streets and squares.

followed by a plunge into the nearest cold lake can be seen almost as a ritualistic preparation for the wintry months to follow.

But Finland is becoming more urbanised. Some 80 percent of Finns live on 2 percent of the land. Domestic emigration is accelerating – Finns are moving from small towns to Greater Helsinki, and the big urban centres of Tampere, Turku and Oulu, although many Helsinki business types are relocating to other countries with warmer climates and lower taxes. The much publicised *etätyö* (distance working via the internet) has its attractions, but despite this growing trend, the majority of people still try to escape to the cities.

ticultural demeanour: an influx of Russian, Estonian, Somalian and Chinese immigrants has boosted the city's foreign population to about 8 percent. However, although the numbers are well below the EU average, Finland is experiencing unrest along with these new citizens, perhaps partially explained by the country's historical experiences of foreign influence. Recent polls reveal that one in two Finns is opposed to further new arrivals, and the right-wing Finns Party (previously True Finns), which even objects to the country's small population of Swedish-speaking Finns, is now the third largest party in the Finnish Parliament, receiving nearly 13 percent of votes in the 2014 European Parliament election. In

2012, Sauli Niinisto, became the first Finnish conservative president since 1956.

Women and men

At least the battle of the sexes is not a major societal concern. *Sisu*, meaning guts or fortitude, is a word synonymous with the Finnish character, and self-reliance, determination and tenacity are national traits that apply equally to men and women. There has never been a strong feminist movement, because there has never been a need for one. In 1906, Finnish women became the first in the world

as Finland's main exports. Moreover, trade with one of its biggest customers, Russia, whose currency slumped to a record low in 2014, slowed to a standstill. Without Norway's oil money, and tied to the flounder-

> As a nation, Finns are great lovers of the outdoors and of sport, and some young Finns, following in the footsteps of the great Finnish runner Paavo Nurmi, live for little else but their athletic activities.

Sami weaver at work.

to gain unrestricted political rights to vote and to stand for election. They were quick to take up the challenge, forming 10 percent of the first Finnish government, and by doing so were directly able to influence government policy. Women MPs now make up 40 percent of parliament, and from 2000 until 2012 Finland had a female president –Tarja Halonen.

Finland today

Nokia largely contributed to Finland's economic growth between 1998 and 2007, so when it was devoured by Microsoft in 2014, only paper-manufacturing goods, which are sensitive to market fluctuations, remained

ing euro (unlike Denmark and Sweden), Finland has experienced an economic slowdown ever since 2014 and public debt has also increased.

The Finns are experts at adjusting themselves to difficult events, gritting their teeth and battling onwards. Adaptation is deep-rooted in the Finnish soul: the big wheel keeps turning, and another year means new opportunities. As the Finns will tell anyone who asks, "The only constant is change."

Sisu is a word synonymous with the Finnish character. Roughly translated it means guts or fortitude, a description which aptly fits the heroic, patriotic and noble warriors of Finland's national epic poem, the Kalevala.

THE ACTIVE LIFE

Scandinavians are passionate about nature and the
outdoors. Unfazed by the weather, they hike, ski,
skate, sail, cycle, fish and climb.

The people of the Nordic countries are so at
home in their natural surroundings that
they seldom pause to consider how intertwined their daily lives are with the climate, the
seasons, and the amazing and diverse beauty of
the northern landscape.

In spring and summer, the mountains
beckon backpackers to scale their heights, the
Swedish archipelago is dotted with thousands
of sailing boats, and serious hikers and day-trip-
pers wend their way through the Nordic forests. Danes head for their magnificent beaches
while Swedes, Norwegians and Finns celebrate
the cool refreshing plunge of the thousands of
lakes that dot the landscape. In recent years,
hordes of Nordic ski enthusiasts have taken to
the open roads and mountain trails.

Winter poses no obstacle to the hardy Scandinavian. They take to their skis to traverse fields
and forests, pull on skates to blaze paths across
icy lakes, fish through the ice and climb frozen
waterfalls just for fun.

Scandinavians often manage to combine a
practical outlook with a sense of adventure and
a sporting spirit – where better to exercise all
three than in the great outdoors?

At the water's edge

Denmark and Sweden offer varied coastlines
and a thriving beach life. There are 8,000km
(5,000 miles) of coastline in Sweden, offering
clean, if often chilly, water to swim in, and rocks
to sun on (but few sandy beaches). The most
spectacular seascape is the Stockholm archipelago, with its 24,000 islands, but nearly as
thrilling are the waves crashing on the rocks of
Bohuslän's archipelago.

The Danes are blessed with sandy beaches.
With more than 7,400km (4,600 miles) of

Hiking in Nuuksio National Park, Finland.

coastline, the waters surrounding Denmark
are a playground for outdoor activities. Kayaks, canoes, rowing boats and smaller sailing
or motor craft may be hired at resorts along
the coasts or on the larger lakes. The air is
hardly still in Denmark, and the windsurfing
is excellent. Seasoned surfers may prefer the
exhilaration of the North Sea, for example the
beaches around Klitmøller; while beginners
can try their hand in the lee of a bay or fjord,
or on a lake.

Norway's fjords can be explored by steamers in summertime. In winter, when the fjords
freeze over, families take Sunday "walks" on
skates among the rocks and islets. Increased
tourism along Finland's lake system is bringing

the steamers back into business. There are now regular passenger routes on several of the lake systems, but the oldest and probably the most romantic are those across Saimaa's vast expanse.

Hitting the walking trails

The Nordic region is known for its great open landscapes and is a mecca for hikers and backpackers. Waymarked footpaths are found in scenically outstanding areas. The Danish countryside offers the most gentle introduction to walkers, with an appealing patchwork of dense forests, coastal dunes, marshes, moors and meticulously manicured farmland. In every type of landscape there are paths or trails that stretch for miles, and a labyrinth of winding country roads.

The greatest proportion of Sweden is virgin country. You can stroll for miles along tracks without seeing another human being. Throughout Sweden, there's an excellent network of waymarked footpaths. Close to Stockholm is the Sörmlandsleden (Sörmland trail), with over 1,000km (620 miles) of pathways, starting at Björkhagen underground station. Carefully laid out, the trail offers hikers constantly changing

Hiking in Norway's fjords is an exhilarating experience.

NATIONAL PARKS

The Nordic region has many national parks, each with its unique native flora and fauna. Denmark's parks are very new – the first opened in 2008 – and contain small but unique environments such as the tidal flats of the Wadden Sea. Parks in the other Scandinavian countries tend to be much bigger, with marked hiking trails. In the more remote parks, you'll often find a chain of mountain stations set a day's walk from one another along waymarked footpaths, providing shelter for walkers. Most are equipped with cooking facilities, a shop and comfortable beds; some have a self-service restaurant and a sauna. They are not hotels, but simple accommodation designed to provide a haven for tired walkers.

Large areas of Norway have been designated as national parks to protect special habitats and support biodiversity. Sweden's 28 national parks cover everything from low-lying marshland to Sarek's trackless mountains and glaciers. For spring flowers and birdsong, head to Dalby Söderskog in Skåne. Store Mosse in Småland is birdwatching heaven with whooper swans, marsh harriers and cranes. Finland's network is mostly administered by the Forest and Park Service, which controls 37 national parks, including the rift valley of Hiidenporrttin Kansallispuisto in Karelia and the Ramsholmen Nature Reserve on the Åland Islands. It also rents out accommodation in isolated wilderness cottages.

vistas of deep forest, historic sites, lookout points and lakes. It passes several camps where you can eat, rest and buy supplies, with shelters at regular intervals. Sörmlandsleden is an easy hike, but it offers plenty of excitement, with deer, elk, capercaillie, hawks and grouse along the way. For the most exotic views, head for the Kungsleden trail which runs for 450km (280 miles) between Abisko and Hemavan.

Norwegians are quite at home in their wild, unspoilt country, and have a great feeling for its mountains. In Norway, the bulk of the trails and lodges are conveniently in the middle of the triangle bounded by the cities of Oslo, Bergen and Trondheim. A central entry point is Finse, situated above the timber line at 1,200 metres (4,000ft). Finse's main street is the station platform; there are no cars because there are no roads.

Finland also offers pristine wilderness, quaint historical attractions and ample peace and quiet. Some of the country's best hiking is along the Karelian Circle Trek, Finland's longest trekking route, with approximately 1,000km (620 miles) of marked trails. It offers genuine wilderness routes, variety in four different national parks, and the possibility to combine walking with mountain biking, canoeing, fishing or hunting. Bears are rare, but walkers are advised to tie a small bell to their backpack to warn them of their presence. Bed-and-breakfast accommodation is available, as are wilderness huts. Pitching a tent is legal (and free) almost everywhere along this route.

Accessible mountaineering

To the north of Finse lie the Jotunheimen Mountains, literally the "Home of the Giants". Nonetheless, even the loftiest of the Jotunheimen peaks, Galdhøpiggen and Glittertind, which are the highest in Northern Europe, with summits rising more than 2,400 metres (7,900ft), rank low on the international scale of noteworthy mountains where sheer altitude, not challenge, is the main criterion. Though this fact has led to relative anonymity – few Norwegian peaks appear in the classic mountaineering literature – it does mean that you can ascend the equivalent of the Matterhorn or Mont Blanc without the problems associated with high altitude.

Some of the glaciers that hewed the Norwegian landscape left offspring. One,

Jostedalsbreen (Jostedal Glacier), is the largest in mainland Europe. Jostedalsbreen and its siblings throughout the country are the places to see crampon-shod parties wielding ice axes from spring until autumn. Contact with the ice that shaped their land is currently the Norwegians' fastest-growing wilderness recreation, and many centres now organise specialist courses.

On two wheels

The bicycle is an important mode of transport for Danes and visitors to Denmark alike. Bikes outnumber cars in some city areas, where the

Scandinavians are keen cyclists.

FREEDOM TO ROAM

The freedom to explore nature is considered a birthright of most Scandinavians, and the politicians have seen fit to put that inheritance into law. Since 1957 Norway has had a *Lov om friluftslivet* (Outdoor Recreations Act), which states succinctly: "At any time of the year, outlying property may be crossed on foot, with consideration and due caution."

In Sweden, the freedom to roam is called *Allemansrätten* (Everyman's Right), and in Finland *Jokamiehenoikeus*. Everyone is permitted to camp anywhere for a night, or to walk, ski or paddle a canoe anywhere, as long as the area is not fenced in or in close proximity to a private home.

In Sweden and Norway, the extensive networks of walking and hiking trails are marked by a red "T". Lodges and cabins offer accommodation along the way.

streets have bicycle lanes and traffic lights. Denmark has thousands of miles of cycle paths, and bikes may be taken on most trains and ferries. Tourist offices can provide detailed maps of routes. Hærvejen is a bicycle and walking trail that stretches from the German border to

is the Sverigeleden (Sweden Bicycle Route), from Stockholm to Göteborg – a distance of 2,600km (1,600 miles).

Cast your line

One of the most remarkable places to fish is right in the centre of Stockholm, in the fast-moving Strömmen channel which links the fresh water of Lake Mälaren with the Baltic Sea. A clean-up programme has brought salmon and sea trout back to the very heart of the capital.

Big salmon and sea trout can be caught almost anywhere in Sweden – in world-famous

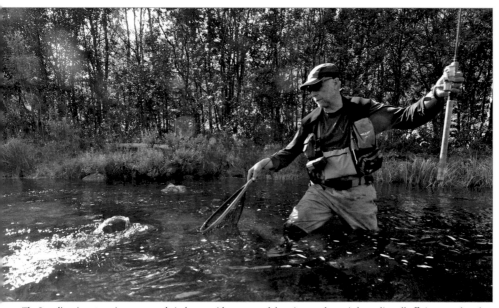

The Scandinavian countries are an angler's dream, with numerous lakes, rivers and a varied coastline all offering a good catch.

Viborg in north-central Jutland. Traders and travellers beat this path a few thousand years ago, and much of it still looks as it did during Viking times. All along the route there are inns, hotels or hostels, as well as shops for provisions.

Cycling is also a popular outdoor sport for Swedes, and there are many well-designed and well-lit routes all over the country. You could spend a week touring the islands of Gotland or Bornholm on a bike. Keen cyclists also head for Östergötland, particularly along the banks of the Göta Kanal where the towpaths make ideal cycling tracks. Bikes can be hired at several places along the canal, and the most popular stretch for cyclists is between Berg and Borensberg. For the truly ambitious, there

waters like the southern Mörrum River, in the large and wild rivers of the north, as well as along the coast when the fish are on their migration. The salmon season varies between rivers, but it usually starts during the summer and continues well into the autumn. The sea trout tend to arrive a little later. Both spinning and fly-fishing can produce good salmon catches, but sturdy tackle is advised.

In Norway the variety of fish and fish products is amazing, and Norwegians look on a proper fresh fish shop as an asset to a community. Norway is a country of fishermen, both commercial and anglers. The long coastline is a mecca for saltwater angling, yet freshwater angling is more popular, and there are a quarter of a million fishable inland lakes and ponds. The most common of around 40 freshwater species are trout and char; in the northernmost parts, and in lakes and ponds at higher elevations, they are the only fish. Grayling and pike are more common in larger lakes and rivers in eastern and central areas.

Ice fishing is a prime wintertime hobby. It's a straightforward form of angling, which requires only a baited hand line or short pole and line, warm clothing and lots of patience.

Winter sports

Long winters, frozen rivers and lakes, and beckoning snow-topped mountains make Sweden, Norway and Finland a fabulous destination for winter sports enthusiasts. It's possible to participate in all kinds of activities, including snowshoeing, ice climbing and snowmobiling, and many ski areas can provide equipment and organise expeditions. Even in the heart of Scandinavia's cities, winter sports abound: in Stockholm, for example, you can fly round the 14 islands on a pair of ice skates.

Naturally, skiing is the biggest winter sport, whether it's downhill (Alpine), cross-country or Telemark. Downhill skiing in Sweden attracts a growing number of visitors thanks to artificially produced snowfall, a variety of slopes and a reduced avalanche risk compared to Alpine resorts. Sälen is the largest ski resort in Sweden, and Åre, where the World Cup Ski Championships are held, attracts skiers from all over Europe with hundreds of top-class, superbly groomed pistes served by high-speed lifts and

cabins. Half-pipes and snow parks are available for snowboarders.

Norway's six-month long skiing season is a boon to fanatics, and there are resorts scattered up and down the country, from Sirdal in the south to Tromsø way up in the Arctic Circle. Halfway between Oslo and Bergen, Hemsedal is the largest Norwegian ski resort, with 51 downhill slopes, cross-country trails and several excellent terrain parks for snowboarders. Although it's only small, the Kvitfjell resort wins kudos for containing the "black diamond" downhill run used in the 1994 Winter Olympics. At

Skiing, both downhill and cross-country, is a national sport in Norway, Sweden and Finland.

Geilo pure adrenalin-seekers can try snowkiting, a hair-raising sport whose stars reach speeds of up to 100kmph (60mph).

Although Finland has no mountains, it too boasts a good collection of resorts – the biggest is Levi, 170km (105 miles) into the Arctic Circle in Lapland. But the country really comes into its own with cross-country skiing: tens of thousands of kilometres of well-marked trails wind their way through forests, over hills and across frozen lakes.

Adventure activities

Scandinavia makes a thrilling playground for the adventurous in any season, and every year

THE VASALOPPET

One of the world's greatest skiing competitions takes place in Mora, in the Dalarna region of Sweden. The Vasaloppet, a 90km (56-mile) cross-country skiing race, is the most popular sporting event in the country. It is held every March to commemorate King Gustav Vasa's flight from his enemies in the 16th century. Each year the race includes around 15,000 competitors, who in the past have included the present Swedish king, Carl XVI Gustaf. The first Vasaloppet was run on 19 March 1922. A Vasaloppet victory is regarded as highly as a podium place in the Olympic Games or the World Championships.

Life in Lapland

The indigenous Sami of northern Scandinavia, a hardy semi-nomadic people, can trace their roots back thousands of years.

The Sami call themselves "the people of the eight seasons". They are indigenous people who live in Sweden, Norway and Finland's most northerly provinces, and can trace their heritage back more

Reindeer herd in Lapland.

than 8,000 years. They have their own language, religious traditions and customs. While the life of the Sami has changed in modern times (snowmobiles have become ubiquitous in the last decade), the annual cycle of the reindeer – rutting, herding, separating, slaughtering, calving, marking – continues to shape the Lapland calendar. The winter round-ups are among Europe's most colourful events, resembling scenes from a Wild West film transposed to an Arctic setting. Visitors can enjoy this ancient culture at festivals and ceremonial occasions held throughout the year, where one can sample reindeer delicacies and marvel at Sami handicrafts.

A vivid way to experience the Sami lifestyle and landscape is in spring and summer, when the

mountains blossom with heather, globe flowers, cloudberries and countless other species, inviting the visitor to take to the trails and woods of the many national parks in the Sami regions of Scandinavia. Padjelanta ("the higher mountain" in Sami) is the biggest national park in Sweden. It is one of Sweden's most beautiful areas, with rolling plains, gently rounded mountain massifs, huge lakes such as Vastenjaure and Virihaure, and small streams, which the Lapps call *jokk*. It has always been an important pasture for their reindeer herds.

For golf enthusiasts, nothing can quite top the thrill of golfing under the Midnight Sun in the glorious days of summer, where (depending on latitude and cloud cover) the sun is visible for up to 70 summer days. Anglers will find a true paradise in the primeval wilderness of the north, laced by swift rivers and streams and punctuated by lakes and pools.

To enjoy the wintry wilderness in an entirely different way, try dog-sledging, which is offered by many firms in northern Scandinavia. Drive the dog-sledge yourself or sit back in the vast silence of the mountains and be driven by a team of huskies. Your guide will tell you how to take care of a sledge dog and share bits of trivia, like the fact that in the Inuit language there are 18 different words for snow. Dog-sledging, common in Greenland, is now well established in Sweden and is growing in popularity in Finland's northern wilderness around Muonio.

The Sami winter vistas can also be enjoyed on reindeer sleigh rides and snowshoe treks. Ice climbing is popular, too. Fishing through the ice is common on most lakes and rivers.

To soak up the hard life of the Sami fully, the visitor can stay in the world's largest igloo, the Jukkasjärvi Ice Hotel in Sweden. Each autumn, as the Arctic temperature plummets, Laplanders rebuild this celebrated igloo from thousands of tons of snow and ice. Inside it houses a church, hotel, gallery, golf room, cinema and bar named, appropriately, Absolut Ice. Guests sleep in warm sleeping bags on mattresses of spruce bough and reindeer skins. Temperatures average −4°C (25°F). The hearty fare served from the kitchen and the activities waiting outdoors don't leave guests much time to feel cold. Next morning, the hotel will issue a certificate of survival. It's not quite the same as herding reindeer, but it brings you one step closer to understanding how climate, custom and sheer human persistence have made the Sami what they are today.

activity companies offer better and better access to the wilderness.

The region's rivers present an exhilarating challenge for white-water rafters: the fast-flowing Gevsjöströmmarna, near Åre, is Sweden's steepest navigable river. In Karelia in Finland, you can work up an appetite by shooting the Ruunaa Rapids on the Lieksanjoki River, before pulling up on the riverbank for a hunter's lunch. Several companies in Norway run rafting trips, including one along

> Golf is the fastest-growing sport in Scandinavia, and its popularity has exploded in Denmark in recent years. In Scandinavia's far north enthusiasts like to play golf under the Midnight Sun.

the lovely Sjoa River, near Rondane National Park: canyoning and riverboarding are also possible here.

In the winter months, visitors can experience dog-sledging, an ancient form of transport believed to have been around for 4,000 years. Hurtling across packed snow on a dog sledge, pulled by teams of almost-wolves, is truly something out of the ordinary. Wrap up warm, and go for a ride in Greenland, in Norway's Finnmark province, or in Finnish or Swedish Lapland.

What the Baltic Sea lacks in tropical reefs, it makes up for in shipwrecks – all well preserved thanks to the low-saline water and an absence of wood-eating worms. Around 40,000 known wrecks lie on its bottom, from Viking vessels to World War II submarines. Diving tourism is just beginning to take off in Sweden and Finland, with several new companies who can lead divers to these sunken treasures.

Europe's unspoilt north contains some of the most fascinating creatures on the planet. Whale-watching is a burgeoning industry, and the north coast of Norway is a prime place to spot orca, minke and sperm whales from May to September. Greenland has even more species to see, including narwhals. Visitors can go on a whale-watching safari in towns such as Nuuk and Kulusuuk, and it's common to see the creatures while walking by the shore or fjord sides.

Sporting heroes

Physical activity is both a pleasure and a serious pursuit to the sporty Scandinavians. Emerging from this broad base of running, jumping, skiing, sailing, puck-thwacking, ball-kicking people come the elite, competitors who enter the many national championships and represent their countries in international sports meetings.

Snowy mountains have naturally given Scandinavians a passionate interest in skiing, and the extended winter season allows them to perfect their sport: unsurprisingly, some of the world's best skiers come from this region. Sla-

Dog-sledding in Lapland.

lom champion Ingemar Stenmark put Sweden on the international skiing map, and Anja Pärson, the World and Olympic champion skier, has kept the country in the spotlight. In 2007, she became the first person to win World Championship gold medals in all five skiing disciplines.

Norwegian Marit Bjørgen is officially the most successful cross-country sprinter in history, and holds 12 World Championship gold medals – the latest four won in 2013 in Val di Fiemme. Bjørgen also picked up three gold medals at the 2010 Winter Olympics in Vancouver and another three in 2014 in Sochi. Aksel Lund Svindal was the world's number one downhill skier in 2013 at the FIS Alpine World Ski Championships; overall he has won eight World Championship medals and three Olympic ones.

Traditionally, Norwegians have excelled in sailing and winter sports, but this athletic nation has won international medals in a wide range of events. A personification of national grit and sporting talent was Grete Waitz, who won the New York marathon nine times – an unbeaten world record. She was given a state funeral on her death in 2011.

In Sweden, great players like Björn Borg, Mats Wilander and Stefan Edberg have made Swedish tennis prowess legendary. Denmark shines in rowing and sailing, winning gold medals in four events at the 2008 Beijing Olympics and five medals of different metals at London 2012.

The runner Paavo Nurmi (1897–1973) first put Finland on the map in the 1920 Olympics, breaking multiple world records and winning four gold medals. Variously known as the Flying Finn, the Phantom Finn and the Phenomenal Finn, he is remembered for his extraordinary running style, speed and tough character. Another tough cookie, Carina Räihä, became the first Finnish woman to scale Mount Everest in 2010.

These days the Finns maintain a strong presence as world-class rally drivers. Mika Häkkinen, Tommi Mäkinen, Kimi Räikkönen and Ari Vatanen may be known only to lovers of motor sports, but probably more non-Finns could name them than could identify Finland's current prime minister.

Ice hockey is one of the most important team sports in Sweden and even more so in Finland. Each country has around 60,000 officially registered federation players, and the countries' national teams constitute two of the International Ice Hockey Federation's "big seven". Around 60 Swedes and 30 Finns play in the North American NHL. One of the highest scoring players in NHL history was the 10-time All-Star Teemu Selänne, also known as the Finnish Flash, who retired in 2014.

And of course, all the Nordic countries share the European passion for football. Clubs are supported through funds from the football pools and from the sale of players to major European leagues.

Cross-country skiing race in Sweden.

TELEMARK SKIING

In the mid-1800s, Sondre Norheim, a young farmer from Morgedal, in the county of Telemark, created a whole new style of skiing. Morgedal is in the mountains, so the ski-makers there sought designs that would perform well in the surrounding rugged terrain, both in everyday winter skiing and for impromptu sporting meetings.

Norheim modified his skis by adding firm bindings, which hold the ski boots to the skis and allow the feet control over them; he also gave them "sidecut", a slight hourglass profile when seen from above, which enables the skis to run true and turn easily.

Norheim and his friends used the adapted skis to perfect new manoeuvres, including landing from airborne flights off snow-covered rooftops and natural outcrops. Soon they were ready to show off their new skills, and this led to the first ski-jumping contest in 1879. The bent-knee stance with one ski trailing soon became known as the "Telemark".

In modern Telemark skiing, the heel is free to lift up from the ski and turns are steered, with one ski trailing and at an angle to the other. Competitive Telemark ski races are now held on packed slopes, as are Alpine ski races, but true Telemark skiing has spawned the revival of skiathlons, in which competitors must ski jump, ski through a slalom course, and run a cross-country ski race, all on the same pair of skis.

The Girl in the Kitchen by Anna Ancher, 1883–6.

ART AND CULTURE

Rich in art, music and literature, and pioneers of modern design, Scandinavians are justifiably proud of their cultural heritage.

The histories of Denmark, Norway, Sweden and Finland have been so intertwined through the centuries that, while each country possesses a unique culture, there are strong similarities, perhaps best seen in design and an overall "feel" for visual expression. A bias towards simplicity pervades, with clean lines, natural materials and a lack of pretence.

Although much of what is considered Scandinavian style is a product of the 20th century, there is an underlying cultural heritage that complements the modern look. Exceptions exist, such as work commissioned by royalty with French design in mind, but the tastes of the people over the past 200 years make the strongest impression on the visitor.

Denmark

The rich cultural history of Denmark finds expression in centuries' worth of art and artefacts, including Viking treasures, numerous castles and manor houses, churches (many from the Middle

Rottneros Manor was the inspiration for Ekeby in Gösta Berlings Saga by Swedish Nobel Laureate Selma Lagerlöf.

LOUISIANA MUSEUM

Small museum treasures may be found throughout Denmark, but the most complete and satisfying of them all is the Louisiana Museum of Modern Art, situated in a sublime spot in Humlebæk, 35km (22 miles) north of Copenhagen. Louisiana houses a splendid collection of 20th-century art, including pieces by Pablo Picasso, Andy Warhol, Alberto Giacometti and Asger Jorn. It lies on the water's edge, and the extensive sculpture garden, featuring work by Henry Moore and Alexander Calder, that surrounds the unassuming building (much of its space is underground) is backdropped by exquisite coastal scenery and landscaping (www.louisiana.dk).

Ages), fortresses, stimulating museums and some of the finest contemporary design in the world.

Denmark's strong literary tradition encompasses sagas and medieval folk songs, the most popular Danish playwright, Ludvig Holberg (1684–1754), the Romantic poet Adam Oehlenschläger (1779–1850) and, in the 19th century, Hans Christian Andersen (1805–75) and Søren Kierkegaard (1813–55). Andersen is probably still the most widely read Danish writer today. His children's tales – including *The Ugly Duckling*, *The Emperor's New Clothes* and *The Princess and the Pea* – gained him worldwide fame, and are a continuing source for plays, ballets, films, visual arts and bedtime reading. In the 20th century, Karen

Blixen (1885–1962), working under the pseudonym Isak Dinesen, gained international recognition for her 1937 memoir of her years in Kenya, *Out of Africa*, which became a Hollywood movie.

> With The Killing (2007), a slow-burn crime drama, political Borgen (2010) and The Legacy's (2014) modern family portrait, TV drama has recently become a popular Danish export product. The latter series was sold abroad before it even premiered on Danish television.

Karen Blixen, Danish author of Out of Africa.

The Danish philosopher Søren Kierkegaard, known as the father of existentialism, wrote in the first half of the 19th century. His work made an impact in the mid-20th century when it was translated into German and English.

Peter Høeg is Denmark's best-known living author. *Miss Smilla's Feeling for Snow* (1992) is his most famous work, an elegant, absorbing literary thriller which begins in Copenhagen and ends in the icy wastes of Greenland. It was made into a film in 1997.

Theatre and dance

Plays are still performed on the old stage of Det Kongelige Teater (Royal Theatre) in Copenhagen, founded in 1748; but it has been superseded by a futuristic waterside playhouse, which opened in 2008. In recent years, Copenhagen's arts scene has also been gifted with a purpose-built opera house (Operaen), which houses the Royal Danish Opera, and the new DR Koncertsalen, where the Royal Danish Orchestra sometimes perform. The Royal Danish Ballet, formed 150 years ago, is one of the most influential worldwide. It has attracted great masters such as August Bournonville (1805–79), creator of today's "classical ballet" and choreographer of more than 50 productions, including the popular *La Sylphide*.

The big screen

Denmark's Nordisk Film Kompagni, founded in 1906, is the oldest film company still in operation. Carl Theodor Dreyer (1889–1968), who started his career here, directed one of the most influential films of all time, *The Passion of Joan of Arc* (1928). Dreyer died believing his masterpiece had been destroyed in a fire, but the original was rediscovered in 1981 in a Norwegian mental institution.

Today the government-supported Danish Film Institute is the heart of a vibrant Danish film industry. Three films have won the Academy Award for Best Foreign Film: *Babette's Feast* (1986), *Pelle the Conqueror* (1987) and *In a Better World* (2010), directed by Susanne Bier.

Other Danish films have attracted international acclaim, including Lars von Trier's *Dancer in the Dark* and Thomas Vinterberg's *The Celebration*. These directors are signatories (along with Kristian Levring) of the Dogma 95 Manifesto. This set of "chastity" rules – films should be made on location without artificial lighting or sound, using hand-held cameras – was intended as a personal challenge to help reinvigorate the art of filmmaking.

Painting and plastic arts

C.W. Eckersberg (1783–1853) is considered the father of Danish painting. At the end of the 19th century, a group of artists – including P.S. Krøyer (1851–1909) and Michael and Anna Ancher (1859–1935) – based themselves in Skagen at the northernmost tip of Jutland. Known as the "Skagen painters", they turned away from Impressionism, the favoured French style of the day, and focused on capturing the special northern light within their maritime landscapes.

In the middle of the 20th century, Asger Jorn (1914–73), a member of the CoBrA art movement, created large, bold, brightly coloured paintings. His expressionistic and experimental works on canvas and ceramics played a key role in the development and promotion of modern Danish art.

Olafur Eliasson (1967–) has created some of the 21st century's most innovative installations, which play with light, water and optical phenomena – for example, *The Weather Project*, a giant "sun" that illuminated London's Tate Modern in 2004.

Norway

After being a world power during the Viking Age, Norway went through various unions with and occupations by Denmark and Sweden until independence in 1905. Over the centuries, "culture" was something the overlords brought with them from foreign capitals... and took away again when they left. Norway's own culture was suppressed: under Danish rule, Norwegian "dialects" were forbidden for official documents and communications. As a result, Norway's early cultural heritage is identified in rural arts and crafts.

Rustic arts

The country's ancient stave churches represent some of the most distinctive examples of Norwegian artistic production. The rich ornamental carvings on door frames, around windows and on capitals in the interior owe more, stylistically, to the design motifs of the Viking period – dragons, tendrils, leaf patterns – than to Christian iconography. There are 28 stave churches in Norway, two of the most striking being the restored church at Urnes, which is on the Unesco list, and the Heddal stave church in Telemark, the largest.

INGMAR BERGMAN

Although Sweden was a cinematic powerhouse in the age of silent films, since the advent of sound it has been a relatively small player, with the exception of exports such as Greta Garbo and Ingrid Bergman, and one of the giants of film and theatre, Ingmar Bergman (1918–2007). Bergman made his breakthrough with *Smiles of a Summer Night* in 1955. His most acclaimed films are *The Seventh Seal* (1956), *Wild Strawberries* (1957) and *Cries and Whispers* (1973). *Fanny and Alexander* (1982) was his last film, although he remained active in the theatre until his death. His work offers a personal perspective on what is Swedish, yet universal.

Another very "Norwegian" visual expression, from the 18th century, is rustic *rosemaling* or "rose painting", of which there are as many styles as villages. Used to adorn household utensils and

One the Academy Awards nominees for Best Foreign Language Film of 2012 was the historical drama Kon-Tiki, Norway's most expensive movie production so far. It tells the story of ethnographer Thor Heyerdahl's three-month-long expedition in 1947.

Ingmar Bergman, internationally acclaimed Swedish playwright and film producer.

interiors, it features organic patterns and flowers, figurative representations and geometric design.

Plays and literature

The re-creation of a national identity began in earnest in the 19th century, inspired by nature, ancient traditions and the heroic Viking sagas of long ago. Henrik Ibsen (1828–1906) wrote many plays based on folklore. His best-known works include *Peer Gynt* (1867), to which Edvard Grieg composed the incidental music, *A Doll's House* (1879) and *Hedda Gabler* (1890). Ibsen commented on Norway's relationship with Denmark and Sweden, as well as on the individual's relationship with a society which would have him conform.

Growth of the Soil, which follows the tribulations of a Norwegian peasant family over 20 years, won its author Knut Hamsun (1859–1952) the Nobel Prize for Literature in 1920. His literary power is unquestioned, but his reputation suffered because of his Nazi beliefs – in the middle of World War II, he sent his Nobel medal to Joseph Goebbels as a token of his support. Eight years later, Sigrid Undset (1882–1949) won the prize for her epic trilogy *Kristin Lavransdatter*, whose eponymous heroine lives, loves and dies in a richly reimagined medieval Norway.

More recently, Mrs Pepperpot, an old lady

book, *Beatles*, is a darkly comic coming-of-age story set in Oslo.

And "Nordic Noir" is alive and well. Anne Holt's Inspector Hanne Wilhelmsen pursues truth and justice at great personal cost in thrillers such as *1222*. Karin Fossum is hailed as the "Norwegian Queen of Crime": one of her latest

> Joik is a form of singing traditional among the Sami. Composed in response to an event or emotion, it sounds like a yodelling chant.

Henry Moore at the Louisiana Museum of Modern Art, Denmark.

who shrinks at inconvenient moments, is another gutsy female character, and brought children's author Alf Prøysen (1914–70) great success. Her world is still rooted in peasant soil; but over the last 50 years, Norway's obsession with its own past has abated over time, and today's writers embrace contemporary genres and worldwide issues. Jostein Gaarder's philosophical novel *Sophie's World* was translated into 60 languages, and was quickly followed to the top of the international book charts by Åsne Seierstad's controversial bestseller, *The Bookseller of Kabul*, set in Afghanistan. Award-winning author Laars Saabye Christensen is considered one of the original voices in contemporary Nordic fiction – his most noted

Inspector Sejer novels, *The Drowned Boy*, was translated into English in 2015. And Jo Nesbø reigns supreme with his dry Oslo detective Harry Hole – *Phantom* and *Police* are his latest white-knuckle page-turners.

From Grieg to Black Metal

Norwegian music also flowered in the early 19th century, mainly influenced by the Royal Swedish Court. The violin virtuoso Ole Bull (1810–80), the "Nordic Paganini", proved a model for musicians and writers alike. The late 1800s became known as the Golden Age of Norwegian music, with such prominent composers as Halfdan Kjerulf (1815–68), Edvard Grieg (1843–1907) and Johan Svendsen

(1840–1911). Generally, they incorporated elements of folk music in their work, including Grieg, who fused folk music with Romanticism.

And classical music still thrives in modern Norway: Oslo's incredible submerged Opera House, opened in 2008, is a must-see. Grieg's work forms the kernel of the Bergen International Festival in late May, a major arts festival bursting with music and theatre performances. In recent times, theatre of a different kind has been provided by one of Norway's most unusual musical exports – the thriving black metal scene, which courts controversy with its violent lyrics and bloody stage performances.

Sweden

As a conqueror rather than one of the conquered, Sweden developed strong cultural traditions, particularly in theatre, music and dance. Diplomatic and commercial links with Europe allowed new ideas to travel into the country. Prosperous Swedish monarchs were patrons of culture, and their private collections became the basis for national art museums.

King Gustav III (1746–92), the "Theatre King", took many of his cues from the royal court of France and patronised drama and the arts. In 1775, construction began on the Kungliga Teatern (Royal Theatre, known today as the Royal Opera), and on the Kungliga Dramatiska Teatern (Royal Dramatic Theatre or *Dramaten*) in 1788. He hired Swedish actors and singers, forming the basis for a tradition of opera and drama performed in Swedish, instead of French or Italian.

The most notable Swedish venue is Drottningholms Slottsteater (Drottningholm

Court Theatre), in the grounds of Drottningholm Palace outside Stockholm. Built in 1766 and restored in the mid-20th century, every summer this intimate stage draws spectators from all over the world eager to see Baroque and rococo operas in an intact 18th-century theatre, complete with original backdrops and stage machinery.

Award-winning writers

One of the best-known (at least among Swedes) and still popular writers of the past is Carl Bellman (1740–95), a troubadour, whose lyrics and

The Scream by Edvard Munch, 1893.

poems immortalised 18th-century daily life.

Works such as *The Red Room* by August Strindberg (1849–1912) and *Gösta Berlings Saga* by Selma Lagerlöf (1858–1940), two of the country's finest writers, set the foundation for modern Swedish literature. Strindberg, whose personal life was marked by a series of failed marriages, alcoholism and instability, produced books, stories, plays and screenplays that often featured social criticism, satire and emotional angst. The creative output of Lagerlöf, the first woman to win a Nobel Prize in Literature (1909), is distinct from Strindberg, depending more on legend, history and childhood memories (*Jerusalem*, 1901–2, *The Wonderful Adventures of Nils*, 1906).

EDVARD MUNCH

Edvard Munch (1863–1944), perhaps Norway's most reproduced artist, is honoured with a museum in Oslo dedicated to his work, as well as an entire floor of the National Gallery. A forerunner of Expressionism, his introspective, symbolist and angst-ridden paintings and prints, such as *The Scream* (1893), *The Kiss* and *The Vampire* (both 1895), verge on the dark side and are a product of Scandinavian themes, artistic developments in France and Germany where he studied, as well as personal idiosyncrasies and obsessions. The Munch Museum will transfer to avant-garde new premises near the Opera House in 2019.

Other Swedes have won Nobel Literature prizes, Eyvind Johnson and Harry Martinson, in 1974, and more recently, Tomas Tranströmer in 2011, whose poetry praises the rhythm of nature and everyday life and has been trans-

> Even the most recalcitrant sopranos come home for the annual Savonlinna Opera Festival. Held in a 500-year-old castle, it is one of the most delightful summer opera festivals in the world.

Inspired by nature, the composer Jean Sibelius (1865–1957) set the scene for modern music in Finland.

lated into over 60 languages. A fascinating read, particularly for US visitors with Swedish ancestors, is Vilhelm Moberg's four-volume epic novel, beginning with *The Emigrants*. The book inspired the musical *Kristina from Duvemåla*, written by former ABBA members Benny Andersson and Björn Ulvaeus.

One of the most widely read Swedish writers is Astrid Lindgren, the indefatigable creative mind behind *Pippi Longstocking*, *Emil of Lönneberga* and other free-spirited child heroes, heroines and anti-heroes and heroines. Currently taking the world by storm is Stieg Larsson's posthumously published Millennium trilogy, *The Girl with the Dragon Tattoo*, *The Girl Who*

Played with Fire and *The Girl Who Kicked the Hornets' Nest*, which have sold around 50 million copies to date. We can only guess what Astrid Lindgren might have made of Lisbeth Salander, the books' violent, antisocial, computer-hacking heroine – created partly through Stieg Larsson imagining Pippi Longstocking as an adult. Another acclaimed Swedish crime writer is Henning Mankell, the creator of inspector Kurt Wallander, whose books have been translated into 40 languages.

Swedish design

The well-known "Swedish look" is greatly indebted to the graphic work and paintings of Carl Larsson (1853–1919), as well as to the design of his home at Sundborn. Larsson's images are marked by strong outline, subdued colours and a gentle curvilinear quality. Today, however, Swedish visual arts are extraordinarily multifaceted. Artists such as Ann-Sofi Sidén, Elin Wikström and Carl Michael von Hausswolff work in a variety of media, addressing complex contemporary issues. These trends can be seen at Moderna Muséet in Stockholm, which reopened in 1998 in a new building by Rafael Moneo, in adjacent ArDes (Swedish Centre for Architecture and Design), and at Moderna Muséet in Malmö, inaugurated in late 2009.

Finland

What may properly be called "Finnish culture" has existed for only a little over a century. Until the late 19th century, the arts in Finland fell under the influence of the invading powers of Sweden and Russia. Prior to Finnish independence (from Russia) in 1917, talented artists and composers normally studied and worked in Stockholm or St Petersburg.

As for all Nordic countries, innovations from France and Germany preoccupied Finland's artists. Many spent time in Montmartre ateliers, like Albert Edelfelt (1854–1905) and the well-travelled Akseli Gallén-Kallela (1865–1931), who returned to their homeland and gave painterly expression to the growing nationalist spirit. Their influence continued into the 20th century, with rural life and landscapes considered to be the worthiest of Finnish themes.

Musical notes

Jean Sibelius (1865–1957) is still the most notable name in music. Sibelius exemplified

19th-century Romanticism in his compositions, which drew inspiration from Finnish nature, folk music and poetry. His career began while Finland was still under Russian rule, and works such as *Finlandia* (1899; revised 1900) provoked such patriotic and nationalistic feelings that they were banned by the Russian authorities. His early symphonies, such as *Kullervo*, used material and motifs from Elias Lönnrot's classic poem *Kalevala*.

A generous funding policy for musicians and musical institutes has spawned a remarkable pool of modern talent. The contemporary classical scene teems with internationally acclaimed figures, snapped up by concert halls, festivals and orchestras across the globe: soprano Karita Mattila graces the stages of the world's major opera houses; Esa-Pekka Salonen is currently the principal conductor of London's Philharmonia Orchestra; Magnus Lindberg was the New York Philharmonic's composer in residence until 2012 and has now moved to the London Philharmonic Orchestra.

At home, the state-of-the-art Helsinki Music Hall (Musiikkikoulu) opened in September 2011, the new residence of the Helsinki

Interior at Sundborn, Sweden, by Carl Larsson

FINNISH ARCHITECTURE AND DESIGN

One of the more prominent architects of Helsinki is Carl Ludwig Engel (1778–1840) from Germany, who designed much of the capital, including Senate Square and the cathedral, as well as other buildings in Finland.

The National Romanticism of Armas Lindgren (1874–1929), Herman Gesellius (1874–1916) and Eliel Saarinen (1873–1950) defined Finnish architecture of the late 19th and early 20th centuries, gradually turning from a Gothic look to embrace Art Nouveau.

Alvar Aalto (1898–1976), Finland's most celebrated architect, designed the Finnish pavilion at the New York World's Fair in 1939, gaining international recognition for himself and the unadorned Functionalist style. In Finland he left his mark on housing, schools, governmental and industrial buildings, theatres and churches. His finest building, Helsinki's Finlandia Hall, was built in 1971 during his "white" period. Alas, critics assailed him for focusing on aesthetics instead of acoustics. Possibly Aalto's most indelible imprint on the world is from his classic chairs and stools and curving glass vase (Alvar Aalto Museo, Alvar Aallon katu 7, Jyväskylä; tel: 014 266 7113; www.alvaraalto.fi).

Industrial designer Yrjö Kukkapuro is known for his timeless furniture designs which are still being produced today by Avarte in leather and steel, and are in the collection of New York's Museum of Modern Art.

Cool Looks

Scandinavian design is elegant, light, sparse, shows respect for natural materials, and is made with superb craftsmanship.

Say "Scandinavian design" and most people visualise furniture, textiles, glass and domestic ware with pure forms and simple, clean lines. The aesthetic is immediately recognisable, in both Nordic architecture and objects, especially since the Swedish home-furnishing giant IKEA invaded the world.

Swedish cloud chair, a soft shape that suits tall and short people alike.

Scandinavian architecture and design have their roots in traditional crafts, but are very much a product of the 20th century and the age of Functionalism. Taking off in the 1920s, led by architects and artists such as Le Corbusier in France and Walter Gropius in Germany, Functionalism applies to various movements such as the International Style and Bauhaus. In Scandinavia it has been a source of inspiration since the 1930s.

The move away from ornamentation in favour of clean shapes and lines, allowing for the pure expression of the essence of structures, was more than a mere change in taste. Adherents to this style, which manifested itself in new materials (tubular metal, steel and glass), also embraced a vision for a new world, one where architecture and design could contribute to the levelling out of injustices in modern society. In Scandinavia, both the aesthetics and the social agenda of the modern, international style were eagerly adopted.

Earlier in the 1900s, Carl and Karin Larsson, taking their cue from the English Arts and Crafts movement, revived an interest in traditional Swedish crafts and craftsmanship. Their home at Sundborn, now a museum of Swedish country style (see page 274), features textiles with simple checked and striped patterns, against a background of sparse wall designs, wooden floors, striped rag runners and furniture brightened with uncomplicated embellishments.

Art Nouveau was an important inspiration. In the hands of Danish designers in the mid-20th century, its fluid decorative lines became part of the quest for a satisfying form that fitted a function, as seen in the chairs of Hans Wegner and Arne Jacobsen from the 1940s and 1950s (see page 128). Designers also began to heed ergonomic research at industrial companies like the car-makers Saab and Volvo.

Today, the adage "form follows function" is taken to a high science in Scandinavia. Aesthetics are fused with efficiency in everything from utensils to welding equipment. Numerous pieces from the early 20th century remain as popular as ever, for example, stools by the Finnish architect and designer Alvar Aalto.

The success of Nordic design has made it a standard far beyond the boundaries of Northern Europe. Smart Scandinavian design is found the world over. Time-tested pieces, such as the Stokke Tripp Trapp chair (1972) by Norwegian Peter Opsvik, are still best-sellers. The multitalented Stefan Lindfors burst onto the scene in the 1980s and since then has created everything from chairs and lamps to prefabricated houses, saunas and sex toys! Much of his crockery and cutlery is sold by the Finnish company Arabia. Other instantly recognisable Finnish designs are Marimekko textiles and Nokia telephones. Swedish glass manufacturers Kosta Boda and Orrefors produce lighting and homeware.

One of the best places to spot up-and-coming talent is Design House Stockholm, which acts as a "publishing house" for around 60 independent designers.

The 19th-century artist Akseli Gallén-Kallela was a seminal figure in Finnish culture whose contribution laid the foundations for contemporary Finnish design.

Symphony Orchestra, the Finnish Radio Symphony Orchestra and the celebrated Sibelius Academy. Festival fever strikes in summer: the international Savonlinna Opera Festival and Pori Jazz Festival are both held in July.

Rock and heavy metal dominate the mod-

work, a heroic epic on the scale of the *Odyssey* or the *Iliad*, inspired the 19th-century nationalistic surge in writing in Finnish, and is a continuing influence on literature, art and music.

A contemporary of Lönnrot, Aleksis Kivi (1834–72) wrote the first proper Finnish novel, *Seven Brothers*, which celebrated rural life and contributed to a burgeoning national consciousness. The stage performance of Kivi's *Leah* in the late 19th century marked the beginning of Finnish drama. F.E. Sillanpää (1888–1964), the only surviving child of a poor farming couple, took home the country's

Alvar Aalto's Finlandia Hall in Helsinki.

ern music scene – bands such as HIM, Nightwish and Eurovision winners Lordi are big in Finland, but less well known abroad. The long-established Ruisrock Festival, held on the island of Ruissalo, and the three-day Provinssirock Festival both attract crowds of tens of thousands, and Helsinki's Tuska Festival is the world's largest heavy-metal festival.

Literary heritage

Until Sweden ceded Finland to Russia in 1809, the Swedish language dominated Finnish culture. All that was to change in 1835 when, after many years of studying and collecting folk poetry, tales and ballads, Elias Lönnrot (1802–84) published his remarkable poem *Kalevala*. The

sole literary Nobel prize (1939) for his depictions of peasant life.

Today, the Moomin books by Tove Jansson are Finland's most famous literary creations, loved by children and adults the world over. Although the contemporary literature scene is vibrant – Finland publishes the second-highest number of books per capita in the world – little is translated into English. One exception is the work of Sofi Oksanen, the newest literary voice to gain international attention. Her third novel, *Purge* (2010), won numerous awards including the European Book Prize and the Nordic Council Literature Prize. In 2013, she was the first Finnish female writer to be awarded the Swedish Academy Nordic Prize.

The New Nordic Cuisine embraces local, organic ingredients all beautifully presented on a plate.

FOOD AND DRINK

Brace yourself for a gastronomic treat: fresh
seafood, wild berries and succulent game washed
down by fiery aquavit is the order of the day.

Magnificent landscapes, clean air and
the Baltic and North Seas have created a natural larder from which
Scandinavians have helped themselves for centuries. Every home chef makes full use of local
fruit, vegetables, grains, fish, meat and game;
and the capitals' restaurants have won plaudits
and Michelin stars galore for their back-to-
basics approach to Nordic cuisine.

Denmark, Sweden, Norway and Finland
have their own food cultures, but share gastronomic ground. Seafood is king, and herring is
the fish most associated with the region. Marinated, spiced, smoked, fried, salted or baked, it
is usually eaten cold and washed down with
aquavit. Elk, venison and reindeer are commonly found on menus, and nearly all Scandinavians do a different kind of hunting in
autumn – for mushrooms, blueberries and
golden cloudberries.

Denmark

In Denmark, model ships hang in every
church, as if to remind parishioners to give
thanks for the fruits of the sea. Fish, particularly herring, is still a mainstay, commonly
smoked, salted or pickled. Traditional Danish food included lots of pork, butter and
dairy products, but Danes today lean towards
a lighter, healthier diet, inspired by modern
Scandinavian cuisine.

Sandwiches and sausages

Denmark is synonymous with *smørrebrød*, for
which it seems there are as many toppings as
tastebuds. Liver pâté, shrimp, herring, caviar,
smoked salmon, roast pork and steak tartare
are combined with pickles, jams, remoulade and herbs in a kaleidoscope of culinary

Danish pastries.

THE NEW NORDIC KITCHEN

In 2004, Scandinavia's finest chefs came together
to devise the New Nordic Kitchen manifesto, focusing on slow food, local organic produce and foraged
ingredients such as birch juice and Arctic bramble.
Behind it lays a healthy appreciation of the Arctic
region's long, cool growing season, its abundance
of fish and game, and forests full of fungi, wild
plants and berries. The manifesto was the start of a
staggering regional-cuisine resurgence. Stockholm,
Oslo, Helsinki and Copenhagen are the focus of
exciting new culinary scenes, exemplified by Denmark's Michelin-starred Noma, named the world's
best restaurant in 2010, 2011, 2012 and 2014.

deliciousness. Specialist *smørrebrød* restaurants usually open at lunchtime.

Bacon makes up over 5 percent of Denmark's exports, but not all pork products are sent abroad. Danes wisely keep the tastiest for themselves: salami, crackling roast pork and *frikadeller* are national institutions. The last (perfect comfort food) are fried meatballs, usually made from minced pork, served with potato salad and pickled red cabbage. Sausages are popular, with each region having its own speciality – in south Jutland *ølpølse* (beer sausage) is a tasty snack found at the local butcher. Blood sausage, *blødpølse*, appears around Christmas time. The *pølsevogn* (sausage wagon) is a common sight around Danish towns, a cheap place to pick up a lurid *rød pølse* (red hotdog).

Sweet treats

Danish pastry (*wienerbrød*) is famous for a reason. Visit a bakery and try rich, chewy "chocolate snail" pastries, layered cream cakes or a waffle cone filled with ice cream, marshmallow topping and marmalade. Scandinavians have a peculiar love of salty liquorice, found in its strongest form in Denmark.

Danish open sandwiches (smørrebrød).

OPEN SANDWICHES

Danish *smørrebrød* (open sandwiches), eaten daintily with cutlery, are miniature works of art with a near-infinite choice of toppings. Slices of dense rye bread, packed with seeds and grains, serve as the base. It's customary to begin with a herring topping, washed down with cold-as-hailstones aquavit. Next comes a little warmth – perhaps fried fish, lemon and remoulade – then beef slices, pâté or meatballs. Cheese and fruit salad round off the meal.

Norwegian *smørbrød*, Swedish *smörgåsbord* and Finnish *voileipäpöytä* are equally artistic hot-and-cold lunch buffets. Finnish dishes tend to be less sweet, and served with a greater variety of bread.

Norway

Norway's long, varied coastline provides ample opportunity for harvesting both "wild" and farm-raised fish. The slow ripening process of everything that grows during the light summer imparts an extraordinary aroma to berries, fruits and vegetables. And animals that graze on the verdant grass provide meat with a distinctive full flavour.

Tasty Norwegian fare

Norway is known for its fish – from cod to monkfish, sea wolf to halibut. Ubiquitous salmon, marinated or smoked, remains a delicacy in this part of the world. Fishballs with new potatoes is a traditional dish, and

Danes, Swedes and Norwegians eat sweet, cured gravlax (raw salmon marinaded in salt, sugar and dill) as a lunchtime delicacy.

fishcakes, which can be bought from the fishmonger, make a delicious snack. Whale is found on some restaurant menus.

Autumn is the time to indulge in game such as reindeer, elk or grouse, ideally served with tangy berries and wild mushrooms. Lamb, though not found on many restaurant menus,

The best way to smoke salmon.

forms the basis of several treasured Christmas dishes like *farikal* (slowly simmered mutton with cabbage and peppercorns) and *pinnekjott* (which combines salted, dried and smoked lamb). Foreign guests are sceptical of *lutefisk*, another holiday "treat", which translates to cod marinated in lye.

Cheese and fruity desserts

Jarlsberg will be familiar to visitors, but *geitost* (brown goat's cheese) is seldom found outside the country and should be experienced. Usually found at breakfast, it is caramel-coloured and slightly sweet.

Desserts are always popular. Try *bløtkake*, a rich sponge cake topped with strawberries,

karamellpudding, similar to flan, and fresh waffles served with fresh fruit and whipped cream. Thanks to the cool climate and clean air, plums, pears, berries, and oversized morello cherries are pure indulgence.

Sweden

Sweden has access to some of the freshest flavours in Europe, farmed in the mellow climate of the south, or hunted in the unspoilt north. Dishes are generally gentle and unchallenging, but Sweden's cuisine throws up a few surprises. There are complex notes in its reindeer, boar and

Herring is a firm favourite.

grouse, and a love of "wild larder" ingredients like angelica, caraway and tart red lingonberries.

Husmanskost

Traditional Swedish dishes (*husmanskost*) are often updated for modern palates at the country's best restaurants. Found on the table on Thursdays, *ärtsoppa* is a hearty pea soup served with pork. *Pytt i panna*, a hash of fried diced meat, onions and potatoes, is another speciality. *Kåldolmar* (stuffed cabbage rolls) are said to have been brought back from Turkey by King Karl XII in the 18th century. Alien to foreign tastebuds, sweet gloopy soups such as rosehip or blueberry soup are served hot or cold.

Swedes eat little pork links (*prinskorv*) at a *smörgåsbord*. Another *smörgåsbord* favourite is herring spiced with sandalwood (*matjes*), frequently eaten with boiled potatoes and sour cream. In

> Crayfish are eaten widely in Finland and Sweden in July and August, when they are boiled, peeled and served at outdoor parties, with plenty of singing and toasting. Guests wear colourful bibs to shield them from crayfish drip.

Skåne in southern Sweden, look out for *spettkaka*, a tower-shaped confectionery of sugar, eggs and potato flour baked over an open fire.

Also particular to Sweden is a delicious baked anchovy-potato-cream casserole known as "Jansson's Temptation".

An acquired taste

A summertime favourite in northern Sweden is *surströmming*, Baltic herring, that is salted and "soured" or fermented, then canned. The *surströmming* tin bulges ominously with still-fermenting gases; and when it is opened (*always*

Herring is usually accompanied by a glass of aquavit.

The Finns love their mushrooms.

DRINKING IN SCANDINAVIA

Alcohol is expensive in Scandinavia, and the sale of strong beer, wine and spirits in Sweden, Norway and Finland is restricted to state alcohol shops (Systembolaget in Sweden, Vinmonopolet in Norway, Alko in Finland), and licensed bars and restaurants. In contrast, alcohol flows freely in Denmark.

No Scandinavian herring dish is complete without aquavit, literally "water of life". Distilled from potatoes or grain and flavoured with herbs and seasonings (caraway seed, cumin, fennel, dill or St John's wort), ice-cold aquavit warms body and soul. One of the best is Norway's Løiten Linie: part of its maturation involves a sea voyage across the equator and back.

In line with the growing local-food movement, micro-breweries have mushroomed all over Scandinavia. At Christmas, out comes the *gløgg* – hot spicy mulled wine, served with gingerbread, cinnamon buns, Danish *æbleskiver* (puff pancakes) or rice pudding.

To gain instant friends in Denmark, Sweden and Norway, lift your drink and say the word for cheers: *"skål"* (pronounced "skoal"). The correct way to skål is to look at the person, say the word, lift the glass slightly, drink and look at the person again. At formal occasions, strict rules of etiquette govern the *"skål"*-ing: for example, never drink until your host has given a welcome toast. The Finns say *"kippis"* when making a toast.

outdoors), the resulting stench often causes the uninitiated to run for the hills.

Finland

Mushrooms, berries, fish, sausages and reindeer are the key elements of Finnish cuisine. In July,

> In Finland, there are late-night kiosks dispensing polsar (hot dogs) to diehard pub crawlers, for sustenance as well as alleviating the next day's hangover.

of vodka (*viini*, or schnapps) and song. Reindeer, the cow of Lapland, is enjoyed as cutlets, steaks, meatballs, liver, smoked, in stew Karelian-style, or as carpaccio or tartare. Hare, elk, bear, wild duck, snow goose and ptarmigan are other game specialities, best served with creamy mashed potatoes, chanterelles and a tangy berry sauce.

Mushroom magic

Around 500 edible varieties of mushrooms exist in Finland, but only 30 are delicious enough to use in sauces, soups and salads. Signs in Hel-

Finnish open sandwiches.

look out for thick asparagus and sweet crunchy peas. New potatoes, tiny and tender, are served with fresh, aromatic dill, often as an accompaniment to fresh-salted salmon (*graavilohi*) or herring. Rhubarb is used in puddings, but there's nothing like fresh lingonberries, blueberries, strawberries or Lappish cloudberries with vanilla ice cream.

Fish and game

Finnish waters boast a variety of fish, from famed Baltic herring and pike perch to ubiquitous whitefish and salmon. Salmon soup is often served as a light meal, with dark crusty bread and sweet butter. In Midsummer, the crayfish season arrives, celebrated with rounds

sinki's market warn that some fungi must be boiled for an hour to detoxify!

Konditorei culture

Scandinavians are some of the world's biggest coffee-drinkers. Finns top the chart, consuming an amazing 12kg (26lb) per person each year. The Finns eat *pulla* (wheat buns) with their coffee and indulge in cream cakes topped with strawberries. The Swedish-speaking Finnish population has contributed to the crossover tradition of konditorei culture: elegant tearooms combine a good bakery and assortment of chocolate, and delicate sandwiches and pastries are enjoyed most afternoons by a mix of generations.

Lapland's snowy beauty in winter.

King crab safari near Kirkenes, Norway.

INTRODUCTION

A detailed guide to the Scandinavian
countries, with principal sites cross-
referenced by number to the maps.

Windmill in Finland.

Whether you're in a car or coach, on a bicycle, boat or train, on foot or on skis, the Scandinavian countries of Denmark, Norway, Sweden and Finland have an enormous variety of sights and scenery to beguile the visitor.

Denmark is neatly beautiful, with its white-sand beaches, well-groomed farmland, gentle hills and fairytale castles. Chilled-out Copenhagen is a particularly enjoyable capital, with pedestrianised streets, pavement cafés, superb shops and entertainment. Every Danish town has its museum and art gallery, every castle its collection. Remote from the rest of Denmark lie the Faroe Islands, a bird-watchers' paradise, and Greenland, a terrific adventure destination.

Norway is made up of mountains etched with beautiful fjords and dramatic valleys. From the southern beaches, the coastline stretches right into the Arctic Circle, dotted with islands, fishing villages and historic towns like Bergen. Inland, the rugged landscape beckons walkers and skiers. The capital, Oslo, offers every city delight, sleek architecture and forests on its doorstep.

Cows grazing in the Fryken Valley, Sweden.

A short drive from Copenhagen brings you to southern Sweden's gentle farmland and sunny islands. At the country's heart lie two vast lakes, Vänern and Vättern, linked by the Göta Kanal, a pleasure-boaters' mecca. Further north, the folklore province of Dalarna gives way to lakes and forests, winter sports centres and rugged Lapland. Stockholm floats majestically on 14 islands, the most sophisticated of Scandinavia's capitals.

Today, independent Finland has a distinct identity, with remnants of Swedish and Russian influence. The south coast is a summer playground of islands and beaches, fortresses and painted towns. The "Daughter of the Baltic", Helsinki, is an architecturally fascinating capital. Lakes and forests cover central Finland, while easterly Karelia is a hiker's delight. Lapland, land of the Midnight Sun, attracts anglers, white-water enthusiasts and those in search of true solitude.

Scandinavia

DENMARK

Small, but perfectly formed, Denmark is a country of fun-loving, environmentally conscious people.

Danish design.

Hamlet was wrong – there is nothing rotten in the State of Denmark. Yes, winters are dreary, but they're mild with little snow, and summers are sunny, with long hours of daylight. Yes, the tax rate is among the world's highest. But taxes are reinvested to help make this a country "where few have too much and fewer too little".

The world's oldest kingdom packs plenty of international clout. The Vikings are gone, but their descendants are spreading their seed far and wide: Denmark is one of the biggest suppliers of frozen human sperm on the planet. It's also a major purveyor of machinery and computer elements, windmills, agricultural products, arts and crafts and skilled professionals.

Denmark is a green nation of cyclists and recyclers. Nine out of 10 Danes own a bicycle, more than half the country's rubbish is recycled, and windmills provide nearly 40 percent of the country's power needs. It aims to be using 100 percent renewable energy by 2050.

Everyone cycles in Denmark.

Nowhere is very far away. The Jutland peninsula and main Danish islands are linked by a network of spectacular road and railway bridges, which even extends across the Øresund to Sweden. Ferries still play their part, linking islands and crossing the larger lakes, for this is a nation with a strong seafaring past.

Zealand, in the east, holds Scandinavia's liveliest capital city, Copenhagen, and Hamlet's castle, Kronborg at Helsingør (Elsinore). Jutland, in the west, is Denmark's link with mainland Europe. North Jutland's seascapes have captivated artists over the centuries, and its beaches draw summer holiday-makers. East Jutland boasts an intricate lake system, well used for canoeing and water sports, and Århus, Denmark's second city, with its esteemed international arts festival. Funen, sandwiched between Jutland and Zealand, is the "garden of Denmark". Out in the Baltic is Bornholm, Denmark's sunniest holiday spot.

Far to the west and north lie the outposts of the Danish kingdom: the windswept Faroe Islands ("Sheep Islands"), a favourite haunt for birdwatchers, and Greenland, offering adventurous travellers stunning scenery and a pristine natural environment.

Denmark

N

0 20 km
0 20 miles

S k a g e r r a k

K a t t e g a t

Anholt
Anholt

Hesselø

Læsø

Læsø Rende

Ålborg Bugt

SWEDEN

Marstrand
Torslanda
Göteborg
Billdal
Möndal
Kungsbacka
Onsala
158
Kungsbackafjord
Åsa
Bua
Varberg
Glommen
Falkenberg
Veddige
Ullared
E6
Tvååker
Vessigebro
Getinge
Skärström
Halmstad
Laholmsbukten
Laholm
Eldsberg
E6
Åsexdrega
Rydboholm
Borås
Hindås
Viskafors
41
Kinna
Skene
Svenljunga
Holsljunga
Överlida
Horred
Lygnern
Kungsäter
Älvsered
26
Nissan
E6

Alingsås
Mölnlycke
Kållered
Anneberg
Lindome
41

Åkulla

Torup

Möndal

Astorp
Bjuv
E6
Helsingborg
Helsingør
Hornbæk
Gilleleje
Fredriksborg
Tisvilde
Höganäs
Jonstorp
Grevie
Torekov
Skälderviken
Ängelholm
Båstad
Mölle
Hälsingborg
K

A
R
M
Gniben

Grenen
Skagen
Skagen
Albæk Bugt
Albæk
Tannis Bugt
Kandestederne
Tversted
Lendum
40
Hirtshals
Lønstrup
Sindal
Tårs
35
Vrå
Østervrå
Vendsyssel
Hjørring
E39
Brønderslev
55
Løkken
Pandrup
Blokhus
Jammerbugten
Vestero Havn
Byrum
Østerby
Hornfiskrøn
Dokkedal
Voersa
Asa
Hals
Østervrå
Ulsted
E45
Sæby
Frederikshavn
Hallund
E39
Kås
Brovst
Fjerritslev
Aggersund
Logstor
11
Hjallerup
Vadum
Aalborg
E45
Nørresundby
Nibe
13
Års
Suldrup
29
Støvring
Skørping
Kongerslev
Gistrup
Øster Hurup
Havndal
Mariager Fjord
Hadsund
Assens
Mariager
Råby
Randers Fjord
Ørsted
Holbæk
Udbyhøj
Bamten
Strand
Fjellerup
Glesborg
Grenå
Trustrup
Hjelm
Ebeltoft
Egsmark
Rønde
16
Djursland
Kalø
Vig
Tved
Århus
Bugt
M

Nordjylland
Limfjorden
Himmerland
Aars
Ålestrup
Hobro
Mølgrup
Hæmmershøj
Onsild
Bjerringbro
Hadsten
Hammel
Resenbro
15
E45
Randers

Viborg
Viborg
Ans
Silkeborg
15
Kolvrå
J y l l a n d
Mid-Jutland
Ikast
18
Bording
Herning
15
Århus
Hornslet
Lystrup
Århus
N
E
D
15

Skals
26
Stoholm
Hald Ege
16
Skive
34
Vinderup
Lem
28
Hvalpsund
Vilsted
Louns Bredning
Rønbjerg
Nykøbing
Erslev
Mors
Redsted
Thisted
26
Sallingsund
Jylland
Venø
Bugt
Struer
Holstebro
Ringkøbing-
Harsyssel
Vildbjerg
Videbæk
13
Skjern
26
Vinderup
Spjald
11
Ulfborg
Tim
16
Ringkøbing
Sønderig
Ringkøbing
Ringkøbing Fjord

Hanstholm
Klitmøller
Thy
Vigsø Bugt
Vorupør
Nørre Vorupør
Agger
Thyborøn
Harboør
Nissum Bredning
Lemvig
Bækmarksbro
Bøvlingbjerg
Torsminde
Husby
Nissum Fjord
Sædding
Bedsted
11
Snedsted
Østerild

On the waterfront in
Christianshavn.

COPENHAGEN

Denmark's capital city is the most exuberant in Scandinavia. Pedestrians and cyclists rule, shopping is a pleasure, cultural sights abound, and by night the city buzzes.

Copenhagen (København) is the "city of green spires". Copper plates, etched green by salt air, clad the spires of castles and churches in the Old City, and tower over the medieval street network and newer houses. The Old Town you visit today would have looked different but for two devastating fires and a terrible bombardment. Blazes in 1728 and 1795 licked and leaped along the straw-roofed houses and turned most of the half-timbered medieval town to ashes. Only a few solidly built structures survived – among them the Round Tower (Rundetårn). When Admiral Lord Nelson and the British fleet bombarded Copenhagen in 1801 the toll was also heavy. Six years later, Wellington besieged the city, destroying 300 houses and capturing the Danish fleet.

Copenhagen is the liveliest – and many claim the most fetching – of the Scandinavian capitals, with things to see and do all the time. With Europe's longest pedestrian mall, this was the first capital to offer the pleasures of ambling through a network of streets free of motor vehicles and exhaust fumes.

A good way to get a first feel of Copenhagen is from the water. Take one of the canal boat trips from Kongens Nytorv/Nyhavn, Gammel

Strand or Vester Voldgade (tel: 32 66 00 00; www.stromma.dk). If you're the adventurous type you could explore the waterways in a kayak for two hours, starting at Strandgade in Christianshavn. A guide paddles ahead of you (Copenhagen Adventure Tours; tel: 40 50 40 06; www.kajakole.dk).

Rådhuspladsen

City Hall Square (Rådhuspladsen) is the nexus of Copenhagen, grandly lit up at night with its coloured

Main Attractions

Tivoli Gardens
Ny Carlsberg Glyptotek (Art Museum)
Strøget
National Museum
Rundetårn (Round Tower)
Nyhavn quayside
Frederikskirke (Marble Church)
Amalienborg
The Little Mermaid

Copenhagen is an urban cycling paradise.

TIP

There is a public bike scheme operating in the city centre of Copenhagen which allows you to rent bikes from 20 docking stations (more opening in 2015) and cycle up to 12 hours. It costs DKK25 per hour, or you can get a monthly subscription for DKK70, and ride for the first half hour free, while every consecutive hour will cost you DKK6. Prior to rental you will need to create a user account, either on www.bycyklen.dk or directly on the bike's tablet. You will need a credit card to register. All bikes have a built-in GPS.

Tivoli Gardens at Christmas.

signs, digital news headlines and blinking neon, with the enormous **City Hall** ❶ (Rådhuset; tel: 33 66 25 82; Mon–Fri 8.30am–4.30pm, Sat 10am–1pm; free; daily tours in English) at its heart. Constructed in the National Romantic style, its inspiration was drawn from medieval Danish and Norwegian architecture with a touch of the palazzo style of northern Italy. The facade and interior are trimmed with historic details from Nordic mythology. For a bird's-eye view of the city's spires and towers, climb the 106-metre (347ft) tower (daily).

Inside the Rådhuset's foyer, look for the entrance to **Jens Olsen's World Clock** (Mon–Fri 8.30am–4.30pm, Sat 10am–1pm). Its star dial mechanism shows the path of the pole star in resettable periods, making it one of the most accurate and complicated clocks in the world. Unsurprisingly, this masterpiece of time-telling took 27 years to build.

Bordering the square to the east on Vester Voldgade are two of Copenhagen's fine traditional hotels. Closest to City Hall is the **Palace Hotel**, one of the few buildings in the *Jugendstil* (Art Nouveau style), and further north, past the square, **Hotel Kong Frederik**, with the smart and pricey Gastro Pub restaurant.

Between the two hotels is the beginning of Strøget, Europe's longest pedestrianised shopping street, and the kingdoms of wonder that are **Hans Christian Andersen's Wonderful World** and **Ripley's Believe It or Not! Museum** (tel: 33 32 31 31; www.ripleys.com/copenhagen; mid-June–Aug daily 10am–10pm, Sept–mid-June Sun–Thu 10am–6pm, Fri–Sat 10am–8pm). Forget educational value, and take the family to marvel at animated tableaux of Andersen's most famous stories, or shrunken heads, optical illusions, and a picture of Queen Margrethe carefully constructed from pocket fluff.

On the western side of Rådhuspladsen is Denmark's most visited attraction, the charming **Tivoli Gardens** ❷ (tel: 33 15 10 01; www.tivoli.dk; in season daily 10am–8pm, off season Mon–Fri 10am–6pm).

Opened in 1843, the amusement park updates its collection of rides and rollercoasters regularly while still retaining the air of a pleasure garden from a bygone age. The fair opening in April marks the beginning of summer. It's a Copenhagen institution, attracting visitors of all generations with its old-fashioned sidestalls, aquarium, gardens, cafés, theatres, an open-air stage, its own symphony orchestra, and a concert hall where classical concerts, jazz and musicals are performed. The park has more than 20 restaurants, including the Michelin-starred restaurant Herman.

Art and design

A two-minute walk south of the City Hall on H.C. Andersens Boulevard is the **Dansk Design Centre ❸** (tel: 33 69 33 69; http://ddc.dk; Mon–Fri 10am–5pm), host to a programme of temporary Danish and international exhibitions (see page 128).

Across the road is the **Ny Carlsberg Glyptotek ❹** (tel: 33 41 81 41; www.glyptoteket.dk; Tue–Sun 11am–5pm). This exquisite museum offers a grand art collection begun by the brewer Carl Jacobsen and maintained by the New Carlsberg Foundation. There are collections of ancient Egyptian, Greek, Roman and Etruscan sculptures, as well as some French masterpieces from Cézanne, Gauguin and Rodin. The lush, palm-lined indoor Winter Garden has a wonderful café.

Vesterbro

On Bernstorffsgade, across from Tivoli's west entrance, is the **Central Railway Station** (Hovedbanegården). Beyond it to the west lies **Vesterbro**, one of Copenhagen's oldest residential districts, today a multicultural community, vibrant with bizarre shops, exotic restaurants and its red-light boulevard, **Istedgade**. Over the last few years, Vesterbro has been the focus of a whole whirl of stylish new bars, clubs, restaurants and contemporary art galleries, based in **Kødbyen**, the meat-packing district. By day, it is still populated by butchers (although rising rents are forcing

City Hall Square (Rådhuspladsen).

TIP

You'll find local news and listings in the weekly English-language tabloid newspaper *The Copenhagen Post* (http://cphpost.dk), distributed free at some hotels and sold at Danish State Railway kiosks and 7-Eleven stores.

many to relocate); by night, it's a place to party.

The **Copenhagen Tourist Office** ❺ lies across the street from Central Station at Vesterbrogade 4. This travellers' ganglion has it all: information on sights, cultural activities, transport, eating places and events. A prime source of information is the city's official website: www.visit copenhagen.com.

East from Vesterbro, visit the famous Carlsberg Brewery and stables (Gamle Carlsberg Vej) in Valby. Marvel at the world's largest beer-bottle collection, meet the stocky Jutland horses traditionally used to cart wooden beer barrels, and sample a glass of the best (tel: 33 27 12 82; www.visitcarlsberg.com; Tue–Sun 10am–5pm).

The medieval city

If Rådhuspladsen is the heart of Copenhagen, then **Strøget** ❻, the 1.8km (1-mile) pedestrian shopping street, is the spine. It has endless shops, street vendors, buskers and cellar galleries. Strøget (*"stroy-yet"*)

is where Copenhageners and visitors alike go to shop or just to promenade. The mainstream shops and eateries are on Strøget proper, while the more quirky boutiques, cafés and restaurants are situated on the quieter side streets.

Starting at Rådhuspladsen, Strøget meanders through five streets and four squares before it runs into **Kongens Nytorv** (King's New Square) the largest square in the Old Town, on which stands an equestrian statue of Kristian V who laid it out in 1670. Good landmarks and meeting places are the squares at **Gammeltorv** (Old Square) and at Strøget's major crossroads, the crane fountain at **Amagertorv**. Here, another main pedestrian artery, **Købmagergade**, branches off to the north.

Near Gammeltorv, the area behind **Vestergade** is one of the few remaining residential areas in the inner city. Living in the picturesque neoclassical houses is a mixture of old-time Copenhageners, artists and students, and here you find some of the more exotic clothes shops and galleries – try Skt Pedersstræde for starters. **St Peter's Church** ❼ (Sankt Petri Kirke; www.sankt-petri.dk), on the corner of Nørregade and Skt Pedersstræde, is the oldest church in Copenhagen, its chancellery built in 1450. Hans Christian Andersen lived at No. 19 Vestergade when, as a young man, he first arrived in Copenhagen from Odense. Another famous Dane, the 19th-century philosopher Søren Kierkegaard, lived in the house on the corner of Nytorv and Frederiksberggade at Gammeltorv.

One block south and running parallel to Strøget is **Kompagnistræde**, with shops specialising in antiques, china and pewter.

Two blocks south, across from the canal on Ny Vestergade, is Denmark's **National Museum** ❽ (Nationalmuseet; tel: 33 13 44 11; www.natmus.dk; Tue–Sun 10am–5pm; free, guided tours in English available),

ON AMAGER ISLAND

Visitors glancing out of the aeroplane window near Copenhagen (Kastrup) airport may be intrigued by what appears to be a swirling vortex on Amager island. The spiralling landmark is actually one of many surprising buildings springing up around Copenhagen. Completed in 2013, it is the state-of-the-art home of Scandinavia's biggest aquarium, The Blue Planet (Den Blå Planet; www.denblaaplanet. dk; daily 10am–6pm, Mon 10am–9pm), with its popular 16-metre (52-feet) long shark tunnel. The aquarium is easily reached by metro.

For years, Amager was a quiet hinterland. Today, it's the scene for some of Denmark's most exciting architecture. A whole "downtown" area, Ørestad, is being created from scratch here: a shining new metro station brings shoppers to one of Denmark's largest malls, and to the DR Koncerthuset, home of the Danish Symphony Orchestra. Nearby, the Øresund bridge uses the island as a launchpad to curve itself over to Swedish shores.

Islandsbrygge, on the west of Amager, has more to offer the casual visitor, with its Havneparken (Harbour Park). The water around Copenhagen is clean enough to swim in, and in the park you'll find five outdoor pools. Even more of a luxury, Amager Strandpark (www. amager-strand.dk) is a beach development on the east, with beaches, an artificial island and a lagoon.

the country's most visited museum, which is largely focused on Danish history. It is highly recommended for its newly revamped collections of ancient "bog" finds from the Stone, Bronze and Iron Ages, and includes unique treasures such as the golden Chariot of the Sun, the enigmatic Gundestrup Cauldron and Egtved Girl. A fascinating and well-structured museum that takes days to cover, it also has an interesting section on Danish cultural history.

From Nytorv, continue along Strøget towards Amagertorv. For a close encounter of the rich and sweet, stop at one of Copenhagen's premier confectioners, **Conditori La Glace**, a few stops from Strøget at Skoubogade (http://laglace.dk). Here, cream layer-cakes reign supreme.

The opposite side of Amagertorv is occupied by the shops most often visited by tourists: **Illums Bolighus** ❾, a showcase for superb Danish and international design, and the flagship stores of **Royal Copenhagen Porcelain** and **Georg Jensen** silver (www.illumsbolighus.dk).

Latin Quarter

The streets to the north of Amagertorv form the old **Latin Quarter**, featuring the cosy **Greyfriars Square** ❿ (Gråbrødretorv). The cobblestone square is a popular place to enjoy lunch at one of several outdoorsy restaurants, or dinner (Peder Oxe is a local favourite; www.pederoxe.dk).

The streets just to the north hold **Copenhagen Cathedral** ⓫ (Københavns Domkirke; http://koebenhavns domkirke.dk) and the main building of the **University of Copenhagen**. The seat of the University Board, beside Nørregade, dates from 1420 and is the oldest building in Copenhagen.

A fun stop for children is the sweet factory on Nørregade 36, **Sømods Bolcher**, where confectioners make old-fashioned boiled sweets by hand (tel: 33 12 60 46; http://soemods-bolcher.dk; demonstrations Mon–Fri 10.15am, noon, 1.30pm, 3pm). **Fiolstræde** is known for its antiquarian bookshops, and **Krystalgade** is the site of Copenhagen's synagogue. Try

TIP

The new City Circle metro line, due to open in 2019, is currently in progress. It will extend Copenhagen's dinky little system with another 15.5km (9.5 miles) of track and 17 city-centre stations. You are bound to come across construction sites across the city, or attractions that have closed temporarily due to building work.

Gråbrødretorv.

a sandwich from the busy, bowler-hatted organic butchers, **Slagteren ved Kultorvet** (Coal Square; www. slagterenvedkultorvet.dk), on the open plaza near the Nørreport subway station, at the top of traffic-free Købmagergade.

On Købmagergade itself is one of Copenhagen's most fascinating buildings. The **Round Tower** ⓬ (Rundetårn; tel: 33 73 03 73; www.rundetaarn. dk; tower: late May–late Sept 10am–8pm, late Sept–late May 10am–6pm; observatory: see website for seasonal times) was built in 1642 as an observatory, possibly inspired by the work of Denmark's world-renowned astronomer, Tycho Brahe. The viewing platform on the top offers a breathtaking panorama on clear days and nights. The tower stands 36 metres (118ft) high, and to reach the roof one walks up a 209-metre (685ft) spiral ramp. In 1716 Tsar Peter the Great rode a horse to the top while his wife followed in a carriage.

Around the corner off Landemærket is the **Danish Film Institute** ⓭ (Det Danske Filminstitut: tel: 33 74 34 00; www.dfi.dk; performances Tue–Fri 9.30am–10pm, Sat noon–10pm, Sun noon–7.30pm), home of Cinemateket, which celebrates Denmark's trailblazing successes in cinematography, and shows a programme of Danish and international films.

King's New Square

The last section of Strøget, from the Crane Fountain to Kongens Nytorv, is the home of the exclusive and expensive: fashion shops, furriers and jewellers.

At the end of Strøget, facing **King's New Square** (Kongens Nytorv), stands the grand old hotel of the city, **Hotel D'Angleterre** ⓮ (www. dangleterre.dk). The majestic buildings dominating the square are the **Royal Theatre** ⓯ (Det Kongelige Teater; http://kglteater.dk) – the national stage for ballet, opera and drama. The present building was designed in the 1870s, taking the Paris Opera Garnier as its ideal.

Next door is **Charlottenborg**, since 1754 the home of the **Royal Academy of Fine Arts**, where painters,

Købmagergade.

sculptors and architects receive their formal training.

Nyhavn quayside

At the narrow waterway of **Nyhavn** ⑯, a famous landmark from 1673, colourful old wooden schooners line the quay, and the north side is a charming combination of sailors' bars and new restaurants. The south side was always the "nice side", but the north side used to be the "naughty side" where sailors on shore leave would spend their liberty drinking, whoring and getting tattooed. Times have changed, and gentrified Nyhavn is now one of the most popular and atmospheric spots in town. It's a fine place to wine, dine and socialise, and the waterfront **Royal Danish Playhouse** ⑰ (Skuespilhuset; www.skuespilhus.dk) adds a cultural element too.

Frederiksstaden

From Nyhavn, Bredgade and its parallel twin, Store Kongensgade, are the main shopping streets of the residential **Frederiksstaden** to the north.

The area was planned and built in the 18th century for the well-to-do who wanted stately homes close to the centre.

At Bredgade 68 is **Designmuseum Danmark** ⑱ (tel: 33 18 56 56; www.designmuseum.dk; Tue–Sun 11am–5pm, Wed 11am–9pm; guided tours in English), featuring classic Danish design as well as European and oriental objects. The building (1757) was originally a hospital. Opposite the museum, three domes tower over **Alexander Nevski Russian Orthodox Church**, which was built in 1881 by the Russian government and contains a number of fine icons.

Close by looms the grand copper dome of **Frederikskirke** ⑲ (tel: 33 15 37 63; www.marmorkirken.dk), popularly known as the **Marble Church**. The church was meant to be a majestic rococo monument, designed to rival St Peter's in Rome, but the king, Frederik V, ran out of money and the project was cancelled in 1770. The church was not completed until 1894, and when the project was resumed it was built not in marble but in limestone.

Guarding Amalienborg Palace.

The colourful quayside at Nyhavn.

FACT

Flame and Citron (2008) is a chilling film noir, directed by Ole Christian Madsen, former member of the Dogme group of Danish film-makers. Set in 1944 Copenhagen, the plot is based on the real lives of two of Denmark's most famous Resistance fighters and explores the moral complexities of war.

Visit the dome for a splendid view across the Sound to Sweden (mid-June–Aug daily 1pm and 3pm, off season Sat–Sun and holidays 1pm and 3pm). The statues outside the church represent important Danish clergymen and theologians.

Amalienborg Palace ⑳ (Amalienborg Slot), across Bredgade towards the harbour, is the winter residence of the royal family, one of Europe's less assuming royal domiciles, built in the 18th century. One wing of the palace houses the **Amalienborg Museum** (tel: 33 12 21 86; http://dkks.dk/amalienborgmuseet, May–Oct daily 10am–4pm, Nov–mid-Dec daily 11am–4pm, Jan–Apr Tue–Sun 11am–4pm, charge), whose reconstructed rooms contain exhibitions on the monarchy from 1863 to 1972.

The Royal Guard are always on duty, and the changing of the guard at noon every day attracts both children and adults. If the flag is flying, then the Queen is in residence and the full ceremony will take place. The exquisite equestrian statue in the square represents Frederik V

and was made by the French sculptor Jacques Saly.

Along the promenade

The other end of the east–west axis through the plaza ends in **Amaliehaven**, a modern park donated to the city by the A.P. Møller shipping company in 1983. Following the promenade to the north, you will find the dazzling fountain, **Gefionspringvandet ㉑**, dedicated to the Nordic goddess Gefion.

At the start of Langelinie is *the* symbol of Copenhagen, **The Little Mermaid ㉒** (Den Lille Havfrue). This bronze statue of the character from the Hans Christian Andersen fairy tale was created by Edvard Eriksen in 1913.

The quay of Langelinie follows, and Europe's busiest cruise-ship pier is to the north of this at **Frihavnen** (Free Harbour). One of the most architecturally interesting of the newer buildings in this area is **Paustians Hus**, designed by Jørn Utzon, who also designed the Sydney Opera House. Paustian is one of Copenhagen's finest furniture stores; the building also houses a good restaurant.

Return to the city centre via **Kastellet ㉓** (The Citadel), a fortification that has kept its old ramparts intact. Part of the area is still military property.

Churchillparken, a tiny park just south of Kastellet, was the home of the **Museum of the Danish Resistance** (Frihedsmuseet), commemorating the Danish resistance fighters of World War II, until 2013, when a fire devastated the exhibition building. Historical artefacts were not damaged and a new venue for the museum is to be constructed on the same site by the end of 2018.

Fine art collections

Continue past Store Kongensgade to visit Denmark's oldest housing development, **Nyboder ㉔**. Construction of the long rows of ochre-coloured houses began in 1631, after Kristian IV addressed the urgent need for housing for Danish Royal Navy

HISTORIC TRADING POST

Although there has been a harbour at Copenhagen since the 8th century, until the Middle Ages it was just a simple trading post called Havn (Harbour), albeit one with an important geographical position. Havn was within easy access of Skåne (Scania), then part of Denmark, across the Sound, and a handy halfway point on the trade route between the growing medieval cities of Roskilde and Lund.

Its fortunes changed dramatically, however, in 1167, when King Valdemar I commanded the local bishop, Absalon of Roskilde, to fortify Havn in order to protect it against Wendic pirates. Absalon built a fortress on the spot where the Parliament building now looms. Copenhagen was on the way to becoming Denmark's biggest and most important town. The fortress became Christiansborg, *borg* meaning castle. Centuries later, it remains the seat of Danish politics, housing the Folketing (Parliament).

During the long reign of Kristian IV (1588–1648), Copenhagen solidified its role as the country's seat of power. This visionary town planner strengthened the city's overseas trade links, enhanced the city's military might with a huge defensive fortification, and made it the country's economic centre by building Børsen, said to be the oldest stock exchange in Europe – a Renaissance structure with a spire of four entwined dragons, steep copper roofs, tiny windows and gables galore.

personnel. The 616 apartments are still used for staff and retired officers.

Nearby, where Øster Voldgade and Sølvgade meet, is the superb **National Museum for Fine Arts** ㉕ (Statens Museum for Kunst; tel: 33 74 84 94; www.smk.dk; Tue–Sun 10am–5pm, Wed until 8pm; permanent collection free, charge for exhibitions). A new extension houses four storeys of modern art within stunning glass and whitewashed walls. Other Danish and European works are displayed permanently, along with changing international exhibitions.

Behind the museum and across the park is the **Hirschsprungske Collection** ㉖ (Den Hirschsprungske Samling; tel: 35 42 03 36; www.hirschsprung. dk; Tue–Sun 11am–4pm), a fine private collection of 19th-century Danish art assembled by tobacco tycoon Heinrich Hirschsprung – including many of the originals from the Skagen painters.

Botanical Gardens and Rosenborg Castle

The **Botanical Gardens** ㉗ (Botanisk Have; tel: 35 32 22 22; http://botanik.snm. ku.dk; daily 8.30am–4pm, May–Sept daily 8.30am–6pm; free) are just across the street. Visit the rosarium, the perennials and a huge conservatory with tropical and subtropical plants.

One of Copenhagen's most attractive sights is **Rosenborg Castle** ㉘ (Rosenborg Slot; tel: 33 15 32 86; http://dkks.dk; times vary usually 10am–4pm; visitors under 18 free), the fairytale castle across from the Botanical Gardens. King Kristian IV's exquisite palace in Dutch Renaissance style is now a museum, and contains three centuries' worth of royal treasures, as well as the crown jewels. The garden surrounding it, **Kongens Have**, has been a favourite with Copenhageners for centuries. In adjacent Kronprinsessegade, located in a neo-classical building at number 30, is **The David Collection** ㉙ (Davids Samling; tel: 33 73 49 49, www.davidmus. dk; Tue–Sun 10am–5pm, Wed until 9pm; free). Overhauled and reopened in 2009, it's a superb small museum boasting marvellous collections of Islamic art, European 18th-century art and Danish early modern art.

Rosenborg Castle.

The ochre-coloured houses of the Nyboder district.

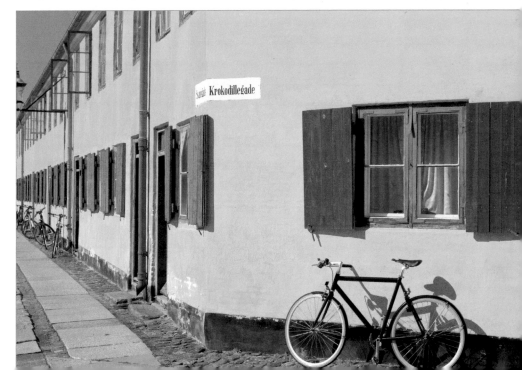

Christiania - the Alternative City

In a beautiful position on Copenhagen's waterfront, Christiania offers a way of life far removed from the bustle of a city.

In 1971, a group of alternative thinkers founded Christiania, a 34-hectare (84-acre) "Free City" with woods, dirt roads, workshops, restaurants and funky houses. The hippie enclave in the heart of the city – only 1km (0.5 mile) from the Parliament buildings – occupies what was previously an abandoned 19th-century military barracks in Christianshavn. The Christianites, about 850 people of all ages, cultures and income levels, have converted barrack blocks, workshops and powder magazines into a place where they can live and work. The basic rules are: no hard drugs, no cars, no gang insignia, no weapons or violence.

Barefoot cyclists, their baskets full of vegetables; earthy-smelling organic markets; recycling warehouses; workshops and stables, resident children

Murals decorate many of the buildings.

playing in an "organic kindergarten" – this image may once have been true, but now the place is far from an idealised hippie paradise.

Since 2004 the Danish government has stepped up measures to "normalise" the area. A police crackdown on "Pusher Street", where marijuana was sold openly, drove the drugs trade underground, yet for a little while only. In 2006 the government proposed that all buildings should be privately owned, a suggestion fiercely rejected by the Christiania collective. When government workers entered Christiania in 2007 with a police guard and began to demolish a derelict building, tension quickly turned to violent protest, with 59 arrests.

In February 2011, the commune was dealt a blow when the Danish Supreme Court declared that the residents had no legal right to occupy the area. Following the ruling, the right-wing government surprisingly gave residents the chance to buy their town for a generous 150m kroner (£18m). It was widely thought that the anti-materialistic inhabitants would reject the offer. But in a further twist, in 2011 the residents agreed to stump up the cash. In order to raise the money they set up a fund and started to issue and sell their own stocks. In 2012, the commune struck the deal with the Copenhagen council. Yet, most of the money to pay off the city came from a 30-year bank loan.

According to police, Christiania has been the centre of organised cannabis sale. In 2014, they raided the community, confiscated the cannabis and arrested 80 people. In January 2015, seven men received jail sentences, and the remaining were awaiting trials in prison in what is considered to be Denmark's largest ever drug case.

As of early 2015, Pusher Street still boasted hash stalls, some in the form of conspicuously covered huts. The smell of smoked pot will hit you as soon as you enter Christiania. Located on Copenhagen's waterfront, in fact it now resembles littered, grim shacks of a breakaway society than a happy commune. A visit there may not be comfortable for all, photography is not allowed and it's definitely not a destination for a family trip.

If you're adventurous, see Christiania for yourself. It has some good restaurants, including SpiseLoppen (The Eating Flea), in the warehouse by the front entrance. In the same building is Loppen, a music club. Månefiskeren (The Moon Fisher; www.maanefiskeren.dk), a café in the heart of the collective, serves excellent coffee in a "far-out" atmosphere.

Castle Island

To the southeast of Strøget and the main shopping area lies **Slotsholmen** (Castle Island). Surrounded by canals, the island is the seat of the Danish Parliament and government ministries.

Bishop Absalon built a fortress on the islet in 1167. The fortress was replaced by a new castle in 1367 and from 1416 it was the home of the Danish king. In the 1730s King Kristian VI ordered a new palace. This one, a magnificent Baroque building, burned in 1794 and was replaced with another new palace which, ill-fated as it was, burned down in 1884.

The present version of **Christiansborg Palace** ③⓪ is around 100 years old and contains Parliament, the prime minister's office, the Supreme Court and the Royal Reception Chambers. The granite facade of this imposing building was made from stones gathered in every parish in the country. The equestrian statue, erected on the Palace Square, depicts King Frederik VII (1843–63).

The public may join conducted tours of the **House of Parliament** (Folketinget; tel: 33 37 32 21; in English, year-round Sun and public holidays 1pm; free; online booking at www.thedanishparliament.dk). The stately **Royal Reception Chambers**. (tel: 33 92 64 92; www.christiansborg. dk; May–Sept 10am–5pm, Oct–Apr Tue–Sun 10am–5pm), still used by the royal family, are richly decorated and contain 11 modern gobelin tapestries commissioned for the Queen's 50th birthday.

The **Ruins of Absalon's Old Fortress** (May–Sept daily 10am–5pm, Oct–Apr Tue–Sun 10am–5pm) and the medieval castle are accessible to visitors and make an interesting "underground" visit.

The **Palace Chapel**, inaugurated in 1826, is located to the north of Christiansborg. Behind the chapel is **Thorvaldsens Museum** ③① (tel: 33 32 15 32; www.thorvaldsensmuseum.dk; Tue–Sun 10am–5pm; Wed free; visitors under 18 free), which contains the works of Denmark's great sculptor, Bertel Thorvaldsen (1770–1844), who lived and worked in Rome for 40 years.

At the National Museum for Fine Arts.

In front of Christiansborg is the **Ridebanen** ㉜, the royal riding grounds from the 1740s bordered by the only surviving buildings from the first Christiansborg. The royal horses are still exercised here, and their stables can be visited on the southeast side of the square – the **Museum of Royal Stables and Coaches** (Kongelige Stalde og Kareter; tel: 33 40 26 76; May–Sept daily 1.30–4pm, Oct–Apr Tue–Sun 1.30–4pm). Adjacent to the stables, the **Teatermuseet** is one of the oldest court theatres in the world, designed in 1766 by the French architect Nicolas-Henri Jardin (tel: 33 11 51 76; www.teatermuseet. dk; Tue–Thur 11am–3pm, Sat–Sun 1–4pm). The equestrian statue on the riding grounds depicts King Kristian IX, who died in 1906.

East of Christiansborg is another of Copenhagen's best-known buildings, the **Stock Exchange** ㉝ (Børsen), built in 1619 in Dutch Renaissance style by Kristian IV. Its prominent spire is formed by the entwined tails of four dragons said to protect the building from fire. On the southeast side of the island is the **Royal Library** ㉞ (Det Kongelige Bibliotek) and its "Black Diamond" – an architectural wonder of old and new. Det Kongelige Bibliotek dates back to 1482 and is the largest library in Scandinavia, with more than 2.5 million volumes. The Black Diamond, completed in 1999, is a modern extension in black polished granite perched on the water's edge.

Christianshavn

Cross the harbour via the Knippelsbro bridge to reach **Christianshavn**, one of Copenhagen's oldest and most colourful residential areas. Christianshavn was built on an island in 1617 by Kristian IV and is surrounded by the original star-shaped ramparts. Along the harbour wall, one of the meticulously restored warehouses is well worth a visit, the **Danish Architecture Centre** ㉟ (Dansk Arkitektur Center; tel: 32 57 19 30; www.dac.dk; daily 10am–5pm, Mon–Fri from 8am, Wed until 9pm; free Wed 5–9pm), which features various exhibitions, a bookshop and café.

Royal thrones at Christiansborg Palace.

Until recently a run-down, working-class area and Denmark's largest shipyard, Christianshavn has changed enormously and now features a mixture of smartly renovated 18th-century city houses, big apartment blocks, old and new industry, a good deal of the state's administration, laidback café-bars, some of the city's finest restaurants and stunning new architecture. It's a real bohemian mixture, home to all kinds of people, and an area just made for wandering: take a stroll down the streets of Christianshavn and glance into the courtyards of some of the old houses on **Strandgade**, stop for a coffee on **Wildersgade** and then to gaze at **Amagergade 11**, surrounded by old galleries and said to have the finest courtyard in town. On the very bottom edge of Christianshavn is the city's first floating hotel, **CPH Living** (www.cphliving.com).

Christianshavn is also the home of **Christiania** ㊱, the hippie-style "free city". The main entrance is on Prinsessegade.

Two of Copenhagen's more notable churches are on Christianshavn.

Christianskirke ㊲ in Strandgade is a rococo building from 1754. It was built as a theatre with boxes, including one for the royal family. The **Church of Our Saviour** ㊳ (Vor Frelsers Kirke; tel: 32 54 68 83; www.vorfrelserskirke. dk; church daily 11am–3.30pm) in Prinsessegade attracts the most attention. Built in red brick in 1694, its tall copper-clad tower with a spiralling, external stairway can be seen from all over the city. The tower is open to visitors who are brave enough to climb through a maze of roof timbers and up the 150 gilded steps.

At the northern end of Christianshavn, a cluster of little islands known as **Holmen** were the Danish Royal Navy's base until the 1990s. Some interesting naval architecture remains, such as the 18th-century **Mastekranen**, used for fixing masts onto sailing ships. But the most recent buzz around Holmen was the creation of Copenhagen's immense new **Operaen** (Opera House). Designed by Henning Larsen, the building contains over 1,000 rooms and cost 2.5 billion Danish kroner.

The Botanic Gardens conservatory.

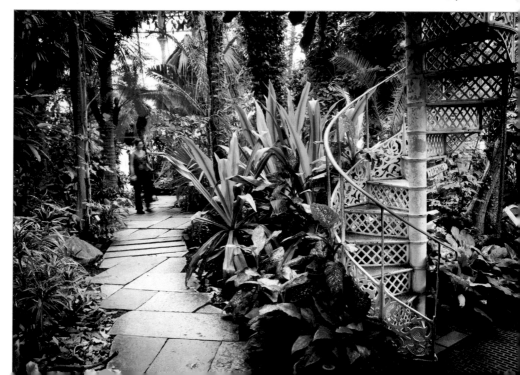

A FLAIR FOR DESIGN: FUNCTION WITH FORM

When a nation of craftsmen mixed with a late move towards industrialisation in the 1900s, an influential new school of design was born.

A chair may be something to sit in, and a lamp may help to light a room, but Danish designers have made these ordinary objects extraordinary. Perhaps their success is linked to the fact that Danish life is so centred around hearth, home and the concept of *hygge* – one's surroundings should always be familiar, functional and beautiful.

Danish design in the 1950s and 1960s brought a whole new look to furniture, lighting and homeware, avoiding the hard, geometrical shapes apparent elsewhere in the design world, and imbuing everyday objects with a tactile, organic quality. This iconic look has survived the test of time – Arne Jacobsen's egg chair is a prime example.

Today, the Danes are still at the forefront of design. Old and new companies alike – such as Fredericia Furniture, Gubi, Normann and Hay – are keen to promote new designers, revitalising the principles of Danish functionalism and creating tomorrow's classics. Whether in museums, conference rooms or homes, Danish design always brings a sense of elegance to everyday life.

"It always starts with a task," says designer Hans J. Wegner. "I never say to myself, I'm going to make a piece of art. I tell myself, I want to make a good chair". Danish designers "subtract and subtract" unnecessary elements from products and tools to find true function and form, says Jens Bernsen of the Danish Design Centre. "Sometimes these designs even turn out to be beautiful."

The iconic Flower Pot lamp by Verner Panton, one of Denmark's most influential 20th-century designers, famous for introducing the Pop aesthetic to furniture and interiors.

A grass vase, a quirky take on a typical home accessory from Normann Copenhagen.

Many of Arne Jacobsen's designs were intended for specific buildings or, in the case of this egg chair, hotel lobbies.

Natural wood grain features heavily in Scandinavian design, and is frequently paired with sleek metal accents, such as the balustrade on this spiral staircase.

DESIGN IN THE HOME

For all its elegance, Danish design is not something limited to galleries and museums. In Denmark, it is found everywhere – hotels, restaurants, cafés, offices and, most importantly, homes. Nearly every Dane, it seems, has some sort of sleek designer lamp hanging over the dinner or coffee table.

For special occasions, such as weddings, birthdays and office receptions, Danes give presents such as arty salad sets, candle holders, salt and pepper grinders, pot holders – even mixing bowls.

"The kitchen drawer is good design's enemy number one," says Erik Bagger, whose wine-serving tools are well known in Denmark. Danish-designed products are meant to be used, however, meaning that Denmark probably has the most stylish contents of kitchen drawers anywhere in the world.

The visually striking sound systems designed by Bang & Olufsen are praised worldwide, and are found in many a Danish home. Even such prosaic items as cupboard handles and other household fittings are given due attention by Danish designers. Organic shapes abound, and recently a certain amount of whimsy has crept in: witness Normann's award-winning grass vase.

This is the PH lamp; Poul Henningsen saw a light fixture as more than just light – as something to create a sense of space.

The architect Arne Jacobsen designed this stainless steel line of household objects, Cylinda Line, for the company Stelton, and it is now one of the most recognised in Denmark.

Bang and Olufsen offers a fine example of contemporary Danish design. The company is well-known for its chic range of electronics.

Roskilde University.

ZEALAND

Venture north from Copenhagen to Hamlet's castle at Helsingør, or south to the white cliffs of Møn, and discover Zealand, a colourful land rich in culture and tradition.

he island of Zealand (Sjælland) is Denmark's largest, yet it is still compact and most of its attractions make ideal day trips from the capital. The area north of Copenhagen makes a classic tour for visitors, with its undulating countryside, beech forests, lakes and good beaches, as well as castles, manor houses, royal hunting lodges, art galleries and museums. The southern and western areas of Zealand have traditionally been entry points for new people and ideas coming from the Continent. This side of the island is an enchanting expanse of rolling hills, woodland and some wonderful seaside scenery.

The Danish Riviera

The coast road from **Copenhagen ❶** (København) to Helsingør, officially called Strandvejen, is also known as the "Danish Riviera" for its stylish houses and fine views across the Øresund to Sweden. Small protected harbours shelter working fishing boats and millionaires' yachts alike, and converted marine buildings house fresh fish restaurants.

While it's true that the essence of North Zealand can be glimpsed in a day, it really warrants more time, either by an overnight stop at a charming Danish *kro* (inn) or by taking several day tours from Copenhagen.

From Copenhagen, drive north through fashionable Charlottenlund to **Klampenborg ❷**. In just 15 minutes you'll come to an ancient deer park, **Klampenborg Dyrhaven** (daily), first mentioned in official documents in 1231. Leave your car and take a horse and carriage through the woods and parkland. Forest walks are indicated by yellow spots painted on trees.

Within the deer park lies the world's oldest funfair, **Bakken** (tel: 39 63 35 44; www.bakken.dk; late Mar–Aug, times vary). **Peter Lieps's** rustic forest

Main Attractions

Louisiana Museum for Modern Art
Helsingør and Kronborg castle
Tisvilde and Liseleje beaches
Vikingeskibsmuseet, Roskilde
Cliffs of Møn

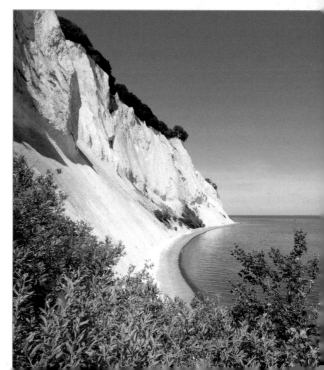

The white cliffs of Møn.

restaurant is where locals go to drink hot chocolate after winter walks (www.peterlieps.dk). Art-lovers will enjoy the quiet elegance of nearby **Ordrupgaard** (Vilvordevej 110; tel: 39 64 11 83; http://ordrupgaard.dk; Tue, Thur, Fri 1–5pm, Wed 1–9pm, Sat–Sun 11am–5pm). Its permanent collection of Danish and French paintings includes works by Matisse and Gauguin. The museum has newly incorporated the home of Finn Juhl, architect and furniture-designer extraordinaire (weekends 11am–5pm).

Karen Blixen's home and the Louisiana Art Museum

A further 12km (7 miles) brings you to **Rungsted ❸**, site of **Rungstedlund** (tel: 45 57 10 57; http://blixen.dk; May–Sept Tue–Sun 10am–5pm, Oct–Apr Wed–Fri 1–4pm, Sat–Sun 11am–4pm; guided tours in English by appointment), the family home of Karen Blixen, the Danish writer known as Isak Dinesen, author of *Babette's Feast* and *Out of Africa*, which later became acclaimed films, winning one and seven Oscars respectively.

At **Humlebæk ❹**, art-lovers could easily spend an entire day at the **Louisiana Museum for Modern Art** (Louisiana Museum for Moderne Kunst, Gl. Strandvej 13; tel: 49 19 07 19; www.louisiana.dk; Tue–Fri 11am–10pm, Sat–Sun 11am–6pm), located in a breathtaking coastal setting overlooking the Øresund. A rich permanent collection, encompassing the work of artists such as Giacometti, Yves Klein, Louise Bourgeois and Picasso, is supplemented by frequent international exhibitions. Various extensions and pavilions stretch into the gardens, their clever designs blurring the distinction between man-made structures and nature.

Hamlet's Helsingør

Helsingør ❺ is best known for its massive Renaissance-style **Kronborg**, Hamlet's "Castle of Elsinore" (tel: 49 21 30 78; www.kronborg.dk; June–Aug daily 10am–5.30pm, Sept–Oct and Apr–May daily 10am–4pm, rest of the year

Tue–Sun 10am–4pm). Originally built by King Eric of Pomerania when he introduced the "Sound Dues" (fees paid to the Danish crown by all ships passing through to the Baltic), Kronborg has been rebuilt several times. It has provided a backdrop for many productions of Shakespeare's *Hamlet*. Inside, the richly decorated King's and Queen's chambers and the 62-metre (203ft) long Great Hall are worth seeing.

Helsingør is one of Denmark's most historic towns, with entire streets of colour-washed buildings. The 15th-century **Skt Mariæ Kirke** (www.sctmariae.dk) and the **Carmelite Kloster** (Convent) are among the best-preserved Gothic buildings in the world. The town is also home to the new **Danish Maritime Museum** located in intriguing underground premises built around an old dry dock (tel: 49 21 06 85; www.mfs.dk; July–Aug daily 10am–5pm, Sept–June Tue–Sun 11am–5pm).

The coast road leads on to **Gilleleje ❻**, the most northerly town of Zealand, a small working fishing port. **Adamsens Fisk**, an unpretentious

The imposing Kronborg Castle is a Unesco World Heritage Site.

Learning to fence at Kronborg Castle.

Historically, Zealand played an important political role in the development of Denmark. The Viking influence was strong, and the town of Roskilde, a trading post in Viking times, became the seat of kings and an important religious centre.

harbourside takeaway, is a great spot for a fish lunch (www.adamsensfisk.dk). If the weather is good, you could stop at the sun-worshippers' beaches of **Tis-vilde ❼** or **Liseleje ❽**.

Turning back towards Copenhagen, Denmark's National History Museum is at the spectacular Renaissance palace **Frederiksborg ❾** (tel: 48 26 04 39; www.dnm.dk; daily, Apr–Oct 10am–5pm, Nov–Mar 11am–3pm; guided tours in English available), built between 1605 and 1621 in **Hillerød**. The most notable rooms are the Council Hall, Knights' Hall and the chapel with its original Compenius organ (1610). Outside is one of the best Baroque gardens in Northern Europe.

Just 9km (5 miles) from Hillerød is the Italianate palace of **Fredensborg ❿** (tel: 33 40 31 87; www.slke. dk; July–mid-Aug daily 1–4.30pm; guided tours in English at 1.45pm and 3.30pm). Built in 1722, it is now used by the Danish royal family as a spring and autumn residence. The astonishing 120 hectares (300 acres) of gardens – long, straight 18th-century avenues interspersed with forest

Exhibit at the Viking Ship Museum.

and seashore – are open to visitors at all times.

Viking town

A major highlight of Zealand is the town of **Roskilde ⓫**, the island's second-largest town, 20 minutes by train west of Copenhagen. The wonderful **Cathedral** (Domkirke; www.roskildedomkirke.dk; Apr–Sept Mon–Sat 9am–6pm, Sun 1–6pm, Oct–Mar Tue–Sat 10am–4pm, Sun 1–4pm), built in 1170, is the burial place of generations of Danish monarchs and a Unesco World Heritage site. The **Viking Ship Museum** (Vikingeskibs-museet; tel: 46 300 200; www.vikingeskibsmuseet.dk; mid-May–late Aug daily 10am–5pm, rest of year 10am–4pm; visitors under 18 free) has five superbly restored ships (including a dreaded Viking man o' war) found in 1962 at the mouth of Roskildefjord – they were sunk by the 11th-century defenders of Roskilde to block the fjord against enemy attack. Costumed re-enactors demonstrate Viking crafts and the restaurant has *mjød* (mead) to quaff.

Vikingeborgen Trelleborg ⓬ (tel: 58 54 95 06; http://vikingeborg.dk; Tue–Sun 10am–5pm), near Slagelse in western Zealand, is an abandoned Viking fortress some 1,000 years old. It was once a huge fortified camp that housed 1,000 Vikings, and one of the houses has been reconstructed.

Southern Zealand

The first stop for modern art enthusiasts south of Copenhagen is the sleek white **Arken Museet for Moderne Kunst** (tel: 43 54 02 22; www.arken. dk; Tue–Sun 10am–5pm, Wed until 9pm; visitors under 18 free) at **Ishøj ⓭**. **Køge ⓮** is popular for its beaches, crowded with sun-loving Danes. Køge is characterised by half-timbered houses. The oldest, dated 1527, stands at 20 Kirkestræde. **Skt Nikolai Kirke** has one of Denmark's most beautiful town church interiors. Not far from the market is **Hugos Vinkælder**, a historic inn serving old-fashioned draught porter (www.hugos.dk).

The cliffs of **Stevns Klint** ⓖ on the south headland of Køge Bay may not be quite as dramatic as those on the island of Møn, but they are impressive when the sun illuminates them in brilliant hues of white.

Inland, 5km (3 miles) south of the ancient town of **Haslev**, Hans Christian Andersen found inspiration for one of his most famous stories, *The Ugly Duckling*, in **Gisselfeld Slot** ⓰ (grounds and stables daily), a castle built in 1554. **Næstved** ⓱, 10km (6 miles) southwest of Haslev, has been an important trading town for most of its history and has an attractive city centre. About 6km (4 miles) to the southwest is **Gavnø Slot** (tel: 55 70 02 00; www. gavnoe.dk; Apr–mid-Oct 10am–5pm, May–Aug 10am–6pm), set among magnificent gardens on a tiny island linked by road. In the 13th century it was used as a pirates' castle; today it houses Scandinavia's largest privately owned picture collection.

Cliffs of Møn

The island of **Møn** ("The Maid") to the east is linked to Zealand by road bridges (www.visitmoen.dk). According to legend, its spectacular stretches of luminous white chalk cliffs, topped with beech woods and studded with fossils, became a refuge for the most powerful of Nordic gods, Odin, when Christianity left him homeless. **Geocenter Møns Klint** (tel: 55 86 36 00; www.moensklint.dk; mid-Apr–Oct 10am–5pm, July–mid-Aug until 6pm) explains Denmark's geological history. There are dinosaurs and a 3D cinema.

Liselund Slot ⓲ (tel: 55 81 21 78; May–Sept Wed–Sun, by guided tour only: 10.30am, 11am, 1.30pm and 2pm) is a thatched mini-chateau, built in 1796. Andersen wrote *The Tinder Box* and *The Little Match Girl* in a summer house on the estate. Møn's churches are noted for their frescoes, particularly those at **Keldby**, **Elmelund** and **Fanefjord** ⓳, the last standing on an isolated hill overlooking the narrows of Grønsund. Beside the church is the

longest barrow grave in Denmark, **Grønjægers Høj**. The main town of **Stege** ⓴ has medieval ramparts.

Falster and Lolland

The Farø bridges connect Zealand to **Falster**, and the ferry routes to Germany. The main town on the island is **Nykøbing** ㉑, noted for the **Czarens Hus** (Tsar's House), where Peter the Great stayed in 1716, which now houses the **Falsters Minder Museum** (tel: 54 84 44 00; Tue–Fri noon–4pm, Sat 10am–1pm, late June–Aug Mon–Fri until 5pm) of local history. The area around **Marielyst** ㉒, to the southeast, has miles of white sand dunes where families take beach holidays. A choice of bridges links Falster to **Lolland**. The 12th-century castle **Aalholm Slot** ㉓ is closed to visitors. From Aalholm, the road north runs past lakes to **Knuthenborg** ㉔ (tel: 54 78 80 89; www.knuthenborg.dk; daily 10am–4pm, in season until 5pm or 6pm, winter closed), a safari park. In the far west, the **Tårs** ㉕ to **Spodsbjerg** crossing connects the island with Langeland and Funen.

Cycling on Lolland.

BORNHOLM

Denmark's Baltic island of Bornholm is a haven for both artists and holidaymakers, attracted by its climate, peaceful lifestyle and natural beauty.

Main Attractions
Hammershus
Rønne
NaturBornholm, Åkirkeby
Svaneke
Gudhjem
Bornholms
  Kunstmuseum
Medieval round churches
Exploring the island by
  bicycle

Hammershus castle ruins.

ornholm is "Scandinavia in a nutshell". Sitting in the middle of the Baltic Sea between Sweden and Poland, this enchanting island features a variety of landscapes typical to different areas of Scandinavia. It is a peaceful place, home to about 42,000 Bornholmers, with no large towns and almost no industry. Visitors have a perfect opportunity to relax, although from early July until the end of August the population swells fourfold with holidaymakers. It is three hours from Copenhagen by train/ferry, and 30 minutes by plane.

Viking strongholds

Bornholm was a maritime centre in the Baltic Sea during the Iron Age. Jewellery, coins and relics from as far away as Rome and the Near East have been discovered on the island, and the scant remains of two forts dating from the Viking period, both known as **Gamleborg**, can be found in **Paradisbakkerne** (The Hills of Paradise) and at **Almindingen Skov**. It is generally believed that Bornholm became a part of the kingdom of Denmark at around that time.

Perched on a huge rocky knoll on the northwest corner of the island are the impressive ruins of **Hammershus** ❶ (daily; free). The castle was built around 1200 to defend the island against attack, and is today Scandinavia's largest castle ruin. At the time the castle was built, Bornholm was owned by the Archbishop of Lund (in what is now southern Sweden, but then part of Denmark); he was openly at war with the kings of Denmark. Strong separatist feelings still exist among some Bornholmers. Their banner is a Danish flag with a green cross instead of the familiar white one. A state-of-the-art Hammershus visitor centre is due to open in 2016.

Around Bornholm

The variety of plant life on Bornholm is astounding. The northern part of the island is extremely rocky and, by radiating heat picked up from the sun, the rocks keep the surface warm enough for figs, grapes, mulberry trees and other plants from Southern Europe to grow well. Sweet cherry trees blossom in June and give a colourful show. Red orchids are common on the banks in the river valleys, and thousands of woodland flowers, especially blue, yellow and white anemones, cover large areas. About 20 percent of Bornholm is woodland: **Almindingen ❷**, in the centre of the island, is Denmark's third-largest forest. **Paradisbakkerne ❸** is wilder in vegetation than Almindingen and is best enjoyed on foot. Small farms are scattered all over the island.

Rønne ❹, with 14,000 inhabitants, is the largest town on Bornholm, and its harbour is one of the largest provincial ports in Denmark. Some parts of the town have been well preserved, especially in the area just east of **Skt Nikolai Kirke**. The beautiful **Kastellet** (citadel) is on the east side of town; today it is a military museum, **Forsvarsmuseet** (tel: 51 33 00 33; http://

bornholmsforsvarsmuseum.dk; mid-May–Sept Tue–Sat 10am–4pm). At Ndr. Kystvej 3 is Bornholm's Visitor Centre (http://bornholm.info).

Bornholm has inspired many Danish painters, as well as having produced a few of its own: Oluf Høst is the best known. **Bornholm's Cultural History Museum** (Kulturhistorisk Museum; Skt Mortensgade 29; tel: 56 95 07 35; www.bornholmsmuseum.dk;Jan–mid-May and late Oct–Dec Mon–Sat Mon–Fri 1–4pm, Sat 11am–3pm, mid-May–June and mid-Aug–late Oct Mon–Sat 10am–5pm, July–mid-Aug daily 10am–5pm) and its collection of paintings and exhibits from prehistory onwards relating to the island's past is worth visiting. It also includes a charming model of the Bornholm railway.

Åkirkeby ❺ (pop. 2,100) is the main town in the southern part of Bornholm, and the only one of the larger towns situated inland. It was an ecclesiastical centre, and its church, **Åkirke**, was built around 1150 as a chapterhouse in the Archbishopric of Lund. The large tower

TIP

In Bornholm you can have a close encounter with a griffon vulture, harris hawk or white-tailed eagle. Head to the Bornholms Rovfugleshow in Nyker where spectacular birdshows are held from April to October. (http://bornholmsrovfugleshow.dk). Alternatively, you may choose to meet the red admiral or small tortoiseshell in the butterfly park in Nexø (www.sommerfugleparken.dk).

Olsker "round church".

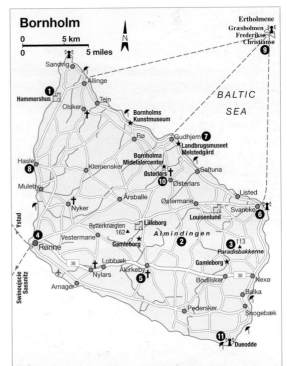

FACT

Bornholm celebrates classical music with a festival from July to mid-August, which attracts music-lovers from around the world (www.wonderfestiwall.dk).

was extended around 1200, and at the same time it was fortified with walls even heavier than those of Hammershus. It is notable for its sandstone baptismal font depicting the life of Christ in 11 relief carvings; the figures are explained in runic script, and end with the signature of the stonecutter, "Sighraf, master".

Åkirkeby's other attraction is **NaturBornholm** (tel: 56 94 04 00; www.naturbornholm.dk; Apr–Oct 10am–5pm, last admission 4pm), a superb interactive visitor centre that explains the island's history, wildlife and geology. The building was designed by Henning Larsen, architect of Copenhagen's Opera House.

The easternmost town in Denmark, **Svaneke** ❻, prospered with the success of its shipping captains. The largest buildings were originally merchants' houses. Today it's the prettiest town on Bornholm, famous for an abundance of **artists' workshops** and its lively **craft market**, from 9am on Wednesdays and Saturdays in summer. North of the town is an old Dutch mill, and nearby an un-traditional

water tower, built by the architect Jørn Utzon in 1951.

Cycling downhill is forbidden in **Gudhjem** ❼ ("good home"), another very picturesque place, built on steep slopes down to the water. Windmills around the town once provided electricity. Bornholm's most famous artist is celebrated at the **Oluf Høst Museum** (tel: 56 48 50 38; www.ohmus. dk; June–Sept 11am–5pm), housed in the painter's former studio. There is an open-air agricultural museum, **Landbrugsmuseet Melstedgård** (tel: 56 48 55 98; www.bornholmsmuseum.dk; mid-May–mid-Oct Sun–Fri 10am–5pm, Jan–mid-May Mon–Fri 1–5pm, Sat 10am–1pm), just southeast of Gudhjem at **Melsted**, complete with horses, pigs and poultry. Northwest of Gudhjem, the excellent **Bornholms Kunstmuseum** (tel: 56 48 43 86; www.bornholms-kunstmuseum. dk; June–Aug 10am–5pm, Apr–May and Sept–Oct Tue–Sun 10am–5pm, Nov–Mar Thu–Fri 1–5pm, Sat 10am–5pm) perches on a craggy outcrop above the sea and houses a worthwhile collection of artwork from the

Gudhjem village, on the north coast.

SALMON AND HERRING

During the summer months, freshly landed herrings are delivered to the island's distinctive white smoke-houses. Here they are turned from their original silver colour into the "golden Bornholmers" dearly loved by Danes, which can often be seen drying on stands outside. Elderwood gives them their special taste. The smoked herrings are either eaten warm from the oven or put on black rye bread, sprinkled with salt, chopped chives, onion and radishes, and topped with a raw egg yolk – this typical Danish open sandwich is known as Sol over Gudhjem – "Sun over Gudhjem".

Pickled herrings are a lunchtime must. The best spiced herrings are produced on Christiansø. Baltic salmon, said to be the finest edible fish in the world, is normally available, too.

Bornholm School, ranging from the 1800s to the present.

Grønbechs Gård (Bornholm Centre of Arts and Crafts; tel: 56 96 18 70; http://groenbechsgaard.dk; late Mar–mid-Oct daily 10am–5pm), an old merchant's house in **Hasle** , showcases the work of the island's artists and designers, with changing wood, ceramics, jewellery, glass and textile exhibitions.

Christiansø

It's an hour's sail from Gudhjem Harbour to the group of islands known as **Ertholmene**. The largest of these are **Christiansø** ❾ and **Frederiksø**. A naval base was constructed here in about 1864, but today only fishermen and their families live on this "fortress in the sea". It makes an interesting place to visit. The islands are quite rocky, with castle towers, batteries and cannon all serving as reminders of the past. Their isolated setting and car-free environment make them attractive to birdlife, particularly eider ducks, which breed all over the islands.

Round churches

Østerlars Kirke ❿ just over 4km (2.5 miles) southwest from Gudhjem, is the largest of the four medieval "round churches" of Bornholm, which include **Nylars**, **Nyker** and **Olsker**. When the Slavic Wends ravaged the island they were occasionally used as places of refuge, and in the 14th–16th century Hanseatic merchants from northern Germany would move in during the herring season. At Østerlars the enormous support pillars create the impression of a fortress, which was the second purpose of the structure. Inside the church (built around 1150), the vault is painted with fine frescoes of biblical scenes. On the north wall of the oval-shaped choir, stone steps lead to the second storey, where the hollow central pillar has two entrances. The outer wall has a watchman's gallery.

The double altarpiece was painted by the local artist Poul Høm.

If you're here with children, drop in on the nearby **Bornholms Middelaldercenter** (tel: 56 49 83 19; www.bornholmsmiddelaldercenter.dk; Apr–mid-Oct daily 10am–4pm, July until 5pm), an activity-packed introduction to the medieval age. The reconstructed town comes alive in summer, with craft demonstrations, performances, a bustling July market, bonfires and booming cannons.

Bornholm by bike

The best way to travel around Bornholm is by bicycle. An extensive network of cycle paths has been established, and it's easy to find houses, hotels and campsites en route. The island's residents often rent rooms or houses to visitors, but remember to book accommodation in advance during the summer months, especially in the southeast part of the island, where the wonderful beaches of **Dueodde** ⓫ and **Balka** in particular attract crowds of holidaymakers in high season.

Cycling is the best way to get around Bornholm, and there are plenty of places you can rent bikes from.

A simple dish of smoked herring.

FUNEN

Bridging the water between Zealand and Jutland is the island of Funen, the "Garden of Denmark", with the buzzing cultural centre of Odense at its heart.

D enmark's central island of **Funen** (Fyn in Danish) is known as "the Garden of Denmark" for its natural beauty, flowered gardens, castles and manor houses. Here, too, lies historic Odense, the birthplace of author Hans Christian Andersen. South Funen and the island archipelago are a paradise for anglers and yachtsmen.

Funen is linked to Zealand by the mighty Store Bælt bridge and to Jutland by the Lille Bælt bridge, and the E20 runs straight across the island. However, the most satisfying way to appreciate Funen's finer aspects is slowly, by the power of your pedalling feet. There are hundreds of kilometres of marked routes, allowing you to lean your bike beside one of the little white-washed churches to take a look inside, and inhale the scent of the wild flowers that lie beneath roadside rose hedges.

Northeast Funen

Nyborg ① is the first Funen town on the eastern coast; before heading north for Kerteminde and the Hindsholm peninsula, take a look at **Nyborg Slot** (tel: 65 31 02 07; www.nyborgslot.dk; June–Aug daily 10am–4pm, Apr–May and Sept–Oct Tue–Sun 10am–3pm), which dates from 1170. It was built to defend the country from the Wends of north Germany and, during the Middle Ages, was the meeting place for the monarchy, nobility and clergy.

A vintage wooden ship.

However, in 1722, much of Nyborg Slot was demolished to provide building materials for Odense Castle. Part of the original ramparts and moat remain, and the castle has a fine interior of great echoing, empty rooms.

About 15km (9 miles) north, near Kerteminde, are the remains of a Viking chieftain's burial ship at the **Viking Museum** (Vikingemuseet; www.viking emuseetladby.dk; June–Aug daily 10am–5pm, Jan–May and Sept–Dec Tue–Sun 10am–4pm) at **Ladby ②**.

Kerteminde ③ is Funen's foremost

Main Attractions
Viking Museum, Ladby
Odense
Den Fynske Landsby
Egeskov Castle
Ærø Island
TICKON sculpture park, Langeland
Langelandsfort, Langeland

FACT

The Kerteminde landscape has attracted some of Denmark's most renowned artists. Their work can be seen at the village's Johannes Larsen Museum at Møllebakken (tel: 65 32 11 77; www. johanneslarsenmuseet.dk).

fishing village, with old half-timbered houses and a reputation for its stoneware and pottery.

Odense

In the centre of Funen lies quaint but lively **Odense ❹**, Denmark's third-largest city (pop. 190,000). The Gothic cathedral, **Skt Knuds Domkirke** (http://odense-domkirke.dk), is one of its most beautiful landmarks. It was named after King Knud (Canute) II, who was murdered in the town in 1086 by his rebellious subjects and later canonised by the Pope. It's adorned with a gilded altarpiece made by Claus Berg in Germany in 1521. In

the crypt lie the remains of Skt Knud.

At **Munkemøllestræde** 3-5, west of the cathedral, is the house where the storyteller Hans Christian Andersen grew up in the early 1800s (July–Aug daily 10am–5pm, rest of the year Tue–Sun 10am–4pm). Northeast of the cathedral is the **Hans Christian Andersen Museum** (Bangs Boder 29; tel: 65 51 46 01; Sept–June Tue–Sun 10am–4pm, July–Aug daily 9am–5pm). The museum's collection is devoted to the writer's life, with manuscripts and other personal belongings.

Denmark's foremost composer, Carl Nielsen, spent his early years in the city, and the **Carl Nielsen Museet**

(Claus Bergs Gade 11; tel: 65 51 46 01; June–Aug Wed–Sun 11am–3pm, Sept–Dec and Jan–Apr Thur–Fri 3–7pm, Sat–Sun 11am–3pm; free) is devoted both to his life and work and to that of his wife, Anne Marie Nielsen, a sculptor. His childhood home can be visited at **Nørre Lyndelse** ⑤ (tel: 65 51 46 01; May–Sept Tue–Sun 11am–3pm), 15km (9 miles) south of Odense.

Few other cities have a river that is clean enough to offer fishermen sea trout and eel: an accomplishment for a once-polluted industrial centre. Today, the quarter around the old factory buildings at Kongensgade and Vestergade has been revitalised and is a popular destination for leisure-seekers. The former textile mill, **Brandts**, off Vestergade, is now a multipurpose cultural centre, complete with **Museet for Fotokunst** (Museum of Photographic Art); **Kunsthallen** art gallery, featuring a varied programme of exhibitions; and **Danmarks Mediemuseum** (Danish Media Museum), which presents the history of Danish print and electronic media (http://brandts.dk; all Tue–Wed, Fri–Sun 10am–5pm, Thur noon–9pm), plus cafés, bars and concert halls. Located nearby at Farvergården 7, **Tidens Samling** (Time Collection) follows Danish daily life and fashion since 1900 (tel: 65 91 19 42; http://tidenssamling. dk; Feb–mid-Dec Mon–Sat daily 10am–4pm, first Sun of month 11am–3pm).

One of the top attractions of Funen is Odense Zoo with an "Oceanium", just south of the centre (tel: 66 11 13 60; www.odensezoo.dk; from 10am until 4–7pm). Little further south of Odense is a delightful spot, **Den Fynske Landsby** (Funen Village, Sejersko-vvej 20; tel: 65 51 46 01; Apr–June and mid-Aug–mid-Oct Tue–Sun 10am–5pm, July–mid-Aug daily 10am–6pm). It contains old farm buildings from different areas, with a vicarage, workshops, a windmill and watermill.

South Funen

Fåborg ⑥ on south Funen is a peaceful little town where **Klokketårnet**,

Europe's largest carillon, chimes out a hymn four times a day. Other low-key attractions include **Fåborg Museum for Fynsk Kunst** (Grønnegade 75; tel: 62 61 06 45; www.faaborgmuseum.dk; June–Aug daily 10am–4pm, Wed until 6pm, Apr–May and Sept–Oct Tue–Sun 10am–4pm, Nov–Mar Tue–Sun 11am–3pm), an art gallery featuring the "Funen artists" (1880–1920), including Peter Hansen, Fritz Syberg and Johannes Larsen, with sculptures by Kai Nielsen.

The heather-covered **Svanninge Bakker** ⑦, about 10km (6 miles) north of Fåborg, is a national park. Heading eastwards, **Svendborg** ⑧ is a beautiful market town and makes a good centre for touring. Along with Fåborg, it is the gateway to the southern islands.

The unmissable **Egeskov Slot** ⑨ (tel: 62 27 10 16; www.egeskov.dk; late Apr–mid-Oct 10am–5, 6 or 7pm, check website for detailed times), 14km (9 miles) north of Svendborg, is one of Denmark's most famous historic sights, a moated castle set in magnificent Baroque and Renaissance gardens. Egeskov means oak forest – legend says that an entire forest of the trees was

Take a ferry to the island of Ærø, where the main town, Ærøskøbing, is filled with cobbled streets and brightly coloured houses.

Beach fun near Fåborg.

TIP

Whether driving, cycling or walking, follow the "Daisy Routes" marked by a flower sign. These guide you past some of the most beautiful scenery in Funen.

felled around 1540 to form the piles the castle stands on. The castle and grounds are filled with wonders, including three **mazes**, a tree-top walk, a unique collection of dresses, old smithy, a motorcycle exhibition and a classic car exhibition.

Along the west coast

From Fåborg, turn northwest to explore Funen's west coast. Around 15km (9 miles) north from Assens on the road to **Middelfart**, a broad west-facing bay at **Tybrind Vig** is a site for underwater archaeology. North of Middelfart, dramatic steep cliffs line the shore.

About 3km (2 miles) east of **Bogense** is the castle of **Gyldensteen**, a late Renaissance building with an impressive gatehouse (closed to the public). Here, Karen Blixen (pen name Isak Dinesen), author of *Out of Africa*, wrote some of her books during the German Occupation of Denmark in World War II. From Bogense, you can complete the Funen circle by touring along the sparsely populated north coast to the Hindsholm peninsula and Kerteminde. At low tide you can walk to the island of **Æbelø** , an unspoilt landscape rich in wildlife.

To the islands

You could spend a lifetime trying to visit all the islands of the Funen archipelago and still miss a few. Only 19 are inhabited permanently, and even the largest hold no more than a few thousand people. You can take day trips aboard wooden sailing ships or longer cruises through the archipelago.

From Fåborg, it is a short trip to the most beautiful island of all, **Ærø**. Hire a bike for the short ride from Søby to **Ærøskøbing** ⑪, the main town of cobbled streets and brightly coloured houses, and on to the old naval port of **Marstal**. Cycling is easy, and the roads wind past fertile fields, thatched farmhouses, medieval churches and windmills. From Fåborg, ferries also run to the smaller islands of **Avernakø** and **Lyø** ⑫; both have good inns.

Svendborg is the ferry port for the southern islands. The first island, reached by a narrow bridge, is **Tåsinge**, with some 6,000 inhabitants. **Valdemars Slot** ⑬ is one of Denmark's oldest privately owned castles, with a wonderful view over Svendborgsund (tel: 62 22 61 06; http://valdemarsslot.dk; June–Aug daily 10am–5pm). It was built in 1640 by King Kristian IV for one of his sons, Prince Valdemar Kristian. Now it hosts a hunting museum and a yachting museum. Most interesting is the castle church, with an excellent restaurant beneath. Beyond the Tea Pavilion, mirrored in its own lake, is a tiny swimming beach beside Lunkebugten Bay. The loveliest village on Tåsinge is **Troense** ⑭.

Langeland ("long land") is linked to Tåsinge by a bridge. H.C. Ørsted, the discoverer of electromagnetism, was born in the main town of **Rudkøbing** ⑮.

North at **Tranekær** ⑯ lies TICKON, a peaceful wooded sculpture park. To the south is fascinating **Langelandsfort** (www.langelandsfortet.dk; May–Sept 10am–5pm, Apr and Oct 10am–4pm, last admission one hour before closing), a Cold War listening station with cannons, bunkers, planes and a U-boat. To the south, **Ristinge** and **Bagenkop** both have excellent bathing beaches.

The majestic Egeskov Castle.

Andersen and Nielsen: Funen's Famous Sons

In the 19th century, two Funen boys, the storyteller Hans Christian Andersen and the composer Carl Nielsen, set off to make their fortunes in the world.

Two of Denmark's most noted literary and musical figures, Hans Christian Andersen and Carl Nielsen respectively, were born on the island of Funen. At the height of his fame, the composer Carl Nielsen (1865–1931) told an audience that his mother had always said to him: "Don't forget that Hans Christian Andersen was a poor boy like you." There may have been something in the Funen air that inspired poor boys to rise to fame, but it is more likely that Nielsen was inspired by Andersen, 60 years his senior. Both came from humble homes, both left Odense to seek their fortune in Copenhagen.

Hans Christian Andersen

Andersen (1805–75) was born in Odense, the son of a shoemaker and a washerwoman, and spent his childhood in a small half-timbered house in Munkemøllestræde, now a museum. Quite apart from his skill as a writer, Andersen had a good singing voice and was a gifted artist. At the age of 14 he set off to Copenhagen to attend the Royal Theatre School. The Theatre Board recognised his skills, and he was found a place at a grammar school in Helsingør.

After school, Andersen travelled widely; *Shadow Picture of a Journey to the Harz Mountains and Saxony* (1831) was the result of his early adventures. Throughout his life he continued to write poems, novels and plays. His autobiographical novel, *The Improvisatore*, described the rise to fortune of a poor Italian boy. His early fairy tales, including *The Tinder Box* and *The Princess and the Pea* (1835), brought him immortality.

In spite of his worldwide fame and extensive travels, Andersen's personal life was a lonely one. In 1840 he met and fell in love with the singer Jenny Lind, "The Swedish Nightingale", but his love was unrequited – she always called him "brother". His fairy tale *The Nightingale* was inspired by her. When he was made an honorary citizen of Odense in 1867, Andersen said it was "an honour greater than I had ever dreamt of".

Carl Nielsen

Carl Nielsen was born in Nørre Lyndelse, where his childhood home is now a museum. He was the seventh of 12 children in a poor family. His father was a house painter and amateur folk musician and Carl played the violin. His earliest compositions, at the age of eight, were two dance tunes. Like Andersen, Nielsen wrote an autobiography, *My Childhood in Funen*.

At the Royal Theatre Orchestra in Copenhagen, where Nielsen became second violinist, the Norwegian conductor Johan Svendsen encouraged him to compose. At 25, Nielsen won a fellowship which allowed him to travel, and went to Dresden to steep himself in Wagner's ideas. Nielsen composed two operas: the dark drama *Saul og David*, and a comic opera, *Maskarade*, along with six symphonies and choral works, such as *Hymnus Amoris*. Like his contemporary, the Finn Jean Sibelius, he studied Renaissance polyphony closely, which accounts for much of the melodic and harmonic content of his music.

Artefacts at the Hans Christian Andersen House.

Dune landscape.

JUTLAND

The dune-fringed shores of Jutland have captured the imagination of both painters and holiday-makers, while music-lovers head for Århus, "the world's smallest big city".

Jutland (Jylland) is the Danish peninsula that juts up above Germany, the "mainland" in this nation of islands. When Copenhageners talk about the provinces, they usually mean Jutland. Nuggets of Denmark's oldest and richest history – prehistoric bog bodies and Viking runestones – are to be found here, as well as youthful attractions like Legoland. Jutland's rolling hills are crisscrossed with rivers, patched with forests, crusted with castles and edged in fine sandy beaches.

Jutland's capital city

Århus ❶ (pop. 311,000), Denmark's second-largest city, is a lively university town known for its music, theatre, ballet, art and cafés, and its fun Festival Week in early autumn (www.visitaarhus. com). In 2017, it will be the European Capital of Culture. The pointed spire of the **Cathedral of St Clement** (Domkirken; http://aarhusdomkirke.dk; May–Sept Mon–Sat 9.30am–4pm, rest of year 10am–3pm, Tue from 10.30am; charge to tower – visit by appointment) is 93 metres (316ft) high and offers a superb view from its belfry. Nearby are the winding, cobblestone streets of the Latin Quarter, with quirky boutiques and trendy cafés and restaurants. **ARoS Århus Art Museum** (Kunstmuseum; www.aros.dk; tel: 87 30 66 00; Tue–Sun 10am–5pm, Wed until 10pm) gives an

overview of Danish art from the 18th century to the present. In 2011, a spectacular circular 150-metre- (492ft-) long glass walkway in all colours of the rainbow was added to the museum, while 2013 saw the opening of a roof pavilion, offering easy access to the walkway as well as great views. The **City Hall** (Rådhus) was built in 1941 and designed by Arne Jacobsen, one of Denmark's most notable architects and designers.

Den Gamle By (Old Town; tel: 86 12 31 88; www.dengamleby.dk; 10am–4 or 6pm, see website for seasonal opening

Main Attractions
Århus
Grauballe Man, Moesgård Museum
Legoland
Ribe
Blåvands Huk
Aalborg
Skagen peninsula and the Grenen headland

The open-air museum in the Old Town of Århus.

Jutland

times; guided tours in English available) is an open-air, national museum of culture and history, with reconstructions of 75 Danish town buildings – with merchant and artisan houses and workshops, gardens, shops, stalls, streets and alleys.

One of the best museum exhibits in Denmark is the 2,000-year-old Grauballe Man at the **Museum of Prehistory ❷** (Moesgård Museum; tel: 89 42 11 00; www.moesgaardmuseum.dk; Tue–Sun 10am–5pm, Wed 10am–9pm), located south of Aarhus in the suburb of Højbjerg. To stand centimetres from the twisted body of this Iron Age man, found perfectly preserved in a peat bog in 1952, is a chilling experience. There is also a new sleek gallery built into the hillside with a sloping grass rooftop that visitors can stroll onto.

The ruins of **Kalø Slot ❸**, built in 1313, stand on a small island north of Århus bay, linked to the mainland by a causeway. The nearby hills of **Mols Bjerge ❹**, where Viking relics abound in beautiful nature, are well worth a visit. Several artists have set up shop on the pretty Djursland peninsula.

Samsø island

West of Mols Bjerge is the immaculate town of **Ebeltoft ❺**, with its small, unaltered town hall from 1789. The island of **Samsø** can be seen from here, but it must be reached by ferry from **Hovu ❻**, 25km (15 miles) south of Århus. A haven for artists, farmers and nature-lovers alike, Samsø is renowned for its new potatoes and cheese – and wind turbines. The Baltic island is one of the first industrialised places in the world to be entirely energy self-sufficient.

Nordby ❼, on the northern tip, contains a wealth of colourful crossbeam houses, as well as small art galleries. Also worth a visit in Nordby is **Samsø Labyrinten**, the world's largest permanent maze (tel: 86 59 66 59; www.samsolabyrinten.com; public holidays and Apr–mid-Oct 11am–3pm, July–mid-Aug until 5pm). Its 5km (3 miles) of passages wind through a dense fir forest covering 6 hectares (15 acres).

Lake district

A series of lakes snake through forested hills west of Århus, and a fun way to see them is from the paddle steamer MS *Hjejlen* (tel: 86 82 07 66; www.hjejlen.com; May–Sept daily 9am–5pm), which has carried passengers from Ry to Silkeborg since 1861. For a bird's-eye view, climb **Himmelbjerget ❽** (Sky Mountain), at 147 metres (482ft) one of Denmark's highest "mountains". The nearby town of **Silkeborg ❾** features **Museum Jorn** (tel: 86 82 53 88; www.museumjorn.dk; Tue–Fri 11am–5pm, Sat–Sun 10am–5pm), built around the glorious, playful work of the painter Asger Jorn and others from the 20th-century CoBrA group. **Silkeborg Museum** (tel: 86 82 14 99; www.museumsilkeborg.dk; May–mid-Oct 10am–5pm, mid-Oct–Apr Sat–Sun noon–4pm) houses one of Denmark's best-known bog bodies, Tollund Man.

Further southeast, historical **Horsens ❿** hosts an annual Middle Ages Festival on the last weekend in August,

Legoland, a miniature world created from more than 59 million Lego bricks. Lego was developed by Ole Kirk Christiansen and his family in Billund in 1949.

The Tollund Man exhibit at Silkeborg Museum.

which is highly recommended (www. middelalderfestival.dk). **Billund**, 50km (31 miles) southwest of Horsens, is the home of **Legoland** ⓫ (tel: 75 33 13 33; www.legoland.dk; Apr–Oct from 10am until 6–9pm).

South Jutland

South Jutland has some of the most patriotic Danes in the country, particularly the generations who remember the area when it was officially part of Germany's Schleswig duchy from 1864 to 1920. **Kolding** ⓬ was a border town on the Danish side at the time, and historical sights abound. Of particular interest are the remains of **Koldinghus Slot** (tel: 76 33 81 00; www.koldinghus.dk; daily 10am–5pm), a castle built in 1268, and **Trapholt** (tel: 76 30 05 30; www.trapholt.dk; Tue–Sun 10am–5pm, Wed until 8pm), with a fine collection of modern art.

Driving south 15km (9 miles), the Danish Moravian town of **Christiansfeld** ⓭ is famous for its scrumptious honey cakes. Further south, close to the German border, **Sønderborg** ⓮ is a striking town on **Als Island**, with

Grenen, where the Baltic and North Seas meet.

a colourful harbour and the mighty **Sønderborg Slot** (tel: 74 42 25 39; June–Sept daily 10am–5pm, Apr, May and Oct Tue–Sun 10am–4pm, Nov–Mar Tue–Sun 1pm–4pm), a fortress built around 1100.

Just to the west, **Dybbøl** ⓯ was a key battlefield in the 1864 war with Germany; the Danish army suffered a huge defeat. **Dybbøl Mill**, restored and painted white, is now a national historic park and its Dybbøl Banke history centre (tel: 74 48 90 00; mid-Apr–mid-Oct daily from 10–11am until 4–6pm), dedicated to the battle, is open to the public.

On the western side of south Jutland is **Tønder** ⓰, a lace-making centre in the 17th century, documented in **Tønder Museum** (tel: 74 72 89 89; June–Aug daily 10am–5pm, Sept–May Tue–Sun 10am–5pm). Tønder has attractive 17th- and 18th-century houses, many with distinctive painted doorways, and hosts Denmark's biggest **folk festival** at the end of August. At **Møgeltønder**, 3km (2 miles) to the west, the village street is lined with lime trees. **Schackenborg Slot** is home to Prince Joachim (fourth in succession) and his second wife, Princess Marie.

VIKING LANDMARKS

Viking sights abound in Jutland. **Lindholm Høje** (tel: 99 31 74 40; Apr–Oct daily 10am–5pm, Nov–Mar Tue–Sun 11am–4pm), just north of Ålborg, is a necropolis with 700 graves, a reconstructed village from the early Iron Age and Viking times, and a museum. Many of the graves have been constructed in the shape of a Viking ship.

Elsewhere, near Hobro, is the Viking fort of **Fyrkat**. Four earth fortifications once enclosed 16 large houses on the site, and one of these longhouses has been reconstructed. Finds from Fyrkat are on display in **Hobro Museum** (tel: 99 82 41 70; May–Sept noon–5pm). On the Mols peninsula near Århus is the **Poskjær Stenhus** barrow, which lies along the road from Agri to Grønfeld.

A memorial referred to as Denmark's "birth certificate" can be found in Jelling. The **Jelling Stones** (Jellingstenene) are covered with runic script that King Harald Bluetooth had carved over 1,000 years ago to proclaim his conversion to Christianity, and to honour his parents, King Gorm the Old and Queen Thyra Danebrod, who were buried in the mounds beside Jelling town church. For a flavour of life in Viking times, re-enactments, including battles and blood oaths, can be experienced at Moesgård, and in Jels in July.

Ribe

Ribe ❼, built around its 12th-century cathedral, celebrated its 1,300th anniversary in 2010 and ranks high on the list of historic centres in Scandinavia (www.visitribe.com). Its brick and half-timbered houses, courtyards and *kroer* (inns) are much as they were hundreds of years ago. **Ribe Cathedral** (Domkirke; tel: 24 66 07 37; http://ribe-domkirke.dk; May–Sept Mon–Sat 10am–5pm, Sun noon–4pm, Apr and Oct Mon–Sat 11am–4pm, Sun noon–4pm, Nov–Mar Mon–Sat 11am–3pm, Sun noon–3pm; church free, charge to tower) stands on the site of one of Denmark's earliest wooden churches, built around AD 860. The "Cat Head Door" was said to be the entrance for the Devil. The choir has been stunningly decorated by CoBrA artist Carl-Henning Petersen, and there are splendid views from the tower.

Ribe continues the medieval tradition of night watchmen. On summer evenings at 8pm and 10pm, the watchman walks around singing the traditional songs that once told the people that all was well and they could sleep soundly.

Around Esbjerg

West Jutland has a sense of space and time different from the rest of the region. In winter, the weather can be rugged, with storms blowing in off a turbulent North Sea. In summer its sandy beaches are popular with holiday-makers. **Esbjerg** ❿ is the biggest port town on the coast, the main gateway for ferries from Britain. The coastline south of here is part of the **Wadden Sea National Park** (National-park Vadehavet) created in 2010 to preserve important wetlands, rich in bird and animal life. They are home to the spring and autumn **"Black Sun"** phenomenon, when up to one million starlings gather, their flight blotting out the sunset.

A 20-minute ferry ride away from Esbjerg is the island of **Fanø**, a major shipbuilding centre in the 18th and 19th centuries. **Sønderho** ❾ village in the south of the island has colourful thatch-roofed cottages, an inn and Seamen's Church (1782). The island is characteristic of west Jutland: a superb stretch of white sandy beach, dunes, heath and forest.

Back on the Jutland coast, 30km (19 miles) northwest, is **Blåvands Huk** ❷⓿ lighthouse, a popular holiday spot with a nature reserve nearby. At the beach during low tide, you'll often see people hunting for nuggets of amber, a golden-coloured petrified tree resin that frequently washes ashore here.

Some 25km (16 miles) to the north, at **Henne Strand** ❷❶, the restaurant **Henne Kirkeby Kro** (tel: 75 25 54 00; http://hennekirkebykro.dk; Easter–Dec) is one of Denmark's finest.

Northwestern shores

A narrow strip of land runs north from Nymindegab to Søndervig, separating the sea from **Ringkøbing Fjord**, a broad, shallow, saltwater "lake". Driving north towards the fishing village of **Hvide Sande** ❷❷, crashing North Sea waves can be heard, but are hidden from view by tall sand dunes. A walk to the top of these dunes is a breathtaking experience.

A boat-shaped grave at the Viking burial site of Lindholm Hoje.

From here to the northern tip at Skagen, the scenery is similar, broken by several attractive fishing villages and bathing resorts. At Sneglevej 9 in **Thyborøn** ㉓, a local has decorated a house with shells, covering all surfaces, inside and out (www.sneglehuset.dk).

Aalborg

At its advantageous location for trade on the Limfjord, **Aalborg** ㉔ – Denmark's fourth-largest city, with a population of 199,000 – is full of historical buildings, castles and Viking monuments. The best-known building in town is the opulent six-storey **Stenhus** (Stone House) on Østerågade, built in 1624 by a merchant, Jens Bang. Bang was annoyed that he had never become a town councillor; on the south facade of Stenhus is a carving of him sticking his tongue out at the town hall across the street. The tourist information centre (tel: 99 31 75 00; www.visitaalborg.com) is across the street.

The town's main entertainment artery is **Jomfru Ane Gade**, lined with restaurants and bars in courtyards and half-timbered buildings. For a complete contrast, wander down to the new harbourfront, dominated by the **Utzon Center** exhibition venue – the last project of architect Jørn Utzon before his death in 2008 (www.utzoncenter.dk; Tue–Sun 10am–5pm). Further down, on Musikkens Plads, is the new impressive concert hall, opened in 2014, which is now home to the Aalborg Symphony Orchestra (www.musikkenshus.dk).

In late May, the whole city goes carnival crazy, as 25,000 costumed revellers dance through Aalborg's streets (http://aalborgkarneval.dk).

Nordic light

Set on a narrow piece of land with the North Sea on one side and the Baltic on the other, **Skagen** ㉕ has a magical quality. The air shimmers with a certain light that inspired the Skagen painters. They made it their home in the late 1800s, with Brøndums Hotel as their rallying ground. Works by Anna and Michael Ancher, P.S. Krøyer and Viggo Johansen can be seen in the renovated **Skagens Museum** (tel: 98 44 64 44; www.skagensmuseum.dk; May–Aug daily 10am–5pm, June–Aug Wed until 9pm, Sept–Oct and Feb–Apr Tue–Sun 10am–5pm) and **Ancher's Hus** (Anchers House; www.anchershus.dk; tel: 98 44 30 09; May–Sept daily 10am–5pm, Apr and Oct Sat–Thur 11am–4pm, Nov and Feb–Mar Sat Thur–Sun 11am–4pm), bought by the Anchers in 1884. Southwest from here is **Gammel Skagen** (Old Skagen), a cosmopolitan resort known for its yellow homes with red-tiled roofs and its fish restaurants.

Just west of Gammel Skagen, is the **Sand-Covered Church** ㉖ (Den Tilsandede Kirke; June–Aug daily 11am–5pm), no longer sand-covered actually. To see migrating dunes up close, you need go no further than **Råbjerg Mile** ㉗, 10km (6 miles) south of Skagen. Pushed by the wind and sea, the dunes travel as much as 20 metres (65ft) every year.

For a thrilling experience of nature, go to **Grenen**, 5km (3 miles) north of Skagen, Denmark's northernmost point. At the tip, you can actually see the North and Baltic Seas crash into each other.

Re-enacting history.

Glacier melting in the sun, Disko Bay.

GREENLAND

In spring and summer when the ice retreats and the temperature rises, Greenland's spectacular landscape becomes accessible to some of the most adventurous travellers.

The world's largest island is a place of stunning natural beauty, dramatic weather and fascinating culture. Greenland (www.greenland.com), like the Faroe Islands, is a former Danish colony, but it's well on its way to full independence, gaining self-government in 2009 (it has been an autonomous country within the Danish Realm since 1979). Notably, Greenland is the only state to ever leave the European Economic Community (EEC, now EU), in 1985, in order to have a better control of its natural resources.

Greenland is like no other place. Its vast Arctic solitude is profound and its silence almost consumes you. Here, where the North Atlantic meets the Arctic Ocean, is the cleanest environment in the world, and measurably the oldest. Where else can you sip a drink cooled by a 1,000-year-old ice cube?

Greenland is called Kalaallit Nunaat (the land of the people) by its own people. They number only about 51,400 (plus an additional 6,300 Danes) in an area of 2,166,000 sq km (836,000 sq miles). The distance north to south is 2,670km (1,655 miles), and the widest part east to west is 1,000km (620 miles). Its closest neighbour is Canada.

More than four-fifths of the country lies under 3km (2 miles) of pack ice; but the southern coastal regions, especially to the west, are green and mild during late spring and summer. Daytime temperatures can climb to a balmy 21°C (70°F) or more, but northerly winds in winter can make the mercury plunge to a bone-cracking –32°C (–25°F). Spring and summer are best for hiking, camping and fishing.

Greenlanders

Greenlanders are Inuit and live in small towns around the coasts, mainly on the milder western side. They still live off fishing and hunting, although oil, gas and aluminium smelting are flagged as future industries. Thanks to its long

Main Attractions

Nuuk
Qeqertarsuaq (Disko Island)
Ittoqqortoormiit
Dog-sledging between
  Sisimiut and
  Kangerlussuaq
Ilulissat Icefjord
Aurora borealis

Coastal settlement.

TIP

Helicopters are an important, often essential, means of transport here. Chopper tours are a breathtakingly beautiful way to travel around Greenland.

Greenland's icy waters.

association with Denmark, Greenland has a modern infrastructure and burgeoning tourist industry.

The capital is **Nuuk** ❶ (Godthåb) on the west coast, the best place to explore the country's human history. The **Greenland National Museum** (tel: +299 32 26 11; mid-June–mid-Sept daily 10am–4pm, mid-Sept–mid-June 1–4pm Tue–Sun) contains various artefacts, including traditional kayaks and Inuit costumes, plus the fascinating 15th-century Greenland mummies, discovered by hunters in 1972.

Dog-sledging and icebergs

The classic way of touring Greenland is by dog sledge, with the season running from late February to May. You can hire a team and driver for a short sightseeing tour or for a longer journey from many towns in western Greenland, including **Sisimiut** ❷, **Qeqertarsuaq** ❸ (Disko Island) and points further north. On the barely populated east coast, you can dog-sledge from **Tasiilaq** ❹ and **Ittoqqortoormiit** ❺. Tasiilaq, the largest town in the east, is also a popular summer destination, with its

"Valley of Flowers" a beautiful spot for hiking, while the area around Ittoqqortoormiit is famous for its hot springs.

A classic, if physically demanding, dog-sledge tour is the three-day trip between Sisimiut and **Kangerlussuaq** ❻ at Søndre Strømfjord on the west coast. The route takes you through the beautiful landscapes of mid-Greenland, across frozen lakes and over hilly terrain. You sleep in hunting huts or tents.

Visitors arriving at Kangerlussuaq international airport don't have far to travel to see their first Greenland glacier. Russells Glacier is a mere 25km (16 miles) away. However, one of Greenland's most dazzling sights, near **Ilulissat** ❼, is the **Icefjord**, a Unesco World Heritage site, which includes the glacier Sermeq Kujalleq – responsible for calving 10 percent of all Greenland's icebergs. There are three marked hiking trails in this protected area; or you can simply watch the huge icebergs from town as they float out into Disko Bay.

Wildlife and nature

Boat tours along the east and west coasts take you through sparkling seas alive with seals, walruses and whales. You can disembark at harbours and settlements for hiking trips, or dog-sledge tours in season. Between ports, you sail past icebergs and glaciers. On land you might see reindeer and musk oxen, or even polar bears. Birdlife is not abundant in Greenland, but you can encounter Arctic terns, ravens, peregrine falcons and eagles.

A novel way of exploring Greenland's nature is aboard a traditional Inuit vessel – the kayak. Although full-on sea-kayaking here is only for experts, beginners can explore sheltered fjord waters from many towns.

This vast, half-frozen island draws an increasing number of anglers for trout and Arctic char in the lowland lakes, rivers and streams; and Greenland halibut, Norway haddock and cod off the coast. Fishing licences are required.

Among the spectacular natural phenomena in Greenland are the Northern Lights and the Midnight Sun. The aurora borealis occurs all year long but is only visible in a clear night sky in autumn and winter. These ethereal lights can appear as colourful curtains, veins of silk ribbon, or as ghostly souls flying to heaven. In summer, the Midnight Sun keeps the night sky blue.

Ruled by the weather

Some cruise ships include Nuuk on their itineraries; otherwise the only way to travel to Greenland is by air, with direct flights from Copenhagen and Reykjavik. Once in Greenland, sailing is an option, but schedules are highly dependent on the weather. The same applies to air services. In a climate which changes from hot sun and clear skies to a deluge of rain in a moment, the weather decides whether it's possible to keep to a plan made the day before. Many a visitor has been forced to "overnight" at **Narsarsuaq** ❽ in the south because aircraft couldn't land.

Most towns in Greenland have modern hotels in various categories of comfort. These and the local tourist offices are the best places to book excursions. The more footloose visitor may prefer a hostel, seaman's home or a cabin. Campsites are appearing; tent-roughing is permitted in most places, so long as campers observe the rules of nature.

Dog-sledging through the snow.

A GREENLANDIC DIET

Traditionally, Greenlandic food is hunted food (seal, whale, reindeer, fish) packed with protein, and eaten frozen, raw, fermented or perhaps boiled over a fire of sticks and smoking heather. The national dish is *svaassat*, seal meat cooked with rice and onions. Another delicacy is *mattak*, pieces of whale skin with a thin layer of blubber.

But "Western" tastebuds won't suffer. Modern Nordic Cuisine has caught on in Greenland, with chefs making full use of the fresh ingredients on their doorstep. Try reindeer venison, honey-roast duck breast, musk-ox steak or Greenlandic lamb cutlets – some of the world's best, and all organic. Greenland's fabulous seafood includes trout, salmon, Atlantic halibut, redfish, whale, bay scallops and world-renowned Greenlandic prawns.

Green Eysturoy.

THE FAROE ISLANDS

The fruits of the sea have brought prosperity to the far-flung Faroe Islands. Visitors are attracted by the natural beauty and remarkable birdlife.

The remote Faroe Islands lie far to the north of mainland Europe, halfway between Iceland and the Shetland Islands. The sailing distance between this self-governing Danish outpost and Copenhagen is around 1,500km (900 miles). But the trip is worth it: craggy, isolated, raw and alive, the Faroes were voted the world's number one travel destination in 2015 by the readers of the *National Geographic* magazine.

Although the Faroe islanders are prosperous with a high standard of living, everything is relative. Around 49,000 live on the 17 inhabited islands – a dozen more are home only to the huge colonies of birds. Much of the surface area is virtually bare rock, and only a few areas are habitable. As though to contrast with the muted blues, greens and greys of rocks, sea and hills, modern Faroese favour brightly painted houses. Traditional, living, green turf roofs are becoming popular once more.

Far north as the islands are, the Gulf Stream keeps the climate mild and moist. In the coldest month the average temperature is around 3°C (37°F), although wind chill makes it feel much colder. In the warmest, it reaches only 13°C (55°F). The weather is very changeable; one minute the sun is warm against the back, the next there is driving rain and mist.

The islands' name in Faroese, Føroyar, means "sheep islands" – there are

Kunoy, in the Northern Isles.

around 20,000 more sheep than people, and lamb is a basic staple. Arable land is extremely limited. Small kitchen gardens have robust plants, leeks, cabbages, carrots. Outside, people hang fish and lamb to dry in the wind.

Tórshavn

The sea is serious business here, and nothing shows that more clearly than **Tórshavn's** ❶ harbour. It is stuffed with boats of all kinds – visiting ships, inter-island ferries, sailing boats and other pleasure craft and, most numerous of

Main Attractions
Tórshavn
Kirkjubøur
Vestmanna bird cliffs
Sailing tour aboard the
    Urðardrangur
Mykines Island
Faroese cultural evenings

The puffin is a Faroese delicacy, caught during the open season in July. The meat has a distinctively tangy flavour.

In traditional dress on St Olav's Day.

all, the fishing boats which disgorge their cargoes at one of the big fish processors scattered around the islands' coasts. The fishing fleet is one of the most modern in Europe. Fish products make up 95 percent of the country's export earnings.

The islands' long seafaring history is traced in the **Føroya Fornminnissavn** (National Museum of the Faroe Islands; mid-May–mid-Sept Mon–Fri 10am–5pm, Sat–Sun 2–5pm) at Hoyvik, 2km (1.25 miles) north of Tórshavn.

Kirkjubøur

The islands' first substantial settlers came from Norway in the 9th century. Even before that time, an early township had been the centre of life for a group of Irish friars who colonised the islands around the 8th century. The township was **Kirkjubøur** ❷, and today this tiny settlement in the south of Streymoy is the islands' most important historical site. The 14th-century ruins of Magnus Cathedral sit in melancholy splendour by the shore; while Roykstovan (Smoke Room) is allegedly the oldest wooden structure in

continued use in the world, built from logs that were towed from Norway.

In 1380, as Norway came under Danish rule, the islands, too, became part of Denmark and, when the union dissolved in 1814, the Faroes continued as a Danish county. The present system of Home Rule dates from 1948, and the Faroe Islands also send two representatives to the Danish Parliament.

The Western Islands

The Faroe Islands' only airport is on the western island of Vágar. Here, the towering faces of the stacks and cliffs are home to thousands of seabirds.

For the seafaring adventurer, boat operators sail from the neighbouring Streymoy village of **Vestmanna**, on an excursion of the islands to view the **Vestmannabjørgini** ❸, or **Enniberg** bird cliffs. The sloop *Urðardrangur* takes visitors on a tour of the islands, sailing into fjords and grottoes.

Boat excursions also run to the traffic-free island of **Mykines** ❹, which attracts birdwatchers from around the world. The hike from pretty Mykines village (the only settlement on the

Faroe Islands

0   10 km
0   10 miles

island) to the Mykineshólmur Lighthouse is an exhilarating experience.

Walking and fishing

The Faroe Islands are full of excellent hiking opportunities through stunning terrain. Footpaths crisscross all the islands and were originally the main routes between settlements. Most of the trails are marked by cairns, but some of them are not regularly maintained, and it's imperative to carry a map and GPS. The tourist information offices on all the islands provide free maps and arrange guided walks and accommodation.

Anglers may find great challenges in the islands' brooks and lochs, which are rich in trout and salmon. The season extends from 1 May to 31 August. Contact the tourist office in Tórshavn for permits and details (tel: +298 20 61 00; www.visitfaroeislands.com).

The Northern Islands

Klaksvík ❺, on Borðoy island, is the Faroes' second-largest town and an excellent base for exploring the northern islands in all their dramatic, windswept beauty. For an insight into life on the islands, visit the **Norðoya Fornminnissavn** (North Islands Museum; mid-May–mid-Sept daily 1–4pm) in a well-preserved 19th-century merchant's house.

Faroese festivals

The Faroese are proud of the rich culture and traditions of their islands, where the language, costumes and customs are kept very much alive. On festive occasions, such as the national St Olav's Day celebrations at the end of July in Tórshavn, everyone joins in the Faroese chain dance, a slow, hypnotic dance accompanied by chanting and schnapps (*akvavit*) drinking.

In the summer months several islands hold **Faroese Cultural Evenings**, encompassing literature, music, theatre and, of course, chain dancing. From early June to mid-August, the **Summartónar Music Festival**, a celebration of classical and contemporary Faroese music, is staged at venues around the islands. There are cultural events galore, from the Knitting Festival to the Winter Jazz Festival.

TIP

You can get around all the islands by the buses or boats from the public transport company Strandfaraskip Landsins. Travelcards can be bought at the airport or at the ferry terminal in Tórshavn. For more information visit www.ssl.fo. In Tórshav, there's a free local (red) bus service.

Historic Kirkjubøur.

Old wooden houses in Bergen.

NORWAY

Breathtaking scenery, historic sights
and modern cities are the big
attractions for the traveller to Norway.

Look up to see the architectural detail.

Norway is synonymous with nature: abundant with majestic mountains and mysterious fjords, imposing waterfalls and glaciers, lakes and rivers, and a coastline littered with bays, inlets and thousands of islands. Its landscape is full of contrasts: beautiful and brutal, hospitable and hostile; barren rock submits to soft fertile plains. The Norwegians themselves have adapted rather quickly – the lusty Vikings have turned into global peacemakers. Norway has both urban excitement and rural tranquillity, and high-technology parallels steadfast tradition. A thriving offshore oil industry has brought prosperity, and, as a consequence, social habits are changing rapidly; however, in a society where the divorce rate is high and cohabitation the norm, the home and family still remain important.

Oslo may be reputed as one of the most expensive cities in the world, but visitors are invited to share the wealth of its cultural and recreational offering. The Norwegian capital boasts some of the finest modern architecture in the world, including a sleek Opera House in the fast-developing Bjørvika district and the Astrup Fearnley Museum of Modern Art,

Souvenir hats.

now in its new location in Tjuvholmen. In less than two hours from the city, one can escape to charming hamlets with historic fortresses, open-air museums and manor houses.

Norway is a long, narrow strip of a country, stretching north from mainland Europe far into the Arctic. The ancient capital of Trondheim is 500km (350 miles) from modern Oslo, yet only a quarter of the way up the country's jagged coast. The southern coast is as far from Monaco as it is from the Nordkapp (North Cape), and Norway's northernmost outpost, the islands of Svalbard (Spitsbergen), are hundreds of kilometres further still. With a population of just less than 5 million, Norway has, above all else, space.

Norway

100 miles

100 km

N

Norwegian Territory

Svalbard (Norway)
Bjørnøya (Norway)
Jan Mayen (Norway)
RUSSIA
FINLAND
SWEDEN
NORWAY
Greenland
ICELAND
UNITED KINGDOM

Svalbard

ARCTIC OCEAN
Kvitøya
Sjuøyane
Lågøya
Nordaustlandet
Kong Karls Land
Svenskøya
Wilhelmøya
Barentsøya
Edgeøya
Newtontoppen 1717
Spitsbergen
Ny-Ålesund
Longyearbyen
Nordvest-Spitsbergen Nasjonalpark
Eidsvollfjellet 1454
Forlandet Nasjonalpark
Sør-Spitsbergen Nasjonalpark
Sørkappøya
BARENTS SEA
NORWEGIAN SEA
100 miles
100 km
0
0

BARENTS SEA

RUSSIA
Lotta
Kirkenes
Vadsø
Vardø
Vadsø
Bátsfjord
Varangerhalvøya
Varangerbotn
E6
Lokan tekojärvi
Lokan tekojärvi
Kemijärvi
Rovaniemi
Kemijoki
Pudasjärvi
Livojoki
20
Oulu
Iijordfjellet
Inari
Olnarijärvi
Ivalo
E75
Vuotso
Sodankylä
E63
Kemijoki
Kemi
Hailuoto
Bottenviken
Honningsvåg
Nordkapp
E69
Havøysund
Hammerfest
Nordkapp
Altaelva
Alta
Karasjok
Lakselv
E6
Tana
Finnmark
Portipandan tekojärvi
Ounasjoki
Yitornio
Tornio
Torneälven
E4
Luleå
Piteå
Sørøya
Finnmarksvidda
Kaaresuvanto
Muonio
Muonioälven
Kittilä
Kolari
Pello
Kalixälven
Överkalix
Kalix
Øvre Soppero
E45
Øvre Soppero
Svappavaara
E10
Gällivare
Luleälven
Boden
Piteälven
Älvsbyn
94
Arnøy
Tromsø
Skibotn
Nordkjosbotn
E8
E8
Kiruna
Malmberget
Stora Lulevatten
Jokkmokk
E45
Käbdalis
Arvidsjaur
95
Ringvassøy
Kvaløya
Finnfjes
E6
Abisko
Torneträsk
Jäkkvik
Uddjaure
Arjeplog
Storavan
Senja
Harstad
Bjerkvik
Narvik
E10
Kraknes
Storfd
E6
Krakmo
Fauske
Lonsdal
Tarnaby
E12
Storuman
Andenes
Lødingen
Skalberget
Svolvær
392
Steigfd
Sortland
Vesterålen
Sørtjord
Svartisen
Umbukta
Rossvatnet
Troms
Nordland
Stokmarknes
Lofoten
Vestfjorden
Bodø
Mo i Rana
Ørnes
E10
Å
Mosjøen
Trofors
Sandnessjøen
Vega
Arctic Circle (Polarsirkel)
NORWEGIAN SEA

Central Oslo

0   200 m
0   200 yds

OSLO AND ITS FJORD

Norway's capital offers a lively mix of galleries, museums, shops, restaurants and nightlife, with magnificent forests, islands, ski trails and the beautiful Oslofjord close at hand.

Oslo still ranks as one of the world's most expensive cities, but the "Nordic City of Light" has awakened to the attractions of city fun, and developed into an unexpected metropolis. Oslo's cultural rebirth in recent years has been in part conscious, in part a natural outcome of injections of money in the right places. On the back of the oil boom came money for the arts and a flourishing of the arts scene. The new face of Oslo is represented by the magnificent white marble and granite Opera House, at the heart of the newly developing Bjørvika waterfront district.

But in many ways Oslo retains the features of the ideal city of the 19th century. Within easy walking distance (and this is a perfect city for walking in), nestled around the northern tip of the fjord and the central boulevard, Karl Johans gate, are all the accoutrements of a capital – the Royal Palace and its park, Parliament, City Hall, a castle, a cathedral, the National Theatre and excellent museums, the city's biggest draw. The attractions not in this compact grid of streets are just a few stops on the tram or T-Bane (Vigeland Park, the Munch Museum, the Nordamarka wilderness), while the sights on the Bygdøy peninsula, Oslo's other big draw, are a short ferry ride away.

Outdoor café, Aker Brygge.

Waterfront Oslo

The ideal way to arrive in **Oslo ①** is by boat, for then you get the most complete picture (though arriving by car from the south along the Mosseveien also offers some impressive views). The view from the fjord is dominated by the **City Hall ④** (Rådhus; tel: 23 46 12 00; Mon–Sun 9am–4pm; June–Aug daily guided tours at 10am, 12pm and 2pm), a large brick building topped by two square towers which overlooks the busy harbour. The imposing Modernist structure took 20 years to build – it

Main Attractions
Akershus Castle and Fortress
Oslo Opera House
Royal Palace
Ibsen Museum
National Gallery
Vigeland Park and Museum
Grønland and Grünerløkka
Munch Museum
Holmenkollen Ski Facility and Ski Jump
Bygdøy peninsula

was begun in the 1930s, but with the interruption of war, wasn't completed until the 1950s. The cavernous main hall is decorated with murals of Norwegian history and mythology, and the courtyard is adorned with bronze statues, a fine carved wooden frieze and the **swan fountain**. Every year on 10 December City Hall hosts the Nobel Peace Prize award ceremony.

On Brynjulf Bulls Plass is the **Nobel Peace Center ❸** (Nobels Fredssenter; www.nobelpeacecenter.org; mid-May–Aug daily 10am–6pm, Thu until 8pm, Jan–mid-May and Sept–Dec Tue–Sun 10am–6pm, Sept–Dec Thur 10am–8pm; guided tours in English Sat–Sun, daily in summer), which opened in 2005 on the site of the Vestbane building, a former railway station. Exhibitions staged here focus on former Peace Prize laureates and topics such as war, peace and conflict resolution.

Just north of the Nobel Peace Center, the **Konserthus** (Concert Hall; Munkedamsveien 14; tel: 23 11 31 00; www.oslokonserthus.no), home of the Oslo Philharmonic, holds concerts most Thursday and Friday nights, except in July. Across the road, the **Stenersen Museum ❸** (Munkedamsveien 15; www.stenersenmuseet.no; Tue–Sun 11am–4pm, Thur 11am–6pm) features three private art collections on Norwegian Realism, Modernism and the avant-garde from the 19th and 20th centuries.

The last remnant of Oslo's heavy industry, the Aker Shipyard, closed in 1982. In its place on the western side of the harbour is **Aker Brygge ❹** (Aker Docks; www.akerbrygge.no), a vibrant complex of shops, offices and apartments overlooking the fjord. The seafront boardwalk lined with cafés and restaurants is one of Oslo's most popular meeting places and teems with people in the summer months.

In 2019, the area will see the opening of the new clean-cut building of the National Museum, next to the Nobel Peace Centre and City Hall. It will be home to visual arts and crafts collections that are currently showcased in three different locations within the city.

A short walk south to the Tjuvholmen peninsula is the new home of the **Astrup Fearnley Museum of Modern Art ❺** (Strandpromenaden 2; tel:

Oslo Opera House.

22 93 60 60; http://afmuseet.no; Tue–Sun noon–5pm, Thur noon–7pm, Sat–Sun 11am–5pm; guided tour in English July–Aug Thur 5.30pm), which focuses on European and American works, with paintings by Francis Bacon and David Hockney among others. The museum's architect Renzo Piano is also responsible for the adjacent **Tjuvholmen Sculpture Park**, featuring works from some of the greatest contemporary sculptors. Part of the revitalisation of the city's waterfront, the Tjuvholmen district has undergone extensive urban renewal in recent years and now boasts some of the finest architecture in Oslo, including the 90-metre (295ft) **Sneak Peak** (Tjuvtitten) tower with a glass elevator open to visitors (www.tjuvholmen.no).

The Akershus complex

Across the harbour, with fine views of the fjord, stands the sprawling **Akershus Castle and Fortress** ❻ (Akershus Slott og Festning; castle: May–Aug Mon–Sat 10am–4pm, Sun noon–4pm, Sept–Apr noon–5pm; bastions and ramparts: May–Sept

6am–9pm, Oct–Apr 7am–9pm; free entrance to grounds). The major complex was begun in 1300, finished in 1308 and extended through the 17th century. It was built principally to defend the city against attack from Sweden. State events are still held in the beautiful ballrooms and the grounds provide the venue for summer concerts and theatrical performances. The Royal Chapel and Royal Mausoleum are open to the public.

In the fortress, the Armed Forces Museum (Forsvarsmuseet; Sept–Apr Tue–Fri 11am–4pm, Sat–Sun 11am–5pm, May–Aug Mon–Fri 10am–5pm, Sat–Sun 11am–5pm; free) covers Norwegian military history from the Viking period on, and provides a fascinating insight into Norway's relationship with neighbouring Denmark and Sweden over the centuries.

Just outside the castle, the **Norway Resistance Museum** (Norges Hjemmefrontmuseum; tel: 23 09 32 80; June–Aug Mon–Sat 10am–5pm, Sun 11am–5pm, rest of year until 4pm, Sat from 11am), located at the place where Resistance members were

FACT

Akershus Castle (tel: 23 09 39 17) and the University Aula (tel: 22 85 97 11) both stage classical music performances in summer. Another small concert venue is Den Gamle Logen (Grev Wedels plassen 2; tel: 22 33 44 70; www. gamlelogen.no), which is closed in summer but stages concerts during the rest of the year.

Guardsman at the Royal Palace.

OSLOMARKA

Oslo's sporty profile is due in part to the closeness of outdoor recreation. On one side there's the fjord, a broad, sheltered expanse of water ideal for windsurfing and boating. On the other side is a huge woodland recreation area known as **Oslomarka** (Oslo's fields; www.oslomarka.no), covering some 1,700 sq km (656 sq miles). Here there are 2,600km (1,600 miles) of ski trails marked with red-painted slashes on trees and rings round sign-poles at trail intersections. The total length of the summertime walking trails is even longer; they are marked in blue, the difference being that red-marked trails can cross lakes and marshes frozen in the winter, while blue-marked trails cannot. Some 110km (68 miles) of these trails are illuminated until 10pm for night skiing, with their trailheads at car parks or underground stations, for ease of after-dark access. All the illuminated trails, as well as some 500km (300 miles) of other trails, are regularly maintained with tracks set by machine. Trail use is free, as cross-country skiing is regarded as part of public recreation. Along the trails, there are some 44 staffed lodges with lounges, cafeterias and toilets; most are open at weekends and during school holidays, and in the winter, some are open in the evening. There are also 16 Alpine ski lift hills and 48 ski jumps. For more information: www.skiforeningen.no.

TIP

An Oslo Pass is recommended for free admission to the city's museums, free public transport and parking, discounts at shops and restaurants and on car hire. You can obtain one from tourist offices and hotels.

executed by the Gestapo, gives a clear and detailed account (with English labels) of the intense and moving story of occupied Norway.

Bankplassen

Overlooking Bankplassen, an attractive square with fountain and trees, housed in the former Bank of Norway headquarters, is the **Museum of Contemporary Art** Ⓖ (Museet for Samtidskunst; Bankplassen 4; www.nasjonalmuseet.no; Tue–Fri 11am–5pm, Thur until 7pm, Sat–Sun noon–5pm; free on Sun). An extensive collection of post-war Norwegian art is exhibited in its light and spacious environs, along with temporary exhibitions featuring top international artists.

In the nearby **National Museum of Architecture** (Norsk Arkitekturmuseet; Bankplassen 3; same hours as Museum of Contemporary Art) exhibitions range from contemporary architecture to historical subjects.

The Bjørvika Quarter

Alfresco diners.

The stunning new **Opera House** Ⓗ (Operahus; Kirsten Flagstads plassen 1; tel: 21 42 21 21; www.operaen.no; 50-minute guided tours in English, Sat–Sun throughout the year, daily in summer) opened in 2008 at a cost of 4.4 billion kroners. This no-expense-spared building is not just a cultural centre, but an inviting public space which draws visitors in their thousands. The Opera House is to be the cornerstone of a dynamic new residential, cultural and commercial district that is emerging in the old industrial port area of Bjørvika. Another landmark development in the district is the glass-and-steel **Akrobaten pedestrian and bicycle bridge**, opened in 2011. This award-winning bridge stretches over the railway line, providing an easy access to Bjørvika from the Grønland area. The Akrobaten is a perfect spot for viewing the controversial **Barcode** – a row of five tall buildings narrowly spaced (hence the name) that have reshaped Oslo's traditionally low-rise skyline. Bjørvika will be welcoming two new buildings of note in the near future: a state-of-the-art main branch of the Oslo public library in 2018 and, in 2019, the new

OSLO OPERA HOUSE

Sloping like an iceberg into the waves, Norway's dramatic harbourside **Opera House** opened in 2008 to international acclaim. The modern structure has pride of place on the waterfront, just a five-minute walk from Oslo S (Central) train station, out the south entrance and over the pedestrian bridge. The award-winning design by Norwegian architects Snøhetta is a truly Nordic concoction, built to resemble snow fields and floating ice, with fabulous acoustics. Norway's largest venue for opera and ballet has three stages, with seating for 1,364 in the main auditorium.

The Opera House was deliberately planned so that even non-opera-goers could find something to enjoy. Two sweeping slopes of Italian Carrara marble flank the main bulk of the building, allowing the public to stroll onto the roof, sunbathe, picnic – in short, to claim the building as their own. There is also a gift shop, bar, brasserie and Argent restaurant, for fine dining.

The harbourside location and radical design have lent the Opera House two unusual features. Much of the building is below sea level – orchestra members in the main auditorium actually sit 15 metres (50ft) "underwater". It's also the only opera house in the world to have its own underwater sea defences, a barrier to protect it should the Oslo–Copenhagen car ferry ever drift off course.

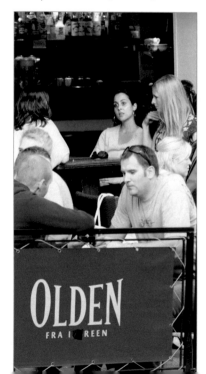

Munch Museum (the Lambda building, only 200 metres (650ft) away from the Opera House.

Karl Johans gate

All the main city sights are within easy walking distance of Karl Johans gate, central Oslo's main axis, which is pedestrianised through its eastern half between the cathedral and Parliament building. Originally designed in 1826 by the royal architect H.D.F. Linstow, it was widened some 50 years later to become Oslo's answer to the Champs-Elysées. Its western end merges into the broad avenue leading to the doors of the **Royal Palace** ❶ (Det Kongelige Slott; tel: 22 04 88 20; www.royalcourt.no; mid-June–mid-Aug, English guided tours daily, tickets on sale from Mar), the cream-coloured domain of the Norwegian royal family. The palace grounds are a pleasant public park (Slottsparken) that's free to enter. The changing of the guard takes place daily at 1.30pm.

Oslo's chic Westside quarter begins behind the Palace, leading up Bygdoy Allé to the Frogner quarter and Vigelandsparken, where many 19th-century mansions housing foreign consulates can be found on romantic tree-lined streets.

On the south side of Dronningsparken, the **Ibsen Museum** ❿ (Henrik Ibsens gate 26; tel: 22 12 35 50; www.ibsenmuseet.no; mid-May–mid-Sept Mon–Sun 11am–6pm, rest of the year until 4pm, Thu until 6pm; guided tours) incorporates the apartment once occupied by Henrik Ibsen (1828–1906), Norway's most famous playwright and one of the world's great pioneers of social drama (see page 85). A comprehensive exhibition opened here in 2006 to commemorate the centenary of Ibsen's death.

A statue of Ibsen stands in front of the rococo **National Theatre** ❿ (Johanne Dybwads plass 1; tel: 22 00 14 00; www.nationaltheatret.no), which opened its doors in 1899. Norway's largest theatre, it is the venue of the International Ibsen Festival.

Alongside the National Theatre, opposite the main university building is the Studenterlunden (Students Park). In warm weather, this is a

Outside the National Theatre.

popular place for nearby office workers to have an alfresco lunch by the **Spikersuppa**, a water feature that converts to an outdoor ice-skating rink in winter.

The Great Hall of the University *(Aula)*, with its celebrated murals by Edvard Munch, is unfortunately no longer open to the public except for concerts and other special events. If you have a chance to go there, it is worth it.

The National Gallery and Historical Musem

Just up the road is the splendid **National Gallery ❶** (tel: 21 98 00 00; www.nasjonalmuseet.no; Tue–Fri 10am–6pm, Thur until 7pm, Sat–Sun 11am–5pm; free on Sun), with a comprehensive collection of 19th-century Norwegian masterpieces, plus some French Impressionist paintings and Russian icons. The main attraction is a version of *Skrik* (*The Scream*) by Edvard Munch on display with some other of his best-known works, but there are many more lesser-known works to discover like the landscapes of J.C. Dahl and Kitty L. Kieland, and the powerful

National Gallery.

domestic portraits by Harriet Backer and Christian Krohg. For a more in-depth exploration of Munch's life and work visit the Munch Museum.

Behind the National Gallery is the **Historical Museum ⓜ** (Frederiks Gate 2; tel: 22 85 19 00; www.khm.uio.no; mid-May–mid-Sept Tue–Sun 10am–5pm, rest of the year 11am–4pm). Dating to 1904, this museum occupies one of Oslo's most elegant Art Nouveau buildings. It covers Norwegian history over 9,000 years, and highlights the Viking Age and medieval times, with Scandinavia's largest collection of Viking gold. There are also displays on indigenous Nordic cultures.

Parliament to Oslo Cathedral

Back on Karl Johans gate, it's a short walk to **Parliament ⓝ** (Stortinget; Akersgate; tel: 23 31 31 80; www.stortinget.no; one-hour guided tours in English on Sat mid-Jan–mid-June, 10am and 11.30am; free; it is advised to come 15 minutes early). The central building is where sessions are held and dates to 1866.

Further east on the pedestrianised section of Karl Johans gate, just before the main station, is **Oslo Cathedral ⓞ** (Domkirken; www.oslodomkirke.no; daily 10am–4pm, Fri night 4pm–6am). It was consecrated in 1697 after a fire destroyed its predecessor. The ruins of an even earlier cathedral, St Hallvard's, named after Oslo's patron saint, lie to the east of the city at Gamle Oslo, where the first city stood. Before going into the Domkirke, take a look at the stone relief to the right of the main entrance (c.1100). The 1718 tower clock is Norway's oldest. The interior owes its appearance mainly to a restoration completed in 1950, but the original design is typified by the organ front which now surrounds a modern organ. The stained-glass windows are the work of Emanuel Vigeland, and the ceilings were painted by Hugo Louis Mohr, depicting various biblical scenes.

The last stretch of Karl Johans gate leads to Oslo Central Station (Sentral-stasjon), or Oslo "S," and a more hectic part of town, with shopping centres and city hotels.

Vigeland Sculpture Park

The works of one of Munch's contemporaries, sculptor Gustav Vigeland (1869–1943), dominate the **Vigeland Sculpture Park** ❶ (Vigelandsparken; www.vigeland.museum.no; year-round; free) in Frogner Park to the west of the city centre, an extensive display of human life and emotion cast in stone and bronze. The most captivating piece here is Vigeland's *Monolith*, a swirl of 121 intertwining figures carved from a single block of granite in a moving tribute to the human condition. A 10-minute walk south of the obelisk, at the edge of the park, is the newly renovated **Vigeland Museum** (Nobels Gate 32; tel: 23 49 37 00; May–Aug Tue–Sun 10am–5pm, Sept–Apr Tue–Sun noon–4pm). This was the artist's atelier and home in the 1920s and is full of sketches, photos, casts and sculptures linked to his work in the the sculpture park. Also within Vigeland Park is the **Oslo City Museum** (Bymuseet; tel: 23 28 41 70; www.oslomuseum.no; Tue–Sun 11am–4pm; free) in the beautiful Frogner Manor House which explores 1,000 years of Oslo's cultural history and urban development.

A few blocks uphill near Slemdal T-Bane station is the **Emanuel Vigeland Museum** (Grimelundsveien 8; tel: 22 14 57 88; www.emanuelvigeland.museum.no; Sun noon–4pm, mid-May–mid-Sept noon–5pm). Gustav Vigeland's brother, painter Emanuel Vigeland (1875–1948), was also fascinated by themes of life and death, and used them in the alfresco decoration of a mausoleum, entitled *Vita (Life)*, the museum's main attraction.

Eastern Oslo

Experience Oslo's multicultural environs by heading east of the centre across the Akerselva River to Grønlandsleiret and Smalgangen in **Grønland** ❷. Here a wide variety of shops run by immigrants offer everything from exotic textiles and gold to kebabs, spices

SHOP

Behind the cathedral is Basarhallene, a round, colonnaded market with food, flower and handicraft stalls, galleries and Café Bacchus, which is open Mon–Sat until 11pm (www.cafebacchus.no).

The extraordinary sculptures at Vigeland Sculpture Park.

and saris. At the corner of Tøyengata and Grønlandsleiret is the **Grønland Bazaar** (www.gronlandbasar.no; Mon–Fri 10am–8pm, Sat until 6pm).

The newest addition to this lively quarter is the **Intercultural Museum** (Interkulturelt Museum; Tøyenbekken 5; tel: 22 05 28 30; Tue–Sun 11am–4pm; free). Housed in a converted police station, renamed the Grønland Culture Station, it produces diverse exhibitions on the history of immigration and cultural changes in Norwegian society. Its aim is to promote respect for cultural diversity.

Follow Storgata north to explore the neighbourhood of **Grünerløkka** Ⓡ. Known as the Greenwich Village of Oslo, this former working-class area by the Akerselva River has been transformed in the last decade into a trendy quarter with cafés, restaurants, eclectic galleries and independent shops. Oslo's hippest bars and nightclubs are in the Grønland and Grünerløkka districts.

Southwest of Grünerløkka across the river the **Norwegian Centre for Design and Architecture** (DogA; Hausmanns gate 16; http://doga.no; tel: 23 29 28 70; Mon–Fri 10am–5pm, Wed and Thur until 8pm, Sat–Sun noon–5pm) occupies a restored power station next to Jakob's church. The changing exhibitions focus on design and architecture, and there is a shop, café and restaurant.

Housed in a former synagogue (1921), the **Jewish Museum** (Jødisk Museum; Calmeyers gate 15; http://jodiskmuseumoslo.no; tel: 22 20 84 00; Tue 10am–3pm, Thur 2–7pm, Sun 11am–4pm) is both a cultural centre and museum tracing the history of Jews in Norway.

The Munch Museum

It's a worthwhile journey to the northeastern suburb of Tøyen to visit the **Munch Museum** Ⓢ (tel: 23 49 35 00; www.munch.museum.no; June–Sept daily 10am–5pm, Oct–May Wed–Mon 10am–4pm; July–Aug guided tours in English at 1pm free with admission ticket), dedicated to the life and works of Edvard Munch (1863–1944), the painter and graphic artist who fathered German Expressionism (see

Hiking in Oslomarka.

page 87). The gallery holds thousands of paintings, drawings, photographs and engravings which the artist bequeathed to the city of Oslo. His *Skrik (The Scream)* is Scandinavia's most reproduced work of art, famously stolen in 2004 then recovered two years later. It was actually painted in two versions. The earlier, from 1893, is in the National Gallery of Oslo. What appears to be a somewhat later version hangs here. More important for promoting and spreading the image was the lithographic version from 1895, which is on display in the graphic section. Plans are afoot to transfer the Munch collection to new premises by the Opera House in the burgeoning Bjørvika quarter, in 2019.

Capital sports

High on the hills offering splendid views of the city is the **Holmenkollen Ski Facility ⓣ** (Kongeveien 5; tel: 22 92 32 00; www.skiforeningen.no; all year; free except during ski meets), which boasts a spectacular new World Cup arena, rebuilt for the 2011 Nordic (Trial) World Ski Championships. This prestigious winter sport event started in 1892 and is the oldest in the world, drawing huge crowds for 21 different competitions. A few weeks later the Great Ski Jump is held, which also traditionally draws a huge crowd.

The centrepiece of the arena is the impressive Holmenkollen Ski Jump, which is part of a complex that includes the world's oldest ski museum and a ski-simulator, where you can experience how it feels to speed down the world's toughest slopes. The **Ski Museum** (tel: 91 67 19 47; www.holmenkollen.com; June–Aug 9am–8pm; Oct–Apr 10am–4pm, May and Sept 10am–5pm), which is situated within the ski jump, traces 4,000 years of skiing history in Norway. Panoramic views of Oslo can be seen from the observation deck on top of the jump tower.

There's a café serving *smørbrød*, and the **Holmenkollen Restaurant** (tel:

22 13 92 00; www.holmenkollenrestaurant. no) serves good Norwegian dishes. The walk down to Holmenkollen station takes 10 minutes, and within half an hour you are back in the city.

The Bygdøy peninsula

It's a short ferry ride (or bus journey in winter) from the harbour across the bay to the Bygdøy peninsula. The first stop is Dronningen dock, a 10-minute walk from the **Viking Ship Museum ⓤ** (Vikingskipshus; Huk aveny 35; tel: 22 13 52 80; www.khm.uio.no; May–Sept daily 9am–6pm, Oct–Apr 11am–4pm) featuring one of Oslo's top attractions: a trio of well-preserved Viking longships unearthed in southern Norway.

The **Norwegian Museum of Cultural History ⓥ** (Norsk Folkemuseum; Museumsveien 10; tel: 22 85 16 30; www.norskfolkemuseum.no; mid-May–mid-Sept daily 10am–6pm, mid-Sept–mid-May Mon–Fri 11am–3pm, Sat–Sun until 4pm) is a sprawling open-air museum with more than 150 historic timber houses from around Norway and a beautifully restored stave church from 1200.

KIDS

Children will enjoy the old-fashioned candy store and horse and carriage rides at the Norsk Folke-museum on Bygdøy peninsula (Museumsveien 10; daily; tel: 22 12 37 00; www.norskfolkemuseum.no).

Folk music and dancing are often performed in summer.

The pines and waters of Oslo were the training ground for Fridtjof Nansen (1861–1930) and Roald Amundsen (1872–1928), two of the greats of the heroic age of polar exploration. Their ships, Fram and Gjøa, are preserved in two other museums on the peninsula, the **Fram Museum** Ⓦ (Bygdøynesveien 36; tel: 23 28 29 50; www.frammuseum.no; daily June–Aug 9am–6pm, May and Sept 10am–5pm, Jan–Apr and Oct–Dec 10am–4pm) and the **Norwegian Maritime Museum** Ⓧ (Norsk Sjøfartsmuseum; Bygdøynesveien 37; tel: 24 11 41 50; www.marmuseum.no; mid-May–Aug daily 10am–6pm, Sept–mid-May Tue–Fri 10am–3pm; charge). Both museums are accessed from the Bygdøynes dock (the next stop after Dronningen dock).

Nearby, the **Kon-Tiki Museum** Ⓨ (Bygdøynesveien 36; tel: 23 08 67 67; www.kon-tiki.no; daily Mar–May and Sept–Oct 10am–5pm, June–Aug 9.30am–6pm, Nov–Feb 10am–4pm) has a fine collection of Easter Island artefacts, as well as detailed displays of the preserved Kon-Tiki and Ra II craft used by ethnographic explorer Thor Heyerdahl (1914–2002).

Outwards and southwards

If you stand at a vantage point in Oslo and look south down the fjord, almost everything in view is in Akershus county. Further south, the fjord is flanked on the east by Østfold county and on the west by Vestfold county. Aside from being home to one in three residents of the country, this area plays a key role in contemporary events and history.

In Akershus county, some 67km (42 miles) north of Oslo, lies **Eidsvoll** ❷, a town that grew around the ironworks built in 1624, and closed in 1825; Eidsvoll might have been just another post-industrial town, save for the happenings of the spring of 1814. Following the dissolution of the union with Denmark, 112 representatives convened at the headquarters of the ironworks, then the only convenient large building, to draw up the Norwegian Constitution. **Eidsvoll 1814** (C. Ankersvei; tel: 63 92 22 10; www.eidsvoll1814.no; May–Aug daily 10am–5pm, Sept–Apr Tue–Fri 10am–3pm, Sat–Sun noon–5pm) is one of Norway's most important cultural monuments. **Eidsvoll Manor** is now a museum to the Constitution and includes the room where the document was signed on 17 May 1814. The country's first railway, built in 1845, connected Oslo and Eidsvoll, and it's now on the E6 highway, the major north–south artery.

Historic provincial cities and towns are scattered throughout Østfold and Vestfold counties. The best way to explore the counties, whether you travel by bus, car or boat, is via **Drøbak** ❸, which has become the Norwegian residence of Santa Claus – there is a shop in the centre (Julehus; www.julehus.no) with a permanent Christmas exhibition and Santa's own post office. By road, you will pass Vinterbro, at the junction

Fredriksten Fort dominates the town of Halden.

of the E6 and E18 highways, the location of **Tusen Fryd** ❹ (tel: 64 97 66 97; http://tusenfryd.no; mid-June–Sept 10/10.30am–4/9pm, see website for exact times), the country's major amusement park.

Picturesque Drøbak grew out of a fishermen's settlement, and fishing vessels still dock to sell fresh catch on the quayside. Places of interest include the open-air **Heritage Museum** (Follo Museum; tel: 66 93 66 36; www.follomuseum.no; mid-Apr–mid-Sept Tue–Fri 11am–4pm, Sun 11am–4pm, mid-Sept–mid-Apr Tue–Fri 9am–3.30pm;) in Belsjøveien, the **Drøbak Aquarium** (tel: 64 98 87 80; http://drobakakvarium.no; daily June–Aug 10am–7pm, rest of the year until 4pm), and **Oscarsborg Fort** (Festning) out in the fjord, (guided boat trips from the harbour). Another point of pride is the cross-timbered **Drøbak Church** built in 1776, with an elaborately carved model of a ship inside, a common church decoration in seafaring towns.

Further south, **Fredrikstad** ❺ is a gem among Østfold towns, and Scandinavia's only completely preserved fortress town, dating from 1567. The **Oldtidsveien** (Highway of the Ancients), the 18km (11-mile) stretch of National Highway 110 between Fredrikstad and Skjeberg, has three **Helleristningsfelt** – literally "rock wall carving areas" with Bronze Age pictographs (free access to grounds).

Halden ❻, south of Skjeberg and close to the Swedish border, is dominated by **Fredriksten Fort** (Festning), a largely intact ruin with many of its buildings serving as small theme museums. In summer, passenger launches travel the **Halden canal** that runs through several sets of massive locks. The **Kanal Museum** (tel: 69 81 10 21; http://ostfoldmuseene.no; mid-late June–mid-Aug daily 11am–5pm) at the locks at **Ørje** ❼ displays the implements of canal operations. It also arranges charter tours on the *Engebret Soot*, named after the

designer of the canal and now the world's oldest propeller-driven steamship in service.

Throughout Østfold, *Olsok* (St Olav's Day, 29 July) is celebrated with a great show of folk costume, music and dance. One of the best displays is at the **Borgarsyssel Museum** (tel: 69 11 56 50; http://ostfoldmuseene.no; June–Aug Tue–Sun noon–5pm, Sept Sun noon–5pm; free) in **Sarpsborg** ❽, north of Skjeberg, which is due to get a new building in 2016.

Drive back to the E6 which takes you northwards to **Moss** ❾ (where you can take the ferry to Horten and the Vestfold), then follow the local road through Moss to reach the small island of **Jeløy**. Visit **Galleri F15** (tel: 69 27 10 33; www.punkto.no; Tue–Sun 11am–5pm), a contemporary art museum in a 19th-century manor house.

Viking Vestfold

The Moss–Horten car ferry connects Østfold and Vestfold in just under an hour. The **Naval Museum** (Marinemuseet; tel: 33 03 33 97; May–Sept daily noon–4pm, Oct–Apr Sun

TIP

For a fun day out for all the family, head for the historic Hadeland Glassworks (Glassverk; www.hadelandglassverk.no) or Blaafarveværket Museum, "The Blue-Colour Works" – a former cobalt mine (www.blaa.no). Both these attractions are set in idyllic locations and can easily be reached by public transport from Oslo's main bus station (https://ruter.no).

Inside the Munch Museum.

noon–4pm; free) at **Horten** ⓾, home port of Sjøforsvaret (the Royal Norwegian Navy), bulges with maritime history. Horten also has the Preuss Museum of Photography (tel: 33 03 16 30; www.preusmuseum.no; Tue–Fri noon–4pm, Sat–Sun noon–5pm, July until 5pm), as well as a museum for vintage cars (tel: 33 04 26 01; www.automobilmuseum.no; Sun noon–5pm, mid-June–mid-Aug daily noon–5pm).

To the south lies the heart of eastern Viking country, and **Borre National Park** (all year; free access to grounds), en route to Tønsberg, contains large turf-covered mounds concealing the graves of Viking kings. Keeping to the coastline along Route 311, **Munch's House** (tel: 469 49 160; www.munchshus.no; May and Sept Sat–Sun 11am–4pm, June–Aug Tue–Sun 11am–6pm) at **Åsgårdstrand** ⓫ is where the artist lived when in Norway. It was a setting for many of his paintings.

Between Åsgårdstrand and Tønsberg is a burial mound, **Oseberghaugen** ⓬, the most important Viking site yet discovered (all year; grounds free). Oslo's Vikingskipshus contains

Åsgårdstrand.

the finds, including the 20-metre (65ft) arch-ended wooden ship. Just south is historic **Tønsberg** ⓭, established in the 9th century. On the 65-metre (200ft) high **Slottsfjellet** are the fortress remains and tower. The main street, **Storgata**, is flanked by Viking graves. These were excavated and incorporated, under glass, into the ground floor of the new library.

The most renowned king to hold court in Tønsberg was Håkon Håkonsson IV (1204–63). The ruins of his court can be seen on **Nordbyen**, a street with historic houses. A more recent native son is Roald Amundsen, the polar explorer. The steamship *Kysten* (built 1909), moored on Byfjord near the old customs house, used to operate island tours out to the skerries but it is still undergoing extensive restoration (www.dskysten.no).

Summer playground

South of Tønsberg, along the eastern side of the fjord, the islands of **Nøtterøy** and **Tjøme**, and the skerries, are fantastic summer hangouts. **World's End** ⓮ (Verdens Ende) is at the end of the chain. The old lighthouse here is a beautifully simple structure made of stone.

On the other side of Tønsbergfjord lies **Sandefjord** ⓯, a whaling town and home to Oslo's second airport. The town centre is compact, and near **Badeparken** are the former spa and the Old Town.

Just outside Sandefjord is another burial site, **Gokstadhaugen** ⓰, in which the *Gokstad* ship, now in Oslo's Viking Ship Museum, was discovered in 1880. The **Vesterøy** peninsula is a supremely peaceful place, ideal for walking, cycling and boating.

Larvik ⓱ was home to two legendary boat-lovers, explorer Thor Heyerdahl (1914–2002) and master boatbuilder Colin Archer (1832–1921), designer of the polar ship *Fram*. Archer's first house was at Tollerodden, on the fjord. At Larvik's back is Farris lake, site of the country's only natural mineral-water spring.

Southern and Central Norway

Lindesnes Fyr (lighthouse), on the southernmost tip of Norway.

SOUTHERN NORWAY

Norway's southern beaches and picturesque seaside towns are a magnet for summer visitors. The west coast is blessed with glorious fjords and the oil-rich city of Stavanger.

D raw an upward arc on the map from Oslo in the east to Bergen in the west, and south of it you see the part of Norway where the majority of Norwegians take their home country holidays. They head for their seaside cottages, camp in the forests and by the lakes, or set sail to explore the islands and inlets. In clockwise order starting at Oslo, southern Norway can be divided into the principal regions of **Sørlandet** (southern country), comprising Telemark, Aust-Agder and Vest-Agder counties and their coasts around to about 7 o'clock; **Rogaland** county centred at the city of Stavanger on the west coast; and **Hordaland** county around Bergen.

Sørlandet

Norway's fifth-largest city, lively **Kristiansand ❶** is the unofficial capital of the southern coast. It's a busy summer resort with ferry connections to Denmark. In 1639, King Christian IV of Denmark and Norway selected the site of the city for a fort to control the approaches to the North Sea and the Baltic. You can visit what remains of **Christiansholm Festning**, which offers views of the harbour and coast from its stocky ramparts.

One of Norway's most visited attractions is **Kristiansand Dyrepark** (www.dyreparken.no; daily from 10am until 3–7pm), 11km (7 miles) east of the

city, incorporating a zoo, wilderness park, water park and amusement park.

West of Kristiansand, the seaside resort and former timber town **Mandal ❷** boasts Norway's best sandy beach and a well-preserved centre of cobbled streets and white clapboard houses characteristic of this area. Beyond, the **Lindesnes Fyr** (lighthouse; www.lindesnesfyr.no) marks the southernmost point of Norway. The last town before Vest-Agder rises to meet Rogaland is the port of **Flekkefjord** and the idyllic island of **Hidra**.

Main Attractions

Christiansholm Fortress
Telemark Museum and Canal Cruise, Skien
Heddal Stave Church
Preikestolen (Pulpit Rock)
Laksestudioet and Ryfylke Museum, Sand
Old Stavanger and cathedral
Skudeneshavn, Karmøy
Langfoss waterfall
Cable Car up Hangurfjell

Breathtaking Trolltunga Rock.

TIP

Express trains speed
between Oslo and
Kristiansand in 4 hours
and 45 minutes, and
between Kristiansand
and Stavanger in 3 hours
and 15 minutes.

The terrain is mountainous, with many splendid waterfalls, especially around **Kvinesdal** ❸.

The Skagerrak coast

East from Kristiansand, the coastline of the Skagerrak strait is made up of islets, skerries and coves. It is relatively protected, but with rocky rather than sandy beaches. The principal centres along the coast, in order, are Lillesand, Grimstad and Arendal. **Lillesand** ❹ is a popular holiday town with a lively harbour overlooked by white clapboard houses. Once a major shipbuilding centre, **Grimstad** ❺ is now a pretty, laidback town, indelibly associated with Ibsen, who served his apprenticeship to a chemist here. Dating to 1916, the **Ibsen Museum** (Henrik Ibsens gate 14; tel: 37 04 04 90; May–Aug daily 11am–5pm) is Norway's oldest museum. **Arendal** ❻ is one of the liveliest towns on this stretch of coast. It was struck by fire in 1863, and lost the houses on stilts that had earned it the nickname "Little Venice", but it still enjoys a lovely setting, surrounded by small islands, and

Heddal Stave Church.

features many restored wooden buildings. The **Arendal Town Museum** (Arendal Bymuseum/Kløckers Hus; tel: 37 02 59 25; Tue–Fri 10am–3pm, Sat 10am–2pm) has extensive displays delineating local history, and the **Town Hall** (Rådhus), previously the home of a merchant, is said to be one of the largest wooden buildings ever constructed in Norway.

Telemark

Best known for its stave churches and canal system, the beautiful, rural Telemark region has much else to recommend it, with lakes, mountains, forests and fjords to explore. The regional capital is **Skien** ❼, where Henrik Ibsen (1828–1906) spent his childhood. His home, Venstøp, forms part of the **Telemark Museum** (Brekke Park; tel: 35 54 45 00; http://telemarkmuseum.no; May–Aug daily 11am–9pm). Tulips bloom en masse in the elegant English gardens in summer, which are surrounded by stylish mansions.

Northwest of Skien lies **Ulefoss**, a village that until the end of the 19th century was a major exporter of ice,

COUNTRY AFLOAT

To the world, Norway and seafaring are synonymous. From the age of sail until after World War II, the Norwegian merchant fleet was one of the world's largest, and Norwegian could be heard in ports worldwide.

Norwegians seem happiest when they are in, on or around the sea. Each year, more than a third of the population spend their summer holidays partly or completely in craft that range from small dinghies to motor launches and ocean-going yachts. In all, there are more than 450,000 boats over 4.5 metres (15ft) in length, and an untold number of smaller boats in the country. Most are motor boats, though sailing is popular on the fjords and as a competitive sport.

Geography and topography are the deciding factors. There are thousands of islands, and the fjords and coastal archipelagos are a paradise for competitive and recreational sailors, king and commoner alike. King Olav V (1903–91), the father of present King Harald V, was an accomplished sailor who won a gold medal in sailing in the 1928 Olympic Games in Amsterdam, which made him the world's only Olympic medallist monarch. Norway's first sailing club was founded in 1868 in Tønsberg, since when the nation has been a major force in championship sailing and regattas worldwide.

which was transported along the waterways of the **Telemark Canal** ⑧, a 105km (65-mile) long waterway linking Skien to Dalen. Blasted out of the rocks over 100 years ago, the canal wends a scenic route through 18 locks. From late May to early September, two venerable passenger launches – the M/V Victoria and M/V Henrik Ibsen – ply the watercourse on pleasure cruises lasting from 2 to 11 hours (tel: 35 90 00 20; www.telemarkskanalen.no or www.visittelemark.com).

The small industrial town of **Notodden** is unremarkable in itself, but just 5km (3 miles) along Route 11 is one of Norway's top attractions, the medieval **Heddal Stave Church** ⑨ (tel: 35 02 04 00; www.heddalstavkirke. no; mid-May–mid-June and mid-Aug–mid-Sept 10am–5pm, mid-June–mid-Aug 9am–7pm). Considered "a masterpiece in wood", its ornate carvings are rivalled only by the beautiful period rose paintings in the Ramberg room of the nearby **Heddal Bygde-tun** open-air museum (http://heddal. visitvemork.no; mid-June–mid-Aug 10am–6pm).

About 10km (6 miles) further on, Route 37 branches north past Tinnsjø lake towards **Rjukan** ⑩. The principal attraction here is the former Vemork hydroelectric plant, just west of Rjukan. Dating from 1910 and surrounded by beautiful scenery, it now houses the **Norwegian Industrial Workers Museum** (Norsk Industriarbeidermuseum; tel: 35 09 90 00; www.visitvemork.com; Oct–Apr Tue–Fri noon–3pm, Sat–Sun 11am–4pm, May–mid-June and mid-Aug–Sept daily 10am–4pm, mid-June–mid-Aug daily 10am–6pm). The museum details the story of the brave attempts of the Norwegian Resistance to sabotage the plant where heavy water was once produced which the Nazis were using to develop nuclear weapons. In 2010, a new exhibition was installed which focuses on the everyday lives of workers from 1950 until the present day.

Rogaland

Though Bergen is known as the capital of fjord country, Rogaland county, centred on the west-coast port of Stavanger, has some of Norway's more spectacular sights. It also has the country's highest average temperature; in winter there is little snow, and the fertile fields are green for most of the year. The Ryfylke area northeast of Stavanger is true fjord country. It starts with Lysefjord and stretches north past long narrow lakes that once were open fjords, until it reaches Vindafjord, Saudafjord and Suldalsvatn.

Every visitor should try to make the trek to stand on **Preikestolen** ⑪ ("Pulpit Rock"), a dramatic table of rock soaring 597 metres (1,958ft) above Lysefjord, and the country's most famous vantage point. It can be reached via a two-hour trail from the Preikestolhytta (hut) along a steep but well-paved path that gives way to steeper, rather soggy terrain, then to thrilling granite slabs and windswept cliffs. There are also buses which link up with ferries, that provide a different perspective from the

Local folk costume.

water below. For more information: www.ryfylke.com or www.regionstavanger.com.

The sheltered bay north of Stavanger, and outer islands such as **Karmøy**, protect Ryfylke's inshore islands from the North Sea. Christianity flourished early here under the protection of the bishops of Stavanger, and the islands are sprinkled with churches, notably the 12th-century Utstein Kloster on Mosterøy.

The many lighthouses are not only landmarks for islanders and seafarers but make excellent bird-watching sites. The waters around these peaceful islands are well trafficked. Most of the island grocers also provide boat services, and it is easy to hire rowing boats and small craft with outboard engines.

In the northeast highlands of Rogaland, the fjords, lakes and rivers are rich in fish and fine for sailing and canoeing. There are good cross-country skiing tracks in winter and excellent Alpine slopes.

Among the best holiday areas is the Suldal district, stretching from

Sand ⓬ on Sandsfjord, along the Suldalslågen River. At the Sand end of Suldalslågen is **Laksestudioet** (mid-May–mid-Aug daily 10am–5pm, rest of Aug noon–4pm, Sept Sat–Sun noon–4pm), an observation studio built under a waterfall. Also worth a visit, the **Kolbeinstveit Old Farmstead Museum** (Ryfylke Museum; tel: 52 79 29 50; www.ryfylkemuseet.no; mid-June–mid-Aug daily 10am–6pm, rest of June and Aug daily 10am–5pm, rest of the year Mon–Fri 9am–3pm) dates to the 1850s and has recreated traditional farm life in a number of authentically restored buildings.

Stavanger

Stavanger ⓭ is Norway's fourth-largest city and its oil capital. As the once-lucrative fishing industry declined, the city discovered North Sea oilfields in 1965, when the city became the base of oil exploration in the North Sea. Nearly one in ten of its 130,000 inhabitants was born abroad, which is rather ironic since in the 19th and early 20th centuries,

Wooden houses in Kristiansand.

Stavanger was the principal port of embarkation for the great waves of Norwegian emigration to the United States: the first 52 emigrants left in 1825, bound for New York on the sloop *Restauration*. Those wishing to trace their roots can contact the **Norwegian Emigration Centre** (Det Norske Utvandrersenteret; www.emigrationcenter.com) for assistance.

The Stavanger *siddis* (colloquialism for a person from Stavanger) claim to be the oldest true Norwegians, tracing their lines to the Battle of Hafrsfjord. This decisive battle that first united the country under King Harald I Hårfagre, *c*.880, took place at a bay just southwest of the city. On the shore is an impressive monument to the event, **Sverd i fjell**, three larger-than-life Viking swords seemingly thrust into bedrock.

The heart of modern Stavanger is the area around **Breiavatnet**, the small lake in the middle of the city, near the Anglo-Norman-style **cathedral**, dating to 1125. Northwest of the cathedral are the winding cobbled streets and old timber houses of **Old (Gamle) Stavanger**. Around 1870, as fishing and shipping were in decline, the fishermen turned their attention to *brisling* (small herring), which were cured and canned in the town and sent as Norwegian "sardines" all over the world. Stavanger thrived on sardines until the 1950s. Today, the **Canning Museum** (Norsk hermetikkmuseum; tel: 407 28 470; mid-May–mid-Sept daily 10am–4pm, rest of the year Tue–Sun 11am–3pm, Thur until 7pm, Sat–Sun 10am–4pm), located in the former cannery, has recreated an authentic 1920s environment. The interactive **Norwegian Petroleum Museum** (Norsk Oljemuseum; tel: 51 93 93 00; www.norskolje.museum.no; June–Aug daily 10am–7pm, Sept–May daily 10am–4pm, Sun until 6pm) provides an insight into the exploration and production of oil and gas.

The west coast

The sea route to **Bergen** is a popular way to see the coast. By taking an express boat from Stavanger to Bergen or Haugesund you can drop off at any

TIP

The 12th-century Utstein Kloster on the island of Mosterøy makes a beautiful setting for concerts (tel: 51 72 00 50; www.museumstavanger.no/museene/utstein-kloster).

Lysefjord.

The Heroes of Telemark

The Norwegian Resistance efforts to sabotage Nazi production of the atomic bomb is a tale of bravery and remarkable survival skills.

When Germany invaded Norway in 1940, the Norwegian defence forces were no match for Hitler's army and the country was quickly occupied. The Norwegian royal family took refuge in London from where King Harald directed operations by the Norwegian underground to obstruct in any way they could their unwanted Nazi occupiers. The most celebrated act of resistance in Norway during World War II was the sabotage of the Vemork heavy water plant at Rjukan, in Telemark, in February 1943 – successful production of heavy water in the plant could conceivably have aided German development of an atomic bomb. No visitor to Rjukan, dwarfed and darkened by mountains all round, could fail to be awed by the audacity of the saboteurs. Their heroic exploits were made into a Hollywood film in 1965, *The Heroes of Telemark*.

Kirk Douglas in the 1965 film The Heroes of Telemark. The movie was shot on location in Norway.

Operation "Freshman"

The operation, named "Freshman", was planned for a joint force of Norwegian volunteers and British commandos in two towed gliders. It ended disastrously when both gliders and one of the aircraft towing them crashed in bad weather, and the survivors were tortured and executed by the Gestapo.

Operation "Gunnerside"

The next attempt was an all-Norwegian affair. "Gunnerside" was the code name for six men who had been trained in England. They parachuted onto a frozen lake where they joined up with "Swallow", an advance party who had been on the ground since the first failed operation, subsisting for almost four winter months on moss, lichen and a single reindeer. The men skied to the ridge above Rjukan for the perilous descent, up to their waists in snow. Just after midnight, the covering party took up positions while the six-man demolition team cut a chain on the gates and crept forward to the basement of the concrete building where the most vital equipment and the heavy water storage tanks were located. The team broke in, surprising a solitary Norwegian guard who agreed to lead them to vital components, laid their charges and began a rapid withdrawal. They had only gone a few yards when there was what members later variously described as "a cataclysmic explosion" and "a tiny, insignificant pop".

The aftermath

Of the 10 saboteurs, six reached Sweden after a 400km (250-mile) journey on skis in indescribably difficult conditions; the other four remained in Norway. Of the Swallow party, Claus Helberg had the liveliest time. He was chased through the mountains by German soldiers, but escaped. Then he fell over a cliff and broke an arm. The next day he walked into a German patrol but had a good enough story to be taken to a hotel to await treatment. Most of the hotel guests (but not the injured Norwegian) were turned out of their rooms to make way for Reichskommissar Joseph Terboven (the Nazi who ruled Norway). Later, he was bundled along with the remaining guests "into a bus and sent off to the Grini concentration camp". Helberg jumped from the bus. Later, he turned up in Britain, reporting for further duties.

of the harbour stops and stay a night or a week according to your whim (tel: 177; www.kolumbus.no). **Karmøy** , the island at the south of the outer islands chain, is big enough to merit its own boat service, which goes to **Skudeneshavn**, an idyllic port with fine sandy beaches at the southern tip. The narrow streets of the Old Town are lined with white wooden houses, dating from the 1800s when the town was a busy herring fishing centre. **St Olafs church at Avaldsnes** is a landmark which dates to 1248; mysterious archaeological remains continue to be discovered here.

The north of the island is linked to the mainland just south of **Haugesund**, in a region known as "Norway's birthplace". It is the first sizeable coastal town north of Stavanger and has long been a centre for fishing, shipping and farming. Today its harbour is filled with pleasure boats and ringed by 19th-century wooden buildings, lively cafés and modern hotels; the town also hosts the Sildajazz international jazz festival (www.sildajazz.no) and the Norwegian Film Festival (www.filmfestivalen. no), both in August.

Don't leave town without climbing **Haraldshaugen**, the national monument constructed at the grave of Harald the Fair-Haired in 1872 to celebrate 1,000 years of Norwegian unification. Ten minutes north of the town centre, the impressive structure sits on a high grassy mound overlooking the sea with a spectacular view of the Tonjer lighthouse. Just south of it is Krosshaugen, an early Christian stone cross.

From Haugesund, the scenic E134 highway winds its way northeastwards via the charming hamlets of **Olen and Etne** to one of the world's most beautiful waterfalls at **Langfoss**. Have lunch in Etne at the reliable Fugl Fønix (www.fuglfonix.no), a unique hotel and restaurant in the heart of the countryside. Route 13, then Route 550 which hugs the western side of the Sør Fjord, lead to **Hardangerfjord**.

Hordaland

Hordaland county includes two of the country's top natural attractions: **Hardangervidda**, Norway's largest national park, whose central mountain plateau is 1,300 metres (4,500ft) above sea level, and **Hardangerfjord**. There are many fine hiking trails, one of which leads past the four giant Husedalen waterfalls which run from the Hardanger plateau down to Sørfjord, an arm of the Hardangerfjord. You can stay overnight in nearby Lofthus or Utne.

In days gone by, the fjords provided west Norway's main transport arteries, and **Utne** was an important junction between east and west. Its economy once centred on the apple, pear and cherry orchards that still cover the slopes of the Sørfjord; but it was also kept afloat by fishing and its charming painted furniture production, which you can still enjoy at the **Utne Hotel**, founded in 1722, the oldest hotel in Norway. The open-air

Shopping in Stavanger.

Hardanger Folk Museum (www.hardangerogvossmuseum.no; May–Aug daily 10am–5pm, Sept–Apr Mon–Fri 9am–3pm) sums up Hardanger life over the past centuries with historic houses, boats, shops and a school.

A ferry service connects Utne with **Kinsarvik** 🛈 on the east side of Sørfjord, or else Kvanndal, where you can connect with Route 7 to Bergen. Heading northeast on Route 13, you'll find a beautiful stretch of water, Eidfjord. It cuts far into the dramatic landscape that includes the beautiful **Skykkjedalsfossen** 🛈 waterfall.

The Hordaland area is also famous for the impressive **Trolltunga rock formation** – a "troll's tongue" jutting out of a cliff. Although it's a several-hours hike one way to get there, some 500 tourists visit it every day in summer.

The Voss district

If you loop back northwest, crossing Eidfjord by ferry and continuing on Route 13, you come to **Voss** 🛈, which lies next to Lake Vangsvatnet in the middle of rich farmland. The

The old fjord village of Utne.

Voss district makes full use of its surroundings to attract visitors, who come in summer for fjord excursions, mountain walking, parachuting, hanggliding and paragliding from **Hangurfjell**, and fishing and watersports on Vangsvatnet. In winter everything changes, and Voss becomes one of the best centres for Alpine and cross-country skiing. At 610 metres (2,000ft) the top station of the cable car (Hangursbanen) gives one of the best prospects of Voss in its bowl-shaped valley.

Around Bergen and north

From Voss the E16 highway or the train take you to **Bergen** 🛈 (see page 199) and its islands. **Askøy** and **Osterøy** islands to the north of the city have their own character, while the long, narrow island of **Sotra** 🛈 to the west shelters Bergen from the North Sea. It is a good base for sea-canoeing in and out of the small offshore islands and rocks and, in good weather, as far as the open sea to combine canoeing with ocean fishing. The area around Bjørnafjord (Bear Fjord) to the south of Bergen is very green and enjoys a particularly mild climate.

Nordhordland is a district of islands north of Bergen that stretches as far as Sognefjord. Fish farming is the economic mainstay here, and the region exports salmon and trout all round the world. There is good sea fishing for cod and coalfish, and rosy-coloured trout inhabit many of the lakes. Diving and sub-aqua fishing are easy in these transparent waters. Oil is a modern, though not conflicting, industry in this area, with the Mongstad refinery illuminated at night.

To the north, the remote island of **Fedje** 🛈 was an important navigation point for many centuries, with two 19th-century lighthouses. Norwegian maritime rules insist that all ships must carry a Norwegian pilot, which here is vital, as tankers serving the Mongstad refinery navigate through the ever-changing waters.

BERGEN

With its relaxed atmosphere, stunning setting and vibrant cultural life, Bergen is an appealing mix of the cosmopolitan and the outdoors, with easy access to the western fjords.

Standing on a peninsula surrounded by seven mountains, beautiful Bergen is Norway's western capital and gateway to the fjords. Its relaxed atmosphere, stunning setting and vibrant cultural life make it an ideal base for a fjord holiday.

The Gulf Stream blesses Bergen with a benign climate and a harbour that is ice-free year-round. But it also brings rain, some 2,250mm (89 inches), making Bergen the country's wettest city, so be sure to pack an umbrella.

Maritime traditions

With a population of 272,500, Bergen is a major port, with 10km (6 miles) of dockside. Until the railway eastwards over the high mountains to Oslo opened in 1909, Bergen was isolated from the rest of Norway. Scotland by ship was closer than Oslo, England less distant than Copenhagen. As the westernmost city in Scandinavia, Bergen soon became a crossroads of the north and, in the 13th century, the capital of a united Norway. Its favourable location with respect to the other ports of Europe drew Hanseatic tradesmen (merchants from medieval German cities), who established a commercial community at the harbour. Fullriggers plied the port, with peak traffic in 1644, when more than 400 ships docked from Scotland alone.

The Ulriksbanen cable car offers great views of Bergen.

A view from the top

The best place to get a feel for the city and take in its amazing natural setting is on the **Fløibanen funicular** Ⓐ (www.floibanen.no; daily every 15–30 minutes, Mon–Fri 7.30am–11.30pm, Sat–Sun 8am–11.30pm), that climbs more than 300 metres (1,000ft) in just eight minutes from the city centre to the top of Fløyen mountain, high above Bergen. At the summit there is a restaurant, gift shop, and a fantastic network of walking paths. Strike out alone or join the "Walk like a

Main Attractions
The Fløibanen funicular and Ulriksbanen cable car
The pastel houses of Hanseatic Bryggen
Fish Market
Aquarium
Concert at Grieg Hall
Troldhaugen, Edvard Grieg's home
Lysøen Island and Ole Bull's Villa

TIP

Invest in a Bergen Card from the Tourist Information Office in Torghallen at the Fish Market. Benefits include free admission or discounts for museums and free public transport.

Norwegian" guided hike through forests, past lakes and breathtaking views, learning about history, traditions and legends on the way (Apr–Sept). Children can go on a free treasure hunt (maps available from the ticket booth at the lower station).

For more breathtaking views of the city, fjords and islands, the **Ulriksbanen** cable car (http://ulriken643.no; Tue–Sun 10am–5pm) goes to the top of Mount Ulriken – at 643 metres (2,109 ft), the highest of the seven peaks that surround the city. You can walk for hours on marked trails while enjoying panoramic views of the city and surrounding sea.

Bryggen

A walk through the atmospheric medieval quarter of **Bryggen B** is a step back in time, to before the Reformation. Many of the Hanseatic buildings remain – a film set in themselves, meticulously preserved and listed as a Unesco World Heritage site. Here, too, are museums, galleries, craft shops, fashion boutiques and eating places, interspersed with sailmakers, a freight company and a scrap metal dealer.

The earliest archaeological remains are in **Bryggen Museum C** (tel: 55 58 80 10; www.bymuseet.no; mid-May–Aug daily 10am–4pm, Sept–Apr Mon–Fri 11am–3pm, Sat noon–3pm, Sun

Bergen

0 ⊢———⊣ 200 m
0 ⊢———⊣ 200 yds

noon–4pm). Guides from the museum conduct tours through the rows of Hansa houses and warehouses that line Bryggen. These were built after the great fire of 1702, which destroyed many buildings. A key to understanding the Hanseatic merchants' way of life is to visit the **Hanseatic Museum** **Ⓓ** (tel: 55 54 46 90; http://hanseatiske museum.museumvest.no; daily from 8.30–11am until 3–6pm), housed in a 1704 trade house complete with original interiors.

Nearby is the oldest building still in use in the city, **St Mary's Church** **Ⓔ** (Mariakirken; www.bergen.kirken. no), built in the early 12th century and justly proud of its rich Baroque pulpit. The other medieval churches to survive the periodic fires are **Domkirke** **Ⓕ** (Bergen Cathedral; http://bergendom kirke.no) and **Korskirken Ⓖ** (Church of the Holy Cross) both merit a visit.

Torget

To buy fish year-round in the open-air **Fish Market Ⓗ** (Fisketorget) on the nearby harbour is to walk in and out of a continuous conversation, as animated fishmongers engage in banter. Just opposite is the **Kjøttbasaren,** a restored 1887 meat market with a food hall, fish restaurants, deli and handicraft shops. Both are good places to make a pit stop before taking a pleasant stroll along the harbour.

Bergenhus

Northwest of Bryggen, overlooking the harbour entrance, stands the Bergen Fortress (Bergenhus Festning), the grounds of which are a public park. Most of the fortifications date from the 19th century. Most impressive of the original medieval buildings is **Håkons Hall Ⓘ** (tel: 47 97 95 77; www.bymuseet.no; mid-May–mid-Sept daily 10am–4pm, mid-Sept–mid-May daily noon–3pm; guided tours to the Hall and Tower every hour in summer). This imposing Gothic ceremonial hall, built in 1261 for King Håkon Håkonsson, is

one of Scandinavia's best examples of medieval secular architecture. The ticket includes entry to the **Rosenkrantz Tower** (Rosenkrantztärnet; tel: 47 97 95 78; mid-May–mid-Sept daily 9am–4pm, mid-Sept–mid-May Sun noon–3pm), built in the 1560s, which served as a combined governor's residence and fortified tower.

Nordnes peninsula

Across the water, the view from the Nordnes peninsula over the town to the mountain of Fløyen is characterised by the contrast between the green woodland, blue sea and the mainly white-painted wooden houses. At the point of the peninsula (along Carl Sundts Gate) is **Bergen Aquarium** **Ⓙ** (Akvariet; tel: 55 55 71 71; www. akvariet.no; May–Aug daily 9am–7pm, Sept–Apr 10am–6pm, feeding time every hour), one of the finest and most extensive collections of marine fauna in Europe. The new shark tunnel which opened in 2010 is a crowd-pleaser, as is feeding time for the seals which takes place every hour from 11am–4pm.

TIP

Explore the unique wooden houses which date back to the 18th and 19th centuries in Bergen's charming old quarters Nordnes, Nøstet, and Fjellsiden, whose narrow alleys and cobbled streets transport you back in time.

At the fish market.

Bergen Art Museum.

A wooden figure at the Museum of Old Bergen.

Musical traditions

Most of the time, the city's backdrop is the glacial quiet of the mountains, but music, one is frequently reminded, is very much a part of its heritage. Norway's greatest composer, Edvard Grieg (1843–1907), and virtuoso violinist, Ole Bull, were both Bergeners. The **Grieghallen** Ⓚ concert hall (www.grieghallen.no) is renowned as the home of the Bergen Philharmonic Orchestra, founded in 1765, and for the annual Bergen International Festival, Norway's oldest such event, held every May–June (www.fib.no).

In more recent years, many Bergen rock and indie bands have gathered a pan-European fan base: Ralph Myerz & the Jack Herren Band, Kings of Convenience, Røyksopp, Kurt Nilsen and Sondra Lerche, to name a few. On the more traditional side, the Buekorps brigade is an organisation for 10–20-year-old boys (and girls, since the 1990s), easily recognised by their natty tunics and tasselled tam-o'-shanter caps. From mid-April until 17 May, the brigades march in formation in the annual Constitution Day parade.

Bergen's art museums

Bergen has several strong art collections, mostly centred on the south side of Lille Lungegårdsvann, an octagonal lake near Grieg Hall, and a focal point for summer festivals. Here the **Bergen Art Museum** Ⓛ, now part of KODE art museums, (Bergen Kunstmuseum – KODE 2 and 3; Rasmus Meyers allé 3, 7 and 9; tel: 55 56 80 00; http://kodebergen.no; mid-May–Aug daily 11am–5pm, Sept–mid-May Tue–Sun 11am–4pm, Sat–Sun until 5pm) boasts a large collection of fine art in three separate buildings: the **Rasmus Meyers Collection**, specialising in Norwegian masterpieces from the 18th to the early 20th century, including masterpieces by Edvard Munch; the **Lysverket** building, which presents Norwegian and international art from the 15th century to the present; and the **Stenersen Gallery**, which stages interesting contemporary art exhibitions.

In between sits the **Bergen Contemporary Art Centre** (Kunsthall, 5

OLD BERGEN

Set in a pretty park in Sandviken, north of the city centre, **Gamle Bergen** (Nyhavnsveien 4; tel: 47 97 95 76; www.bymuseet.no; mid-May–Aug daily 9am–4pm) takes you on a journey back in time to the 18th and 19th centuries. This evocative old town reconstruction comprises some 50 restored and transplanted wooden houses, shops and businesses set on streets and narrow lanes, including a bakery, dentist, photographer's studio, shop and jeweller. It's a family-friendly place with activities for children, entertainments in the open-air theatre and a restaurant. Gamle Bergen is just a 7-minute bus ride (20, 24) from the tourist information office by the harbour (Strandkaien 3, in Torghallen at the Fish Market).

Rasmus Meyers allé; tel: 55 55 93 10; www.kunsthall.no; Tue–Sun 11am–5pm, Thu until 8pm; Thu after 5pm free), in a spectacular Modernist building by Ole Landmark, with a buzzing café, bar and nightclub.

Nearby, the **West Norway Museum of Decorative Art** (Vestlandske Kunstindustrimuseum – KODE 1; Nordahl Brunsgate 9; tel: 55 33 66 33; http://kode bergen.no; closed until 2017) features an art and design collection spanning 500 years, with a focus on furniture, silverware, jewellery, and Ole Bull's famous violin made by Gasparo de Salo in 1562.

South of Bergen

Annual summer concerts attract music-lovers from all over the world to **Troldhaugen** (tel: 55 92 29 92; http://griegmuseum.no; May–Sept daily 9am–6pm, Oct–mid-Dec and Jan–Apr daily 10am–4pm), the home of Edvard Grieg 8km (5 miles) south of the city. It is said that the composer of Peer Gynt was inspired by folk music, but it is clear that nature was his main muse. Take a stroll to the lakefront

spot behind his house where he used to fish to take a break from composing. He once said: "My music has the taste of codfish in it."

Not to be missed is the **Fantoft Stave Church** (tel: 55 28 07 10; http://fantoftstavkirke.com; mid-May–mid-Sept daily 10.30am–6pm), 8km (5 miles) south of the city in Paradis. Built in 1150 in Sogn (see page 209), it was moved to Fantoft in 1883, destroyed by arson in 1992 and completely restored in 1997.

It's a short ferry ride across Lysefjord to the beautiful island of **Lysøen** (Island of Light) and the onion-domed summer residence of composer and violinist Ole Bull (1810–80), who called the villa, built in 1873, his "Little Alhambra" (http://lysoen.no/ole-bull). Bull's charismatic personality and musical excellence had a great influence on contemporary artists and musicians who were often guests here. In summer, the old music room resounds to the music Bull played here. Take the passenger ferry from Buena Quay at Lysekloster.

TIP

Bergen makes a perfect base for exploring the fjords. To experience one of the great sea journeys of the world, join a Hurtigruten cruise, which makes 34 ports of call along the stunning coast between Bergen and Kirkenes near the Russian border (see page 214).

Bryggen, on the quayside.

THE HEART OF NORWAY

Central Norway encompasses a remarkable landscape, from the shimmering fjords of the west across the peaks, plateaux and valleys that have inspired great writers and composers.

The heartland of Norway is the upper part of the southern bulge of the country, extending from above Oslo and Bergen to below Trondheim. The area encompasses the highest mountains in Scandinavia, and freshwater lakes and watercourses abound. To the east there are two long valleys, **Østerdalen** (literally "Easterly Valley") and **Gudbrandsdalen**, orientated roughly parallel to the border with Sweden and knifing through the high interior cordillera to provide the major north–south land transport arteries. In the middle there are the lofty peaks and high plateaus of the Rondane and Jotunheimen ranges, and to the west lies the coast with its fjords and archipelago in waters plied by boats since the land was first settled.

Lake Mjøsa

The glaciers that gouged the fjords also worked the inland and left **Mjøsa** ❷, a jewel of a lake. Its southern end is at Minnesund just north of Eidsvoll, and its northern tip is at Lillehammer, 101km (63 miles) to the northwest. It's slender – only 15km (9 miles) at its broadest – and like a fjord, deep – up to 449 metres (1,472ft). Around Mjøsa lies some of the best arable land in the country, and its shores greet undulating countryside with large farms backed by densely forested hills. One of the best ways to

enjoy the lake and its surroundings is a trip on the **Skibladner**, the world's oldest paddle-wheel steamship still in service. In summer, the *Skibladner* carries up to 230 passengers on excursions five days a week (tel: 61 14 40 80; www.skibladner.no); her home port is at **Gjøvik**.

Nearby **Hamar** ❷ was a medieval centre of Roman Catholicism in Norway and the seat of a bishop. It is still a bishopric, but only ruins remain of its imposing cathedral, now protected under a spectacular glass structure at

Main Attractions
Skibladner steamship
  excursion, Hamar
Lillehammer
Sognefjord
Jostedalsbreen Glacier and
  Glacier Museum
Kvinfoss, "Lady's Waterfall"
Flåm railway
Briksdalsbreen Glacier
Ålesund Art Nouveau
  architecture
Røros

Lake Mjøsa.

There are miles and miles of skiing tracks around Lillehammer.

Hedemark Museum and Cathedral Point (Hedemarks-museet og Dom-kirkeodden; www.hedmarksmuseet.no; mid-June–mid-Aug daily 10am–5pm, mid-May–mid-June and rest of Aug Tue–Sun 10am–4pm). In the 19th century Hamar became a railway junction with a locomotive works. The works are gone, but there's a reminder: the **Norwegian Railway Museum** (Norsk Jernbanemuseum; Strandveien 163; tel: 40 44 88 80; www.norsk-jernbanemuseum.no; Tue–Sun 11am–3pm, Sun until 4pm, July–mid-Aug daily 10am–5pm), with stations, railway buildings and vintage rolling stock. There are regular excursions on a narrow-gauge steam train.

Fertile local lands long ago led to cities and towns producing comestibles. Most stimulating, perhaps, is that seven of the country's eight distilleries are located hereabouts. One of them, **Løten Brænderi** (tel: 90 18 99 05; www.lbr.no; Mon–Sat 10am–6pm, Sun noon–6pm; guided tours), at **Løten** ㉕, 13km (8 miles) east of Hamar, is open to the public. A fascinating one-man show recounts the history of

the distillery and the production of *akevitt*, the Norwegian liquor made from potato and caraway seeds. Also worth visiting on the same site is **Løiten Lys** (www.loiten-lys.no; Mon–Fri 10am–6pm, Sat 10am–6pm, Sun noon–6pm), a candle factory with a display of candles in every conceivable shape and size.

Lillehammer

Lillehammer ㉖ is best known in the world of winter sports as the venue of the 1994 Olympic Winter Games. Many of the Olympic facilities still stand, such as the ice event rinks at Hamar and Gjøvik, and luge and bobsleigh tracks. There's also an Alpine ski area at nearby **Hafjell**, and 500km (300 miles) of cross-country skiing tracks. The cross-country arena now is the finish for the annual trans-mountain Birke-beiner race, one of the world's oldest citizens' races.

For summer visitors, the biggest attraction is the open-air museum, **Maihaugen** (www.maihaugen.no; June–Aug daily 10am–5pm, Sept Tue–Sun 11am–5pm, Oct–May Tue–Sun 11am–4pm), with some 185 vintage buildings brought into the 40-hectare (100-acre) site from all over Gudbrandsdalen, including a stave church and two farms. The museum was the life's work of Anders Sandvig. He came to Lillehammer in 1885 suffering from tuberculosis and with a life expectancy of just two years. Whether or not it was his interest in the museum he founded in 1887 which kept him alive, he lived another 65 years.

Housed in a sleek modern building designed by the same architects as the award-winning Oslo Opera House, **Lillehammer Art Museum** (tel: 61 05 44 60; www.lillehammerartmuseum.com; July–Aug daily 11am–5pm, Sept–June Tue–Sun until 5pm) pays homage to some of Norway's finest 19th-century painters, from Krohg to Munch. The **Road Transport Museum** (Norsk Vegmuseum; Hunderfossvegen 757;

FJORD FORMATION

Fjords are found in Alaska, Canada, Chile, Greenland, New Zealand, Norway and Scotland. But nowhere are they more prominent than in Norway. A direct line along the coast measures 2,650km (1,645 miles), but the stretch of the entire coastline, including the archipelago, is 57,260km (35,580 miles), a third more than the distance around the earth at the equator. The coast of Norway is more jagged than any other, and Norway can lay claim to giving the word fjord to other languages of the world.

The fjords were formed about 100,000 years ago, during the last Ice Age. Glaciers gouged valleys from the land, to depths that lessened at the coast, where the ice was thinner. When the ice eventually retreated, the sea inundated. So a typical fjord is deepest at its midpoint and far less deep at its mouth: the Sognefjord, for instance, reaches a depth of 1,244 metres (4,080ft), but is only 158 metres (518ft) deep at its mouth.

The fame of these fjords has made them part of the myth of science fiction. In *The Hitchhiker's Guide to the Galaxy*, the venerable planet-builder Slartibartfast recalls: "Doing the coastlines was always my favourite, used to have endless fun doing all the little fiddly bits in fjords… did you ever go to a place… I think it's called Norway?"

tel: 61 28 52 50; mid-June–mid-Aug daily 11am–5pm, rest of the year Tue–Sun 11am–3pm; free) at **Fåberg**, to the north of Lillehammer on the E6 highway, has everything from horse-drawn sleighs to modern cars.

Østerdalen

To the east of Lake Mjøsa lies **Østerdalen**, carved through the mountains by the Glomma – the country's longest river – stretching 617km (383 miles). The valley carries one of the north–south railway lines, as well as National Highway 3. It starts at **Elverum** ❷ in the south and continues northwards for 250km (150 miles), becoming broader and more open further north. Just south of **Aursunden**, one of the source lakes for the Glomma River, lies the old copper-mining town of **Røros** ❷, a Unesco World Heritage site.

Gudbrandsdalen

To the west of Østerdalen lies **Gudbrandsdalen**, the country's second-longest valley, cut by the River Lågen flowing south to Lillehammer. Perhaps because mountains surround it, the valley has a long tradition of folk dancing and folk music and is known for its woodcarving and rose painting. For Norwegians everywhere, as well as for curious visitors, Gudbrandsdalen is best remembered as the place where the indigenous Norwegian *geitost* (whey cheese made from goat's milk) was first made in the mid-19th century. The real variety, *ekte geitost*, made entirely of goat's milk, is still produced in the valley and elsewhere in the country; it is ubiquitous at all breakfast tables, from humble bed and breakfasts to the best of hotels.

About midway along the valley lies **Dombås** ❷, a principal rail and road junction just southwest of the **Dovrefjell** (Dovre Mountains). The Dovre summits are lofty, but even the highest, **Snøhetta**, at 2,286 metres (7,498ft), is lower than the

peaks of the Jotunheimen. Yet the Dovre Mountains have a place in the national psyche like no other, embodied in the saying about the strength of the country "United and faithful until Dovre falls".

The Jotunheimen Mountains

South of Dombås is an extensive area of peak and plateau. The Norwegian mountains are made for walking. As explorer Paul Belloni Du Chaillu observed in *Land of the Midnight Sun* (1881): "The difference between the mountains of Switzerland and Norway is this: those of the former are much higher, more bold and pointed, and sharp in the outlines of their thousand forms. On the other hand, the Norwegian mountains have a grave and sombre character, appearing like a gigantic stony wave, with a peak here and there, impressing more by their vastness than their height and ruggedness."

The many hiking trails are marked by red letter 'Ts' painted on rocks and cairns. They meander between *hytte*

Young musicians in Molde.

(lodges), mostly above the timberline, between 950 and 1,600 metres (3,100–5,250ft) above sea level, and the highest summits are around 2,400 metres (7,900ft), hence the lack of mention in mountaineering anthologies, where sheer elevation is the criterion. Therein lies part of the secret: you can enjoy the high-altitude experience without needing high-altitude lungs.

Moreover, in summer you can travel to the heart of the range in only a few steps, by boarding one of the passenger launches that ply the waters of lakes Gjende and Bygdin. In the late 19th century, the composer Edvard Grieg remarked that "when I contemplate the possibility of a future visit to the [Jotunheimen] mountains, I shudder with joy and expectation, as if it were a matter of hearing Beethoven's 10th Symphony". That attraction was in part why Grieg wrote the incidental music for Henrik Ibsen's play *Peer Gynt*, based on a traditional legend of Gudbrandsdalen, in which braggart Peer leaps astride a reindeer, from a knife ridge into the lake below. The knife ridge and the lake are real:

Røros' characteristic turf roofs are now preserved.

Besseggen and Gjende in the Jotunheimen, literally "Home of the Giants". The reindeer are equally real, as herds of them still graze here. One reminder of them is the reindeer pattern on the Gjende brand biscuits, sold throughout the country.

Hiking and skiing trails

Accessibility is another allure of these wilderness areas. To the south of the Jotunheimen lies the hamlet of **Finse** ③⓪, the high point at 1,225 metres (4,000ft) on the Oslo–Bergen railway line. Its high street is the station platform; trains are the local traffic, as there are neither cars nor roads. It's a small speck in a seemingly boundless expanse of ice and snow. So remote yet accessible is this place that it was chosen for the filming of the initial sequences of *The Empire Strikes Back*. Finse has the country's largest *hytte* for hikers and skiers, as well as a full-service hotel, as suits its location as the junction between two giant trail networks, north to the **Jotunheimen** and south to **Hardangervidda** (Hardanger plateau). As the crow flies, the trail

THE HYTTE

The word *hytte*, pronounced "hutta", describes a simple cabin in a tranquil, preferably remote setting in the wilds of nature. In this area the hytte is a mountain lodge with comfortable bunk beds (you need only bring a sleeping bag), which usually provides meals for hungry, weary hikers.

Most of these lodges are owned and operated by Den Norske Turistforening (DNT) and its affiliated local organisations, hence the red Ts on rocks and cairns. You need not be a member to stay in a DNT *hytte*, but membership is a good investment, as the price is soon offset by the accumulated discounts on accommodation. You can join DNT at any of the *hytte* or at the head office in Oslo (tel: 40 00 18 70; www.turist foreningen.no).

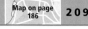

networks stretch 225km (140 miles) to the north and 100km (60 miles) to the south, and in all have more than 5,000km (3,000 miles) of T-marked hiking trails and, at Easter-time, some 2,000km (1,240 miles) of ski trails, marked by poles in the snow.

To the north and east of the Jotunheimen, on the other side of the Gudbrandsdalen Valley, lies the **Rondane** range, which offers some of the country's finest hiking and cross-country skiing. The trails are less steep, the peaks not as high, the walks not as long and the *hytte* not as numerous as in the Jotunheimen. But the connection to the Gudbrandsdalen legend remains, as there is a Peer Gynt *hytte* here. Moreover, to the south and on the west flank of the valley there is a **Peer Gyntveien** (Peer Gynt Way) which leads from Gausdal north of Lillehammer to Golå south of Vinstra.

The trails and the *hytte* reflect the Norwegian view of wilderness: it is for everyone. Pristine perhaps is the best word; only the red 'Ts' and an occasional electric power line betray modern times. Little has changed

since three English adventurers, with the pseudonyms Skipper, Essau and John, came to the Jotunheimen in the 1880s. Their subsequent book, *Three in Norway by Two of Them*, became one of the classic travelogues of the Victorian age. The remnants of their camp are carefully preserved near **Memurubu** ③ on Lake Gjende in the Jotunheimen, one of the *hytte* that dot these wilderness areas.

From Sogn to Nordfjord

The county of **Sogn og Fjordane** lies between the coast and the Jotunheimen Mountains. Narrow fingers of water push inland from the main fjords to reach far into the mountains, and waterfalls tumble hundreds of metres into the fjords below. In the past, the terrain was impassable in winter. Today travel is easier thanks to the network of ferries, tunnels and bridges. The county is easily accessible from Bergen. Indeed, until 1918, it was named Northern Bergen province (Nordre Bergenhus).

The **Sognefjord** is unmatched. On both sides of it small villages cling to

TIP

The railway from Myrdal to Flåm winds through spectacular mountain scenery. The train ride is part of the "Norway in a Nutshell" journey using a variety of forms of transport to take in some of Norway's best beauty spots (see page 376).

Inside the Jostedal Glacier.

RØROS: TIMELESS MINING TOWN

Røros, a Unesco World Heritage site on the E30 north of Alvdal, was until recently the archetypal company town, with life and society revolving around the mining business. Isolated, exposed, nearly 600 metres (2,000ft) above sea level and surrounded by mountains, it owed its existence to copper, which was mined here from 1644 to 1972. Now the inhabitants make their living from sawmills, furniture-making, wool-processing and reindeer meat, as well as tourism. It is a harsh spot; the lowest temperatures in the whole of Norway are often recorded here.

By some miracle Røros escaped the fires that so often laid waste to the wooden buildings in Norwegian towns, and it has retained much of its mining town atmosphere. The wealthy folk lived to the east of the river in Bergmannsgate, while the miners had to make do with the area beneath the slagheaps and the smelter. Picturesque log houses remain, while the crooked houses in Slaggveien are particularly interesting. The most noticeable feature is the stone church, "the pride of the mining town", which was dedicated in 1784. Paintings of clergymen and mining officials decorate the interior. The smelter was the focal point of the town and has been restored as a museum. The town is well known for its artists and craftsmen – glass-blowers, woodcarvers, cabinetmakers, potters and painters – and the atmospheric old streets are full of shops selling their wares.

TIP

In summer, guides from the Jostedalsbreen National Park Centre, 20km (12 miles) from Stryn, lead tours and glacier hikes and kayaking explorations to the great Jostedal. The Glacier Bus travels throughout the Sognefjord region and Glacier National Park from mid-June–mid-Sept (tel: 57 68 32 50; www. sognefjord.no).

Sledging at Lillehammer.

the land, each with its atmosphere. **Balestrand ②** has been a favourite since the 19th century and has an English church, St Olav's. A narrow side-fjord leads to **Fjærland ③**, near the two southernmost tongues of the **Jostedalsbreen Glacier**. Nestling at its base is the **Norwegian Glacier Museum** (Norsk Bremuseum and Ulltveit-Moe Climate Centre; tel: 57 69 32 88; www.bre.museum.no; Apr, May, Sept and Oct daily 10am–4pm, June–Aug daily 9am–7pm, Nov–Mar on request), where interactive models, displays and films provide an insight into Europe's largest glacier.

Going east from Balestrand, a short crossing takes you to **Hella** and past the glistening arc of **Kvinnfoss** (Lady's Waterfall) close to the main road. At the head of the fjord, **Sogndal ③** is the centre for trade and administration. It swells considerably during term-time because it is also a centre for education, with universities and Norway's oldest folk high school.

In **Luster ③**, 25km (15 miles) to the northeast of Sogndal, is the finest of Sogn's many stave churches, **Urnes Stavkirke**. Built around 1130 and believed to be the oldest stave church in Norway, this beautifully preserved church with Viking carvings is now a Unesco World Heritage site (May–Sept daily 10.30am–5.45pm).

The Flåmsbana branch line

Aurlandsvangen, Flåm and Gudvangen lie along the innermost recesses of the fjord, which stretches south from the main fjord like an upside-down "Y". Not to be missed is the mountain railway from Myrdal (on the Bergen line), at 866 metres (2,841 ft) above sea level, to **Flåm ③**, which spirals down the steep mountain gorge through 20 tunnels. The 20km (12-mile) train ride is one of Europe's most scenic stretches of railway (www.flaamsbana.no). When disembarking from the train at Flåm, resist the impulse to jump back on and leave the tourists and troll souvenirs behind. Beyond the crowded, ugly harbourside, Flåm with its mountainous backdrop and lovely surroundings of orchards and meadows is worth exploring.

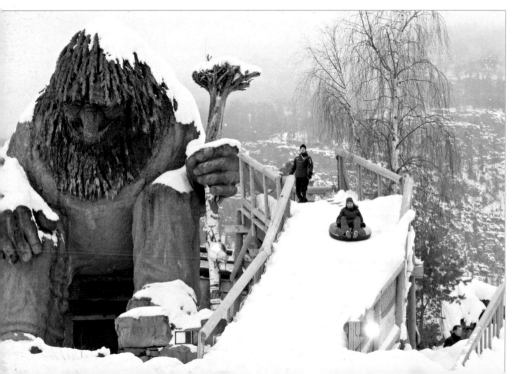

Jølstravatnet

Heading northwest from Balestrand towards **Førde** ➌ and the coast, you cross a region of many lakes – Jølstravatnet – that penetrate the foothills of the high tops in the east and feed into the fjords in the west. One of the rivers, the Jølstra, said to be one of the best salmon rivers in the area, drops precipitously before reaching Førde on **Førdefjord**. Here is **Sunnfjord Museum** (tel: 57 72 12 20; www.sunnfjord.museum.no; July–mid-Aug Mon–Fri 10am–6pm, Sat–Sun noon–5pm, June and rest of Aug Mon–Fri 10am–4pm, Sat–Sun noon–5pm, Sept–May Sat–Sun 10am–3pm), a collection of 26 historic buildings.

Oddly, **Florø** ➌, the only community in this large county big enough to be called a town, lies on the remote edge of the sea, but not so odd considering that Norway has always depended on the sea for food, trade and transport. The **Coastal Museum** (Sogn og Fjordane Kystmuseet; tel: 57 74 22 33; www.kyst.museum.no; mid-June–mid-Aug Mon–Fri 11am–6pm, Sat–Sun noon–4pm, mid-Aug–mid-June Mon–Fri 10am–3pm, Sun noon–3pm) in Florø has a fine collection of old boats.

Inland along Nordfjord

Nordfjord is 100km (60 miles) shorter than Sognefjord. With so many side-fjords, lakes and valleys it is easy to get into the mountains or make the journey up **Briksdalsbreen**, one of the most beautiful glaciers in the fjord country. Even better is that you can climb up to the base of the glacier in the two-wheeled farm carriages, *stolkjaerrer*, pulled by small, sturdy, cream-coloured *fjording* (fjord horses) native to Nordfjord.

The traditional home of the *fjording* is the Eid district, centred around Nord-fjordeid, where Nordfjord proper has already divided itself into Eidsfjord and Isefjord. **Eid** ➌, which is also connected to the coast

by Road 15, is known for Firdariket, the seat of the last Viking chief. The town has white-painted buildings, and the church, which dates from 1849, is decorated with beautiful rose painting.

Further along you reach the Inner Nordfjord, where the fjord system ends at Stryn, Loen and Olden, the start of three spectacular valleys stretching up to the northwest edges of the Jostedalsbreen. Three tunnels out of the Stryn Valley cut right through the mountain to the renowned **Geirangerfjord** to the north. **Stryn** ➍ is known for summer skiing on the northeast of Strynsvatn, where the ground rises to Tystigbreen.

Ålesund to Kristiansund

Coastal vessels have long called at Ålesund, Molde and Kristiansund on their way to Trondheim and the north. Looking at the coastline, islands and fjord mouths on a map, it is difficult to distinguish where sea and islands end and fjords and mainland begin.

The railway from Myrdal to Flåm winds through spectacular mountain scenery. The train ride is part of the "Norway in a Nutshell" journey using a variety of forms of transport to take in some of Norway's best beauty spots.

TIP

Explore the colourful Art
Nouveau town of
Ålesund: guided walks
depart Saturdays at noon
from the Tourist
Information Office
(Rådhus; tel: 70 16 34
30; www.visitalesund.com;
mid-June–mid-Aug).

Ålesund **41** is Norway's largest fishing town. Yet it is best known for its *Jugendstil* architecture, built in 1904 after fire destroyed its centre. If you arrive here by ferry, which most travellers do, you are pleasantly taken aback by the pastel-hued dwellings embellished with towers, turrets and charming decorative elements: from human faces to docile dragons. Credit for the creative and colourful restoration must go to Kaiser Wilhelm II of Germany, who sent architecture students and four ships laden with supplies and building materials. With help and donations from all over Europe, the people of Ålesund completed the rebuilding of their town within three years.

Until the 1950s, fishing supported Ålesund, and *klippfisk* (traditional Norwegian split dried cod) was its principal export, mainly to the Mediterranean. But as fishing changed so did Ålesund, which added fish processing and aquaculture. Many former warehouses are now offices and restaurants, where you can try one of the more unlikely local specialities such as *bacalao* (Spanish for cod), made from boned *klippfisk*.

There are several attractions worth seeing here: the wonderfully preserved **Aalesunds Art Museum** (tel: 70 12 31 70; Mon–Fri 9am–3pm, in summer until 4pm, Sat 11am–3pm, Sun noon–4pm) features exhibitions on the fire and subsequent rebuilding; in the former Norwegian Bank building next to the Art Nouveau centre, **Art Museum KUBE** (Apotekergate 16; tel: 70 10 49 70; www.jugendstilsenteret.no; Sept and May Tue–Sat 11am–4pm, June–Aug daily 10am–5pm; combined ticket with the Art Nouveau centre) focuses on art, architecture and design; **Stiftinga Sunnmøre Museum** (tel: 70 17 40 00; http://sunnmoremuseum.no; May–Sept Mon–Fri 10am–4pm, Sun noon–4pm and Sat in July noon–4pm, Oct–Dec and Feb–Apr Tue–Fri 10am–3pm, Sun noon–4pm) is an open-air attraction which consists of 50 houses and 40 boats that depict life in the seafaring area until the 1900s; the **Atlantic Sea Park** (Atlanterhavsparken; tel: 70 10 70 60; www.atlanterhavsparken. no; June–Aug Sun–Fri 10am–6pm, Sat 10am–4pm, Sept–May Mon–Sat 11am–4pm, Sun 11am–6pm) is one of the largest saltwater aquariums in Northern Europe.

To the southwest of Ålesund is **Runde 42**, the island that draws naturalists from around the world, as more than 200 bird species have been recorded here. Take a four-hour tour on one of the boats departing from **Ulsteinvik** daily from June to August. As a bonus, the waters round the island close over myriad wrecks; in 1972, divers found a hoard of gold and silver coins on board the *Akerendam*, a Dutch vessel that sank in 1725.

Molde 43, halfway along the coast from Ålesund north to Kristiansund, is part of an archipelago sheltered from the Norwegian Sea; its mild climate, lush vegetation and rose gardens earn it the title "Town of Roses".

Looking down on Geirangerfjord.

This modern town was almost entirely rebuilt after German bombing in World War II. It is an excellent base for touring the fjords by boat or car. It is known at home for the might of its football team and for the annual Molde Jazz Festival (mid-July; www.moldejazz.no; many free concerts).

From **Bud** on the coast west of Molde, a road leads to the **Atlanterhavsveien** (Atlantic Road) to Kristiansund, over **Averøya** ❹, the biggest island in the area. It heads north across the rim of the ocean, so driving seems like a voyage. Archaeologists believe that this was one of the first places to be settled after the last Ice Age, and their finds include remnants of the early Fosna culture that existed around 7000 BC.

Kristiansund

Unlike Ålesund and Molde, **Kristiansund** ❺ is vulnerably situated on the coast, with weather-beaten rocks pounded by the sea, yet not far inland are grassy areas and small woods. This is the *klippfisk* town, for long the biggest exporter of Norwegian dried cod. A recent census counted just more than 24,000 inhabitants but, because of the centuries-old links with other countries through its sailors and fishermen, and the foreign merchants who settled here, the atmosphere is cosmopolitan. Like most Norwegian towns with "Kristian" in their title, Kristiansund was named after King Christian VI. A good introduction is by *sundbåtene*, the harbour boats that for more than 100 years have linked four of the town's five islands.

Mellemverftet, once one of four shipyards in Vågen, is working again as a centre for preserving the craft of shipbuilding, carefully restoring the beautiful lines of traditional Norwegian boats. The **Klippfish Museum** (tel: 71 58 70 00; www.nordmore.museum.no; mid-June–early-Aug daily noon–5pm) exhibits archaeological finds from the Fosna culture and the

history of *klippfisk* processing. Kristiansund's main church was destroyed by bombing in 1940, and the architect named its replacement "Rock Crystal in Roses". Like it or loathe it, you cannot ignore this stark white building known as the **Atlantic Ocean Cathedral** (Atlanterhavskatedralen), which boasts 320 stained-glass panels and a 30-metre (100ft) choir wall.

Trollheimen

Inland, the northern part of Møre og Romsdal county ends in a crisscross of fjords eating into the islands and peninsulas which lead to **Trollheimen**, the "Home of the Trolls", where the mountains reach nearly 1,600 metres (5,000ft). This haunt of climbers and skiers is bounded by two important valleys, Surnadalen and Sunndalen, with between them the tiny Todalfjord. Beside the last is the surprise of the **Svinvik Arboretum** ❻ (tel: 71 66 35 80; mid-May–mid-Aug Wed–Sun 11am–4pm, Wed in July until 8pm), beautiful gardens with thousands of rhododendrons, conifers and other plants.

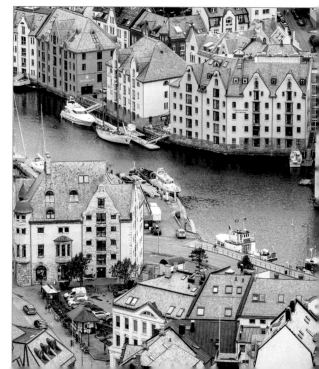

Ålesund.

NORWAY'S MOST BEAUTIFUL VOYAGE

The splendid coastal voyage from Bergen to the North Cape and beyond has long been regarded as one of the most beautiful sea journeys in the world.

To travel on board the Hurtigruten (literally "swift route") steamships is to partake in a voyage with infinite beauty spots (www.hurtigruten.com). What began in 1891 as an idea to provide an express shipping service along the rugged Norwegian coast between Trondheim and Hammerfest has evolved into a lucrative form of tourism. Yet part of the charm is watching a working ship going about its business. It is also possible to jump ship while in port and enjoy a unique excursion: to the Nidaros Cathedral or Ålesund's Jugendstil quarter, for example. Out of season, it reverts to its traditional role of carrying west-coast Norwegians, who treat it as a bus, for business and pleasure. In season it is extremely popular with retirees from the UK and Europe.

From fjords to open sea, fertile land to barren rock, fishing hamlets to cities, the voyage is a mix of the workaday and the spectacular.

Ports of call

In spring and autumn, the 12-day round trip from Bergen across the Arctic Circle to the Nordkapp (North Cape) and Kirkenes lets you feast on the dramatic seasonal changes. In May, the fjord valleys are brilliantly in bloom, and the hills and the mountains of the north are still covered with snow. The Hurtigruten makes 34 ports of call along this ever-changing coast, some at places no bigger than a handful of houses round a harbour, others at cities such as Trondheim and Tromsø with time ashore to explore.

A boat rounds a corner of Geirangerfjord, where it's about to get a close-up view of Seven Sisters waterfall. This fjord, in the county of Møre og Romsdal, is one of Norway's most visited.

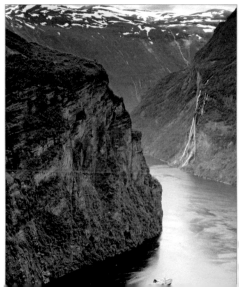

Commemorative plaques at the North Cape.

The dramatic Lofoten Islands.

COMMUNICATIONS REVOLUTION

Over the past century more than 70 ships have served in the Hurtigruten fleet. Before the days of internet and mobile phones, these diverse vessels led a communications revolution, enabling the population and industries along the rugged Norwegian coast to keep in touch in a new way. Previously, it took three weeks in summer or five months in winter to send a letter from Trondheim to Hammerfest; the Coastal Express reduced this time to a few days.

Places such as the Lofoten Islands (pictured above), Trollfjord and the North Cape became accessible to travellers who wanted to see the Midnight Sun. Nature-lovers and birdwatchers are attracted by the scenery and the many bird colonies, which include puffins, kittiwakes and guillemots. Far-flung Tromsø attracts many visitors to its annual film festival. As time went by, ships were built specifically with cold storage and freezer rooms, vehicle roll-on/roll-off capacity and conference facilities, as well as comfortable cabins.

Two companies now run 11 ships, ranging from the grand old *M/S Lofoten* to the *M/S Midnatsol*. They run year-round, and each season offers different landscapes and perspectives.

With thousands of islands and skerries, mountains and glaciers, the landscape is constantly changing and no two days are alike.

Steering the ship into harbour.

The West Finnmark plateau provides summer grazing for the Sami's reindeer herds.

The coloured warehouses of Trondheim.

THE NORTHWEST COAST

North of Trondheim, Norway's religious and
cultural capital, lies a beautiful but often
harsh landscape that crosses the Arctic Circle
into the land of the Midnight Sun.

The northwest coast is where
Norway gets thinner, from
Trondheim – a large city for its
latitude and the gateway to the north
– up to Bodø, which lies beyond the
Arctic Circle. The land along this narrow conduit is mostly forested, with
the benign influence of the Gulf
Stream ensuring temperate conditions
persist far to the north.

Trondheim ❶ is a pleasant city
with clean air, wide streets, low buildings and a compact centre. You get
a reminder of the early days by the
wharves and narrow streets that run
between the wooden buildings. They
may date only to the 18th century, but
these coloured warehouses echo the
architecture of medieval times when
fish and timber were the economic
mainstays of the city. These days
Trondheim has a relatively modest
population of 176,000, which swells
by nearly a sixth in term-time, as this is
a university town, as well as the country's leading hi-tech research centre.

As with all Norwegian cities, the
outdoors is close at hand. Trondheim's back garden is Bymarka to the
west, where **Gråkallen** (Old Man) at
520 metres (1,700ft) high is a favourite walking and cross-country skiing
area. Indeed, outdoor sports are a
leading local pastime, and the city has
acted as host to the World Nordic Ski
Championships.

The west wall of Nidaros Cathedral.

Nidaros Cathedral

Until the 16th century, Trondheim,
known as Nidaros ("mouth of the
River Nid"), was the capital of Norway.
In 997 the settlers of Nidaros could not
have known, but the sheltered site they
picked was to become a pivotal city in
Europe. In the late 11th century, work
started on a major church at Nidaros,
erected over the grave of St Olav, the
king who brought Christianity to the
Vikings. Apparently the Pope found
that fact auspicious, as he appointed
an archbishop there and made the

Main Attractions
Nidaros Cathedral
Hell Blues Festival
Stiklestad
Arctic Circle Centre

Northwest Coast

0   20 km
0   20 miles

bishops of Greenland, Iceland, the Isle of Man, Orkney and the Faroe Islands, and the bishops in Norway answerable to him. The church became the imposing **Nidaros Cathedral** (Nidarosdomen; www.nidarosdomen.no; June–Aug Mon–Fri 9am–6pm, Sat 9am–2pm, Sun 9am–5pm, Sept–Mar Mon–Fri 9am–2pm, Sun until 4pm, Apr Mon–Fri 9am–1pm, Sat 9am–2pm, Sun 9am–4pm; charge includes admission to adjacent Archbishop's Palace), Norway's national shrine and the venue for the coronation of Norwegian kings – most recently King Harald V in 1991.

The **Norwegian Crown Jewels** (June–Aug Mon–Fri 10am–5pm, Sat 10am–3pm, Sun noon–4pm, Sept–Apr Mon–Fri 11am–2pm, Sat 11am–3pm, Sun noon–4pm, Apr Mon closed) may be seen in the cathedral museum, and the regalia for king, queen and crown prince are on display in the **Archbishop's Palace**, next to the cathedral.

City for cyclists

Trondheim has done much to relieve traffic congestion, including implementing a toll ring round the city. Cycling is encouraged on a network of dedicated cycle paths. Yet topography challenges cycling: the flat centre is surrounded by steep hills. So in 1995, the resourceful city built **Trampe** (http://trampe.no), the world's first bicycle lift, 130 metres (426ft) up Brubakken Hill. The lift operates like a ski tow, and cyclists pay using keycards at the bottom of the hill. Not surprisingly, the annual **Styrkeprøven** (Trial of Strength) trans-mountain bicycle race (June) starts in Trondheim. It finishes 540km (336 miles) south, in Oslo.

Rockheim

The newest addition to the city is **Rockheim** (Brattørkaia 14; tel: 73 60 50 70; www.rockheim.no; Tue–Fri 11am–7pm, Sat–Sun 11am–6pm), a rock and pop museum housed in an eye-catching modern building just north of the central train station. The permanent exhibition traces Norway's pop music heritage from the 1950s to the present day. Temporary exhibitions focus on aspects of music history and pop culture. Concerts are held in a hall that seats 350, and there is a restaurant and shop on site.

Hell

Some Norwegian words tempt *double entendre* in English, most notably the name of the village closest to Trondheim's Værnes airport. It's **Hell ❷**. Notwithstanding the derivation of the name from the Old Norse word for cavern, postcards of the railway station at Hell sell astonishingly well. So when in Trondheim, you can indeed go to Hell; it's only 33 minutes east by train. The station here is one of the most photographed in the country. In September Hell hosts an annual blues festival which attracts international stars and fans to this otherwise quiet settlement.

St Olav's battleground

Many European countries claim histories highlighted by a decisive medieval battle. For Norway, it's the **Battle of Stiklestad** on 29 July 1030, some 36 years before England's momentous Battle of Hastings. Unlike Hastings, which enabled the winning Normans to conquer the country, at **Stiklestad ❸** it was the loser who ultimately won. The forces of King Canute of Denmark and England were victorious and King Olav Haraldsson of Norway was slain. Olav was later to become a saint, and it was his martyrdom that triggered the building of Nidaros Cathedral in Trondheim. Stiklestad, set east of the E6 highway about 100km (60 miles) north of Trondheim, is the venue for the annual St Olav's Play performed every July in an open-air amphitheatre during the St Olav Festival. A 12th-century church marks the spot where King Olav died, and the St Olav's Kulturhus (museum) chronicles the events.

Trade and industry

Despite their reputation as marauders, the Vikings were principally farmers and traders who settled and worked the land wherever they went. **Steinkjer ❹**, north of Trondheim, was a trading centre in Viking times, and in 1857 it became an export port for timber and agricultural produce.

Wannabe rockstars at Rockheim.

Hurtigruten boat moored in Bodø.

FACT

The Arctic Circle at 66°N is defined not by temperature, but by light. It is the latitude at which the sun is above the horizon at noon on 21 June. At Bødo, the "Mørketid" (Arctic Night) lasts from 15 to 29 December.

North of Steinkjer, the railway and the E6 highway follow the sheltered Namdalen Valley to **Mosjøen** ❺ at the head of the Vefsnfjord and then to **Mo i Rana** ❻ at the head of Ranafjord. The word *Mo*, meaning sand or gravel flats, is a common place name in Norway. Today the towns support heavy industries, starting in the mid-1950s with the former **Norsk Jernverk** (ironworks) at Mo i Rana and **Mosjøen Aluminumverk** (aluminium plant) at Mosjøen. From a business viewpoint, the locations of these industries in small northern towns may be questioned. They are there as part of the government's efforts to provide jobs that keep people in the region. A similar effort is the more recent centralisation of the nine principal government registers at **Brønnøysund** ❼, on the coast south of Mosjøen.

Crossing the Arctic Circle

Most people experience an inexplicable thrill as they cross the **Arctic Circle** (Polarsirkel). Perhaps the reason is celestial: unlike the equator, set by geometry, or the International Date Line, drawn by

Trondheim at night.

timekeepers, the Arctic Circle marks the southern boundary of a different sort of world, the Land of the Midnight Sun.

The only building in this landscape is the **Arctic Circle Centre** ❽ (Polarsirkelsenteret 66 33" N; tel: 91 85 38 33; www.polarsirkelsenteret.no; May–1 Sept daily 8am–10pm; free). Situated on the Circle, alongside the railway and the E6 highway, the unique architecture has been adapted to the natural surroundings. It has a cafeteria, cinema, gift shop and exhibition hall.

Further north, **Bodø** ❾ was founded as a trading centre, in an ill-fated attempt to compete with Bergen. Today the Hurtigruten coastal steamers call on their way from Bergen. Bodø also features the world's strongest maelstrom – Saltstraumen – with whirlpools up to 10 metres (30ft) in diameter. It is the northern end of the rail network and a staging post for summer visitors. Some 40km (25 miles) to the north on the coast is the old trading centre at Kjerringøy (www.kjerringoy.info; late May–Aug, mid-June–mid-Aug daily 11am–5pm), with 15 preserved buildings, and some typical Nordland boats.

Stiklestad: the Making of a Saint

The site of the Battle of Stiklestad near Trondheim in 1030 marks a pivotal point in the history of the Norwegian nation and the adoption of Christianity.

The ancient battlefield of Stiklestad, north of Trondheim, is the place that saw the foundation of Norwegian unity and the adoption of the Christian faith. In the 11th century Norway was a country constantly disrupted by disputes between rival chieftains. The ambition of the reigning king, Olav Haraldsson, was a united Norway. He also wanted to create a Christian country with Christian laws and churches and clergy.

A first failed attempt at Christianity

He was not the first to attempt this. In the previous century Olav Tryggvason had been converted to Christianity in England. He returned to Norway in 995 with the express purpose of crushing the chieftains and imposing his new-found faith.

But Olav Tryggvason's conversion had not swept away all his Viking instincts, and in his zeal he used great cruelty in his crusade to convert the populace. His chieftains became disenchanted, and Olav was killed in the Battle of Svolder in the year 1000.

Enters King Olav

Olav Haraldsson ascended the throne in 1015 but, like Olav Tryggvason before him, he foolishly made too great a use of the sword to establish Christianity. King Canute of Denmark and England, with his eye on the Norwegian throne, gave his support to discontented factions within the country and in 1028 invaded Norway, forcing King Olav to flee to Russia.

Undaunted, Olav returned with a few followers, but his support had dwindled. He met his end on 29 July 1030 at the Battle of Stiklestad. Olav's corpse was taken to the then capital, Nidaros, and buried on the banks of the Nidelva River.

When the body was disinterred a year later, it showed no signs of corruption: his face was unchanged and his nails and hair had grown. This was taken as a sign of sanctity. Following this revelation, Olav was proclaimed a saint and his body placed in a silver shrine in Nidaros Cathedral. Faith in the holiness of King Olav – St Olav – spread and his shrine became a centre of pilgrimage.

Canute's victory at the Battle of Stiklestad was brief. He ceded power to his son, Svejn, but as rumours of Olav's sanctity grew, popular support for Canute evaporated and Svejn was consequently exiled to Denmark in 1035. Meanwhile, St Olav's son, Magnus, had been in exile in Russia. Norway now invited him to return and accept the crown.

A place of pilgrimage

From that time Stiklestad has been a place of pilgrimage. It now has a beautiful open-air theatre, the largest in Scandinavia, and on the anniversary of the battle a cast of 300 actors, dancers and musicians re-enact the events of July 1030 in the annual St Olav Play, which has been staged every year since 1954, drawing some 20,000 tourists to the area.

King Olav (1016–28) became St Olav, patron saint of Norway.

NORWAY'S FAR NORTH

Far removed from the rest of Europe, Norway's spectacular north extends through Arctic latitudes from the rugged Lofoten Islands to the Russian border. Beyond is the remote archipelago of Svalbard.

Oslo

The far north of Norway, comprising Troms and Finnmark counties and the Lofoten Islands, is unique in the Arctic, thanks to the warming currents of the Gulf Stream. Here lies more than a third of the land of Norway, which one resident in 20 calls home.

The Lofoten Islands

Viewed from the mainland across Vestfjord north of Bodø, the **Lofoten Islands** present an imposing wall of rugged peaks rising from the sea. On the west, these mountains form a mighty shield against the onslaught of Norwegian Sea weather, so most of their habitation is along their east coasts, facing the mainland. **Svolvær ❶**, the main town, has been a trading and fishing centre since the 17th century. Fishing has long been the traditional calling of the islanders, and today *Lofot torsk* (Lofoten cod) remains prized throughout the country. **Kabelvåg**, to the south, is the undisputed fishing capital of northern Norway. Up to 10,000 vessels make for Vestfjord between February and April for the colourful *Lofotfiske*, the annual cod-fishing event. From May to September, it is possible to observe sperm whales, minkes and orcas on a whale safari.

The southernmost of the larger Lofoten Islands, **Moskenesøya** is the most photographed, perhaps because of the picturesque fishing village of **Reine ❷**. Between Lofotodden, its

southern cape, and the islet of Mosken lies **Moskenstraumen ❸**, a 4km (2.5-mile) wide, shallow channel. Here tidal currents reach speeds of up to 6 knots in their alternating flow between the Norwegian Sea and Vestfjord, and water always swirls around a submerged rock in the middle of the channel. Sailing here is risky, as Dutch navigators first noted on maps published in 1595 in *Mercator's Atlas*, where the current was called "*Maelstrom*". It is now a synonym for a whirlpool treacherous to navigation and, by extension, turbulent confusion.

Main Attractions
Lofoten Islands
Tromsø, Polaria and the Arctic Ocean Cathedral
Alta, World Heritage Rock Art Centre
North Cape Hall and Museum

Stilt houses on the islands.

TIP

For panoramic views of Tromsø, take the Fjellheisen cable car 420 metres (1,378ft) above sea level (www.fjellheisen. no). It even operates until 1am when the Midnight Sun is shining.

Tromsø

Tromsø ❹, "Gateway to the Arctic", has long been a leading city in northern Norway and is now regarded as the region's unofficial capital and the cultural centre of the north. International trade and influence came early, and by the 1860s the women of the town were so stylishly dressed as to cause a visiting tourist to remark that the city seemed to be the "Paris of the North". That nickname persists, and now may apply as well to Tromsø's abundant and varied nightlife, with an average of one seat in an eatery or place of entertainment for every three residents. Though it is in the Arctic, the city enjoys a benign climate. The average midday temperature in January is the same as in Oslo, and summer temperatures are about the same as in Trondheim.

The city is built mostly on an island between the mainland and the larger coastal island of **Kvaløya**. The sheltered location made it an ideal port for commercial operations in Arctic waters as well as the last port of call for polar expeditions. Polar exploration, trapping and seal hunting are the main focus of the **Polar Museum** (tel: 77 62 33 60; www.polarmuseum.no; mid-June–mid-Aug daily 9am–6pm, rest of the year daily 11am–5pm), situated in a former customs house (1830) in the historic harbour area. The **Tromsø Museum** (Lars Thørings veg 10; tel: 77 64 50 00; June–Aug daily 9am–6pm, Sept–May Mon–Fri 10am–4.30pm, Sat noon–3pm, Sun 11am–4pm) on the university campus has some enlightening exhibits on Sami culture and a mesmerising simulation of the Northern Lights.

Sami and northern Norwegian art is well represented in the permanent collection of the **Art Museum of Northern Norway** (Nordnorsk Kunstmuseum; Sjøgata 1; tel: 77 64 70 20; http://nnkm.no; Mon–Fri 10am–5pm, Sat–Sun noon–5pm; free) housed in a neoclassical building facing Roald Amundsen's Square.

Tromsø's most visited tourist attraction is **Polaria** (tel: 77 75 01 00; www.polaria.no; daily 18 May–31 Aug 10am–7pm, 1 Sept–17 May 10am–5pm; charge) an Arctic-themed experience centre occupying a distinctive futuristic building. After watching the panoramic

The Far North

0   50 km
0   50 miles

film Svalbard – Arctic Wilderness, stroll the "Arctic Walkway" to witness elements of Arctic nature, from a snowstorm to the tundra; then observe the local bearded seals in the Aquarium.

Just over the bridge on the mainland, a 25-minute walk from the harbour (or a ride on no. 28 bus) is the striking **Arctic Ocean Cathedral** (Ishavskatedral; tel: 47 68 06 68; www.ishavskatedralen. no; June–mid-Aug Mon–Sat 9am–7pm, Sun 1pm–7pm, mid-Aug–Jan and Apr–May daily 3–6pm, Feb–Mar daily 2–6pm), an impressive modern work by the architect Jan Inge Hovig. Inspired by Arctic landscape, it resembles an elegant iceberg or whale in repose. Midnight Sun concerts are held here both in summer and winter.

Tromsø is also home to Europe's northernmost brewery, **Macks Ølbryggeri** (Muségata 1; tel: 77 62 45 00; www. mack.no), established in 1845, where you can sample the famous Arctic ale, *Mackøl*.

Alta rock carvings

Alta ❺, the largest town in Finnmark, is known among fishermen for having one of the world's best salmon rivers. It is also home to the **Alta Museum, World Heritage Rock Art Centre at Hjemmeluft** (Verdensarvsenter For Bergkunst; Altaveien 19; tel: 41 75 63 30; www.alta.museum.no; mid-May–mid-Sept daily 8am–5pm, mid-June–mid-Aug until 8pm, mid-Sept–mid-May 9am–3pm) on the southern outskirts, a collection of rock carvings dating from 4200 to 500 BC. These remarkable "stories in pictures" of people, animals (particularly reindeer), boats and weapons are now a Unesco World Heritage site.

Sami centre

South of Alta on the E93 lies **Kautokeino** ❻, a centre for the Sami, the indigenous people of northern Scandinavia and the Kola peninsula of Russia. The Sami population is conservatively estimated at 70,000, of whom about half live in Norway. Their native languages are related to Finnish, Hungarian and Estonian and have little in common with Norwegian. Traditionally, the Sami have been hunters, fishermen and reindeer herders. Like indigenous minorities elsewhere, the

The Arctic Cathedral (Ishavskatedralen) in Tromsø represents the shape of a Sami tent and the iciness of a glacier.

Sami were long suppressed, but now have their own flag and own Parliament, *Sámediggi*, at **Karasjok ❼**.

Northernmost point

Nordkapp ❽ (The North Cape) at 71°10' 21"N is considered by many to be the most northerly point of mainland Europe. But in fact the tip of **Knivskjelodden**, a low, slim peninsula to the west of Nordkapp, lies 47 seconds of latitude farther north. No matter: the North Cape is the imposing headland that draws visitors from around the world. Wrap up and walk along the cliffs for views from the continent's edge. The tourist complex, **North Cape Hall** (Nordkappallen; tel: 78 47 68 60; www.nordkapp.no; mid-May–mid-Aug daily 11am–1pm, rest of Aug 11am–10pm, Sept–mid-Oct 11am–3pm, mid-Oct–mid-May noon–2.30pm) features a panoramic film about the North Cape through the seasons. The **North Cape Museum** (tel: 78 47 72 00; www.nordkappmuseet. no; June–mid-Aug Mon–Sat 10am–7pm, Sun 11.30am–7pm, rest of the year Mon–Fri 11am–3pm), near the

Hurtigruten quay in **Honningsvag**, has a variety of displays about the cape and its fishing history, and aspects of everyday life.

North to Svalbard

The **Svalbard** (Spitsbergen) archipelago lies 640km (400 miles) north of the mainland. In 1596, the Dutch navigator Willem Barents, searching for the Northeast Passage, sighted the largest of its four main islands, which he called Spitsbergen (Pointed Peaks). Indeed, the terrain resembles that of the Alps, and Spitsbergen covers an area almost as large as Switzerland. In 1906, John Longyear, an American industrialist, founded the Arctic Coal Company on Spitsbergen. Today, the principal village, **Longyearbyen** (pop. 2,100) is named after him, but only Norway and Russia remain as mine operators.

The climate is relatively mild for the Arctic: midday temperatures at Longyearbyen average –7°C (19°F) in February and 7°C (45°F) in July. But permafrost prevails year-round. In 1998 it made the international news, when Canadian pathologists exhumed the well-preserved corpses of six Svalbard coal miners who had died in the 1918 influenza pandemic, to search for clues that might reveal its origin.

Today, technology is supplanting mining as the main economic activity. The **Svalbard Satellite Station** near Longyearbyen is positioned to download images from all earth observation satellites in polar orbits, and the **Rocket Range** at **Ny-Ålesund** is now instrumental in weather research.

With daily flights (weather permitting) between Tromsø and Longyearbyen, tourism is growing. In summer, the stark mountains around the village are offset by a valley which has meadows spangled with flowers. The polar winter is another matter. The sun does not rise above the horizon, and everything is locked in darkness, lit only by the moon and the multicoloured rays of the Northern Lights.

The North Cape – a major tourist attraction 300 metres (1,000ft) above the Arctic Ocean.

Regal details on the Royal Palace gates, Stockholm.

SWEDEN

From sophisticated Stockholm to mountain wilderness, Sweden offers the traveller immense variety.

The ubiquitous Dalahäst (Dala Horse).

Not so long ago, Sweden was an introverted country perched uneasily on the edge of Western Europe. Many Swedes talked about travelling "to Europe" as if it was on a different continent. All that changed with the country's admission to the European Union in the 1990s and the opening in 2000 of the Öresund bridge between Sweden and Denmark.

The Swedes finally became "good Europeans"; in turn, the outside world began to discover the country's hidden delights. More visitors every year flock to the bustling cultural centres of Stockholm, Göteborg and Malmö, or escape into the rural regions or the vast wilderness areas of Lapland.

The Bohuslän coast.

Sweden is ideal for those who like the great outdoors and activities such as angling, golf, riding, fell-walking, skiing, sailing or canoeing. Even the capital city, Stockholm, is a place of waterways and green spaces, flanked by thousands of uninhabited islands. The flat, fertile south, including Skåne, was part of Denmark for centuries: a faintly Danish accent persists. South-central Sweden is dominated by the great lakes of Vänern and Vättern, the hub of a vast waterway network. Visitors can sail across the widest part of the country along the Göta Kanal, which links Stockholm to Göteborg.

Sweden's heartland holds Dalarna, a province that guards the country's oldest folk traditions. From here, the lovely Inlandsbanan railway runs north into the Arctic, home to the indigenous Sami, many of whom still herd reindeer across Scandinavia's remote mountains.

Culturally, state-of-the-art museums, well-preserved historical sites like the Viking capital Birka, and the homes of artists such as Carl Larsson, who inspired the clean lines of contemporary Swedish design, are unique attractions. Göteborg's Symphony Orchestra is in the top rank of world orchestras, and Sweden is increasingly admired as a centre of gastronomic excellence.

In winter, visitors are lured by the Northern Lights, the renowned Icehotel… and the magic of a Swedish Christmas, with its traditional markets, brightly decorated streets and St Lucia processions.

Sweden

100 km

100 miles

N

Arctic Circle

NORWEGIAN SEA

FINLAND

SWEDEN

Lapland

Norrbotten

Västerbotten

Ångermanland

Jämtland

Härjedalen

Medelpad

Bottenviken
Perämeri

Gulf of Bothnia

Vesterålen

Lofoten

Oulu
Muhos
Kemi
Tornio
Haparanda
Rovaniemi
Kalix
Töre
Luleå
Boden
Piteå
Skellefteå
Umeå
Örnsköldsvik
Härnösand
Östersund
Trondheim

Kiruna
Gällivare
Jokkmokk
Kebnekaise 2111
Sarektjåkkå 2090

Tromsø
Narvik
Harstad
Bodø
Mo i Rana
Storfjorsei

Karlavägen
Karlavägen
Östermalmsg.
Greygatan
Nybrogatan
Skeppargatan
Kommendörsgatan
Jungfrugatan
Artillerigatan
Nybrogatan
Linnégatan
Linnégatan

Lindarängsvägen
Lindarängsvägen
Valhallavägen
Valhallavägen
Oxenstiernsgatan
Gärdesgatan

DROTTNINGBERGET

LADUGÅRDSGÄRDET

SKANSBERGET

TV-huset
Radiohuset

Kaknästornet
(Kaknäs
TV Tower)

Karlaplan
Karlaplan
Karlavägen

Maximteatern

Berwaldhallen

Strandvägen

Djurgårdsbrunnsvägen

Statens
Sjöhistoriska
Muséet
(National Maritime
Museum)

Tekniska
Muséet

Folkens
Museum
Entografiska

Östermalmstorg
Öster-
malmstorg
rmalms
en

Marie
Bebadelse

Nobelgatan

Djurgårdsbrunnsviken

Storgatan

Hedvig
Eleonora

ÖSTERMALM

Historiska Muséet
(Museum of National
Antiquities)

LADUGÅRDSGÄRDET

Armémuseum

Strandvägen

Styrmansgatan

Storgatan

Grev Magnigatan

Torstensonsgatan

DJURGÅRDEN

0   500 m
0   500 yds

Musik-
muséet

Riddargatan

Kungliga
Hovstallet

Käptens-
gatan

Artilleri-
gatan

Skeppargatan

Greygatan

gatan

Riddargatan

Barnängatan

Narvavägen

Ulrikagatan

Berwaldhallen

Engelska

Strandvägen

nargatan

Strandvägen

Strandvägen

Storgatan

NOBELPARKEN

Nobelgatan

rokviken

Strandvägen

Djurgårds-
bron

Djurgårdsvägen

Kaknästornet
(Kaknäs TV Tower)
Statens Sjöhistoriska Muséet
(National Maritime Museum)

rokjen

Ladugårdslandsviken

Junibacken

Djurgårdsbrunnsviken

EIPARKEN
onalmuseum
onal Museum
f Fine Art)

Blasieholmen

Galärvarvsvägen

GALÄRPARKEN

Nordiska
Muséet
(Nordic Museum)

Stockholms
Universitet

Rosendalsvägen

useum

Östasiatiska
Muséet

Slupskjulsvägen

Vasamuséet

Hazeliusporten

DJURGÅRDEN

Skeppsholms

Moderna Muséet
(Museum of Modern Art)

Biologiska
Muséet

Skansen

Seglora

af Chapman

Exercis-
plan

ArkDes

Svensksundsvägen

Alkärret

Aquaria
Vattenmuseum

Liljevalchs Konsthall
(Liljevalch Art Gallery)

Cirkus

Skogaholm

SKEPPSHOLMEN

Långa Raden

Östra Brobänken

Falkenbergsg.

ABBA the Museum

Tobaksmuséet

Akvarium

Hazeliusbacken

trömmen

Södra Brobänken

Kastellholms-
bron

Gröna
Lund

Sollidsbacken

Djurgårdsvägen

Andréeg.

Beckholmsvägen

Kastellholmsvägen

Örlogsvägen

Kastellet

Kastellholmen

Prins Eugens
Waldemarsudde

Thielska Galleriet
(Thiel Gallery)

Beckholms-
bron

Beckholmen

Vaxholm

S A L T S J Ö N

Fotografiska

Stockholm

N

0   200 m
0   200 yds

rinavägen
nskagatan

Stadsgårdsleden

ogbergsgatan

Fjällgatan

"SoFo"

City Hall (Stadshus).

STOCKHOLM

Sweden's capital is a city of islands where palaces and peaceful hideaways line the shores, and where cobbled streets lead to chic shops, cafés and lively cultural attractions.

The novelist Selma Lagerlöf called Stockholm "the city that floats on water". Nowhere do you see this more clearly than from the dizzy observation platform on top of the **Kaknäs Television Tower ❶** (Kaknästornet; tel: 08 667 21 80; www.kaknastornet.se; daily 9–10am until 5–8pm), Ladugårdsgärdet, which rises 155 metres (508ft). Below, Stockholm spreads out in a panorama of blue water, the red of the old buildings contrasting with the stark white and glass of the new, and swathes of trees and grass. This pretty low-rise city, designated Europe's first Green Capital in 2010, rests on its 14 islands, for all the world like a raft traveller drifting down a lazy river.

Fresh and salt water are separated by the island of Gamla Stan (Old Town) and the great lock gates of Slussen at the southern end. This island barrier is where Stockholm originated some time before the 13th century. Today, with a population of 2 million in the greater metropolitan area, Stockholm is a modern and sophisticated metropolis, famous for Scandinavian design in furniture, textiles and interiors and a hotbed of innovation in information technology. The city features some of the most exciting cuisine in Europe. Stockholm's nightlife has exploded into an array of young, hip clubs and older, more sedate nightspots. Infusing the old with the new is a speciality of today's vibrant Stockholm.

Stockholm's gorgeous townhouses.

The Vasa capital

Stockholm's history starts in **Gamla Stan** (Old Town), which still has the character of a medieval city. Its narrow lanes follow the same curves along which the seamen of former times carried their goods. The best place to start a tour is **Stortorget**, the centre of the original city, from which narrow streets fan out in all directions.

In medieval times, Gamla Stan's Stortorget was a crowded, noisy place of trade, where German merchants, stallholders, craftsmen and young servant

Main Attractions

Gamla Stan (Old Town)
Royal Palace (Kungliga Slottet)
Museum of Modern Art
Skansen Open-Air Museum
Vasa Museum
City Hall (Stadshus)
Södermalm
Drottningholms Slott
Uppsala

TIP

See more and pay less with a Stockholm Card, available from the Stockholm Visitor Centre, Sergels Torg 5. It offers free travel, free admission to museums and sights, discounts and a guidebook.

girls and boys jostled and shouted. In the cobbled square today, people laze on benches or sit at one of the outdoor cafés, and it is hard to visualise that in 1520 the cobbles ran with blood during the Stockholm Bloodbath. Despite a guarantee of safety, the Danish King Kristian II, known as The Tyrant, murdered 82 people, not only nobles but innocent civilians unlucky enough to have a shop or a business nearby. This gory incident triggered the demise of the Kalmar Union, which had united Sweden with Denmark and Norway. Three years later, Sweden's first heroic king, Gustav Vasa, put an end to the union and made Stockholm his capital.

From the square, it's a short walk to the **Cathedral** ❷ (Storkyrkan; tel: 08 723 30 00; www.stockholmsdomkyrkoforsamling.se; daily 9am–4pm, June–July Mon–Fri 9am–5pm, Aug Mon–Fri 9am–6pm). This awesome Gothic structure is the oldest building in Gamla Stan, in part dating to the 12th century. It has high vaulted arches and sturdy pillars stripped back to their original red brick. Its most famous statue is St George and the Dragon, the largest

A stone cherub inside the Royal Palace.

medieval monument in Scandinavia, a wooden sculpture carved by Bernt Notke in 1489, which has retained its original colouring. The cathedral was the setting for the June 2010 royal wedding between Crown Princess Victoria and commoner Daniel Westling: crowds of around half a million lined the streets to watch the procession.

Våsterlånggatan is a favourite shopping street for locals and tourists alike. Here and on nearly every other cobbled lane in the Old Town you will find shops, restaurants and cafés to suit every taste. Particularly enjoyable are the cellar restaurants with their musty smell and stone walls. It's easy to imagine the Swedish troubadour Evert Taube (1890–1976) raising a beer stein to his compatriots as he composed yet another lyric to the Swedish way of life.

Royal residences

The present **Royal Palace** ❸ (Kungliga Slott; tel: 08 402 61 30; www.kungahuset. se; mid-May–mid-Sept daily 10am–5pm, mid-Sept–mid-May Tue–Sun 10am–4pm) was built on the site of the Tre Kronor Palace, which burnt down

---

UNUSUAL VIEWS OF STOCKHOLM

Stockholm is an unusual city, and visitors may want to explore its delights in an unusual way. There are certainly plenty of opportunities. The city sails along on its 14 islands – join its watery dance by taking to the Riddarfjärden or Saltsjön in a kayak, rowing boat, paddle boat or canoe. Djurgårdsbron Sjöcafe (Galärvarvsvägen; tel: 08 660 57 57; www. sjocafeet.se) is a central hire place, or contact Kanotcenter Svima Sport (Ekelundsvägen 26; tel: 08 730 22 10; www.svima.se).

The **Millenniumtour** run by the Stadsmuséet (Ryssgården, tel. 08 508 316 20; www.stadsmuseet.stockholm.se) takes thriller-lovers on a walk round Södermalm. Here you can see the sights of Stockholm's trendiest district through the eyes of Lisbeth Salander and Mikael Blomkvist, the characters from Stieg Larsson's wildly popular series.

Vertigo sufferers may pale at the idea of a rooftop tour (English tours late Apr–Aug; tel: 08 22 30 05; www.upplevmer.se), but Upplev Mer's ladders and catwalks allow access to the dizzy heights of Riddarholmen, with views over Gamla Stan.

If you're here in winter, you can experience the nearest thing to flying with tour skating. Although routes depend on which parts of the archipelago are solidly frozen, tours usually end with a skate through central Stockholm, right past the Stadshus (City Hall). ICEguide (tel: 730 89 47 63; www.iceguide.se) runs a five-hour introduction from January to March.

in 1697, some say not without the help of Nicodemus Tessin the Younger, who had already built a new northern wing and who obviously relished the glory of rebuilding the palace to his Renaissance designs. His father, Nicodemus the Elder, had been architect to the old Tre Kronor Palace, and the grandson, Carl Gustaf, was responsible for supervising the completion of the new palace many years later. The palace comprises 608 rooms. Various suites are open to the public – the stunning Royal Apartments are what most people go to see – and the sprawling palace houses three museums. Lovers of military uniforms and marching can watch the 40-minute Changing of the Guard ceremony in the outer courtyard (May–Aug Mon–Sat 12.15pm, Sun 1.15pm).

For more of Sweden's aristocratic heritage, head for the **House of Nobility** ❹ (Riddarhuset; tel: 08 723 39 90; www.riddarhuset.se; Mon–Fri 11am–noon) on the nearby island of **Riddarholmen**, built in 1641 as a meeting place for the nobles. It is arguably the most beautiful building in Gamla Stan, with two pavilions looking out across the water. Inside, the nobles deliberated in the grandeur of the Main Chamber, watched from above by a painting of Mother Svea, who symbolises Sweden.

On the opposite side of Centralbron is **Riddarholmskyrkan** ❺ (www.kungahuset.se; mid-May–mid-Sept 10am–5pm), an iron-spired 13th-century monastery church (the oldest in Stockholm) that serves as the burial place for Sweden's monarchs.

Medieval Museum

The refurbishment of the Swedish Parliament Building (Riksdaghus) on Helgeandsholmen to the north of Gamla Stan some years ago led to a remarkable archaeological find and a new museum. When the builders started to excavate the Riksdaghus terrace to form an underground car park, they discovered layer upon layer of the past, including part of the medieval wall and the cellars of an apothecary shop. Stockholm's **Medieval Museum** ❻ (Medeltidsmuseum, Strömparterren; tel: 08 508 317 90; www.medeltidsmuseet.stockholm.se; Tue, Thur and Sun noon–5pm, Wed noon–8pm; free), incorporates the old wall

The majestic cathedral in Gamla Stan.

and other treasures uncovered during the excavations.

Skeppsholmen

To the east of Gamla Stan lies Skeppsholmen. The sleek schooner moored off the island is the 100-year-old **af Chapman** , now a youth hostel and a café. Also on the island is the spectacular new building of the **Museum of Modern Art** ❽ (Moderna Muséet; tel: 08 5202 3500; www.modernamuseet.se; Tue and Fri 10am–8pm, Wed–Thur and Sat–Sun 10am–6pm), designed by the Spanish architect Rafael Moneo, with a collection of 20th-century art that is considered one of the finest in the world, and includes works by Dalí, Picasso and Magritte among others. Its large restaurant-café is worth visiting for a beautiful panorama of the city skyline. Next door, the **ArkDes** (the Swedish Centre for Architecture and Design; tel: 08 587 270 00; www.arkdes.se; Tue 10am–8pm, Wed–Sun 10am–6pm) delves into the design aesthetics of Sweden's buildings.

A bridge links Skeppsholmen to the **Blasieholmen** waterfront area, where the sumptuous big building is one of

Break into song at the ABBA Museum.

Scandinavia's most famous hotels, the **Grand** ❾. Nearby is the **National Museum of Fine Arts** ❿ (Nationalmuseum; Södra Blasieholmshamnen; tel: 08 519 543 00; www.nationalmuseum.se; closed for renovation until 2017), featuring Sweden's national collection of art, with most of the great masters from 1500–1900. Rembrandt is particularly well represented. In summer, the museum holds concerts in the evening, a lovely setting for music.

Djurgården

From Gamla Stan, it is just 10 minutes by boat across the harbour to the island of **Djurgården**. Once a royal deer park, much of Djurgården is still in its natural state, with paths and woods where you may spot small creatures, both everyday and rare, such as hares and the occasional deer. The island is part of **Ekoparken**, the world's first city national park. A good way to get around is to hire a bike at the bridge which forms the road entrance (also the place to hire kayaks and rowing boats when the lure of Stockholm's glittering waters proves overwhelming).

As the ferry slides into the Djurgården quay, there is no mistaking that this is an island devoted to enjoyment. On the right is **Gröna Lund** ⓫ (tel: 010 708 91 00; www.gronalund.com; May–Sept and over Christmas, hours vary), an amusement park with 18th-century roots and up-to-the-minute rides, including its seventh roller-coaster, Twister, and the House of Nightmares, a horror experience new for 2015. At Djurgårdsvägen 68, unleash your inner Dancing Queen at **ABBA the Museum** ⓬ (tel: 771 75 75 75; www.abbathemuseum.com; daily 10am–6pm, Wed–Fri and every day in summer until 8pm), dedicated to Sweden's most popular band ever. Opened in 2013, the museum's popularity has been growing ever since.

Heading south on Djurgården, where the island rises in steps to a hilltop, is **Skansen** ⓭ (tel: 08 442 80 00; www.skansen.se; 10am until 2–10pm), the oldest open-air museum in the world. In 1891, Artur Hazelius decided to preserve the fast-disappearing Swedish way of life by collecting traditional buildings. Today there are some 150, including an 18th-century church, still used for services and weddings. In summer, costumed craftspeople meander round the steep cobbled town and demonstrate traditional crafts such as glassblowing in the little workshops. Skansen's **zoo** contains Nordic fauna, such as bears, elk, reindeer, wolves and wild boar; and its **aquarium** holds some distinctly un-Nordic creatures such as monkeys and crocodiles.

While on Djurgården it's worth visiting the lovely former home and collection of the "Painter Prince" **Prins Eugens Waldemarsudde** ⓮ (Prins Eugens väg 6; tel: 08 545 837 00; www.waldemarsudde.se; Tue–Sun 11am–5pm, Thur until 8pm; charge), which overlooks the sea.

On the far side of the island, fans of Nordic art should make time for the **Thielska Galleriet** (tel: 08 662 58 84; noon–4pm; charge): Ernest Thiel was pals with Carl Larsson, Edvard Munch and Bruno Liljefors, and accumulated a fine collection of his friends' work.

If you choose bus instead of boat and enter the island over Djurgårdsbron from Strandvägen, the first museum you come to is the **Nordic Museum** ⓯ (Nordiska Muséet; tel: 08 519 546 00; June–Aug daily 10am–5pm, rest of year Mon–Fri 10am–4pm, Sat–Sun 11am–5pm, Wed until 8pm), which depicts Nordic life from the 16th century. It has peasant costumes, a collection of bridal gowns and the traditional silver and gold crowns worn by Swedish brides, exhibits on Lapland culture, folk art, and more.

To the west of the Nordiska Muséet on the waterfront is the huge, oddly shaped **Vasa Museum** ⓰ (Vasamuséet; Galärvarvet; tel: 08 519 548 00; www.vasamuseet.se; June–Aug daily 8.30am–6pm, Sept–May Thur–Mon 10am–5pm, Wed 10am–8pm). Inaugurated in 1990, the must-see museum houses the *Vasa* warship, built in the 1620s for

the Thirty Years War, on the orders of Sweden's warrior king, Gustav II Adolf. She was a magnificent ship, decorated with 700 sculptures and carvings, but her oak was too solid. In 1628 she sank in Stockholm harbour on her maiden voyage. In 1956 the Swedish marine archaeologist Anders Franzén found her and, in 1961, brought her up from the depths. More than 24,000 objects have been salvaged from the seabed, including skeletons, sails, cannon, clothing, tools, coins, butter, rum and many everyday utensils. With the ticket to the Vasa museum you can also go onboard a steam-powered 1915 icebreaker and a light ship dating from 1903 moored on the quayside.

Fans of Astrid Lindgren's children's books should not miss **Junibacken** ⓱ (tel: 08 587 230 00; www.junibacken.se; Sept, Nov, March–Apr Tue–Sun 10am–5pm, half Jan, half Feb, May, June and late Aug, Dec daily 10am–5pm, July–mid-Aug daily 10am–6pm), a children's attraction/theatre dedicated to her eccentric characters. An electrically operated indoor tram, with narration in English, allows the rider to experience

TIP

A trip on tram No.7 is a superb way to discover the city. The line is called Spårväg City and will take you from Segels Torg to the museums of Djurgården.

The walk up to Skansen.

FACT

Tunnelbanan, Stockholm's metro system, is described as the "world's longest art gallery". Many stations have paintings, sculptures, mosaics and engravings – and all can be seen for the price of a ticket. A free English guide to the artworks in 90 of its stations can be downloaded from the SL website (http://sl.se).

One of the gravity-defying rides at the amusement park Gröna Lund.

Astrid's World, floating over miniature scenes from her books with moving figures, lights and sound, as familiar characters suddenly pop out of corners.

A short walk across the bridge is the spectacular **Guldrummet** (Gold Room), an underground vault featuring more than 3,000 prehistoric gold and silver artefacts, inside the **Museum of National Antiquities** (Historiska Muséet; Narvavägen; tel: 08 519 556 00; www.historiska.se; June–Aug daily 10am–6pm, Sept–May Tue–Sun 11am–5pm, Wed until 8pm).

Kungsträdgården

It's anyone's guess what the Swedish sculptor John Tobias Sergel (1740–1814) might have thought of the huge illuminated obelisk, fountain and square that bear his name, and of the modern city around it. The heart of this business and commercial area is not large, but it sits somewhat uneasily with the rest. From **Sergels Torg** it is hard to miss the five towering office blocks on Sveavägen, which cast their shadow over the other buildings. In the 1960s, Stockholm City Council, like so many others, succumbed to the temptation to knock things down and build concrete and glass high-rise buildings.

The destruction of many fine old buildings continued until it threatened the **King's Garden** (Kungsträdgården) with the statue of the warrior king Karl XII on its southern side. At this point the Stockholmers had had enough. Normally placid and biddable, they mustered at the King's Garden, climbed the trees that were in danger of the axe, and swore that if the trees went so did the people. The City Fathers retreated, and Kungsträdgården survives to soften the edges of the new buildings and harmonise with the older buildings that are left. This is the place to take a leisurely stroll or sit beside the fountains on a summer day and enjoy a coffee at its outdoor café. In summer it is the venue of many outdoor festivals and rock concerts. In winter, part of Kungsträdgården is flooded with water and becomes a popular ice rink, and the restaurant moves indoors.

A short stroll east is the early 20th-century private palace housing one of Stockholm's most unusual museums,

ROYAL PARKS AND GARDENS

Ekoparken is the world's first national city park, a huge set of green lungs that stretch out in a 12km (7-mile) long arch from Djurgården (where the Vasamuséet, Gröna Lund and Skansen are situated) in the south, up to Ulriksdals Slott (castle) in the north. This green swathe is so large you'll need a full day of serious hiking to explore it, by foot during the warmer months or on skis or long-distance skates in the winter. Bus tours to the northerly Haga Royal Park, run by Strömma Turism (www.stromma.se), include a free boat tour on Brunnsviken Lake.

The Ekopark includes three royal parks, Djurgården, Haga and Ulriksdal, with palaces to tour (Ulriksdals Slott, Gustav III's Paviljong, Rosendals Slott). Visit the tropical Fjärilshus (Butterfly House), where hundreds of colourful species land lightly upon your shoulder, the Bergianska (Bergianska Botanical Gardens), which contains the world's largest water lily, and Naturhistoriska Riksmuseet (Museum of Natural History), where you'll also find Sweden's only IMAX cinema.

For a pleasant retreat on northern Djurgården, you'll find Rosendalsträgård (Rosendals Garden), with orchards, flowers and vegetables, garden shops and a café. For many Stockholmers this has become the ideal retreat after a day on Djurgården. For Ekoparken information, call the Stockholm tourist office (tel: 08 508 285 08).

the **Hallwyl Collection** ⑳ (Hallwyl-ska Muséet; Hamngatan 4; tel: 08 402 30 99; http://hallwylskamuseet.se; June–Aug Tue–Sun 10am–4pm, rest of the year Tue, Thur–Sun noon–4pm, Wed noon–7pm; guided tours in English: June–Aug daily Tue–Sun 12.30pm, Sept–Dec Sat 1.30pm). It's the magpie collection of one person, Countess von Hallwyl, from her ornate piano to china, beautiful furniture and personal knick-knacks.

Just north of the museum on Östermalmstorg, stop to snack at **Östermalmshallen**, a classy deli-style market.

Stockholm's shopping centres

Sweden's equivalent of Harrods or Bloomingdales is **Nordiska Kompaniet (NK)** ㉑, on Hamngatan, whose rooftop illuminated sign, constantly rotating, is visible from far and wide in the city (www.nk.se). NK sells everything from shoes to sporting equipment, men's and women's clothing, glass, pottery and silver, jewellery and perfume; its services range from personal shoppers to post office

and travel agency, and multilingual staff are always on hand to assist with changing currency and shipping your purchases back home.

Just across the street is **Illums Bolighus**, an interior design shop (www.illumsbolighus.se), and heading slightly west along Hamngatan, you come to **Gallerian** ㉒, a huge covered shopping arcade that stretches to Jakobsgatan (http://gallerian.se). A block west is Sergels Torg, on whose southern side is **Culture House** ㉓ (Kulturhuset; http://kulturhusetstadsteatern.se; Mon–Fri 9am–7pm, Sat–Sun 11am–5pm), a popular meeting place and venue for entertainment, which also houses theatres, the **Stockholm Visitor Centre** and the Café Panorama, which boasts a fine view of the city.

Åhléns City ㉔ is on the corner of Sergels Torg and Drottninggatan (www.ahlens.se). It has a similar range and quality to NK, and a visit to its supermarket food department is a sightseeing tour in itself.

The third of this trio of huge department stores is **PUB**, on Drottninggatan at Hötorget, a galleria featuring a

The Vasa warship, one of the most important shipwrecks in the world.

variety of Swedish and international brand shops (www.pub.se).

Drottninggatan

Drottninggatan (Queen's Street), an old street which leads directly through the Riksdagshus and over the bridge from the Royal Palace, is one of Stockholm's main pedestrian ways. In summer, it is full of casual crowds strolling or sitting at one of the outdoor cafés.

At its northern end is the excellent **Strindberg Museum** ㉕ (Strindbergs-muséet; Drottninggatan 85; tel: 08 411 53 54; www.strindbergsmuseet.se; July–Aug Tue–Sun 10am–4pm, rest of year Tue–Sun noon–4pm), housed in the top-floor flat of the **Blåtornet** (Blue Tower) where Sweden's greatest playwright spent his last years and wrote his last epic play, *The Great Highway*, in 1908. Even at the end of his life, Strindberg was astonishingly prolific; he produced some 20 books in his four years in the Blue Tower.

Walking south along Drottninggatan to Kungsgatan, on your left you'll come to **Hötorget** ㉖, with its open-air food stalls and indoor market. This is where Swedes shop for food. Here you can find Swedish delicacies such as elk steak and reindeer and the many varieties of Scandinavian cured herring.

Stadshuset

A city as lovely, unusual and pioneering as Stockholm deserves a fitting symbol. And that symbol is the **Stadshuset** ㉗ (City Hall, 1923). Lying across the Stadshubron bridge on the island of Kungsholmen, this city landmark was built in the truest spirit of national romanticism. The building is made from around 8 million decorated bricks, and garnished with spires, domes and minarets of green-tinged copper. One corner of the building rises into a 106-metre (450ft) tower; and at the very pinnacle of the tower shine three golden crowns (Tre Kronor), Sweden's emblem.

Inside this brick behemoth, the Blue Hall, with its sweeping marble staircase and colonnades, is used as the banqueting hall for the Nobel Prize ceremony, held in December each year. After the 1,300 guests have finished dining, they move upstairs to the Stadshus's most jaw-dropping room, the shimmering

The gleaming interior of the Stadshus.

Golden Hall, where 19 million gold mosaic tiles decorate the walls.

Other notable features include a series of frescoes by Prins Eugens Waldemarsudde – the "Painter Prince" – the 10,000-pipe organ and mechanical figures of St George and the Dragon on the north front of the building, which spring into action at noon and 6pm.

Stadshus is the work of architect Ragnar Östberg, who devoted 12 years of his life to the building. You can admire the interior of his masterpiece by guided tour only. There are usually at least six 45-minute English tours daily (depending on municipal events; www.stockholm.se/stadshuset); it's well worth joining one if you can, as is going up the City Hall Tower, which offers spectacular views of Stockholm (daily May–Sept).

Södermalm: artistic centre

From Gamla Stan, take the Tunnelbanan (underground railway) on a five-minute journey south to Slussen station on **Södermalm** ㉘, commonly referred to as "Söder". Once this was the great working-class area of the city, but today it is the coolest, most bohemian part of Stockholm, popular with local artists and bursting with new cafés, restaurants, boutiques and design shops. There is a concentration of galleries on the steep slope of **Hornsgatan** ㉙, a popular street on which to buy locally made art, glass and ceramics. The inner circle of cool, though, is the **"SoFo"** area (south of Folkungsgagatan), the place to head for cafés and nightlife.

Right next to the Slussen underground station is the **City Museum** ㉚ (Stadsmuséet; Ryssgården; tel: 08 508 316 00; www.stadsmuseet.stockholm.se; closed for renovation until autumn 2017). While Stockholm received virtually no mention until the 13th century, the museum makes it clear that this strategic spot had been inhabited for many centuries. Södermalm forms the backdrop for much of the action in Stieg Larsson's best-selling *The Girl with the Dragon Tattoo* and its follow-ups: the Stadsmuséet runs walking tours that point out pertinent landmarks from the books and films.

The district is also home to **Katarinahissen**, a 19th-century lift rebuilt in 1935 that used to carry passengers

Gamla Stan.

to the heights of Södermalm. It shut down in 2010, but should resume its operations in 2019 after renovation.

Opened in 2010, the fabulous **Fotografiska** ㉛ (Stora Tullhus; Stadsgårdshamnen 22; tel: 08-50 900 500; http://fotografiska.eu; daily 9am–11pm) exhibition space is wowing visitors. Housed within the impressive Art-Nouveau Customs House (1906), Fotografiska puts on four major photographic exhibitions per year, and around 20 smaller shows and video installations. Previous exhibitions hosted within its superb spaces have included everything from the portraiture of Annie Leibovitz and Sandy Skoglund's weird tableaux, to contemporary reportage on conflicts in Guatemala and Rwanda.

Just west of Södermalm, the former prison island **Långholmen** is now a lush green space with its own little **beaches**. And sitting off to the south, like a giant golfball on Stockholm's skyline, the **Ericsson Globe** (tel: 0771 811 000; www.globearenas.se; Skyview: Mon–Fri 9am–6pm, Sat–Sun 10–4pm) is the world's largest spherical building. Since its inauguration in 1989, it has mainly been used as the national ice-hockey arena and as a concert venue, but in 2010, the new Skyview attraction added another dimension. This highly unusual funicular railway takes visitors up the curving sides of the 130-metre (426ft) high Globe in two glass-sided gondolas.

Woodland Cemetery

A short distance south of the Globe is **Woodland Cemetery** ㉜ (Skogskyrkogården; www.skogskyrkogarden.se; open 24hrs, visitors centre: late May–Aug 11am–4pm, Sept Sun 11am–4pm; guided tours in English July–Sept Sun at 10.30am), in the southern suburb of Enskede. This is another of Stockholm's Unesco World Heritage sites and well worth a visit. Skogs-kyrkogården is a place of immense calm and beauty, with five striking chapels, and where every curve in every pathway was built with care and purpose. The work of two of Sweden's most important architects, Gunnar Asplund and Sigurd Lewerentz, this masterpiece of Modernist design took 25 years (1915–40) to create. Greta Garbo is buried here, as is Asplund himself.

Around Stockholm

The Stockholm archipelago

It is a rare city that has 24,000 islands on its doorstep and 100km (60 miles) of lake at its heart, but this is Stockholm's eternal good fortune. Until the building of the Tunnelbanen, boats were the only means of getting around these vast expanses of water, and today boats are still part of Stockholm life. Boat operators Waxholmsbolaget (www.waxholmsbolaget.se) and Strömma Kanalbolaget (www.stromma.se) transport passengers around the archipelago in a variety of craft, from old coal-fired steamers to modern ferries.

The most popular place to visit in the archipelago is the royal palace, **Drottningholms Slott** ❸ on Lovön (see page 251), to the west of the city. West of Lovön is **Björkö** ❹, the site of Sweden's oldest city, **Birka**, now a Unesco World Heritage site. Between AD 790 and 975, Birka was the trading centre for the 40,000 inhabitants of the rich Mälaren area and the meeting point for traders. This was also where Christianity first came to Sweden, when Ansgar, the Saxon missionary, landed in the 9th century. Almost nothing is left of Birka above ground, but archaeological digs have revealed much of the town's story: **Birka Vikingastaden** (tel: 08 560 514 40; www.raa.se; mid-May–mid-Sept 10am–5pm) features the most recent finds, and Viking-based activities in summer add life to the island.

Although it is now easy to get there by underground train (T–Ropsten), in summer it is worthwhile taking the boat to the island suburb of **Lidingö** ❺, to visit **Millesgården** (tel: 08 446 75 90; www.millesgarden.se; May–Sept 11am–5pm, Oct–Apr Tue–Sun 11am–5pm), the summer home of sculptor Carl Milles and his wife, the Austrian painter Olga Granner. Here, Milles patiently reproduced the statues that had made him more famous in his adopted country of the US than in Sweden. His creations seem to defy gravity: they appear to soar and fly, emphasised by their position on terraces carved from the cliffs.

North of Stockholm

Less than an hour's drive north of Stockholm on the E4 lies **Uppsala** ❻, Sweden's ancient capital, seat of one of Europe's greatest universities. This is the birthplace of Ingmar Bergman and the setting for his film *Fanny and Alexander*. The town also has the largest Gothic cathedral to be found in Scandinavia, **Domkyrka** (www.uppsaladomkyrka.se; daily 8am–6pm; free). Its vaults, from 1435, house the shrine of Saint Erik, a former king and the patron saint of Sweden.

Across the town's lush parks rises **Uppsala Slott**, a fortress from the days of the Vasa dynasty, now housing the **Uppsala Museum of Art** (tel: 018 727 24 82; www.uppsalakonstmuseum.se; Tue–Sun noon–4pm, Wed until 8pm, Sat–Sun until 4.30pm; Wed after 4pm free). A few minutes north of the town lies **Gamla Uppsala** (Old Uppsala), 5th-century bastion of the Yngling dynasty. The three huge grave mounds of kings Aun, Egil and Adils (described in *Beowulf*) dominate the grave fields beyond the **Gamla Uppsala Museum** (tel: 018 23 93 12; www.

A blacksmith at the Birka Viking museum.

There are plenty of outdoor restaurants for alfresco refreshments on Gamla Stan.

raa.se; Apr–Sept daily 11am–5pm, Oct–Mar Mon, Wed, Sat–Sun noon–4pm), which does a good job of explaining the Viking world.

Near Uppsala, where the sea meets the forest, you'll find **Sigtuna** , Sweden's oldest town. In the 11th century this was the commercial centre for the Svea and Vandal tribes. Merchant ships from as far away as Asia dropped anchor here; monasteries and abbeys competed with one another in building glorious churches. Today, Sigtuna is a picturesque town with crooked lanes, quaint wooden houses and a miniature town hall. Tant Brun's café on the main pedestrian lane is a lovely place to stop for a cup of strong Swedish coffee and a freshly baked cinnamon bun.

South and west of Stockholm

To the south of Stockholm is **Norrköping** ❸, with its tree-lined avenues, outdoor cafés, 19th-century canalscape, trams and elegant architecture. The town's main attraction is **Kolmården Djurpark** ❸, Scandinavia's

Uppsala archway.

wildlife safari, natural habitat and amusement park supreme (tel: 010 708 7000; www.kolmarden.com; late Apr–late Sept 10am until 5–7pm).

Heading west of Stockholm towards Lake Mälaren's bays and inlets, you come to idyllic **Mariefred** ❹ and the impressive **Gripsholms Slott** (Castle; tel: 0159 101 94; mid-May–Sept daily 10am–4pm, mid-Apr–mid-May and Oct–Nov Sat–Sun noon–3pm; guided tour in English mid-May–Sept daily at 3pm), which contains the royal portrait collections and a marvellous theatre from the late 1700s. Best of all is the architecture of this fortress, begun in the 1370s and continually updated. Around the edge of the moat is a collection of runestones carved with serpents, ships and inscriptions. Mariefred is a lazy summer lake town, with cafés and restaurants to suit all tastes, and ferry connections to Stockholm.

Further west around the lakeshore is **Strängnäs** ❹, a delightful small town dominated by a magnificent Gothic cathedral. Next to the church at **Boglösa**, 20km (12 miles) north, are hundreds of Bronze Age rock carvings.

A Royal Treat: Drottningholm Palace

Often referred to as Sweden's "mini Versailles", the island palace of Drottningholm with its exquisite gardens and historic theatre is not to be missed.

The most popular place to visit in Stockholm's archipelago is Drottningholms Slott (tel: 08 402 62 80; www.kungahuset.se; May–Sept daily 10am–4.30pm, Apr daily 11am–3.30pm, Oct Fri–Sun 11am–3.30pm, Nov–Mar Sat–Sun noon–3.30pm; guided tours in English) on Lovön. Now the main home of the Swedish royal family, the 17th-century palace is a Unesco World Heritage site, surrounded by formal Baroque and rococo gardens of fountains, statues, flowerbeds, box hedges and a variety of trees.

Eleonora's castle

The palace was built for Eleonora, the widow of King Karl X, by the Tessin family of architects headed by Nicodemus the Elder (1615–81). Work began in 1662 and was completed by his son, Nicodemus the Younger.

Highlights

Although the royal family live at Drottningholm, much of the palace is open to the public.

Interior highlights include a magnificent Grand Staircase with trompe l'œil paintings by Johan Sylvius, the Baroque Karl X Gallery, Queen Hedwig Eleonora's State Bedroom with its richly painted ceiling, and the library of Queen Louisa Ulrika, who married King Adolf Fredrik in 1744.

In the parkland stands the exotic pagoda roofs and ornamental balconies of the Kina Slott (Chinese Pavilion; tel: 08 402 62 00; May–Aug daily 11am–4.30pm, Sept daily noon–3.30pm), a birthday present to Queen Louisa Ulrika from her husband. In one of four adjoining pavilions the king had his carpentry workshop.

In Kanton, a small village that was purposely established next to Kina Slott, silkworms that had been introduced perished in the freezing winter, thwarting the Swedish court's attempt to produce cheap silk.

The Drottningholms Slottsteater

The island's greatest treasure is undoubtedly the 18th-century Drottningholms Slottsteater (Court Theatre; tel: 08 759 04 06; www.dtm.se; May–Sept guided tours only). The theatre was designed for Queen Louisa Ulrika by Carl Fredrik Adelcrantz and opened in 1766.

The queen's son, Gustav III, was an actor and playwright who became known as the "Theatre King". He invited French troupes of actors to perform at Drottningholm, and the royal theatre rapidly became an important and influential centre for performing arts. Gustav went on to found Stockholm's Dramatic Theatre and developed a native theatre and opera.

The building fell into disrepair in the 19th century, then in the early 20th century it underwent extensive restoration. Today it is the oldest theatre in the world still using its original backdrops and stage machinery for productions.

In summer, the annual opera festival stages works from the time of the theatre's glory days, with the music performed on period instruments – attending one of these performances is a magical experience.

The State bedchamber in the Royal Palace.

STEAMING OUT AMONG THE SKERRIES

When summer comes, the Swedes set off by boat to the thousands of idyllic islands that dot the waterways between Stockholm and the Baltic.

Every summer thousands of Swedes in boats navigate carefully through waters loaded with the 24,000 islands, rocks and islets of the Stockholm archipelago. The brackish waters start in the centre of Stockholm and extend 80km (50 miles) out into the open Baltic Sea. Close to the mainland, the islands are larger and more lush, the bays and channels wider. Hidden here are idyllic island communities, farmlands and small forests. But as you travel further out, the scenery becomes more rugged, finally ending in sparse windblown islets formed by the last Ice Age.

Island retreats

In the middle of the 19th century affluent Stockholm families began to build their second homes along the shores of the various islands in the archipelago. Over the years, "commoners" had more money and leisure time and soon they, too, sought their way to the archipelago. The combination of wilderness, sea, fresh air and closeness to the city satisfied many leisure needs. Today, Swedes either own their cottages or rent them, and enjoy swimming, fishing, boating, nature walks and socialising with friends.

Many Swedes learn to sail from a very early age; getting out on the water is almost considered a birthright.

Crayfish parties, with much drinking of schnapps and singing of folk songs, are held throughout Sweden to celebrate the summer.

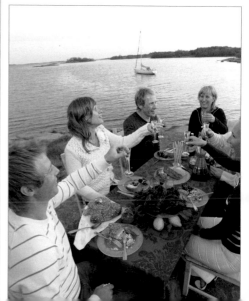

More than 50,000 second homes offering varying degrees of comfort are spread throughout Stockholm's archipelago.

Kayaking is also a great way of exploring the archipelago.

A QUICK GUIDE TO ISLAND-HOPPING

The archipelago can be explored on guided tours from Stockholm's city centre. But if you want to travel like the locals, then buy a *Waxholmsholmsbolaget's* 5 day travelcard from the Waxholm boat company (tel: 08 679 58 30; www.waxholmsbolaget.se), which allows you to see as many islands as you can, including:

Sandön: with its attractive sailing centre village of Sandhamn, sandy beaches and some good restaurants (3 hours by boat from Stockholm).

Fjäderholmarna: featuring a boat museum, fish-smoking plant, restaurants and crafts shops (20 minutes by boat).

Vaxholm: with its famous fortress (1 hour by boat).

Utö: where a 12th-century iron mine is the main attraction, a great place for bike-riding (3.5 hours by boat).

Sailing on Lake Malaren; such is the importance of water to the Swedes that one in ten residents owns a boat.

There are plenty of ferries to help you get around.

Valholm, one of the most popular islands in the archipelago.

SOUTHERN SWEDEN

Across the Öresund bridge from Denmark,
southern Sweden is home to the lively city of
Malmö. Castles and Stone Age sites abound, while
bathers and birdwatchers head for Öland.

Skåne is Sweden's most southerly province, so close to Denmark across the narrow sound that even the accent is faintly Danish. For centuries Swedes and Danes fought over this area, along with the provinces of Halland and Blekinge, until Sweden established its sovereignty in 1658. Since 2000, however, the two countries have been joined by the Öresund road and rail bridge that links Malmö and Copenhagen. The project has prompted a renaissance for southern Sweden as a centre of the Danish–Swedish Öresund region, with a total of 3 million people and one-fifth of the total combined GNP of Sweden and Denmark.

Skåne is often called Sweden's food store because of its rich farmland, mild climate and good fishing. Along the coast the landscape is undulating and lush, and especially spectacular in the southeast corner, Österlen. Inland, there are lakes and three large ridges with lovely walks.

Skåne is renowned for its castles and manor houses. There are said to be 240 in the province, most of which are in private ownership, but it is usually possible to walk round parts of the house and/or gardens such as at **Sofiero ❶**, 4km (2.5 miles) north of Helsingborg (tel: 042 10 25 00; www. sofiero.se; daily mid-Apr–mid-Sept 10am–6pm, mid-Sept–mid-Apr park

only). Built in 1857, Sofiero was used by King Gustav VI Adolf as his summer palace until his death in 1973. He was a keen botanist, as the gardens show – they were awarded the title of Europe's most beautiful park in 2010.

Malmö: city of the south

Malmö ❷ is Sweden's third city, a lively, multicultural place with a population of about 304,000 and a bubbling restaurant scene. In the 16th century, Malmö competed with Copenhagen to be Scandinavia's leading capital. In those days it

Main Attractions
Moderna Muséet, Malmö
Lund Cathedral
Öland
Kalmar Castle
Glasriket (Glass Kingdom)

Cycling in Lund.

The town hall, Malmö.

was an important port, not far from rich fishing grounds. Today, the harbour is still busy and many of the old buildings remain. **Malmöhus**, the dominating castle built by King Christian III when Skåne was still part of Denmark, is Scandinavia's oldest remaining Renaissance castle. It houses the **Malmö Museer** (Malmö Museums; tel: 040 34 44 00; daily 10am–5pm), which include the Art Museum, history exhibitions, an aquarium, the Science and Technology/Maritime Museum and the **Kommendants Hus** (Commander's House).

From the same period is **Rådhus** (City Hall; tel: 040 34 34 34; Mon–Fri 8am–4.30pm), which you will find in **Stortorget**, one of the largest squares in Scandinavia. It was built in 1546 in genuine Dutch Renaissance style. In 1860 it was given a facelift with niches, bays, allegorical paintings and colonnades. Northeast from Stortorget is **St Petri Kyrka**, Göran Olsgatan 1, built in the Baltic Gothic style and dating from the 13th century, although its towers were built in the 15th century and its copper spires in 1890 (www.svenskakyrkan.se). This elegant cathedral features a

beautiful altar area created by sculptors in 1611.

A particularly idyllic place to sit and relax is **Lilla Torg** (Little Square), with its cobblestones, carefully restored houses and 16th-century charm. Through an arch on the south side of the square is Hemanska Gården. Once a merchant's home and trading yard, it now houses the **Form/Design Center** (tel: 040 664 51 50; www.formdesigncenter. com; Tue–Sat 11am–5pm, Sun noon–4pm; free), where Swedish industrial design and handicrafts are displayed.

Walking east from Lilla Torg, make sure you don't miss Malmö's exciting new cultural hub, the **Moderna Muséet** (Ola Billgrens plats 2–4; tel: 040 685 7937; www.modernamuseet.se/malmo; Tue–Sun 11am–6pm), which opened at the end of 2009. This former power station now contains one of the most comprehensive 20th-century art collections in Scandinavia, and hosts changing exhibitions of local and international artists.

Malmö's most impressive modern building is without doubt the **Turning Torso**, Sweden's tallest building at 190 metres (620ft), designed by Spanish architect Santiago Calatrava (www.turn-ingtorso.se). This unique structure, which twists 90° from bottom to top, has revitalised the West Harbour area of the city, now a popular summer dining spot.

Towards Helsingborg

Heading northeast from Malmö, **Lund** ❸ is a university town with a fine cathedral, **Domkyrkan**, built in the 12th century. Don't miss **Kulturen** (Cultural History Museum; Tegnérplatsen; tel: 046 35 04 00; www.kulturen.com; May–Aug daily 11am–5pm, Sept–Apr Tue–Sun noon–4pm), an open-air museum with dozens of buildings, silver, textiles, ceramics and art. Along with the University of Uppsala, Lund is one of the two ancient Swedish universities. About 30km (19 miles) north along the coast, **Glumslöv** ❹ offers memorable views. From the hill above the church, on a clear day you can see 30 churches and seven towns, including Copenhagen and Helsingør in Denmark.

Helsingborg ❺, 60km (37 miles) north of Malmö, is an interesting town of cobbled streets, dominated by the ruined castle, **Kärnan**. Frequent ferries to Helsingør in Denmark leave from its busy harbour. **Höganäs** ❻, 20km (12 miles) north, is devoted to potters and artists. The large pottery merits a visit.

Along the south coast

Some 40km (25 miles) southwest of Malmö are the summer idylls of **Skanör** and **Falsterbo** ❼. **Skanörs Ljung** is recommended for bird-lovers, particularly in September and October, when a large number of migrating birds gather.

Southeast of Kivik is **Bredarör** ❽, site of the Bronze Age **Kiviksgraven** (King's Grave). Scientists still debate the mysterious markings on the stones, unearthed in 1748, which are different from any others found in the region.

Kristianstad ❾ is the birthplace of the Swedish film industry, which started around 1910. The original studio is intact and is now a museum where you can watch old films on video (**Filmmuséet**; Östra Storgatan 53; tel:

044 13 57 29; mid-June–mid-Aug Mon–Fri noon–5pm, mid-Aug–mid-June Sun noon–5pm; free). Nearby, **Kristianstad Vattenriket** (Water Kingdom) is a rich wetland on the Helge River, with a diversity of birds, wildlife and plants.

Blekinge is a tiny province with sandy beaches and Sweden's most southerly archipelago. It is excellent for sea fishing. You can enjoy peaceful angling in some of the lakes, or good sport for salmon in the Mörrum River. Canoeing is popular. Driving to Blekinge from Skåne, you first reach **Sölvesborg** ❿ , and the ruins of 13th-century **Sölvesborg Castle** (Slott).

Mörrum ⓫ , 30km (19 miles) north of Sölvesborg, is noted for its salmon fishing: at **Mörrums Kronolaxfiske** you can see salmon and trout at different stages of their development; fishing fans can cast a line here too (tel: 0454 501 23; www.morrum.com).

The biggest town in Blekinge is **Karlskrona** ⓬, a naval centre built in the 17th century, with wide streets and impressive buildings. In the Björkholmen district you'll find quaint 18th-century cottages built by ships'

Map on page 256

TIP

Råå, on the outskirts of Helsingborg, is a picturesque fishing village with an excellent inn.

Lund's 12th-century cathedral.

FACT

In 2017, Halmstad, a town 80km (50 miles) north of Helsingborg, will be one of the ports welcoming the Tall Ships' Races, a spectacular event with large sailing ships from many countries participating. Other harbours on the 2017 route include Kotka and Turku (Finland), Klaipèda (Lithuania) and Szczecin (Poland).

carpenters. The nearby village of **Kristianopel** 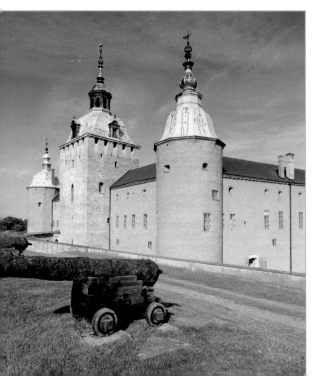 is renowned for its smoked herring.

Öland island

The island of **Öland**, off the east coast, is one of the most visited areas of Sweden and, with its diverse landscape and superb beaches, it is a paradise for birdwatchers, nature-lovers and sun-worshippers. Above the main town of **Borgholm** ⓮ rise the huge ruins of **Borgholm Slott** (Castle), a once splendid residence from the 12th century (tel: 0485 12333; www.borgholmsslott.se; May–Aug daily 10am–6pm, Apr and Sept 10am–4pm).

The island has many ancient burial places, and there are remains of 16 fortified dwellings from earlier times. The most interesting is **Eketorp** ⓯ (tel: 0485 66 20 00; www.eketorp.se; mid-June–mid-Aug 10.30am–6pm) in the south, which has been reconstructed and now hums with medieval re-enactors and craftspeople in summer. Sweden's prime bird-watching can be enjoyed at the **Ottenby Bird Station**, on the island's southerly tip, where more than 370 species have

been recorded. Nearby, you can see **Karl Xs Mur** (Karl X's Wall), impressive for its sheer size; it was built in 1650 to distinguish Ottenby's domain and keep out the peasants' animals. **Stora Alvaret**, an expanse of bare limestone soil in central southern Öland, is a starkly beautiful landscape offering rare flowers and flocks of cranes in the autumn.

Kalmar ⓰, one of Sweden's oldest cities, was of great importance in the Swedish–Danish wars. Sweden's best-preserved Renaissance castle, **Kalmar Slott** (tel: 0480 451 490; www.kalmarslott.se; Apr and Oct–Dec Sat–Sun 10am–4pm, May–mid-June daily 10am–4pm, July–Aug 10am–6pm, Sept and Jan–Mar 10am–4pm; English guided tours in summer), was begun in the 12th century but was completely renovated during the 16th century by the Vasa kings. The castle's coffered ceilings, panelled halls, fresco paintings and magnificent stonework have inspired the Renaissance Festival, held every July, featuring tournament games, market, music and theatre.

Kingdom of glass

Northwest of Kalmar, about 20km (12 miles) is **Orrefors** ⓱, part of Sweden's **Glasriket** (Glass Kingdom). The first glass was melted in Sweden in 1556 but it was not established as an industry until 1742, when **Kosta**, the oldest works, was founded to the west of Orrefors. Today, the Kosta, Orrefors and Åfors glassworks have merged to create one mighty glass-making company: you will find its wares marketed under both the brand names "Kosta Boda" and "Orrefors". Most of the 13 glassworks in the area are open to visitors for demonstrations, and many have shops – for further information, see the Glasriket website www.glasriket.se.

Also look out for *hyttsill* ("glassworks herring") evenings. In bygone times the glassworks were a social centre where locals would gather to bake herring and potatoes in the furnace, with music provided by an accordionist or fiddler. Some glassworks have revived this tradition for visitors.

Kalmar Castle.

Gotland: the Sunshine Island

With its medieval towns, sandy beaches and curious rock formations, tranquil Gotland – the largest island in the Baltic – is a favourite holiday spot.

Gotland is an island of gaunt rocks, forests, wild flowers, cliffs and sandy beaches, blessed with more hours of sunshine than anywhere else in the country. Swedes naturally flock here for their summer holidays.

Gotland was created over thousands of years as the animals and plants of the ancient Silurian sea slowly sank into the sediment that was to become the limestone platform of modern Gotland. Million-year-old fossils and the island's monumental sea-stacks *(raukar)* can still be found on the coast.

Visby

In the Viking Age the island was a busy trading post. **Visby** 🔞, the principal centre of population, later became a prosperous Hanseatic town. Great stone houses were erected, churches were founded and a city wall was built. Today, 3km (2 miles) of the medieval limestone wall remains virtually intact, interspersed with 44 towers and numerous gates. It is now a Unesco World Heritage site.

Limestone has created one of the island's major attractions – the impressive subterranean tunnels and stalactite caves of **Lummelundagrottan** 🔟 (tel: 0498 27 30 50; www.lummelundagrottan.se; May–Sept daily; guided tours only), 13km (8 miles) to the north of Visby, which should not be missed. Dress warmly, as it's 8°C (46°F) inside.

Fårö

About 50km (30 miles) north of Visby lies **Fårö** 🔟, the "island of sheep". Take a ferry to the island from Fårösund, and enjoy sites such as Gamlehamn, a medieval harbour, and the ruins of a chapel to St Olof. You can also see one of Gotland's most bizarrely shaped *raukar*, "The Camel", and visit the beach of Sundersand. After you have been here a little while, you will begin to understand why Fårö was Ingmar Bergman's favourite place.

Horsing around

Sweden's most primitive horse, the Russ, has lived in the forests of the island from time immemorial. The name Russ comes from the Old Norse *hross*, and it is thought that the horse is a descendant of the wild Tarpan. Modern Gotland ponies make excellent riding ponies for children and harness-racing ponies. They also excel at show jumping, dressage, and eventing.

You can see them, only 123–126cm (46–52 inches) tall, roaming in the enclosed Lojsta moor where they live all year round.

Myriad churches

Wherever you travel in Gotland, you'll come across at least one of its 92 medieval churches. At **Romakloster** 🔟, in the centre of the island, there is a ruined monastery from the 12th century. There are many other relics of the past, including runic stones and burial mounds.

If you reach Gotland's southernmost tip, you'll see some of the most impressive *raukar* on the island.

Stana Kerlso in Gotland, the perfect getaway island.

SWEDEN'S WEST COAST

From the sandy beaches of Halland to the bustling city of Göteborg and the rocky shores of Bohuslän, the west coast has long been a summer playground for Swedes.

T he west coast of Sweden, generously dotted with beaches and fishing villages, is 400km (250 miles) of glorious coastline divided in two by the city of Göteborg (Gothenburg). It has been a favourite holiday spot since the early 20th century. The best beaches are in the southern province of Halland. North of Göteborg, in Bohuslän, is a majestic coast of granite rocks and islands.

The E6 connects all the larger cities, but follow the small coastal roads to discover the gems. Starting along the coast in the northwestern corner of the county of Skåne, a number of small towns offer views into the past. **Gamla Viken ❶** 15km (9 miles) north of Helsingborg on Highway 22, is a picturesque fishing village. **Torekov**, at the tip of the next peninsula, has a seaside golf course and boats to the island of **Hallands Väderö**, where you can spot seals basking offshore.

Halland coast

Halmstad ❷, the largest town in Halland and Sweden's "golf capital", lies on the River Nissan. **Halmstads Slott** (Castle), the provincial governor's residence, was built in the 17th century by the Danish king Kristian IV. Other sights include **St Nikolai**, a 13th-century church. **Tylösand**, 8km (5 miles) west of Halmstad, is

a popular holiday resort with a predominantly sandy beach and two golf courses. There are good beaches at **Östra Strand**, **Ringenäs** and **Haverdalsstrand**.

Falkenberg ❸, 40km (25 miles) north of Halmstad, is on the Ätran, a river famous for its salmon. The old part of the town with its 18th-century wooden houses and cobbled streets is centred on the 14th-century **St Laurenti Church**. There is an old toll bridge (*tullbron*) from 1756 and Sweden's oldest pottery, **Törngrens**

Main Attractions

Tylösand beach resort
Varberg
Maritiman ship museum, Göteborg
Liseberg amusement park, Göteborg
Marstrand
Islands of Tjörn and Orust
Smögen harbour

Fiskebäckskil.

Krukmakeri, run by the Törngren family since 1789 (tel: 0346 103 54; www.torngrens-krukmakeri.se; Mon–Fri 10am–6pm, Sat 10am–2pm). Good beaches are found at **Olofsby** (north of the town) and **Skrea Strand** (south of the town).

Continue 30km (19 miles) north on the E6 to **Varberg ❹**, a bustling place combining spa, resort, port and commercial centre with a ferry service to Grenå in Denmark. **Varbergs Fästning** (Fortress) stands beside the water and houses a youth hostel, restaurant, apartments and a **museum** (tel: 0340 828 30; www.museumhalland.se; mid-June–mid-Aug 10am–6pm, mid-Aug–mid-June Tue–Sun noon–4pm). Pride of place goes to the Bocksten Man, the only preserved figure in the world wearing a complete costume from the Middle Ages. Reminders of Varberg's late 19th-century development as a spa resort include **Societetshus** (1883), an elaborate wooden pavilion in the park, and the bathing station (1903), a rectangular wooden structure open to the sea, with changing huts and deck chairs round the sides. After a quick plunge in the pool, bathers can relax over coffee and waffles.

North to Särö

Heading 30km (19 miles) north towards **Kungsbacka**, you will pass the most out-of-character building along the entire coast. **Tjolöholm Castle ❺** (tel: 0300 40 46 00; www.tjoloholm.se; June–Aug daily 11am–4pm, Feb–May and Sept–mid-Nov by guided tour only Sat–Sun noon, 1.30pm and 3pm) was built in the early 20th century in an English Tudor style, with a splendid Art Nouveau interior.

Instead of beaches, a dramatic landscape of rocks, inlets and islands takes over at the little seaside resort of **Särö ❻** (immediately north of Kungsbacka). In the early 19th century Särö was a fashionable resort, popular with the Swedish royal family. It remains in a time warp. You can walk along the Strandpromenaden and

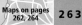

through **Särö Västerskog**, one of the oldest oak woods on the west coast.

Göteborg

Göteborg ❼ (Gothenburg) is the second-largest city in Sweden, with 540,000 inhabitants. Once a gritty industrial seaport, Göteborg has evolved into a sophisticated 21st-century city, with a thriving cultural life (including a growing reputation for world-class cuisine) and beautiful parks (there are reputedly 175 sq metres (1,880 sq ft) of green space per citizen). Dutch architects planned the city in the 17th century for King Gustav II Adolf, and it grew in stature during the 18th century, when the Swedish East India Company began shipping luxury goods from the Orient. Göteborg is still Scandinavia's largest port: the harbour area is its soul and a good place to start your sightseeing.

The bold **Göteborgsoperan** ❹ (Opera House; tel: 031 13 13 00; http://sv.opera.se) stands on the water just west of the commercial centre. Built in ship-like style in 1994, it is well worth a visit for its architecture alone. Near the Opera is Göteborg's **Maritiman** ❺ (Maritime Centre; tel: 031 10 59 50; www.maritiman.se; May and Sept daily 11am–5pm June–Aug daily 10am–6pm, Apr and Oct some weekends) on Packhuskajen. The world's largest floating ship museum, it features 20 ships, including a submarine, destroyer and lightship. Göteborg got its own Ferris wheel, the 60-metre (200ft) high **Wheel of Göteborg** ❻ in Lisebergs Nojespark (http://liseberg.se; June–mid-Aug 10–11am until 10–11pm, May and mid-Aug–Sept Wed–Sun 11am–3pm until 8–10pm, Oct irregular days) in 2010, giving great views of the area.

The heart of Göteborg lies along Östra Hamngatan and Kungsportsavenyn. Start at the northern end of Östra Hamngatan; heading south you will pass **Nordstan**, one of Northern Europe's largest covered shopping centres (www.nordstan. se). Along the intersecting streets of Norra and Södra Hamngatan are dozens of small and inviting

Göteborg's waterfront Opera House.

Take a ride on the Wheel of Göteborg for great views of the city.

boutiques. Cross Stora Hamnkanalen (Great Harbour Canal) and continue south to **Kungsportsplatsen**, where you can pop into the **Göteborgs Turistbyrå D** (Tourist Office; tel: 031 368 42 00, daily 9.30–10am until 2–8pm).

Across the street is **Saluhallen E**, a large indoor marketplace (1886–9) stocked with Swedish specialities such as seafood, cheese and meats (www.storasaluhallen.se). This is a good place to enjoy a cup of coffee or a full lunch.

Kungsportsplatsen is also the place to embark on a **Paddan** (Swedish for "toad"), one of the flat-bottomed sightseeing boats that cruise through the old moat, along 17th-century canals, under 20 bridges, out into the harbour and back again (tel: 031 60 96 70; www.stromma.se/paddan; mid-Apr–mid-Oct).

From Kungsportsplatsen, cross the moat into Kungsportsavenyn – known as "**Avenyn**" **F** (The Avenue), a long, wide boulevard lined with trees, restaurants, pubs and cafés. Halfway along the Avenyn, you are just a block away from the **Röhsska**

Muséet G (Vasagatan 37–39; tel: 031 36 83 150; http://rohsska.se; Tue noon–8pm, Wed–Fri noon–5pm, Sat–Sun 11am–5pm), the Swedish museum for design and handicrafts.

At the southern end of the Avenyn is Göteborg's cultural centre, **Götaplatsen**, with the Poseidon fountain by the Swedish sculptor Carl Milles. Götaplatsen is flanked by the **Konstmuseum H** (Art Museum; tel: 031 368 35 00; http://konstmuseum.goteborg.se; Tue and Thur 11am–6pm, Wed 11am–8pm, Fri–Sun 11am–5pm), with an extensive collection of Scandinavian art, including work by Munch, Zorn, as well as works by Rembrandt, Rubens and the French Impressionists. Also on the square is the **Konserthus I** (Concert Hall), home of the Göteborg Symphony Orchestra.

Liseberg J (tel: 031 40 01 00; http://liseberg.se; late Apr–early Sept and Christmas), in the middle of town, is the largest amusement park in Scandinavia, with 43 attractions including AtmosFear, the highest freefall plummet in Europe and, brand new in

2015, the star-shaped Mechanica with six gondolas.

Also great for families is **Univer- seum Ⓚ** (tel: 031 335 64 50; www. universeum.se; daily 10am–6pm mid- June–mid-Aug 10am–8pm), an impressive science and nature centre with shark tunnel and rainforest zone.

For a calmer experience, wander through the picturesque little 18th- century neighbourhood of Haga on the way to the **Botaniska Trädgården Ⓛ** (Botanical Gardens; www.gotbot.se; daily 9am–sunset) or **Slottsskogen Ⓜ**, just two of Göteborg's 20 parks (www. goteborg.se/slottsskogen).

The rugged coast

The province of Bohuslän begins north of Göteborg. To see the coast, head 15km (9 miles) west from Kungälv on route 168 past Tjuvkil, where you can catch a ferry to **Mar- strand Ⓑ**, a car-free town and a popu- lar holiday resort and sailing centre. **Carlstens Fästning** (Fortress) domi- nates the town and offers the best views of the island.

Beyond Marstrand lie the islands of Tjörn and Orust, connected by bridge to the mainland. **Tjörn Ⓨ** is beauti- ful, with some barren areas inland and a fascinating coastline. A magnificent curved bridge links Tjörn and **Orust Ⓩ**. This island, the third-largest in Sweden, has its quota of fishing villages, includ- ing Mollösund, Ellös and Käringön.

Returning to the mainland, take a ferry across the **Gullmarn**, Sweden's only genuine fjord, from **Fiskebäck- skil Ⓚ** to **Lysekil Ⓛ**. Lysekil comes to life in the summer with boat excur- sions to the islands and sea fishing trips. **Havets Hus** (sea aquarium; tel: 0523 66 81 61; www.havetshus.se; mid-June–late Aug daily 10am–6pm, late Aug–mid-Oct and mid-Feb–mid- June 10am–4pm, Jan–mid-Feb and Nov–mid-Dec Sat–Sun 10am–6pm) includes a tunnel aquarium contain- ing rays and sharks.

North of Lysekil on the Sotenäs peninsula, the small harbour of

Smögen Ⓥ is a favourite stop for boats. The main attraction is the wooden, waterside boardwalk, where you can shop, stroll and lounge. The other attraction is fresh shrimp. Watch a fish auction and then go round the corner to buy some of the catch.

At **Åby Säteri Ⓦ**, 17km (11 miles) northeast of Smögen, is **Nordens Ark** (tel: 0523 795 45; www.nordensark.se; daily mid-June–mid-Aug 10am–7pm, Apr–mid-June and mid-Aug–Sept 10am–5pm, Jan–Mar and Oct–Dec 10am–4pm), a nature park featuring endangered species and old breeds of Nordic farm animals.

Towards Norway

The last town before the Norwegian frontier is **Strömstad Ⓧ**, a health resort noted for its long hours of sunshine. Strömstad shrimps are considered by the local inhabitants to be in a class of their own, with a distinctive mild flavour. The district has more than a touch of Norwegian about it, having been part of Norway until 1717.

Smögen's wooded waterside boardwalk.

SWEDEN'S GREAT LAKES

Two of Europe's largest lakes, Vänern and Vättern, lie at the heart of southern Sweden. In this area of farmland and forests, painted churches, grand castles and literary hideaways abound.

Two enormous lakes, Vänern and Vättern, dominate the map of Sweden. The larger of the two is Vänern, a vast stretch of water with an area of 5,585 sq km (2,156 sq miles) and the largest lake in Western Europe. Its western shore embraces two provinces, Dalsland and Värmland.

Dalsland is a province of neat farms and prosperous small towns and villages, with empty roads running through its forests. The greatest attraction here is nature and, thus, the most interesting activities are outdoors: namely, camping, hiking and canoeing. The upland area of **Kroppefjällen** ❶ is a nature reserve, and one of the best ways to explore the region is to hike along the 15km (9-mile) **Karl XIIs Väg** (Karolinerleden), a historic walking trail; maps can be obtained from the tourist office in Mellerud (Storgatan 13, tel: 0530 189 00; www.vastsverige.com).

A local feature is the **Dalslands Kanal**, a network of interconnected lakes and rivers. It was designed by Nils Ericsson and built between 1864 and 1868 to provide better transport for the local ironworks and sawmills. Today, it is popular for sailing and canoeing.

The aqueduct at **Håverud** ❷, 14km (9 miles) north of Mellerud, is a dramatic piece of engineering. Made of iron and 33 metres (108ft) long, it carries the canal over the rapids of the River Upperud.

Along the Klarälven

The Värmland region is covered with spruce and pine and crisscrossed with narrow lakes and rivers; the **Klarälven** is among its most beautiful. The river begins turbulently in Norway, where it is called Trysilelva, but gradually becomes broader, winding and sluggish before emptying into Lake Vänern near the province's largest town, **Karlstad** ❸. Highlights of Karlstad include the cathedral (1730), the longest arched stone bridge in Sweden (168 metres/550ft), and a popular park,

Main Attractions

Nobel Museum
Örebro
Mariestad
Läckö Castle
Trollhättan
Karlsborg Fortress
Göta Kanal

The scenic Fryk Valley.

Mariebergsskogen. The Klarälven was the last Swedish river used for floating logs. The practice ended in 1991, but in **Dyvelsten** ❹, 17km (10 miles) north of Karlstad, the **Flottningsmuseum** (Log Rafting Museum; tel: 054 701 19 20; Mon–Fri 10am–6pm, Wed 10am–8pm, Sat–Sun 11am–6pm) shows how it was done. You can drift down the gentle Klarälven yourself on a self-assembled raft: contact the Karlstad tourist office (Västra Torggatan 26; tel: 054 540 24 70; http://visitkarlstad.se) for details.

At **Ransäter** ❺, 40km (25 miles) north of Karlstad on the Klarälven, the **Hembygdsgården** (Heritage Village; tel: 0552 303 43) includes museums devoted to mining, forestry, agriculture and rural life, which paint a fascinating picture of the Värmland of yesteryear. Ransäter hosts an annual folk music festival in June and the largest accordion festival in Scandinavia in July.

Nobel laureates and inventors

West of Ransäter, on the eastern shore of Mellan-Fryken, is **Mårbacka** ❻ (tel: 0565 310 27; www.marbacka.com; guided tour only July daily 10am–5pm, June and Aug daily 11am–4pm, rest of the year mostly Sat 1pm), the manor home of Swedish writer Selma Lagerlöf, the first woman to receive a Nobel

Prize for literature, in 1909. Through her books, she made famous the Fryk Valley and lakes. On the western side of the lake is **Rottneros Park** ❼ (tel: 0565 602 95; www.rottnerospark.se; mid-June–July 10am–6pm, late May–mid-June and Aug–early Sept 9–10am until 4–5pm), whose elegant manor house appears as Ekeby in Lagerlöf's *The Story of Gösta Berling*. This beautiful park has an arboretum and works by Scandinavian sculptors, including Milles, Eriksson and Vigeland.

North of Lake Vänern, the bedrock is rich in minerals, and this area has long been associated with Sweden's early industrial development. Many Americans make the pilgrimage to **Filipstad** ❽, which has the mausoleum of John Ericsson, the gifted inventor and engineer. **Björkborn Herrgård** ❾, near Karlskoga, was the home of Swedish inventor Alfred Nobel. The manor house is now a museum, **Nobelmuséet** (tel: 0586 834 94; http://nobelmuseetikarlskoga.se; open for group visits and during summer holidays). At **Kristinehamn** ❿, 24km (15 miles) west of Karlskoga, a 15-metre (49ft) high sculpture by Picasso is the most striking feature on Lake Vänern (www.visitkristinehamn.se).

To the east, in the province of Närke, is **Örebro** ⓫, with a dramatic 17th-century lakeside **castle** (tel: 019 21 21 21; guided tours July–Aug several daily, rest of the year Sat–Sun 1pm).

Between the lakes

The region separating Lake Vänern from Lake Vättern offers rich pickings for the visitor. This is the province of Västergötland. In 1746 the indefatigable Swedish botanist Carolus Linnaeus said: "Truly no one could ever imagine such splendour as in Västergötland who had not seen it for himself."

Heading south along the eastern shore of Vänern, you come to **Mariestad** ⓬, dominated by the spire of the 17th-century Renaissance-style cathedral, one of the few churches of this period remaining in Sweden.

Most Swedes learn in school that the king who first united the Svea and Göta tribes, Olof Skötkonung (994–1022), was baptised in 1008 at Husaby Källa (Husaby Spring) at the southern tip of Kinnekulle. True or not, Husaby is considered to be the cradle of the Swedish state. Next to the spring, 12th-century **Husaby Church** ⓭ (tel: 0511 285 00; May–Aug Mon–Fri 8am–8pm, Sat–Sun 9am–8pm, Apr and Sept Mon–Fri 8am–4pm, Sat–Sun 9am–4pm) is an imposing three-spired edifice with beautiful ceiling paintings inside.

Nestled into Kinneviken (Kinne Bay), 51km (32 miles) south of Mariestad, is **Lidköping** ⓮, a town founded in 1446 and once renowned for its porcelain. Its most famous company, **Rörstrand**, the maker of the Nobel china, no longer has a factory here (its fine china is now manufactured in Hungary and Sri Lanka), but there is a museum (tel: 0510 250 80; Mon–Fri 10am–7pm, Sat 10am–4pm, Sun noon–4pm), a factory shop and a café. Lidköping has other fine cafés, including the renowned Garströms Konditori, established in 1859, on the main square (www.garstroms.se).

Fun at Läckö Castle, near Lidköping.

A guided tour of Rottneros Park.

TIP

On the east of Lake Vättern, historic sites of note include the stone of Rök at Rökeskyrka with its 800 runes (E4 north of Ödeshög) and Alvastra Kloster, Sweden's first Cistercian monastery (route 50 north of Ödeshög).

North of Lidköping on the Kållandsö peninsula stands the restored Baroque-style 17th-century **Läckö Slott** ⑮ (tel: 0510 48 46 60; www.lackoslott.se; guided tour only May–Sept daily), one of the most impressive castles in Sweden. In summer it holds cultural exhibitions and is a venue for outdoor concerts.

Trollhättan ⑯, at the southern tip of Lake Vänern (www.trollhattan.se), is the hometown of Saab Automobile and has a rich industrial heritage: it's also known as "Trollywood" thanks to its film production! The town has long been famous for the magnificent 32-metre (105ft) falls of the Göta River. Today, the river is diverted to generate electricity and the falls are silent. But during the annual Falls Festival in July it is released to follow the old course, providing an impressive spectacle (www.fallensdagar.com).

The southern part of Västergötland is still the heartland of Sweden's textile industry, with the focal point at **Borås** ⑰, where there is a **Textilmuséet** (Textile Museum; tel: 033 35 89 50; http://textilmuseet.se; Tue noon–8pm, Wed–Fri noon–5pm Sat–Sun noon–4pm).

Karlsborg Fortress.

Around Lake Vättern

Lake Vättern covers an area of 1,912 sq km (738 sq miles). Near the southern tip of the lake, on the west side, is the 14th-century timber-built **Habo Kyrka** ⑱ (Habo Church), southwest of Habo village. It features an outstanding painted interior, the work of Johan Christian Peterson and Johan Kinnerus, between 1741 and 1743, illustrating Luther's catechism and biblical scenes.

Travelling north along the lake, stop at the small waterside resort of **Hjo** ⑲ to enjoy freshly smoked whitefish. Then tour the town in a horse-drawn carriage, or cruise on the lake in the 1892 steamer *Trafik*. In summer, Hjo hosts Scandinavia's largest craft festival. **Skara** ⑳, 50km (31 miles) to the west of Hjo, has Sweden's second-oldest cathedral (after Lund), dating from the 11th century. **Skara Sommarland** (tel: 010 708 7000; www.sommarland.se; June 10am–5pm, July10am–Aug 10am until 5–7pm), 8km (5 miles) east of Skara on route 49, is a delight for children, with numerous attractions from lunar vehicles to a giant water park.

Some 10km (6 miles) southeast of Skara is **Hornborgasjön**, a wildlife area with over 100 species of birds and a stopover for migrating cranes.

Karlsborg fortress

Karlsborg ㉑, on the western shore of Lake Vättern, 30km (19 miles) north of Hjo, is dominated by its huge fortress (**Karlsborg Fästning**; tel: 0505 173 50; www.karlsborgsturism.se; all year, June–Aug daily guided tours). In 1809, when Sweden lost Finland to the Russians, the Swedes decided to build two fortresses to house the government and the treasury. The first, at Karlsborg, was started in 1819 and required 250,000 tons of limestone. It was quarried by prison labour on the eastern side of the lake and ferried across by boat. The castle has walls 2 metres (6.5ft) thick with 5km (3 miles) of ramparts, but by the time the building was finished, in 1909, fortresses were out of fashion. The second castle was never built.

Crossing Sweden by Canal

One of the most leisurely ways of sampling the country's history is to cruise along the Göta Kanal between Stockholm and Göteborg.

Kings and industrialists alike spent centuries pondering how to link inland Sweden's lakes and rivers, from Stockholm on the east coast to Göteborg on the west coast, before Baltzar von Platen, naval officer and statesman, succeeded in the early 19th century.

At the time, the country needed this new east–west artery to transport timber, iron and food, and to build up local industry. For 22 years, 58,000 soldiers laboured to build the 190km (118-mile) long **Göta Kanal** ㉒. The canal was designated an "International Historic Civil Engineering Landmark", giving it the same status as the Golden Gate Bridge and the Panama Canal, and in 2007 was officially recognised as Sweden's greatest feat of engineering. Today, there is no commercial traffic on the canal... but there are plenty of pleasure craft!

A typical cruise

For the visitor, the classic way is to take a cruise between Stockholm and Göteborg on one of the vintage vessels operated by the Göta Kanal Rederiaktiebolaget (Göta Kanal Steamship Company; tel: 031 806 315; www.stromma.se/en/gota-canal). The oldest of the three vessels is M/S Juno, built in 1874.

The four-day cruise westbound starts from Stockholm, finishing the first day at the village of Trosa. On the second day the boat passes through Mem – where the canal was officially inaugurated in 1832 – before reaching Berg, where there's time to visit the historic monastery church at nearby Vreta, once the richest religious establishment in Sweden.

The route crosses two picturesque lakes, Asplången and Roxen, where there are ospreys and herons during the breeding season. The canal then takes you through 15 locks in 3km (2 miles), lifting you 37 metres (120ft). The next night is spent at Motala, a town founded by Baltzar von Platen.

On the third morning the boat crosses Lake Vättern to Karlsborg, site of a huge fortress, and

Forsvik, an old metalworking village and the site of the canal's oldest lock, built in 1813. Here, the boat is often greeted by a local family singing hymns and offering passengers wild flowers. This 100-year-old custom originated as a blessing for passengers as they embarked on the once hazardous crossing of Vättern. In the evening the boat reaches Sjötorp, marking the beginning of Lake Vänern.

At the south side of Lake Vänern, the boat enters the gorge at Trollhättan for the last day of the voyage down the Göta River to Göteborg.

Under your own steam

It's all very leisurely, but if you prefer to take a more hands-on approach, how about chartering your own motor boat? It's also possible to hire a canoe and paddle along the waterway – several companies offer a pick-up service so you don't have to retrace your route.

For landlubbers, the Göta Kanal is Sweden's most popular cycling path. For all these forms of do-it-yourself transport, see the website www.gotakanal.se.

M/S Juno, the oldest ship to cruise on the Göta Kanal.

DALARNA

Dalarna is Sweden's folklore province, as famous for its scarlet Dala horses as its music and merrymaking at Midsummer. Winter attracts skiers challenged by championship events.

Dalarna represents all that is quintessentially Swedish. With its colourful costumes, centuries-old traditions of music and dance, Midsummer festivals and evocative rural landscape, its folklore and beauty attract an increasing number of visitors each year (www.visitdalarna.se).

Dalarna is the third-largest tourist site in Sweden, after Stockholm and Göteborg. The culture that gave us the red-painted Dalahäst (Dala horse) and inspired two of Sweden's most beloved artists, Carl Larsson and Anders Zorn, can best be experienced in the twilight of *fäbodar*, the old pasture cottages nestled in the hills, in the company of elderly but amazingly energetic fiddlers.

Musical traditions

Music is one of the most defining characteristics of Dala culture. Music on Lake Siljan (Musik vid Siljan; www.musikvidsiljan.se) is a huge annual festival, held in late June/early July, that attracts visitors from all over Sweden and abroad. Distinctly Dala are the *spelmansstämmor*, folk musicians' rallies, particularly the one held each July in **Bingsjö ❶**, 30km (19 miles) east of Rättvik, where fiddlers turn the classic polka into a musical performance that rivals any blues master.

An exotic setting for listening to music is **Dalhalla** (tel: 0248 79 79 50; http://dalhalla.se, see website for seasonal opening times), a cavernous outdoor concert arena set in the depths of an abandoned limestone quarry near the town of **Rättvik ❷**. The annual summer festivals here feature artists of international standing.

Farm cottages

For a change of pace, the gentle quiet of the region's *fäbodar* offer a taste of back-to-the-land living. These pasture cottages and surrounding buildings, dating from the 15th and 16th centuries, are found all over Sweden but are most often

Carving Dalahästen (wooden horses) in Nusnäs.

associated with Dalarna. They constitute a living museum, where cows are milked, butter is churned, *messmör* (a type of goat's cheese) is made, and *tunnbröd* (thin bread) is baked. Many *fäbodar* also sell products or serve food.

One worth visiting is **Ljusbodarnas Fäbod** (tel: 073 048 06 08; mid-summer–early Aug), about 20km (12 miles) south of Leksand on route 70 towards Mockfjärd, where children are encouraged to pet the cows, hens, sheep and pigs.

If trying your own hand at 15th-century farming appeals, **Prästbodarnas Fäbod** (tel: 0246 910 91; June–Aug daily, book in advance), near Bingsjö, has a variety of native Swedish farm animals, and offers one-day courses in butter-churning, milking and cheese-making.

At the northern extremity of Dalarna is the deceptively gentle start of the mountain range which marches north, gaining height all the time until it culminates in the snow-topped peaks of the Kebnekaise range in Lapland. Dalarna is a transition zone between the softer landscapes of southern Sweden and the more dramatic, but harsher north.

Copper mine at Falun.

Industrial traditions

Dalarna is not exclusively rural. The Bergslagen district has been mined for a millennium, and the whole area is now a Unesco World Heritage site. The most impressive industrial site is the 17th-century **Falu Gruva** (Falu Mine; tel: 023 78 20 30; www.falugruva. se; year-round, extra attractions in summer, phone or see website for times), on the edge of the provincial capital, **Falun** ❸, with machinery, museum and 1.5-hour tours into the depths. Copper was extracted here, as were the iron pigments used to colour the iconic Falu Red paint, liberally applied to all Sweden's little red houses.

Hedemora ❹ claims to be the oldest town in Dalarna, with a charter dated 1459; its privileges as a market town go back even further than that, while parts of the church are 13th-century. The locals have devised **Husbyringen**, a 56km (35-mile) "museum trail" which you can take by car through the area northeast of the town to explore a number of industrial archaeology sites (http://husbyringen.se).

Also worth visiting is **Säter** ❺, one of the seven best-preserved wooden towns in Sweden. Compared with Hedemora it is quite an upstart, with a town charter dated 1642. The ravines of the Säter Valley were created at the end of the Ice Age and are of interest for their flora.

Handicrafts

This is the province that inspired the distinctive Dala horse, still being made at the Grannas workshop in **Nusnäs** ❻ (tel: 0250 372 50; www.grannas.com; mid-June–mid-Aug Mon–Fri 9am–6pm, Sat–Sun 9am–4pm, mid-Aug–mid-June Mon–Fri 9am–4pm, Sat 10am–1pm; free), so it is not surprising that the region is known for its abundance of carvers, potters, silversmiths, weavers, painters and bakers. This is a mecca for *hemslöjd* (crafts), all of which have their ancient roots in the farming culture.

At **Säterglänan** ❼, 3km (2 miles) south of Insjön Lake, **Hemslöjdens Gård** (tel: 0247 645 70; www.saterglantan. se) offers handicrafts and courses. At **Nittsjö Keramik** (http://nittsjokeramik. se; tel: 0248 171 30; Mon–Fri 10am–6pm, Sat 10am–2pm, June–Aug Sun 11am–3pm), 6km (4 miles) north of Rättvik, clay goods are made following a 100-year-old tradition.

Ski resorts

With plenty of snow from December to April, Dalarna's ski resorts are the main winter tourist attraction, both for cross-country skiing and downhill (some slopes are illuminated for the dark winter days). **Romme Alpin** ❽ is Sweden's most visited ski resort outside the proper mountain areas, with some 200,000 visitors annually. Together, **Sälen** ❾ and Idre, in northwest Dalarna, have almost half of Sweden's ski-lift facilities, and Sälen is the starting point for the very popular Vasaloppet – an 85km (53-mile) cross-country skiing race to **Mora** ❿ on Lake Siljan.

Nearby, the skiing area at Orsa has an added attraction. **Orsa Björnpark** (tel: 0250 462 00; www.orsabjornpark.se; July and early Aug daily 10am–6pm; rest of year daily 10am–3pm) is Europe's largest bear park, and your best chance of seeing large predators (brown bears, polar bears, wolves, lynx, wolverines and even leopards) in natural surroundings.

A self-portrait by Carl Larsson.

CARL LARSSON

Carl Larsson (1853–1919) is Sweden's best-loved artist. The greatest source of inspiration for Larsson was the life he shared with his wife Karin, a textile artist, and their children at their home at **Sundborn** ⓫ (tel: 023 600 53; www.clg.se; by guided tour only: May–Sept daily 10am–5pm, Oct–Apr Mon–Fri 11am, Sat–Sun 1pm).

Carl Larsson was born to a poor family in Stockholm, and during his youth he suffered all the deprivations of poverty, a period he later described as "hell on earth". He was determined to leave those hard times behind him and thus it was no coincidence that he became the artist who would best portray the happy, harmonious Swedish family, bathed in light, colour and joyous celebration of home and hearth. In their wooden farmhouse, where Karin and Carl lived with their eight children, they created the simple interiors that were to influence so much of modern design. Stripped floors strewn with rugs, brightly painted furniture and hand-painted friezes were the key elements.

Larsson's paintings were strongly influenced by the local Dalarna folk-art traditions. In his autobiography, Larsson wrote, "My art: it is just like my home; there is no place there for fine furniture… it is simple, but harmonious. Nothing extravagant… just good, strong work."

Helpful sign in Jämtland.

CENTRAL SWEDEN

Brilliant blue lakes, rushing rivers, the mysterious outlines of mountains and, above all, the space and silence beckon hikers and anglers to this untouched landscape.

Five provinces stretch across central Sweden. In the east are Gästrikland, Hälsingland and Medelpad, which share the long coastline known as Jungfrukusten (Virgin Coast). Further inland come Härjedalen and Jämtland, which stretch west to the Norwegian border, the land of lakes and coniferous or birch forests. Härjedalen marks the beginning of the great northern mountain ranges and the further north you go, the more dramatic the scenery is.

Gästrikland

The small province of **Gästrikland** has one major town, **Gävle ❶** in the southeast corner of the region. Gävle was one of Sweden's great shipping towns, and the most treasured exhibit at the local museum, **Länsmuséet** (tel: 026 65 56 00; www.lansmuseetgavleborg.se; Tue–Fri 10am–6pm, Sat–Sun noon–4pm; free), is the Björke boat, a rare find from around AD 400. Other exhibits include displays on local industry and handicrafts, plus a surprisingly extensive collection of paintings by notable Swedish artists from the 17th century to the present day, including works by Carl Larsson.

Railway enthusiasts should make a point of visiting the **Sveriges Järnvägsmuseum** (Swedish Railway Museum; tel: 010 123 21 00; June–Aug daily 10am–5pm, Sept–May Tue–Sun

10am–4pm) on the outskirts of Gävle. The collection embraces gleaming locomotives from the golden age of steam, including the stately 1874 coach of King Oscar II, and comes up-to-the-minute with an X2000 simulator.

For children, **Furuviksparken** (tel: 026 17 73 00; late May–mid-June and mid-Aug–late Aug 10am–5pm, mid-June–mid-Aug 10am–7pm), 10km (6 miles) south of Gävle, combines extensive zoological gardens with a variety of other attractions, including a theatre and a circus.

Main Attractions

Sveriges Järnvägsmuseum (Swedish Railway Museum)
Boat trips from Söderhamn
Frösön
Jamtli Open-Air Museum
Jämtland hiking trails
Åre ski resort

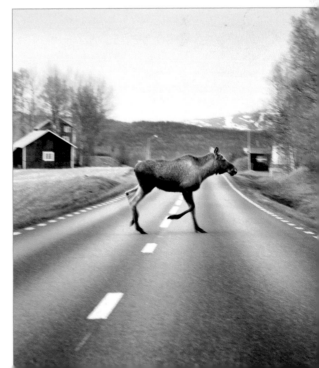

Moose crossing the road.

Grilled herring and potatoes with dill butter is a favourite dish all along the Virgin Coast. At **Bönan**, 10km (6 miles) northeast of Gävle, visit **Engeltofta** (www.engeltofta.se) to sample the town's famous golden-brown smoked herring, cured over spruce wood – in summer you can catch the boat over from Gävle.

Gästrikland is at the eastern end of the swathe of land which gave Sweden its early mining and smelting industries. On summer Sundays, vintage steam trains ply the 4.5km (2.75 miles) from **Jädraås** ❷, northwest of Gävle, to **Tallås** (www.jtj.org). The railway is typical of those used to haul minerals or timber, and the coach used by King Oscar II (ruled 1872–1907) when he went hunting bears in Dalarna is still in service.

Follow the E4 north to **Söderhamn** ❸, the starting point for boat trips around the archipelago. Söderhamn was founded in 1620 as an armoury for the Swedish army, and the museum is situated in part of what was the gun and rifle factory. Although a commercial centre, the town has an impressive town hall, plus a church to match and a pleasant riverside park.

Lynx, resident of northern Scandinavia.

Hälsingland

Around 120 years ago, when the timber industry was at its peak, **Hudiksvall** ❹ had a reputation for high living. A reminder of the era is the town's theatre, opened in 1882. Hudiksvall also has a group of the best-preserved 19th-century wooden buildings in Sweden, the Fiskarstan.

The interior of **Hälsingland** province has the best scenery, particularly the Ljusnandalen River Valley, which is laced with lakes along its entire length. West of **Ljusdal** ❺, where the Ljusnan meets the Hennan River, the forests begin.

On the first weekend in July, **Delsbo** ❻ attracts thousands of visitors for the annual **Delsbostämman** (www.delsbostamman.nu), where folk fiddlers, dancers and costumed actors air the region's traditional culture. Surrounded by dark forests, the **Dellenbygden** area is rural Sweden at its best. It's worth doing a circuit through Friggesund and Hassela and back to the coast, taking in the Dellen lakes area, with its boat and canoe trips, and walking trails.

THE INLAND RAILWAY

Atrip on the Inlandsbanan (Inland Railway) is an enjoyable way of seeing some of Sweden's most dramatic scenery. The route stretches through the Central Heartlands from Mora in Dalarna to Gällivare in Lapland.

The idea of building such a long railway through a harsh and inaccessible landscape was first promoted in 1894, but it was to take another 40 years of hard labour before it was completed. The 1,100km (680-mile) line was finally inaugurated in Jokkmokk in Lapland on 6 August 1937, and a monument was erected to commemorate the event.

Today the train stops along the way so passengers can visit local artists and craftspeople or simply admire the views. Sometimes it has to halt to avoid running into herds of reindeer resting on the track. With luck, passengers may also spot elks or bears.

It is possible to make stopovers along the route and stay for a night or two in local towns and villages to do some walking in the mountains, or just enjoy the magnificent landscape. Various packages are available combining rail travel with hotel accommodation, or trekking. For more information contact Inlandsbanan AB: tel: 0771 53 53 53; www.inlandsbanan.se.

The following Sunday, **Hårga** ❼ 50km (30 miles) further south, used to host one of Sweden's best-known dance competitions, Hälsingehambo, epitomised by the catchy polka *Hårgalåten*. It was a fitting setting: the legend has it, the devil had lured a group of young folk out onto Hårgaberget with his bewitching fiddle music, where they had danced themselves to death. The festival shut down in 2011, but the residents miss it so much that every year on the same day they organise traditional Hårga dances at Hembygdsgården Ol-Nils.

Härjedalen

Together the provinces of **Härjedalen** and **Jämtland** are as big as Denmark, but with a population of only 123,000. To the east and southeast are extensive forests with hills, rivers and lakes. The higher mountains begin in Härjedalen. This heartland has four main rivers, the Ångermanälven, Indalsälven, Ljungan and Ljusnan, all well stocked with fish, especially trout and grayling. Perch, pike and whitefish are the most common in the forested regions, but many

tarns have been stocked with trout. It is an anglers' paradise – fishing permits can be bought cheaply nearby or at any local tourist office. The vast tracts of near-uninhabited territory are also home to wildlife such as bears, wolverine, lynx and the ubiquitous elk.

When tourism was in its infancy, Härjedalen was one of the first Swedish provinces to attract skiers, who still return to pit their skills against its varied terrain, and come back in the summer for mountain walking. The scenery is impressive and, north of **Funäsdalen**, not far from the Norwegian border, the province has Sweden's highest road over the **Flatruet plateau**, up to 1,000 metres (3,280ft) high.

At the crossroads of the north–south route, highway 45, and east–west, highway 84, is **Sveg**, a small town but Härjedalen's largest, with a population of around 2,600. **Vemdalen** ❽, 60km (37 miles) northwest, has an eight-sided wooden church with a separate onion-domed bell tower. Beyond the village the road climbs between two mountains, **Vemdalsfjällen**, before entering Jämtland.

FACT

The E14 from Östersund to the Norwegian frontier is an age-old route once used by pilgrims on their trek to the grave of St Olav at Trondheim (see page 217).

The open-air museum, Jamtli.

Jämtland

Jämtland is the biggest province in central Sweden, a huge territory of lakes, rivers and mountains. Its heart is the lake of Storsjön, the fifth-largest stretch of inland water in the country, which is reputed to have its own monster, a Swedish version of Scotland's "Nessie". Present-day monster-seekers can take a cruise on the lake in the 1875 steamer Thomée.

On the banks of Storsjön is Jämtland's largest town, **Östersund 9**, connected by a bridge to the beautiful island of **Frösön**. The island was home to the noted Swedish composer and critic Wilhelm Peterson-Berger (1867–1942). His most popular work, the opera *Arnljot*, is performed every summer on the island as a theatrical, rather than a musical, work. Östersund hosts one of Sweden's biggest international music festivals, Storsjöyran (http://storsjoyran.se), at the end of July: past artists have included Lady Gaga, B.B. King and Motörhead.

In Östersund, **Jamtli** (tel: 063 15 01 00; www.jamtli.com; all year) is one of the biggest open-air museums in the country, an interesting collection of 18th- and 19th-century buildings including a *shieling* (summer farm), baker's cottage, smithy, and an old inn, and myriad activities for children. The food in the café is recommended.

North of Storsjön, on the north bank of Lake Alsensjön at **Glösa 10**, are a number of *hällristningar*, primitive rock carvings.

In western Jämtland, the peaks rise up to nearly 1,800 metres (6,000ft). It is a splendid area for trekking in summer and skiing in winter. Centuries ago, melting ice left many strange and unusual formations, such as the deep canyon between the Drommen and Falkfångarfjället mountains. The region is also rich in waterfalls, such as **Ristafallet** near Hålland, **Storfallet** northwest of Höglekardalen and **Tännforsen**, to the west of **Åre 11**.

Åre (www.are360.com) is a popular winter sports resort with a funicular railway that goes from the town centre partway up the local mountain, Åreskutan, and a cable car that continues almost to the summit. Lakes and mountains on every side make up a superb view.

Plouging the fields near Delsbo.

Sarek National Park, a Unesco World Heritage Site

NORTHERN SWEDEN

Lapland, land of the Midnight Sun and home to the Sami, offers a richly rewarding experience for the traveller. Fishing villages and holiday islands dot the Bothnian coast.

I n the search for natural landscapes Lapland, which stretches across northern Sweden and Finland, offers some of the finest, wildest lakes and mountains in Europe; and although distances are great, there are quality roads and a rail link. Anglers are guaranteed excellent river fishing, and sea fishing along the coast of Bottenviken (Gulf of Bothnia), the stretch of water that separates Sweden from Finland. Holidaymakers and sailors gravitate to its sheltered coves and islands.

Highway 45

The best way to absorb the immensity of Swedish Lapland is to take the inland highway 45, from south to north. The first town across the border from Ångermanland is **Dorotea ❶**, at the heart of bear country – the animals sometimes wander into town in search of food. **Vilhelmina ❷**, 100km (60 miles) north on the Ångermanälven River, has a well-preserved church village where travellers can find accommodation in its wooden houses.

West of Vilhelmina is the **Kittelfjäll** mountain region and the border with Norway. To the north lies an important road junction at **Storuman ❸**, where the 45 is bisected by the E12, known as the Blå Vägen (Blue Highway) because it follows a succession of lakes and the Umeälven River on its route from the east coast. It passes

Sami and reindeer.

through **Lycksele ❹**, where there is a zoo, **Lycksele Djurpark** (tel: 0950 163 63; www.lyckseledjurpark.se; May–mid-Sept daily 10am–4pm or 5pm, mid-Sept–late Dec Mar–Apr noon until 3–5pm), that has Nordic species including bear, elk, musk ox, wolf and reindeer. From Storuman the E12 continues west through Tärnaby to Mo i Rana in Norway.

The Silver Road

From Slagnäs, on highway 45, a secondary road leads through glorious

Main Attractions

Arjeplog Silver Museum
Lappstaden (Sami church village)
Gällivare
Laponia World Heritage area
Ice Hotel, Jukkasjärvi
Höga Kusten (High Coast)
Umeå
Gammelstad

drop to –35°C (–31°F). First held in 1605, the market soon became a meeting place for the Sami and merchants from the coastal communities. Today it is as much a social occasion as an opportunity to trade, and weddings and baptisms often take place. The **Ájtte Fjäll-och Samemuseum** (Swedish Mountain and Sami Museum; tel: 0971 170 70; www.ajtte.com; mid-June–mid-Aug daily 9am–6pm, Feb–mid-June and mid-Aug–Dec Tue–Fri 10am–4pm, Sat 10am–2pm) portrays the local culture as well as the mountain world, placing mankind in a natural, cultural and ecological perspective.

Highway 45 continues through a sparsely populated area to **Porjus** ❽, a major centre for hydroelectric power. To the east of the town is **Muddus National Park** (certain areas are closed during the breeding season, mid-Mar–July; tel: 0971 222 50; http://destinationjokkmokk.se), home of bear, lynx and wolverine. **Dundret Mountain**, 820 metres (2,690ft) high, northeast of the park, is a bustling ski centre from November to April. In summer, the region abounds with activities – riding, walking, windsurfing, fishing, golf and rafting – contact Gällivare tourist office (tel: 0970 166 60; www.gellivarelapland.se) for details.

To the Finnish frontier

Gällivare ❾ (pop. 18,400), and its twin town, Malmberget, owe their growth to the discovery of iron ore. Gällivare is the end of the railway line, Inlandsbanan, that follows highway 45 north from Östersund. It is a popular tourist route and jumping-off point for treks into the region that include the Padjelanta, Stora Sjöfallet and Sarek national parks, which together with Muddus form the Laponia Unesco World Heritage site. The town has a museum and an 18th-century Sami church. Beyond Gällivare, the 45 joins the E10 and continues north to **Svappavaara**, a former mining centre, and **Karesuando** ❿, on the Finnish frontier. Many place names in Swedish Lapland owe more to Finnish than to Swedish. In Kiruna, for example, a fifth of the population are Finnish immigrants.

The most northerly church in Sweden can be found in Karesuando, which also has the lowest average winter temperatures and Sweden's only tundra. From the top of **Kaarevaara mountain**, 517 metres (1,696ft) high, you can see three countries: Sweden, Finland and Norway.

Kiruna and the Ice Hotel

Beyond Svappavaara, the E10 swings northwest to **Kiruna** ⓫ (pop. 18,200), Sweden's most northerly town. Mining began here in 1900 and is still the main industry. Such is the extent of the underground workings that Kiruna is subsiding, and plans are under way to move the entire town east of its current location. The **LKAB InfoMine** is the world's largest iron-ore mine, with 400km (250 miles) of underground roadways. Tours of the mine can be booked all year round; contact the tourist office (tel: 0980 188 80; www.kirunalapland.se).

Also visitable through Kiruna tourist office, the **Esrange Space Center**

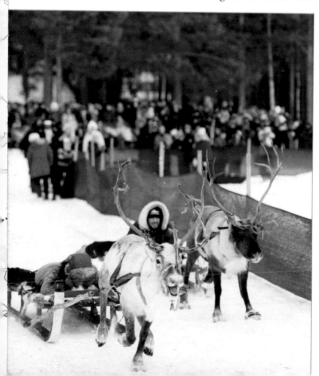

Reindeer race at the Jokkmokk winter fair.

is Europe's only civilian space centre, launching around five to 10 test rockets per year.

East of Kiruna, **Jukkasjärvi** ⓬ is famous for its Ice Hotel (www.icehotel.com), built afresh every winter. Activities in the region include dog-sledging in the snow-covered wilderness and white-water rafting in summer.

The E10 (Nordkalottvägen), from Kiruna via the Norwegian frontier to Narvik, penetrates one of Europe's last wilderness areas. The mountains southwest of the highway can only be reached on foot or by pony, and it is here that **Kebnekaise**, Sweden's highest peak at 2,117 metres (6,945ft), reigns supreme. **Abisko** ⓭, 150km (93 miles) from Kiruna, is a popular base from which to set out along the **Kungsleden** (King's Trail), which enables even inexperienced walkers to see the mountains.

The Bothnian coast

The Bottenviken (Gulf of Bothnia) coastline ranges from polished rock to sand and shingle beaches. Islands form an almost continuous archipelago – a playground for holidaymakers passionate about sailing and the sea. Inland, lakes provide tranquil blue oases in the dense forests.

Starting in the south, the main coastal town of Ångermanland is **Härnösand** ⓮, which is modern except for the town hall, the Domkyrkan (Cathedral) and some 18th-century wooden houses. Overlooking the harbour at Murberget is a large open-air historical museum (www.murberget.se; Tue–Sun 11am–4pm; free). Slightly inland, the 13th-century church, near **Ytterlännäs** on highway 90, is an antiquarian wonder.

Travelling north on the E4, the Höga Kusten (High Coast) Bridge, modelled partly on San Francisco's Golden Gate Bridge, is an impressive structure, 1.8km (1 mile) long. It marks the start of the most beautiful stretch of coast, the **Höga Kusten**, a Unesco World Heritage site. Its towering cliffs are Sweden's highest, created at the end of the last Ice Age.

Here you'll find the **Nordingrå peninsula** ⓯, whose bedrock is an intense red *rapakivi* granite. Its scenic treasures include **Omne Bay**, the villages of **Måviken** and **Norrfällsviken**, and the view from the church over Vagsfjärden. **Bönhamn** is a tiny place among the rocks, where **Arnes Sjöbod** is renowned for fresh fish and mashed potatoes and **Mannaminne**, near Häggvik, provides home-baked delicacies, handicrafts and musical evenings. The **Höga Kusten walk**, at 25km (16 miles), starts at Fjordbotten with bathing places at Storsand, Norrfällsviken, Hörsång and Noraström. Between the E4 and the coast lies the majestic **Skuleskogen National Park** ⓰ (all year; www.skuleskogen.se), noted for its rare birds and mammals.

Örnsköldsvik ⓱, known as Övik, is an industrial town and one of Sweden's leading winter sports areas. The islands offshore include **Ulvön**, with one of the oldest fishermen's chapels in Sweden, **Trysunda**, a favourite with the sailing fraternity, and **Högbonden**, whose former lighthouse is now a cosy clifftop youth hostel, accessible by boat from Bönhamn.

TIP

The mosquitoes are rapacious in summer in northern Sweden, so don't forget to pack insect repellent.

Höga Kusten Bridge.

Sami items hand carved out of reindeer bone; a knife and a box on a string.

The Ice Hotel in Jukkasjärvi.

A new high-speed railway line makes **Umeå** ⑱ easily accessible from Stockholm. This is a young, lively place which was European Capital of Culture in 2014. The main attraction here is the open-air **Friluftsmuseum Gammlia**, part of the adjacent **Västerbotten Museum** (tel: 090 16 39 00 18 00; www.vbm.se; Tue–Fri 10am–5pm, Wed 10am–9pm, Sat–Sun 11am–5pm; free), which explores local history and has the oldest ski in the world – over 5,000 years old. Umeå also boasts an acclaimed museum of contemporary art and visual culture, housed in a modern seven-floor building on the Umeå Arts Campus (Bildmuseet; www.bildmuseet.umu.se; Tue 11am–8pm, Wed–Sun 11am–6pm; free).

Continuing north, **Piteå** ⑲ can come as a culture shock. Some 17th-century wooden houses remain, but today it is a centre for timber, paper and pulp industries. Norwegians come in flocks from their calm northern fjords to the large holiday resort of Pite Havsbad.

From Piteå, the road leads northwest through Älvsbyn to Bredsel and **Storforsen**, Europe's longest natural rapids, with an 81m (265ft) drop over 5km (3 miles). You can get close to the rushing water via wooden walkways and bridges; it is an awe-inspiring sight. The hotel nearby offers superb views.

Luleå and the Lule Valley

Luleå ⑳ was moved 10km (6 miles) by the king in 1649 and stands now at the mouth of the Luleälven River. The old church town, **Gammelstad**, was left on its original site; it is a Unesco World Heritage site with 400 red-painted cottages and a 15th-century church still used on important religious occasions. Beside the original harbour the open-air museum, **Friluftsmuséet Hägnan** (tel: 0920 45 38 09; Tue–Fri 11am–3pm; free), has a hay shed typical of Norrbotten. The **Norrbottens Museum** (tel: 0920 24 35 02; www.norrbottensmuseum.se; June–Aug daily 11am–5pm, Sept–May Tue–Fri 10am–4pm, Sat–Sun 11am–4pm; free) in Hermelin Park provides a picture of the province and has Sami artefacts.

In the 19th century, **Boden** ㉑, 35km (22 miles) inland from Luleå on the Luleälven River, was referred to as "one of the strongest fortresses of Europe – that is to say, in the whole world". Today, Boden is still the largest garrison town in Sweden.

For a complete change of scene, head 45km (28 miles) northwest to the peaceful Lule Valley near **Harads** ㉒, where you'll find some of Sweden's weirdest accommodation. If you've ever wanted to sleep in a bird's nest or have a sauna up a tree, here's your chance.

The eastern frontier

Haparanda ㉓, Sweden's easternmost town, was built opposite Finnish Tornio on the Torneälven River, which forms the border between the two countries. Road 400 goes north along the river on the Swedish side into the Tornedalen Valley to the Kukkolaforsen waterfall. West of there, on the Kalixälven River, is **Överkalix** ㉔, with fine views from the top of Brännaberget. At the end of June, this is the place to see the amazing tradition of netting whitefish and salmon.

Peaceful Lakeland waters.

FINLAND

The serenity of Finland's lakes and forests remain timeless, but change is always in the air.

Finnish fare.

For a country of just over 5.5 million people, Finland has produced an astonishing number of architects, artists, sculptors, musicians and athletes; the tradition continues. Helsinki was named World Design Capital 2012, a biennial honour given to a city for merits in successful utilisation of design for cultural, social and economic improvement. In 2011, Helsinki opened a new Music Centre next to Alvar Aalto's Finlandia Hall, and in 2012, the state-of-the-art Helsinki University Main Library in Kaisaniemenkatu. The city's restaurant scene continues to evolve, with several Michelin-star restaurants and a lively dining out culture.

This drive and tenacity may also explain why the World Economic Forum deemed Finland "the seventh-most competitive country in the world". Sisu is a Finnish word that is synonymous with having guts and being resilient; one Finn described it as pushing open a door that says "pull", but it is the extra ingredient in the Finnish DNA that helps them survive climactic and economic challenges. Long known for its substantial pulp and paper industry, Finland is also considered a worldwide force with technological innovations: from mobile phones to state-of-the-art medical equipment and progressive internet services. After mobile phones were overtaken in the market by smart phones, Nokia found itself at a critical juncture. In 2010, they began a new partnership with Microsoft, designing and manufacturing new products in Finland, but in 2014 the American corporation effectively swallowed Nokia's mobile device business.

Iittala glassware.

Finns may work hard, but they also know how to wind down. The endless expanses of untouched landscape soothe the soul of the urban Finn, who escapes to the country at the weekend, and enjoys each season accordingly. The silence of the forests provides reflection, as the sauna provides solace. With fishing, swimming and a small boat in summer, and skis, snowshoes or snowmobile in the winter, Finland remains a paradise for all.

Finland

Pukkisaaret

Seurasaarentie

Seurasaarensalmi

MEILAHDEN PUISTO

Humallahti

Ulkomuseo
★ (Open-Air Museum)

31

Seurasaari

Rajasaari

Mustasaari

Seurasaarenselkä

Taivalluoto

Porsas

Ourit

Pieni-Porsas

Lapinlahti

Messeniuksenk.

Stenbäckinkatu

Tavaststjernank.
M. Lybeckink.

Topeliuksenkatu

Nordenskiöldinkatu

Mannerheimintie

Urheilukatu

Paavo Nurmentie

Mäntymäent.

**Olympia-
stadion**

Talkontie

KAUPUNI
PUIITAR

Linnankoskenkatu

Rajasaarent.

SIBELIUKSEN
PUISTO

Sibeliusmonumentti **32**

7

Markkanniemi

Mechelininkatu

Sibeliuksenk.

Kesäk.

TAKA-TÖÖLÖ

Eino Leinon k.

Humalistonkatu

Töölönk.

Ruusulankatu

Helsinginkatu

Kivelänk.

Mannerheimintie

10

**Suomen
Kansallisooj**
(Finnish Natio
Opera House)

Töölönk.

Töölönla

Sammonk.

Töölönt.

Pohj.Hesperiankatu

Apollonkatu

Caloniuk.

Runeberginkatu

Museokatu

Eteläinen Hesperiankatu

Hietaniemenkatu

Krematoriont.

HIETANIEMEN
HAUTAUSMAA

Hiekkarannantie

Vähänliisankatu

Tunturik.

Temppelik.

Nervanderink.

11

6

Temppeliaukion
kirkko

Kansallismuseo
(National Museum)

**Hakasalmi Vil
Eduskuntatal**
(Parliamen
Building

Finlandiatal
(Finlandia Ha

5

Luonnontieteellinen museo
(Natural History Museum)

Hietaniemenk.atu

Leppäsuork.

Pohj. Rautatiekatu

Malminkatu

Lastenk.k.

Mechelininkatu

Lapinlahdentie

Tennispalatsi
(Tennis Palace)

4

Fredrikink.

Salomon

M

Kamppi

Kan
(Shop
Cen

24

Lapinlahdenk.

Työnk.

Ruoholahdenk.

Eerikink.

Kalevank.

Lönnrotink.

Aleksanterin teatteri
(Aleksander Theatre)

Hietalahdentori
(Hietalahti Flea
Market)

Sinebrych
Taidemus

Abrahamink.

LÄNSIVÄYLÄ

Länsiväylä

SALMISAARI

Pohjoiskaar

Salmisaar
renranta

Tallberr

Itämerenkatu

Porkkalankatu

**Suomen Valokuvataiteen
museo & Teatterimuseo**
(Photography &
Theatre Museums)

14

M
Ruoholahti

Kellosaarenkatu

Itämerenkatu

Santakatu

Selkämerenk.

Tammasaarenranta

Kaapeli
(Cable Factory)

Jaalaranta

Messitytönkatu

Laivapojankatu

Hietalahti

Ruoholahdenranta

PUNAVUC

Kansallisarkisto
(National Archives)

Vironkatu

Shelmaninkatu

Unioninkatu

Fabianinkatu

Rauhankatu

Rauhankatu

Säätytalo
(House of Estates)

Sörnäinkatu

Kaisaniemi

M

**Helsinki University
Main Library**

Vuorikatu

Suomen Pankki
(Bank of Finland)

Kirkkokatu

Kirkkokatu

Tuomiokirkko
(Cathedral)

19

KRUUNUNHAKA

Yliopistonkatu

Kluuvikatu

Yliopiston kirjasto
(University Library)

Yliopisto
(University)

Aleksanteri II

Hallituskatu

Regeringsgatan
Senaatintori
(Senate Sq.)

Katarinank.

Valtioneuvoston linna
(Council of State)

Mariankatu

Ritarihuone
(House of Nobility)

Meritullintori

Aleksanterinkatu

Helsingin Kaupunginmuseo
(Helsinki City Museum) **21**

**Kaupungin
matkailutoimisto**
(Helsinki City
Tourist Office) **16**

Sederholmin Talo
(Sederholm House) **20**

Kaupungintalo
(City Hall) **18**

Bockin talo
(Bock House)

Presidentinlinna
(Presidential Palace)

Hietaniemi

**Uspenskin
katedraali**
(Uspenski
Cathedral) **22**

LÄNSISATAMA

Poseidoninkuja

Kellosaarenkuja

**Länsi-
terminaali**

MUNKKISAARI

Pohjoisesplanadi

J.L. Runeberg

Havis
Amanda

ESPLANADIN
PUISTO **13**

15

**Kappeli
Restaurant**

Pohjoisesplanadi

Kauppatori
(Central
Market Sq.)

17

Obeliski Keisarinnan kivi
(Czarinas Obelisk)

KAARTINKAUPUNKI

Fabianinkatu

Eteläranta

KATAJANOKKA

Vanha Kauppahalli
(Old Market Hall)

P. makasiinkatu

Eteläsatama

0   200 m
0   200 yds

Suomenlinna, Korkeasaari

Kanavakatu

**Kanava-
terminaali**

Stockholm,
Marienhamn,
Tallinn

Tallinn

Pihlajasaari **36**

Helsinki

0 — 500 m
0 — 500 yds

Työväenasuntomuseo
(Museum of Worker Housing)

Linnanmäki

Aleksis Kiven katu

Porvoonk.
Flemingink.
Vaasankatu

Teollisuuskatu
Hämeentie
Lautatarhankatu
Pääskylänkatu
Työpajakatu
Varastok.

HARJU

L.Brahenk.

M Sörnäinen

SÖRNÄINEN

Helsinginkatu

Kaarlenkatu k.
Franzénin k.
Torkkelinkatu
Pengerkatu
Käenkuja

Hämeentie
Vilhonvuorenk.

Itäväylä

Helsinginkatu
Alppikatu

Alppikatu
Castreninkatu
Kolmas linja
Toinen linja
Ensi linja Wallininkatu
Neljäs linja
Vidas linja
Irja
Agricolank.

Sompasaarensalmi

MUSTIKKAMAA

KALLIO

Hämeentie
Suoniontie
Siltasaarenkatu
Haapaniemenkatu
Häkäniemi
Häkän. tork.

Hämeentie
Hämeentie
Näkinkuja
Lintulahdenkuja
Sörnäisten rantatie
Hanssaarenkatu

SOMPASAARI

Kaupunginteatteri
(City Theatre)

Eläintarhanlahti
Hakaniemi

Näkinsilta

Mustikkamaansalmi

Siltasa. ranta
Pitkänsillanr.
Kaisaniemenranta

M

HAKANIEMI

Hakaniemenranta

Sörnäisten satama

NIEMI

Kaisaniemenranta
Pitkäsilta
Siltavuorenranta

Sörnäisten satama

KORKEASAARI

Korkeasaaren
eläintarha
(Zoo)
30

KASVITIETEELLINEN
PUUTARHA
(UNIVERSITY BOTANICAL
GARDENS)

Ruiskumestarin talo
(Burgher's House)

Kristianink.

Maurinkatu

Sotamuseo
(Military Museum)

Tervasaarenkannas

Tervasaari

Hylkysaarensalmi

Hylkysaari

Töölönlahdenk.

Rautatieasema
Järnvägs-
stationen
(Central Railway
Station)

Suomen
Kansallisteatteri
(Finnish National
Theatre)

Liisankatu

Maneesikatu
Vironk.
Rauhankatu

Mariankatu
Snellmaninkatu
Merikatu

Pohjoisranta

Tervasaarenkannas

Pohjoissatama

C.G.E.
Mannerheim
Rautatientori
1

Vilhonkatu

Unioninkatu

Kirkkokatu

Kruunuvuorenselkä

Mannerheimintie

Ateneum
(Finnish National
Gallery)

M Kaisaniemi

Yliopistonkatu

Tuomiokirkko

Senaatintori

Uspenskin
katedraali

Laivastokatu

Luotsikatu

Merikasarmi
(Ex-Naval Barracks)

Palace
Kaivokatu

Aleksanterinkatu

2
12 Stockmann

Yliopisto
Galleria
Esplanad

Aleksanterinkatu

Presidentinlinna

KRUUNUNHAKA

Kaup.k.

Merikasarminkatu

Pohjoisesplanadi

Tulli ja tullimakasiini
(Customs and
Bonded Warehouse)

Kanavakatu

Linnankatu

Svenska Teatern
(Swedish Theatre)

Eteläesplanadi

Kanava-
termi-
naali

23

Katajanokanlaituri

Kruununvuorenkatu

Katajanokanranta

KATAJANOKKA

Vanha
kirkko

Unioninkatu
Eteläranta
Korkeavuorenkatu
Kasarmikatu

Uudenmaankatu

Designmuseo
(Design Museum)
25

Suomen
Rakennustaiteen
museo
(Museum of Finnish
Architecture)
26

Makasiini-
terminaali

Eteläsatama

Katajanokan
terminaali

Katajanokanluoto

Johanneksen
kirkko

Tähtitorni
(Observatory)

Olympia-
terminaali
28

Valkosaari
Blekholmen

Ryssänsaari

Kruunuvuorenselkä

Tarkk'ampujankatu
Jääkärinkatu

ULLANLINNA

Pyhän Henrikin
kirkko

Cygnaeuksen
galleria

Mannerheim-
museo

33
Luoto

Vuorimiehenk.

Itäinen
Läntinen puistotie
Iso puistotie

Siltatie

Puolimatkansaari

EIRA

Tehtaankatu

Pietarinkatu
Neitsytpolku
Kaivopuistonk.

Laivanvar.k.

27

KAIVOPUISTO

Lonna

Laivurink.

Huvilakatu

Ehrenströmintie

Merisatamanranta
Merisatama

Pormestarinluodot

Sirpalesalmi

35 Uunisaari

rpalesaari

Liuskasaari

37
Harakka

34
Särkkä

Pikku-Musta

Vanha-Räntty

Länsi-Musta

29

SUOMENLINNA

Suomenlinna

Rostock, Stockholm, Tallinn, Mariehamn

Tram passing by an Art Nouveau building.

HELSINKI

An intriguing mix of Swedish and Russian influences combine with an ultramodern architectural stamp to make Finland's unique capital a gem of the northern Baltic.

Helsinki

Aproud and active member of the EU, Finland's capital city continues to evolve as a lively, cosmopolitan city with its own unique identity, beyond the Swedish and Russian influences of the past.

Flying over Helsinki, one sees nothing but lakes and forests. Arriving in the city centre, one is pleasantly confronted with stately granite buildings and a potpourri of impressive architecture styles: from neoclassical and neo-Renaissance to Art Nouveau, National Romanticism and Functionalism. People bustle along purposefully, stylishly or outrageously dressed, fueled by high-octane doses of *kahvi* (coffee).

After a complex 460-year history, Helsinki has grown from a picturesque village with a harbour to a modern, confident capital where the quality of life has been ranked as among the highest in Europe. It's accessible, surprisingly quiet, and less intense, proceeding at its own steady pace. The "Daughter of the Baltic" has gained her own identity and wears it with pride.

Building a capital

Before gaining independence in 1917, Finland lived through 500 years of Swedish rule, and more than 100 years under the Russians. These diverse influences from the west and then from the east have contributed

Festival fun, Esplanadi Park.

to Helsinki's character. Helsinki was founded in 1550 by the Swedish King Gustav Vasa, but the monumental city centre was built in the early 19th century, thanks largely to the talents of the German-born architect Carl Ludwig Engel. Engel's first commission was a new administrative centre, followed by the cathedral, senate building, university and university library. Engel's neoclassical work can also be seen in St Petersburg and Tallinn. At the same time, Helsinki became the seat of a nationalist movement. Native

Main Attractions

Central Railway Station
Ateneum Art Museum
Kiasma Contemporary Art Museum
Temppeliaukion Kirkko "Rock Church"
Central Market Square and Old Market Hall
Senate Square, Helsinki Cathedral
Uspenski Cathedral
Design Museum and Design District
Suomenlinna Fortress

architects such as Eliel Saarinen and Alvar Aalto emerged and, after independence in 1917, Finnish Functionalism replaced Art Nouveau as Helsinki's predominant architectural style.

Nothing could completely protect the city from the massive Russian air raids of 1944 – nor from fervent, and not always lovely, post-war reconstruction. But Helsinki's position on the sea soon helped it to regain and then increase its stature, not only as a major port, but also as the important site for shipbuilding and international meetings it is today.

Helsinki Central

Modern Helsinki is a tranquil but still growing city with some 622,000 occupants. The heart of the city pulses around the **Central Railway Station** ❶ (Rautatieasema), a memorable Helsinki landmark, which also contains a metro station and an underground shopping complex. Designed by Eliel Saarinen, who travelled through Europe to study railway stations, and completed in 1919, it links two of Helsinki's most prevalent styles: National Romanticism and Functionalism. The broad entrance is guarded on either side by two giant figures – the work of leading sculptor Emil Wikström (1864–1942) – each holding a globe lantern to light the way for the passengers ebbing and flowing through its doors.

While in the vicinity of the station, take a look at the Finnish National Theatre (Suomen Kansallisteatteri; www.kansallisteatteri.fi) located on the northeastern side of the station, another impressive building in the National Romantic style.

To the southeast of the station in another stately building is the **Ateneum** ❷ (Finnish National Gallery; Kaivokatu 2; tel: 0294 500 401; www.ateneum.fi; Tue and Fri 10am–6pm, Wed and Thur 10am–8pm, Sat–Sun 10am–5pm), built in 1887. The museum's fine collection of Finnish paintings, sculpture and graphic art covers the years 1750 to 1960 and includes works by such prominent Finnish artists as Akseli Gallen-Kallela, Hugo Simberg, and Albert Edelfelt, alongside a small international collection with works by Van Gogh, Munch, Cézanne, Goya and Delacroix. Also worth singling out are some evocative Finnish landscapes by Pekka Halonen, and the collection of Finnish prints and Japanese woodcuts. The temporary exhibitions throughout the year are impressive, too.

Mannerheimintie

To orientate yourself in Helsinki, just remember that all roads lead to **Mannerheimintie**, the city's main thoroughfare and the longest street in Finland. It was named after Carl Gustav Mannerheim, commander-in-chief of Finnish forces during World War II, and post-war president.

From the railway station turn north into Mannerheimintie and on the right is Finland's most visited museum **Kiasma** ❸ (Museum of Contemporary Art; tel: 0294 500 501; www.kiasma.fi; Tue 10am–5pm, Wed–Fri 10am–8pm, Sat–Sun 10am–6pm;

Wikström's massive figures adorning Helsinki Railway Station.

first Fri of the month free after 4pm). This remarkable curvaceous structure with its bright-white, naturally lit interior was designed by American architect Steven Holl as a showcase for contemporary art, which is displayed in a series of rotating exhibitions. Its bar and outdoor terrace are a popular meeting place.

Joining Kiasma to create a triangle of Functionalist architecture are two other cultural institutions: **Lasipalatsi** (Glass Palace) across Mannerheimintie and the former **Tennispalatsi** ❹ (Tennis Palace) at the other end of the new Kamppi underground and bus station. Built for the 1940 Helsinki Olympics, the Lasipalatsi building (www.lasipalatsi. fi) has been rejuvenated to create a Film and Media Centre, designed to "bring the services of modern technology and IT close to people". It incorporates an internet library, television studios, cinema, fine cafés and the Ravintola restaurant, restored to its 1930s glory (www.ravintolalasipalatsi.fi).

Built in the same period, the Tennispalatsi was used during the 1952 Olympic Games and was extensively renovated to house Finland's largest cinema complex (14 screens; www.finnkino.fi) and two museums – a branch of the **City Art Museum** (Helsingin Kaupungin Taidemuseo; tel: 09 3108 7041; http://taidemuseo.hel. fi; Wed–Sun 11am–6pm; free), used for temporary exhibitions, and the **Museum of Cultures** (tel: 040 128 6469; www.nba.fi; Tue–Sun 11am–6pm; Fri free after 4pm), which holds ethnographic collections from around the world, with the emphasis on Finno-Ugric peoples.

Near the Lasipalatsi building, take a moment away from the rushing crowds and step into another of Helsinki's one-of-a-kind churches. The award-winning **Kamppi Chapel of Silence** (Mon–Fri 8am–8pm, Sat–Sun 10am–6pm; free) is an astonishing building, constructed from curving strips of spruce. Opened in 2012 as part of the World Design Capital

programme, it has attracted half a million visitors in its first two years of existence.

Opposite Kiasma is the **Parliament Building** ❺, built between 1925 and 1930 and distinguished by an impressive sweep of steps and a facade of 14 columns of grey granite.

Just behind the Parliament Building, the extensively refurbished **Natural History Museum** ❻ (Pohjoinen Rautatiekatu 13; tel: 09 1912 8800; www.luomus.fi; June–Aug Tue–Sun 10am–5pm, Thur 10am–7pm, Sept–May Tue–Fri 9am–4pm, Thur 9am–7pm, Sat–Sun 10am–4pm) has turned the University of Helsinki's vast zoological collection of animal specimens into engaging exhibits on Finnish flora and fauna.

Museums of History

Statues of former Finnish presidents scatter the area between Parliament and the **National Museum of Finland** ❼ (Kansallismuseo; tel: 040 128 6469; www.nba.fi; Tue–Sun 11am–6pm; visitors under 18 free, Fri free after 4pm), two blocks to the north. It

Kiasma, the Museum of Contemporary Art.

focuses on Finnish history, with interesting displays on life in pre-industrial Finland, and Finnish folk culture. The museum's decoration and the stone bear by the entrance are by Emil Wikström, and the frescoes on the foyer ceiling, depicting scenes from Finland's national epic, the *Kalevala*, are by renowned Finnish artist Gallen-Kallela (1865–1931).

Across Mannerheimintie is a branch of the **Helsinki City Museum** (Mannerheimintie 13b; tel: 09 3107 8519; Wed–Sun 11am–5pm, Thur 11am–7pm; free). Housed in the fine **Hakasalmi Villa** (1843) designed in the Italian neoclassical style, it stages interesting exhibitions on different aspects of the capital's history.

World-class venues

Finlandia Hall ❽ (Mannerheimintie 13e; tel: 09 40 241; www.finlandiatalo. fi; guided tours only), opposite the National Museum, is undoubtedly the most famous building in Helsinki with its clean lines and Carrara marble exterior, designed by Alvar Aalto. It was long the residence of the Helsinki Philharmonic Orchestra and a venue for various congress events, but that changed radically in September 2011 with the opening of the long-awaited, overdue and much-debated **Helsinki Music Centre ❾** (Musiikkitalo; www. musiikkitalo.fi), a state-of-the-art concert hall whose main occupants are the Helsinki Philharmonic and the Finnish Radio Symphony orchestras, and **Sibelius Academy**, Helsinki's famous musical conservatory.

Continuing north along Mannerheimintie to where Hesperia Park and Töölö Bay come to an end, the contemporary **Finnish National Opera House ❿** (Helsinginkatu 58; tel: 09 4030 2211; www.ooppera.fi), which opened in 1993, offers an ambitious season with many international performers. In 2011, the Finnish National Opera celebrated its centenary with several world premieres and prominent guest artists.

Nestling, literally, into a small hill west of the Parliament Building behind Mannerheimintie and the winding streets of Töölö, is the ultra-modern Lutheran church, **Temppeliaukion Kirkko,** or "Rock Church"

The Olympic stadium.

⓫ (Lutherinkatu 3; tel: 09 2340 5940; June–Aug Mon–Sat 10am–5.45pm, Sun 11.45am–5.45pm, Sept–May Mon–Sat 10am–5pm, Sun 11.45–5pm), which reopened in 2011 after extensive repair work. It is not only an architectural oddity – built as it is directly into the granite rocks, with inner walls of stone and an impressive copper-covered dome – but it is also the site of many good concerts. A service for English-speakers is held every Sunday at 2pm.

Around Esplanadi

Heading south, back to town on Mannerheimintie, you'll find **Stockmann** ⓬, Finland's largest department store (https://stockmann.com), which has an excellent food hall on the lower level. Behind it, on Keskuskatu, is Scandinavia's largest bookshop, **Akateeminen Kirjakauppa** (https://akateeminen.com), a great place to browse or to take a break in the stylish café designed by Alvar Aalto.

The bookshop faces another Helsinki landmark, **Esplanadi Park and Boulevards** ⓭, which was first laid out in 1831 and runs between Mannerheimintie and South Harbour. In summer its narrow lawns and benches are filled with people relaxing and eating ice creams, while being entertained by buskers. Summer concerts are held on the bandstand and come winter, it's the setting for the annual Christmas Fair.

Two boulevards stretch east–west along either side of the park. Nowadays the fine 19th-century buildings along Pohjoisesplanadi (North Esplanade) mostly house Finnish design shops, including Marimekko, Arabia and Aarikka.

The **Swedish Theatre** (Svenska Teatern; www.svenskateatern.fi), an elegant semicircular stone building dating from 1866, commands Esplanadi's western head on Mannerheimintie. In front of the theatre, bus no. 20 will take you just five minutes out of the centre to the **Ruoholahti** area and the **Cable Factory** (Kaapeli; www.kaapelitehdas.fi), a lively cultural complex (with café and restaurant), where the **Finnish Museum of Photography** and **Theatre Museum** ⓮

The tubular Sibelius Monument by Eila Hiltunen honours Finland's finest composer.

HELSINKI CARD

If you plan on doing lots of sightseeing in and around Helsinki, consider investing in a Helsinki Card, which can be purchased from the City Tourist Office (Tour Shop), Pohjoisesplanadi 19, hotels, sightseeing departure points, Airport Travel Services (at the airport, arrivals area 2b, open 24 hours) and railway station – or online, with a €3 discount (www.helsinkicard.com). The card provides free admission to museums and sights, an audio bus tour, free travel to Suomenlinna Sea Fortress and entry to the main sights, entry to Helsinki Zoo, and free travel on city buses, trams, trains and the metro. It also includes various other discounts and benefits. The card can be purchased for periods of 24, 48 and 72 hours; for adults €44, €54 and €64; for children 7–16 years old, €22, €27 and €32 respectively.

The stylish Kappeli restaurant by Esplanadi Park.

Busy Esplanadi Park.

are located (Tallberginkatu 1; tel: 09 6866 3621, www.valokuvataiteenmuseo.fi for photography; 0207 96 1670, www.teatterimuseo.fi for theatre; Tue–Sun 11am–6pm, Wed 11am–8pm; photography museum: last Wed of the month free after 5pm; theatre museum: closed in July).

Heading east through Esplanadi, past the central statue of J.L. Runeberg, Finland's national poet, you come to the historic café-restaurant and former haunt of Sibelius, **Kappeli** ⓯ (Eteläesplanadi 1; tel: 010 76 63880; www.kappeli.fi). It is a popular meeting place near the harbour with a pleasant outdoor terrace.

The nearby **Helsinki City Tourist Office** ⓰ (Pohjoisesplanadi 19; tel 09 3101 3300; www.visithelsinki.fi; mid-May–mid-Sept Mon–Fri 9am–8pm, Sat–Sun 9am–6pm, mid-Sept–mid-May Mon–Fri 9am–6pm, Sat–Sun 10am–4pm) offers tour advice, maps and brochures, and there's a booking desk here too.

In 1999 the **Hotel Kämp**, Pohjoisesplanadi 29, a popular rendezvous in Helsinki at the end of the 19th century, reopened its doors as a luxury hotel. The **Galleria Esplanad** is an exclusive shopping complex on the street and lower levels (www.galleriaesplanad.fi).

Market Square

Across the road from the Kappeli restaurant is the **Havis Amanda Fountain**, which created quite a stir when it was first erected in 1908. The bronze statue of a nubile mermaid represents the city of Helsinki rising from the sea, innocent and naked. Opposite the fountain is the bustling **Central Market Square** ⓱ (Kauppatori; Mon–Fri 6.30am–6pm, Sat until 4pm, in summer also Sun 10am–5pm). This is where locals buy their fruits, vegetables, flowers and fish. The small tents serve tasty cinnamon buns or meat pastries and there's a heated coffee tent. Other stalls sell arts and crafts, including Sami handicrafts. Every year in October, the traditional Herring Market is held on the square.

To the south of the square at the 100-year-old, yellow-and-red-brick **Old Market Hall** (Vanha Kauppahalli; http://vanhakauppahalli.fi; Mon–Sat 8m–6pm), you can buy salmon, reindeer cold-cuts, and even Vietnamese *loempia* (egg rolls).

Behind the market are the long blue **City Hall** ⓲ designed by Engel in 1833, and **Presidential Palace**, designed in 1818 as a private home and turned into a tsarist palace by Engel in 1843. The Finnish president no longer resides here.

To the cathedral

Another major landmark, **Senate Square**, stands one block north of here, on the busy **Aleksanterinkatu** shopping street. Over the centuries the square has remained a very impressive spot, where thousands gathered for the funeral of Jean Sibelius.

Helsinki Cathedral ⓳ (Tuomiokirkko; Mon–Sat 9am–6pm, Sun noon–7pm), at the top of a flight of steep steps on the north side, is a point of pride for Finns, and the exterior – with its five green cupolas, numerous white Corinthian columns and sprinkling of important figurines posing on its roof – is certainly impressive.

At the southeastern corner of the square stands the city's oldest stone building, dating from 1757, the small blue-grey **Sederholm House** 20 (Sederholmin Talo; Aleksanterinkatu), which used to contain the Children's Town exhibition. In May 2016, the new Helsinki City Museum will open in its place with a renewed children's exhibition and collections moved from other locations (www. uusikaupunginmuseo.fi).

If you are visiting prior to May 2016, you should head one block south to the **Helsinki City Museum**'s location at the time of printing 21 (Sofiankatu 4; tel: 09 3103 6630; Mon–Fri 9am–5pm, Thur 9am–7pm, Sat–Sun 11am–5pm; free).

Contemporary architecture buffs should not miss the Helsinki University Main Library, completed in 2012 in the very heart of city centre in Kaisaniemenkatu. A curved brick facade hides an imposing interior with state-of-the-art facilities.

Katajanokka

After exploring Helsinki's centre, venture into one of the surrounding districts, each of which has its own particular character. **Katajanokka** lies on a small promontory sticking out into the sea a few blocks east from Senate Square, connected by two short bridges. The spires and onion-shaped domes of the Russian Orthodox **Uspenski Cathedral** 22 (Uspenskin Katedraali), built in 1868, tower above a popular restaurant complex across the street. Helsinki's oldest Russian restaurant (1917), the **Bellevue** (www.restaurantbellevue.com), sits at the base of the cathedral, across from Katajanokka Park.

Jugendstil (Art Nouveau) architecture dominates **Luotsikatu** street, just east of the cathedral. Don't miss the

charming griffin doorway at No. 5.

In recent years, many of the old warehouses have been converted to restaurants, shops and a hotel. The **Customs and Bonded Warehouse** 23 (Katajanokkan Laituri 5) from 1900 remains the same, with its imaginative *Jugendstil* architecture.

West of Esplanadi

Head west from Esplanadi along **Bulevardi** and explore the neighbouring streets like Eerikinkatu, Fredrikinkatu and Uudenmaankatu, a fashionable quarter known for its galleries, boutiques, antique bookshops and restaurants. At the end of Bulevardi, past the old Opera House, don't miss the **Hietalahti flea market** 24 (Mon–Fri 9am–6pm, Sat 8am–4pm, also Sun 10am–4pm in summer), a popular open-air market in the summer months.

To the south of Bulevardi are the exclusive **Eira** and **Ullanlinna** districts. The **Design Museum** 25 (Korkeavuorenkatu 23; tel: 09 622 0540; www.designmuseum.fi; Tue 11am–8pm, Wed–Sun 11am–6pm,

Helsinki's fine cathedral, Tuomiokirkko.

On the Trail of Jugendstil

Helsinki offers a wealth of interest for lovers of architecture, especially among its flamboyant Art Nouveau buildings.

Helsinki has a wealth of architecture, which can be discovered in different quarters of the city. From Baroque Classicism and neo-Renaissance to neo-classical Empire and Modernist design. However, for the first-time visitor, it is the *Jugend* style which really makes an impression. It was around the turn of the 20th century that a younger generation of architects, inspired by the Arts and Crafts movement, rose in revolt against Classicism and older styles which recreated the past. These included: Lars Sonck (1870–1956), Bertel Jung (1872–1946), and the trio Herman Gesellius (1874–1916), Armas Lindgren (1874–1929) and Eliel Saarinen (1873–1950), who were committed to creating "a more domestic, freer and more authentic world" with their work.

In France, the name of this new style was Art Nouveau, and in Germany *Jugendstil*. It is

A classic example of Art Nouveau (Jugend) style in Katajanokka.

recognised by its own unique elements which have taken on a more local form in Finland known as National Romanticism, characterised by visually striking windows, heavy ornamentation, serious figurative components, the use of natural materials like timber and granite, and castle-inspired features like spires and towers.

Where to find *Jugendstil* in Helsinki

With its four globe-bearing figures by Emil Wikström and imposing facade, Helsinki Central Station, designed by Eliel Saarinen, is a memorable example of the National Romantic style. Arrive in good time before your train leaves to look at the striking murals in the Eliel restaurant.

The National Museum with its spires, distinctive clock tower, carved bear at the entrance also by Wikström and ceiling painting by Akseli Gallen-Kallela, both prominent artists of the period, was jointly designed by Saarinen and his partners Herman Gesellius and Armas Lindgren, who won an architectural competition for the project in 1902. They also created Hvitträsk, in Kirkkonummi, a stone and log structure in an idyllic lakeside setting on a forested hill, just west of Helsinki. The villa served as their country home and studio until their tumultuous personal relationships ended their collaboration in 1905; it is one of the masterpieces of Finnish architecture. The National Theatre is another example of their work, as is Pohjola House at Aleksanterinkatu 44, former HQ of the Helsinki Telephone Company, now head office of Pohjola Insurance.

Examples of *Jugendstil* architecture can be found all around Helsinki, like Katajanokka (east of Senate Square), Kruununhaka (just to the south) and the stylish Eira neighbourhood, just south of Kaivopuisto Park, known for its splendid embassy mansions. Other buildings to look out for include the hospital at Laivurinkatu 27, designed by Lars Sonck, Lindahl and Thomé's Linna Hotel (now GLO Hotel Art), Lönnrottinkatu 29, and the Otava publishing house at Uudenmaankatu 10.

National Romanticism was not just expressed through architecture, but in the visual arts and classical music (most notably in the Karelia Suite by Sibelius). Architects looked to their national history for inspiration, like Karelia, the province that spans Russia and Finland, of great historic importance, and to the national epic, the Kalevala, which is rich in mythology and symbolism.

For dedicated walks and tours of Jugendstil sights, visit www.archtours.com.

June–Aug daily 11am–6pm) provides an overview of modern Finnish style and the roots of its aesthetic, showcasing Finland's leading designers of the 20th and 21st century who transform everyday items – lamps, chairs, glasses, toys – into objects of simple, functional beauty. In the same block is the **Museum of Finnish Architecture** ㉖ (Kasarmikatu 24; tel: 09 8567 5100; www.mfa.fi; Tue–Sun 11am–6pm, Wed until 8pm; free first Fri of the month), which has an excellent archive of architectural drawings and changing exhibitions focusing on Finnish architectural movements.

The southernmost end of the peninsula is lined by parkland, frequented by joggers, skaters and cyclists. In summer, the city sponsors free concerts in **Kaivopuisto Park** ㉗. Strollers head for refreshment at the **Café Ursula** (www.ursula.fi) whose terrace offers a stunning view of the Suomenlinna Castle, or the seafront **Café Carusel** (www.carusel.fi). In winter, when the sea is frozen, you can actually walk out to some of the closer offshore islands. On the eastern point, the grand villas of foreign embassies fill the chic Ullanlinna district. **Olympia Quay** ㉘ (Olympia terminaali) is a mooring place for the huge Silja and Viking liners. The fast ferries that ply the route to medieval Tallin, the Estonian capital, board at the West Terminal.

Suomenlinna

Suomenlinna ㉙ (Fortress of Finland) consists of five islands, over which the ruins of a naval fortress and its fortifications are spread. Suomenlinna has played an integral part in Helsinki's life since its construction started in 1748. Listed by Unesco as a World Heritage site, today it is a thriving local artists' community with the restored bastions being used as studios and showrooms. Visitors arrive here year-round by ferry which departs from Market Square every half-hour. They dock on **Iso Mustasaari**, from where a hilly path leads up through **Rantakasarmi** (Jetty Barracks), which houses art exhibitions and the restaurant and microbrewery **Panimo**.

Try your hand at dinghy sailing around Helsinki's islands.

Suomenlinna.

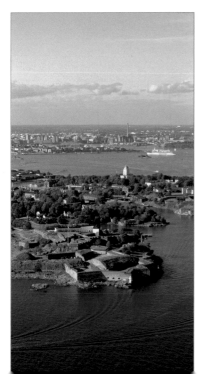

FERRIES TO ESTONIA, TRAINS TO RUSSIA

Across the Gulf of Finland lies the northernmost of the Baltic states, Estonia. Its capital, Tallinn, is 85km (53 miles) from Helsinki and about 130km (80 miles) from St Petersburg. Finns have long taken advantage of Estonia's proximity and relative cheapness, making the ferry crossing in droves. It is easy to see the attraction: Tallinn has the prettiest Old Town in the Baltics, a medieval enclave set on a hillock above its port. Within the fairytale walls and towers and beneath the Gothic spires are winding cobbled lanes, artisan shops, historic buildings, charming cafés and breathtaking vistas – a wonderful contrast to the modern city centre, where a rapidly developing commercial district has redrawn the city's skyline. For information on organised day trips visit www.stromma.fi; for information on fast boat services visit www.tallink.com (the journey takes 2 hours each way).

For an alternative, land-based excursion across the Russian border take the fast train from Helsinki and St Petersburg. The ultramodern Allegro train takes you on a 3.5-hour journey from city centre to city centre (www.russiantrains.com). There are four daily services. Border formalities are conducted during the journey on board the train, and you can also exchange currency during the trip. Most nationals will need a Russian entry visa, yet there are some exemptions for organised groups; contact your travel agent for more details.

TIP

Helsinki has a number of public saunas, but the only wood-heated one is Kotiharjun Sauna, Harjutorinkatu 1 in Kallio, near Sörnäinen metro station (tel: 09 753 1535; www.kotiharjunsauna.fi; Tue–Sun 2–8pm, sauna time until 9.30pm).

For information on the island's museums, stop by the Visitor Centre (daily; entrance to fortress free, charge to museums; tel: 0295 338 410; www.suomenlinna.fi; guided tours in English). The expansive **Suomenlinna Museum** covers the history of the sea fortress from the 18th century to the present. The castle courtyard, the best-preserved section of the fortress, contains the 1788 sarcophagus of Count Ehrensvärd, commander of the fort, whose former home is now the Ehrensvärd Museum with period furniture, arms and lithographs. Other museums include a **Toy Museum, Artillery Museum, Customs Museum** and the fascinating **Vesikko**, a World War II submarine (all open in summer only). Try to visit the atmospheric summer restaurant **Walhalla**, where on a clear day it is possible to see Estonia, some 80km (50 miles) away.

Korkeasaari

In summer, **Helsinki Zoo** ㉚ (Korkeasaari island; tel: 09 3101 615; www.korkeasaari.fi; daily May–Aug 10am–8pm, Oct–Mar until 4pm, Apr and Sept until 6pm) can be reached by boat from Market Square or on bus no. 11 from the Railway Square. The zoo, unsurprisingly, specialises in "cold climate animals", although there's an interesting enclosure of South American species.

Seurasaari

The island of **Seurasaari** ㉛ is eminently atmospheric. A pretty, forested place with a national park (all year), its northeastern side has been made into an **Open-Air Museum** (tel: 04 0509 660; June–Aug daily 11am–5pm) containing wooden buildings from provinces all over Finland from the 17th to 19th centuries.

To get to the island, take either bus no. 24 from Erottaja (in front of the Swedish Theatre), or cycle along the Meilahti coastal drive which takes you past the lovely **Sibelius Park** ㉜ and its silvery tubular **Sibelius Monument** to the bridge connecting Seurasaari with the mainland.

Other islands

Less well known are the smaller islands that form a string around Helsinki's southern peninsula. Across the "Olympic Harbour" are **Luoto** ㉝ and **Valkosaari**, restaurant islands with romantic villas. A long pier outside Kaivopuisto offers a boat service to **Särkkä** ㉞, another island with a popular restaurant. **Uunisaari** ㉟ is accessible at the southern end of Neitsytpolku Street. It's a popular recreational island with a beach, sauna and restaurant.

Pihlajasaari ㊱ is Helsinki's favourite island for swimming. It actually comprises two islands, with a sandy beach, café and changing cabins on the larger island's western shore. Helsinki's only nudist beach is on the smaller island. Boats to Pihlajasaari depart in summer every 15 to 30 minutes from outside Café Carusel in Eira.

The former military island of **Harakka** ㊲, south of Kaivopuisto, is now a wildlife reserve.

Kaivopuisto Park.

Alfresco lunch by the harbour.

THE TRADITIONAL FINNISH SAUNA

An old Finnish proverb says: "First you build the sauna, then you build the house". Even today, there is nothing so uniquely Finnish as a sauna.

There are some things along the way which a traveller does not forget – and a real Finnish sauna is one of them. Although its origin is obscure and legend claims that the sauna came to Finland over 2,000 years ago, credit must go to the Karelian people for introducing the sauna to Finnish culture (see page 341). Official statistics now estimate that there are over 1.6 million saunas in Finland, not counting those in private houses or summer cottages that dot the shoreline of the country's lakes. The actual figure could easily be over 2 million in a country of over 5 million people.

Business and pleasure

The sauna outgrew its rural roots long ago. Today, be it city or village, you will find public saunas, and it is safe to assume that every new apartment block has a sauna for its tenants. Many companies also have saunas for their employees, most hotels have them for guests, and there is even one in Helsinki's Parliament building.

A Finnish sauna is not a meeting place for sex, as it is in some countries; codes of behaviour are strict, and public saunas are not for both genders at the same time. It is not unusual for board meetings and government cabinet meetings to be held in a sauna – perhaps because it's "not done" to swear or raise one's voice. Titles and position are, they say, left hanging in the changing room along with the clothes.

In 2010, this national institution was honoured with a documentary film *Steam of Life*, which was a big hit on the festival circuit.

Cooling off after a sauna in Lapland.

The sauna has become an integral part of Finnish life, where friends meet and business deals are struck. A popular seasonal option is to spring into a lake between steam sessions.

Birch leaves, cut in early summer when they are green, are tied up in bundles and used in the sauna as switches to increase blood circulation.

Some brave souls dive into icy water or jump through holes in the ice – not recommended practice for people with high blood pressure.

HOW TO TAKE A SAUNA

There is no "right way" to take a sauna – temperature and style vary. The ideal temperature is between 60–80°C (140–175°F), although it can be a cooler 30°C (85°F) on the bottom platform, reserved for children. A common practice is to brush oneself with a wet birch switch, called the *vihta*. This not only gives off a fresh fragrance but increases blood circulation and perspiration.

How long you sit in the sauna is entirely up to you. When you have had enough, you move on to stage two: cooling off. A cold shower is the most common way but, if the sauna is by a lake or the sea, a quick plunge into the cool water is stimulating.

The final stage is to dry off, which should be done naturally, to avoid further perspiration. It is also time for a beer or coffee and a snack to complete the ritual.

Soaking up the heat in a sauna is a refreshing and revitalising experience, good for the skin and the psyche.

Saunas are generally same sex only; mixed ones are either for families or groups of close friends.

Finnish musician M. A. Numminen giving a concert in the country's largest sauna, at the Naval Academy in Suomenlinna.

SOUTHERN FINLAND

Follow the route of the Nordic kings from west
to east across southern Finland, through a gentle
landscape of painted villages, ancient castles
and an island-studded coast.

The route once travelled by Nordic kings and princes to St Petersburg is known as the King's Road; it passes through mainly flat coastal country covered with farmland and dense forest. From Pargas (Parainen), south of **Turku ❶** (Åbo; see page 323) at the head of the Turunmaa archipelago chain, through Hanko (Hangö), Ekenäs (Tammisaari), Karis (Karjaa) and further east via Porvoo (Borgå) through a cluster of small villages on the approach to Kotka, you will hear a great deal of Swedish being spoken and read it as the first language on signposts.

Exploring the islands

Richly vegetated but sparsely populated, the archipelago of **Turunmaa ❷** is quieter than the Ålands in terms of tourism, and the islands are reached more quickly from the mainland by local bus or car. They are linked by a series of bridges and then ferries, which also service some of the smaller islands that spin off south from the main chain. Many Finnish families have their own islands – the ultimate refuge.

Turunmaa's finest harbour is on the northern spur of **Nagu**. An old wooden house overlooking the marina has been made into a guesthouse-style hotel. Also to be found in Nagu is a small **Hembygdsmuseum** and the 15th-century **St Olof's Church**.

As you approach **Pargas ❸** (Parainen) from the west or the south you come to **Sattmark**, on the island of Stortervolandet. Here you can lodge in a tiny log cabin that was once a sailor's quarters, or just stop for some refreshment in the charming café (tel: 044 9702 599; www.sattmarkinfo.fi).

Continuing east towards Piikkiö, it is worth making a detour to **Kuusisto Castle ❹** (Kuusiston Linna) on the Kuusisto peninsula. This medieval bishop's castle stood stoutly until Gustav Vasa ordered its demolition

Main Attractions

Turunmaa archipelago
Hanko harbour and
  19th-century villas
Bengtskär Lighthouse
Ekenäs/Tammisaari Old
  Town and National Park
Fiskars village
Hvitträsk
Gallen-Kallela Museum
Porvoo Old Town
Åland Islands

Ekenäs.

Southern Finland and the Lakes

in 1528, but enough remains to have encouraged restoration.

Salo and Sammatti

Salo **⑤**, to the east on the mainland, has a lively market and is set off by a triad of churches – the Lutheran **Uskela** (1832) by C.L. Engel, the Greek Orthodox **Tsasouna** at its foot, and the stunningly modern **Helisnummi Church** about 4km (2.5 miles) outside the town. At **Sammatti ⑥**, 48km (30 miles) east of Salo, look out for the sign to **Paikkari Cottage** (Paikkarin Torppa; www.paikka rintorpantuki.fi), the home of Elias Lönnrot who collected the legends and tales for the *Kalevala* (see page 89).

The coast: west of Helsinki

Southwest of Salo is **Hanko ⑦** (Hangö), Finland's southernmost town, once a popular spa resort, and now frequented for its annual regatta and its beaches. Hanko is distinguished by an abundance of turreted villas in pastel shades which grace the stretch of beach behind a line of charming white changing huts. These stately homes were built in the late 19th century for the Russian nobility who came for health cures; several offer bed and breakfast accommodation.

The City Hall Gallery and Municipal Library Gallery offer a range of exhibitions. Just a stone's throw away at Villa Orrmanissa you can indulge in freshly baked pastries at **Alan's Cafe**, and browse in the antiquarian bookshop and crafts gallery. There are two fish restaurants on the harbourfront and several in the adjacent renovated warehouses. On 26 August, the annual Night of the Bonfires takes place and launches the Hanko Days Weekend Festival (note that at the end of August hotels and restaurants virtually shut down, however some villas may be hired privately).

In summer, seal safaris take off from the eastern harbour Thur and Sun at 11am. Book at the tourist office (tel: 019 2203 411; http://tourism.hanko.fi). There are also boat excursions to the adjacent town of Ekenäs (www.marine lines.fi), or to **Bengtskär Lighthouse**, 25km (15 miles) south of Hanko, which make a memorable day's adventure. Built in 1906, the massive stone structure is Scandinavia's tallest lighthouse at 52 metres (170ft) high. The climb to the top of the 252 steps is worth it for the view. There is a café and gift shop, and it is also possible to lodge here.

Ekenäs ⑧ (Tammisaari) is the next main coastal stop along the King's Road. It is a finely laid out old town, with 18th- and 19th-century cobbled streets and charming wooden buildings, and is a great place for a stroll. Just to the south is the **Tammisaari National Park**, resplendent with marshes, forests and water birds.

There is an extremely active boating life in and around Ekenäs, and numerous outdoor concerts in summer. The **Knipan** summer restaurant (http://knipan.fi) and the steeple of the old granite church (1680) are the town's main landmarks. Visit **Ekenäs Museum** (Tammisaari, Wasas gata 11; tel: 019 289 2512; Wed–Sun 11am–5pm) for some local history. Boat tours depart

The Monument of Liberty in Hanko, erected in 1921.

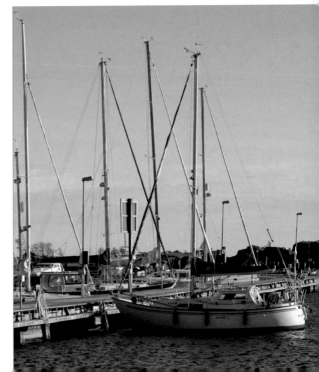

The harbour at Hanko, Finland's southernmost town.

Hvitträsk interior.

Fiskars.

from the North Harbour in July and August.

From Ekenäs, take a detour north to the picturesque village of **Fiskars** ❾, a craft, design and art centre and the original home of Fiskars knives and scissors, founded in 1649. The **Fiskars Museum** (tel: 019 237 013; www.fiskarsmuseum.fi; May–Sept Mon–Fri 11am–5pm, Sat–Sun until 6pm) portrays the company's history.

A few kilometres east from Ekenäs is **Snappertuna**, a farming village 15km (10 miles) from the late 14th-century castle at **Raasepori** ❿. The outdoor theatre in the Raseborg dale stages dramatic and musical evenings. Further east beyond Snappertuna is **Fagervik** ⓫, the site of a tremendous old manor overlooking an inlet. The nearby fishing village of **Ingå** (Inkoo) has pretty cafés and craft shops.

Hvitträsk and Tarvaspää

Just outside Espoo, **Hvitträsk** ⓬ (tel: 040 128 6359; May–Sept daily 11am–5pm, Oct–Apr Wed–Sun 11am–5pm) merits a visit. This Jugendstil jewel was designed by Eliel Saarinen (1901–3) and his colleagues, Herman Gesellius and

Armas Lindgren, and for a time served as the architects' communal residence and studio, and was frequented by the likes of Sibelius, Gallen-Kallela and Gorki. Set on a forested hill by a lake, this fantastic and fanciful creation of timber and granite now functions as a museum with a café that serves local specialities.

A little further west, approaching Helsinki, **Tarvaspää** ⓭ was the home of Finland's national artist, Akseli Gallen-Kallela (1865–1931). His *Jugendstil*-inspired studio has been converted into the **Gallen-Kallela Museum** (tel: 09 849 2340; www.gallen-kallela.fi; mid-May–Aug daily 11am–6pm, Sept–mid-May Tue–Sat 11am–4pm, Sun 11am–5pm), displaying the artist's paintings, stained glass, tools and objects collected on his travels. There is an outdoor café and nearby walking trails.

Porvoo

East of Helsinki, **Porvoo** ⓮ (Borgå) is one of Finland's most important historical towns. The Swedish king Magnus Eriksson gave Porvoo a royal charter in 1346; it soon became a busy trading post and, ultimately, it was the place where the Diet of Porvoo (1809) convened to transfer Finland from Swedish to Russian hands. The striking 15th-century **Porvoo Cathedral** (May–Sept Mon–Fri 10am–6pm, Sat 10am–2pm, Sun 2–5pm, Oct–Apr Tue–Sat 10am–2pm, Sun 2–4pm) is where this momentous event took place.

While its rich history made the town important, Porvoo's writers and artists gave it its real character. The former residence of Finland's national poet, **J.L. Runeberg** (Aleksanterinkatu 3; tel: 019 574 7500; May–Aug Mon–Sun 10am–4pm, Sept–Apr Wed–Sun 10am–4pm) opened to the public as a museum in 1882, and its well-preserved interior contains original antiques, books, manuscripts and memorabilia. The **Walter Runeberg Sculpture Collection** (Aleksanterinkatu 5; tel: 040 489 1770; May–Sept Mon–Sun 10am–4pmhas over 100 sculptures by J.L Runeberg's son, a respected sculptor

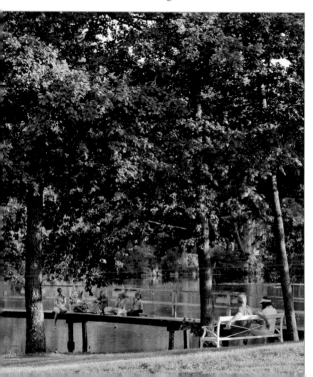

who was commissioned to make statues of his father and Tsar Alexander II.

Porvoo Museum (tel: 019 574 7500; May–Aug Mon–Sat 10am–4pm, Sun 11am–4pm, Sept–Apr Wed–Sun noon–4pm) occupies two buildings (1763) on the cobbled old town square. It focuses on life as lived by a wealthy 18th-century merchant family.

For scenery, the medieval atmosphere of **Old Porvoo** has few rivals: its riverbanks are lined with redochre warehouses and pastel-coloured wooden houses. On summer weekdays, guided walking tours of the Old Town start from the town hall on the square at 2pm (tel: 040 489 9801; www.visitporvoo.fi). From mid-May until mid-Sept, the M/S J.L. Runeberg operates cruises from Helsinki to Porvoo (tel: 019 524 3331; www.msjlruneberg.fi).

The **Albert Edelfelt Atelier** (Edelfeltinpolku 3; tel: 040 552 9083; June–Aug Tue–Sun 10am–4pm, 15–31 May and 1–15 Sept Tue–Sun 10am–2pm) built in 1883 in Haikko, 6km (4 miles) south of Porvoo, exhibits the *oeuvre* of one of Finland's finest 19th-century artists.

East of Porvoo, the landscape becomes more rural and less populated. In summer the grassy hillocks bristle with wild flowers. **Loviisa** ⓯ is a pretty coastal town with an esplanade headed by the New Gothic Church. A town museum tells the local history, including the role of the Rosen and Ungern bastions, built in the 18th century to protect the trade route between Vyborg and Turku. Just 10km (6 miles) from the centre of town on an island at the mouth of Loviisa Bay is the **Svartholma** sea fortress, built in 1748.

Kotka

Kotka ⓰ is the next important destination on the King's Road and is one of the most beautifully situated cities in Finland. Here, the fast-flowing Kymi River breaks up into five branches before rushing off into the sea, making for perfect salmon and trout fishing. The local fish species can also be found in the **Kotka Aquarium** (Maretarium; tel: 040 311 0330; www.maretarium.fi; Mon–Tue and Thu–Sun 10am–5pm, Wed noon–7pm).

Tourists flock to the modern town of Kotka every July to join in the fun at

TIP

Good stopping points on the journey east from Loviisa to Kotka are the excellent sandy beaches of Pyhtää and the holiday island of Kaunissaari, with its interesting fishing village.

Old cottages in Porvoo in winter.

the largest maritime festival in Finland (www.meripaivat.com). The pleasant **Sapokka Marina** has a nice park, with a high artificial waterfall. Step aboard a water bus for a tour of the beautiful Kotka archipelago (www.visitkotka.fi).

The **Kymenlaakso** (Kymi River Valley) extends further inland, where there are forest trails, fishing and white-water rafting. Enquire for details at the Kotka Tourist Office (Keskuskatu 6, tel: 040 135 6588; www.southeast135.fi).

The main attraction at nearby **Langinkoski** is the impressive **Imperial Fishing Lodge Museum** (tel: 05 211 1600; www.langinkoskimuseo.com; June–Aug daily 10am–6pm, May and Sept daily 10am–4pm), in a beautiful wooded setting, by the Kymi River, some 5km (3 miles) north of the town centre. This striking two-storey log building was crafted by the Finns for Tsar Alexander III (1845–94), who used it to break his journeys between Helsinki and St Petersburg.

It's another 5km (3 miles) from here to the Siikakoski rapids, an ideal spot for fishing, and Restaurant Munkkisaari, built on the site of an Orthodox monastery. The restaurant sells fishing licences and has boats and cabins for hire (tel: 05 210 7400).

In summer, **Kärkisaari**, just west of Kotka, makes for a lovely excursion. The long swimming dock leads into the island-filled inlet of the Gulf of Finland. On the adjacent peninsula is **Santalahti**; the crescent-shaped beach has grassy knolls at the edge of a sandy bay.

To the Russian border

Kotka is only 70km (45 miles) from the nearest Russian city, Viipuri (Vyborg), and 270km (170 miles) from St Petersburg. Various trips to Russia can be arranged with the Kotka Tourist Board; remember to plan overnight trips well in advance so that your visa will be ready.

The streets of the 350-year-old town of **Hamina** ⓱ are laid out in concentric circles and lined with beautiful wooden buildings, small restaurants, cafés and craft shops.

Further east lies **Vaalimaa**, a busy border station with huge supermarkets selling goods to Russians and Finns crossing the frontier.

Main street, Porvoo.

Åland Islands: the Ultimate Retreat

To the west of Finland, the Ålands are a perfect island-hopping destination. Catch a ferry, hire a bike and discover this little-known paradise.

The Åland Islands (Ahvenanmaa in Finnish) are a collection of granite skerries made up of over 6,000 islands in the Baltic Sea, between the west coast of Finland and the east coast of Sweden. Ålanders have inhabited their islands for thousands of years, and have a strong ethnic culture and a formidable pride in their identity. The population of 28,000 has had its own flag since 1954 (a red cross within a yellow cross against a blue background) and its own postage stamps since 1984. Today, the islands are an autonomous demilitarised zone represented both in the Finnish Parliament and the Nordic Council, with Swedish being the official language. Although part of the EU, Åland remains outside the tax union agreement, so tax-free shopping is available to travellers.

The islands are a paradise for hiking, fishing, golfing, swimming and other watersports, and, because they are mostly flat, are ideally explored by bike. The bicycle ferry *M/S Silvana* (mid-June–mid-Aug) links bike routes between islands (tel: 18 37 212). You can hire bicycles from the Mariehamn harbours and campsites.

June to August is the ideal time to visit. A high point of the summer are the midsummer celebrations held in almost every village with the traditional raising of the Midsummer pole and dancing.

Take a Viking (www.vikingline.fi) or Silja Line (www.tallinksilja.com) ferry from Turku, Helsinki, or Stockholm to **Mariehamn** ⑱, the Åland capital, sailing through the maze of skerries en route. There are also Next Jet and SAS flights from Stockholm to Mariehamm.

With 11,000 inhabitants in total, Mariehamm is the only town-sized settlement on the archipelago. It is known as "the town of a thousand linden trees" due to its broad tree-lined trees. In the West Harbour, the four-masted museum ship Pommern (May–Sept), built in Glasgow in 1904, is worth a visit, as is the nearby Maritime Museum (www.sjofartsmuseum.ax; June–Aug daily 10am–5pm, Sept–May 10am–4pm). Other museums in the

town focus on Ice and Bronze Age life, photography, hunting, fishing – there's even a museum on the postal service.

Most notable in Åland's northeast is the historic **Kastelholm Castle** ⑲ (www.kastelholm.ax; May–mid-Sept daily 10am–5pm, July until 6pm), a medieval fortress built in the 14th century; it was once the administrative centre for the islands, and of strategic importance to Swedish control of the Baltic. Badly damaged in a fire in 1745, the castle was massively restored in the 1980s. With the adjacent **Jan Karlsgården Open-Air Museum** (May–mid-Sept daily 10am–5pm), and nearby ruins of the Russian-built fortress Bomarsund, it is a major attraction.

To the southeast of Åland lies the lush island of **Föglö** ⑳, once an important vodka-smuggling destination. Its eastern side is a seabird reserve (the name Föglö means "the place of many birds"). There are scenic hiking trails around Jyddö and Hastersboda, which also offers excellent birdwatching opportunities. Canoeing in the bays and canals of the island is a popular leisure activity.

Hotels, guesthouses, cottages and camping facilities are available throughout Åland. For more information, contact the Åland Tourism Board, Storagatan 8; tel: 018 24 000; www.visitaland.com.

Mariehamn.

Floating restaurant in Turku.

TURKU

Ancient and modern coexist in Turku, Finland's former historic capital. Colourful restaurant boats line the river; museums, bars and galleries intermingle in the city centre.

In 2011, Turku (Åbo in Swedish) celebrated its role as the European Capital of Culture, jointly with Tallinn in Estonia, hosting an unparalleled year of cultural events which put this "small town with a big soul" in the spotlight. Surrounded by islands, river and sea, Finland's former capital is a town for all seasons. The River Aura divides the modern city in two, and you can cross its five main bridges or take the little city ferry (year-round) that still carries pedestrians and bicycles free of charge (www.visitturku.fi).

Medieval Turku is Finland's oldest city and yet many of the buildings go back only to the Great Fire of 1827 which destroyed a town then largely made of wood. In 1300, when it acquired a new cathedral, Turku became the spiritual centre of Finland. Around the same time, the solid lines of a castle began to rise near the mouth of the River Aura as the heart of royal power in Finland, where the Swedish governor lived and visiting dignitaries paid their respects.

After the Great Fire, the market and town moved away from the cathedral to the west bank of the Aura, much of it designed and built to the plan of Carl Ludwig Engel. Turku had the first university in Finland, founded by the 17th-century Governor General of Finland, Count Per Brahe.

Take a step back in time to 18th-century Finland at Luostarinmäki.

Exploring the town

A good place to begin a walking tour of the town is the **Turku Art Museum** Ⓐ (Aurakatu 26; tel: 02 262 7100; www.turuntaidemuseo.fi; Tue–Fri 11am–7pm, Sat–Sun 11am–5pm; Fri after 4pm free), an impressive Art Nouveau building which presents works from the Golden Age of Finnish art (1880–1910) by Gallen-Kallela, Victor Westerholm, Pekka Halonen, Albert Edelfelt and others.

Follow Aurakatu to the **Orthodox Cathedral** Ⓑ, built in 1838 on the

Main Attractions
Turku Art Museum
Luostarinmäki Handicrafts Museum
Turku Cathedral
Abo Vetus & Ars Nova
Turku Castle

FACT

Turku has become known for its unusual bars in the city centre, housed in buildings that have been converted from a pharmacy, bank, schoolhouse, and even a public toilet.

orders of Tsar Nicholas I. The church is next to the bustling market square (Kauppatori) flanked by Sokos and Stockmann department stores. Be sure to visit the 19th-century **Kauppahalli** **C** (Indoor Market Hall; www.kauppa halli.fi), across the street in Eerikinkatu, an ideal spot for a quick lunch or coffee and pastry.

Turning down Aurakatu, the Auransilta (bridge) gives the first view of the numerous restaurant boats moored along the river. Across the bridge is a Turku must-see – the **Luostarinmäki Handicrafts Museum** **D** (tel: 02 262 0350; June–Aug daily 10am–6pm, May, Sept Tue–Sun 10am–6pm, mid-Nov–mid-Jan Tue–Sun 10am–4pm), an authentic open-air museum in the only 18th-century area to survive the Great Fire. Here you can wander down unpaved streets past traditional wooden houses and watch artisans in period costume at work.

Around Old Great Square

Until the Great Fire of 1827, Old Great Square (Vanha Suurtori) was the heart of Turku, its administrative centre and main market place. Today the square stages the summer Medieval Market and Finland's oldest Christmas Market. Nearby **Turku Cathedral** **E** (Tuomiokirkko; daily 16 Sept–15 Apr 9am–7pm, 16 Apr–15 Sept until 8pm) maintains a stately presence. Consecrated in 1300, it is the country's national shrine and its most important medieval structure. Outside the cathedral stands a statue of Per Brahe, governor of Finland from 1637, who introduced welfare reforms and founded Finland's first university.

Beyond the museum towards the river, the **Sibelius Museum** **F** (Piispankatu 17; tel: 02 215 4494; www. sibeliusmuseum.abo.fi; Tue–Sun 11am– 4pm, extended hours Wed 6–8pm) chronicles the life and times of the great composer, with an interesting collection of instruments housed in a sleek Modernist building. In spring and autumn, evening concerts are held every Wednesday.

On the riverbank south of the Old Great Square stands **Rettig Palace**, built in 1928 for one of Turku's aristocratic families. It now houses the

Turku

two-in-one museum **Aboa Vetus & Ars Nova** (Museum of History and Contemporary Art; Itäinen Rantakatu 4–6; tel: 02 0718 1640; www.aboavetusarsnova.fi; daily 11am–7pm), which translates as "Old City, New Art". The museum's contemporary art exhibits are juxtaposed with the excavated remains of medieval Turku (discovered during building works) to great effect, providing insight into Turku both as a historical city and forward-thinking cultural centre.

Along the riverbank

For a riverside tour, return to the north bank and **Qwensel House** , Turku's oldest wooden building (1695), which now houses the **Pharmacy Museum** (Läntinen Rantakatu 13; tel: 02 262 0280; May–Aug Tue–Sun 10am–6pm, Dec Tue–Sun 10am–4pm) and a popular courtyard café. Walk past **Mill Bridge** (Myllysilta) to the next bridge, Martinsilta, where the *S/S Ukkopekka* is moored (www.ukkopekka.fi). Between June and August, pleasant excursions through the archipelago aboard the steamship run from the quay at the bridge. Continue on this side of the river as far as Turku Castle and the modern harbour area, with merchant tugs and tankers and Viking and Silja Lines terminals.

On your way to the harbour is the **Maritime Museum** (Forum Marinarum; Linnankatu 74; tel: 02 267 9511; www.forum-marinum.fi; exhibitions: June–Aug daily 11am–7pm, Sept–May Tue–Sun 11am–6pm; ships: June–Aug daily 11am–7pm), which documents Turku's shipping history, and a fleet of museum ships moored outside, including the handsome three-masted barque *Sigyn* and the sleek white hull of the sailing ship *Suomen Joutsen* (Swan of Finland) which once plied the ocean between Europe and South America.

The riverside walk culminates at **Turku Castle** (Turun linna; Linnankatu 80; tel: 02 262 0300; Tue–Sun 10am–6pm, June–Aug daily), some

3km (2 miles) from the centre. In its labyrinth of rooms, Turku's history from medieval times is relayed.

Heading back towards the centre along the opposite bank you come to the **Wäinö Aaltonen Museum** (Itäinen Rantakatu 38, tel: 02 262 0850; www.wam.fi; Tue–Sun 10am–6pm), exhibiting works by one of Finland's most important sculptors, Wäinö Aaltonen (1894–1966). In **Urheilupuisto** , the surrounding park, the windmill on Samppalinnanmäki is the last of its kind in Turku. Next to it is the running track where the champion long-distance runner and Olympic gold medallist Paavo Nurmi (1897–1973) trained. His statue stands on the Auransilta (bridge).

Ruissalo Island

Boat services depart several times daily for **Ruissalo Island** . An ideal excursion for cyclists, walkers and nature- and beach-lovers. If you are also fond of the exotic flora, visit the Turku University Botanical Garden located here (http://puutarha.utu.fi). In summer, the island hosts **Ruisrock**, the annual rock festival (www.ruisrock.fi).

TIP

One of the best ways to see the archipelago is on a cruise aboard the steamship *S/S Ukkopekka* (tel: 02 515 3300; www.ukkopekka.fi). The two-hour cruise to Naantali, a charming seaside town north of Turku, is popular in the summer. Children come in droves to visit nearby Moomin World (tel: 02 511 1111; www.muumimaailma.fi), a theme park based on Tove Jansson's Moomintroll stories.

The bustling university town is a good base from which to explore.

Olavinlinna, Savonlinna.

FINLAND'S LAKELAND

A labyrinth of lakes and pine-covered islands extends north from Helsinki. The landscape that was home to Sibelius rewards exploration by lake steamer and canoe.

With some 33,000 islands and peninsulas, the Great Lakes of Saimaa and Päijänne in central Finland provide a diverse waterscape of lakes, rivers and canals to form Europe's largest waterway system. This varied landscape owes its beauty to the Ice Age, when glaciers carved out the shape of lakes and ridges. The area attracts thousands of visitors each year yet never appears crowded.

The best approach to the lakes is via industrial **Kouvola** ㉑, about 140km (86 miles) northeast of Helsinki and a junction of road and rail routes into Saimaa. Although not the most interesting town in Finland, Kouvola's Kaunisnurmi quarters house quaint handicraft shops and several museums.

To capture the spirit of Saimaa, ignore the direct routes to Kuopio in the north and head east on route 6 to **Lappeenranta** ㉒, south Karelia's main town. The fortress next to the harbour, in the Linnoitus quarter, was built by the Russians in 1775 and today houses the **South Karelian Museum** (Etelä-Karjalan Museo, Linnoitus; tel: 05 616 2261; June–mid-Aug Mon–Fri 10am–6pm, Sat–Sun 11am–5pm, mid-Aug–May Tue–Sun 11am–5pm). Its permanent "On the Border" exhibition chronicles the history of Lappeenranta and Vyborg, formerly in Karelia but now just a few miles south in Russia, whose fate was sealed by the 1939–40 Winter War between Russia and Finland. The **Cavalry Museum** (Ratsuväkimuseo; tel: 05 616 2257; June–mid-Aug Mon–Fri 10am–6pm, Sat–Sun 11am–5pm) details the history and distinctive red uniforms of Finland's proud soldiers. Also in Linnoitus is Finland's oldest Orthodox church (1785).

Day cruises to Russia operate from Lappeenranta, for which visitors do not require visas (since this is an organised tour and they will be

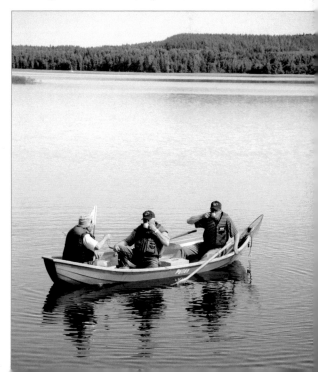

Fishing in the Lakeland.

staying less than 72 hours), although they are obligatory for other visits.

A few miles further east is the industrial city of **Imatra** ㉓, once erroneously described as the "Niagara of Finland", but worth a brief visit to see the impressive **Imatrankoski** (Rapids).

Punkaharju

About 50km (30 miles) north of Imatra, route 6 passes within a few hundred metres of the Russian border. Switching to route 14, you soon come to **Punkaharju** ㉔, one of countless ridges bequeathed to Finland by the last Ice Age. It's around 7km (4 miles) long and in places is just wide enough to carry the road; elsewhere it widens to accommodate magnificent pine and birch woods. **Lusto** – the Finnish Forest Museum (tel: 015 345 100; www.lusto.fi; May and Sept daily 10am–5pm, June–Aug 10am–7pm, Oct–Apr Tue–Sun 10am–5pm) documents the relationship between the Finns and their forests, past and present. Nearby, in Kerimäki, it is possible to visit the world's largest Christian wooden church, built in 1847. In summer, a

Steamships on the lake.

lake steamer sails between Punkaharju and Savonlinna from Retretti. The two-hour trip is a delightful mini-voyage through the islands. There is also an enjoyable diesel rail tour connecting tourist attractions in this area.

Savonlinna

Savonlinna ㉕ is the most charming of Finland's main lakeland towns and the best base in Saimaa for making trips. The medieval castle of **Olavinlinna** (tel: 015 531 164; tours June–mid-Aug daily 10am–6pm, on opera days in July until 5pm, mid-Aug–May Mon–Fri 10am–4pm, Sat–Sun 11am–4pm), is the site of the annual Opera Festival that takes place throughout July. Its massive granite walls, ramparts and round towers provide a dramatic stage setting. Tickets for, and accommodation during, the festival should be booked well ahead (tel: 0600 900 900; www.operafestival.fi).

Near the castle, the museum ship *Salama* – a steam schooner built in 1874, shipwrecked in 1898 and raised from the lake in 1971 – is one of four converted old ships that form the inland navigation section of the **Savonlinna Provincial Museum** (Riihisaari; tel: 044 417 4466; Sept–May Tue–Sun 11am–6pm, June–Aug daily 10am–6pm; charge).

Scenic routes to Kuopio

From Savonlinna to Kuopio by lake steamer is a full day's journey. Road travellers have a choice of continuing west from Savonlinna on routes 14 and 5 to Mikkeli or staying with Saimaa to its northern limits beyond Kuopio.

Mikkeli ㉖, a pleasant provincial capital, is a historic army town. Near Mikkeli, **Visulahti** amusement park has a vintage car exhibition, plastic dinosaurs and waxworks (tel: 015 182 81; www.visulahti.fi; park and waxworks year-round, Mon–Sat 10am–5pm, Dinosauria Water Park and vintage car exhibition summer only).

The recommended scenic route to Kuopio from Savonlinna is via Varkaus on route 464. Then take route 23 heading northeast towards Joensuu in north Karelia, passing by the Orthodox monastery of **Valamon Luostari** ㉗ (tel: 017 570 111; www.valamo.fi; Sun–Thur 8am–5pm, Fri–Sat until 9pm) and the nearby convent, **Lintulan Luostari** (tel: 0206 100 500; www.lintulanluostari.fi; June–Aug daily 9am–6pm). On all three counts of history, culture and scenery, these merit a visit. *M/S Sergei* cruises along the canal between the two in high summer.

The monastery was formed by monks fleeing from Lake Lagoda in 1940, after the Finno-Russian Winter War. There is a fine chapel, completed in 1977, a cafeteria, souvenir shop and a modern hotel.

Kuopio

Kuopio ㉘ hosts the International Dance and Music Festival in June. Sights to see include the **Old Kuopio Museum** (Kuopion Kortellimuseo; Kirkkokatu 22; tel: 017 182 625; http://korttelimuseo.kuopio.fi; mid-May–Aug Tue–Sun 10am–5pm, Sept–mid-May Tue–Sat 10am–3pm). The open-air

museum comprises 11 original dwellings complete with authentic furniture, warehouses and even gardens dating from the late 18th–19th centuries.

The **Kuopio Art Museum** (Kuopion Museo; Kauppakatu 35; http://kuopionmuseo.fi; tel: 017 182 603; Tue–Fri 10am–5pm; visitors under 18 free) exhibits art from the late 19th century to the present day. Nearby at no. 23 is a lovely Art Nouveau castle-like structure which is the shared home of the **Kuopio Museums of Cultural and Natural History** (same telephone and opening hours).

At **Iisalmi** ㉙, 80km (50 miles) north of Kuopio on route 5, the **Karelian Orthodox Centre** (Kyllikinkatu 8; tel: 017 816 441; mid-June–mid-Aug Tue–Sat 10am–4pm, rest of the year Mon–Fri same times) displays valuable relics recovered from territory now in Russia. Dine and drink with a view at **Olutmestari** (Savonkatu 18), a popular summer restaurant in the harbour.

Lake Päijänne

To the west of the region lies Päijänne, Finland's deepest lake and its longest

Opera performance at Olavinlinna.

Sailing in Lappeenranta harbour.

TIP

The traditional woodsmoke sauna is enjoying something of a revival in Finland, and there are a number of places in the Kuopio region where you can enjoy the real thing. For a truly memorable sauna experience, visit the world's biggest smoke sauna in an atmospheric log-built lodge in Rauhalaht (www. rauhalahti.fi).

Olavinlinna is the dramatic setting for the Savonlinna Opera Festival.

at 119km (74 miles). At the southern and northern ends of the lake system are two of Finland's more substantial towns, Lahti and Jyväskylä respectively, which are linked to the west of Päijänne by one of Europe's main highways, E24, and to the east of it by a network of slower, more attractive routes.

Lahti ㉚, a modern town and winter sports centre (www.lahtiregion.fi), lies 103km (64 miles) north of Helsinki on route 4 (E75). The **Lahden Urhei-lukeskus** sports centre is the venue for the annual (March) Finlandia Ski Race and the Ski Games; it's also a major tourist attraction featuring **Lahti Ski Museum** (Tue, Thur and Fri 9am–5pm, Wed 10.30am–7pm, Sat 11am–5pm). One of Lahti's few older buildings is the Art Nouveau **Town Hall** (Kaupungintalo) designed by Eliel Saarinen in 1912. Three blocks north is the market, and two blocks further north, at Kirkkokatu 4, the highly individualistic **Ristinkirkko** (Church of the Cross; mid-May–Aug daily 9.30am–6pm), built in 1978, and the last church in Finland designed by Alvar Aalto. Built in 2000, the

award-winning **Sibelius Concert Hall and Congress Centre** (Ankkurikatu 7) on the Vesijärvi waterfront is made entirely of wood, its design inspired by Finnish forests. The **Lahti Historical Museum** (Lahdenkatu 4; tel: 03 814 4536; www.lahdenmuseot.fi; Tue, Thu and Fri 9am–5pm, Wed 10.30am–7pm, Sat 11am–5pm) exhibits regional ethnographical and cultural history collections in a 19th-century manor house.

From Lahti it's only 35km (21 miles) northeast on Route 4 to the pleasant little town of **Heinola ㉛**. Taking the summer lake route, it's four hours by steamer. The **Jyrängönkoski** (rapids) provide good sport for local canoeists and for fishermen casting for lake and rainbow trout. Rent a rod at the **Siltasaari Fishing Centre** and have your catch smoked to eat on the spot or take it away (www.heinola.fi).

An attractive route to Jyväskylä is along the minor road 314 from Asikkala. This will take you along the **Pulkkilanharju** (Ridge), offering magnificent views en route. Continue via Sysmä and Luhanka, through various waterscapes to rejoin route 9 (E63) at Korpilahti. For the final leg to Jyväskylä you can use the enormous bridge across Kärkistensalmi, one of Päijänne's many narrow straits.

A beauty spot inside the **Päijänne National Park** is the long, slender island of **Kelvenne** ㉜, 60km (37 miles) north of Lahti, with its lakes, lagoons and curious geological formations. You can reach it from the Ravintola Laivaranta camping area at Padasjoki.

Jyväskylä, Alvar Aalto's city

Jyväskylä ㉝ is situated on the northern shore of Lake Päijänne. Alvar Aalto grew up here, and there are no fewer than 30 of his buildings around the area, including the university, theatre and the Museum of Central Finland. The **Alvar Aalto Museum** (7 Alvar Aallonkatu; tel: 014 266 7113; www.alvaraalto.fi; Tue–Sun 11am–6pm, July–Aug Tue–Fri 10am–6pm, Sat–Sun from 11am) has a collection of architectural plans, photographs, scale models and furniture designs.

There are a number of winter and summer sports facilities in Jyväskylä, but the town is best known internationally as the venue for the well-attended Neste Rally, Finland's premier motor-racing event, in August. The Jyväskylä Arts Festival is a major cultural event held in July, always with a different theme.

Tampere

Tampere ㉞, Finland's industrial capital and Scandinavia's largest inland city, lies 150km (94 miles) southwest of Jyväskylä. Situated between lakes Nasijärvi and Pyhäjärvi, it is the gateway to southern Finland. Of the 200 lakes in the area, these two are the largest.

Tampere was officially founded in 1779 by King Gustav III of Sweden-Finland and owes its fortunes to the Tammerkoski rapids, which divide the city and first brought power and a booming textile industry to the area.

Hence it's description as the "Manchester" or "Pittsburgh" of Finland. It is an appealing city, enjoying a beautiful natural setting that's actually enhanced by the landmarks of its past in the form of brick-built textile mills dotted along the river. A rich cultural heritage, interesting architecture and a thriving arts scene all add to Tampere's appeal.

The historic **Tampere Cathedral** Ⓐ (Tuomiokirkonkatu 12; daily May–Aug 10am–5pm, rest of the year 11am–3pm), designed by Lars Sonck and completed in 1907, is one of the finest examples of the National Romantic style in Finland. It contains works by two key artists of the period: an altar fresco of the Resurrection by Magnus Enckell, and Hugo Simberg's masterpiece, *The Wounded Angel*.

West of the cathedral, on the banks of the Tammerkoski River, stands the old Tampella foundry and linen mill. Built in 1850, it remained productive until the 1990s (though fabric manufacture ceased in the 1970s). It was transformed in 1996 into an impressive museum centre and renamed **Vapriikki** Ⓑ (Alaverstaanraitti 5; tel:

Tampere Orthodox Church, showing the Russian influence in Finland's second city.

Jyväskylä.

TIP

With over 200 lakes in the area, make sure to take a boat journey from Tampere, either south on the Silverline route, or north on the Poet's Way, or hop on a boat to Viikinsaari to retreat into nature.

03 5656 6966; http://vapriikki.fi; Tue–Sun 10am–6pm; Fri after 3pm free) – the Finnish word for fabric. It features unique exhibitions on the region from archaeology to technology and the natural sciences, and houses a quirky collection of museums to hockey, dolls, minerals and even shoes on its extensive premises. There is a café-restaurant and museum shop. Across the river, the old Finlayson Factory, built in 1899 (named after the Scot James Finlayson who set up the first engineering workshop here) has been converted into a cultural and business centre, with restaurants and bars, computer and technology firms, a polytechnic, a newspaper headquarters… and a **Spy Museum** (Vakoilumuseo; Satakunnankatu 18; tel: 03 212 3007; www.vakoilumuseo.fi; Sept–May Mon–Sat noon–6pm, Sun 11am–5pm, June–Aug Mon–Sat 10am–6pm, Sun 11am–5pm). This intriguing little museum unlocks some of the secrets and tricks of the espionage trade adopted by Finnish spies during the Cold War. Another museum worth a look is the **Lenin Museum**

(Hämeenpuisto 28; tel: 010 420 9222; www.lenin.fi; daily 11am–4pm, in summer until 6pm), housed in the Workers' Hall where Lenin and Stalin met for the first time in 1905. The exhibit focuses on Lenin's life in Tampere before the Russian Revolution.

Among the city's significant modern landmarks is the 20th-century **Kirjasto** (City Library) by husband and wife architects, Reima and Raili Pietilä, the design of which is said to be based on the open wings and spread tail feathers of a wood grouse. In a park on the eastern side of town is another Pietilä design, the stark **Kaleva Church** (Liisanpuisto 1; daily July–Aug 11am–5pm, rest of the year until 3pm). Built in 1966, its most striking feature is the organ with 3,000 pipes shaped like a sail. In Sorsapuisto Park, just east of the station, **Tampere-talo** (Tampere Hall; www.tampere-talo.fi) is a spectacular concert venue designed in 1990 by Esa Piiroinen and Sakari Aartelo.

At the northern harbour entrance, at the centre of **Särkänniemi Park**, stands the **Näsinneula Observation Tower** (Tue–Sun 11am–11.30pm, summer daily). At 120 metres (400ft), it is the highest viewpoint in Finland. The park is a favourite place for children with its aquarium, dolphinarium, planetarium, children's zoo and amusement park (tel: 02 0713 0200; www.sarkanniemi.fi; Mon–Fri 11am until 5–7pm, Sat–Sun 11am–noon until 5–8pm).

Viikinsaari island

A favourite summer getaway from Tampere is Viikinsaari island. Just 3km (2 miles) from the city in Lake Pyhäjärvi, it has a nature trail, beach, playground, sauna, sports field, rowing boats and fishing-rod hire. After a full day, visitors usually enjoy a meal at Wanha Kaidesaari, an atmospheric dance pavilion serving Finnish specialities. On Saturday nights, there is traditional dancing with an orchestra. Open June–late Aug; the boat leaves on the hour from Tampere's Laukuntori quay and returns on the half hour. The trip takes 25 minutes.

South of Tampere

From Tampere, the 175km (110-mile) route back to Helsinki passes through the industrial centre of **Valkeakoski** ㉟. In the Middle Ages, it was a hamlet, and later a mining village in the parish of Sääksmäki; but, even then, it had the rapids that meant water power, first to grind corn and then to make paper.

The old **Voipaala Manor** on Rapola Hill was once the home of the sculptor Elias Ilkka and is now where the Valkeakoski Summer Theatre performs. Make your way to **Visavuori** (www.visavuori.com; June–Aug daily 10am–6pm, Sept–mid-Dec Tue–Sun 10am–4pm, Jan–Mar Tue–Fri 10am–4pm), the lakeside studio-home complex of one of Finland's best-known sculptors, Emil Wikström (1864–1942). It is a fine example of Karelian architecture built in the National Romantic Style. In summer, it is also accessible by Silverline ferry from Tampere or Hämeenlinna (www.runoilijantie.fi.)

Glass-making centres

Of all Finland's glassmakers, **Iittala** ㊱ is the most famous. Beautiful, functional glassware and objets

Dusk in Tampere.

Häme Castle, Hämeenlinna.

d'art are made at the **Iittala Glass Centre** (tel: 02 0439 6230; www.iittala.com; daily 9am–6pm, free guided tours June–Aug Tue–Fri at noon and 3pm, July–mid-Aug daily), and put on display along with designs by Alvar Aalto, Timo Sarpaneva and other glass artists. Visit the Iittala factory outlet, where seconds are often indistinguishable to the inexpert eye and less than half the price of perfect work.

It's also worth visiting the **Finnish Glass Museum** (Suomen Lasimuseo; www.finnishglassmuseum.fi; tel: 019 758 4108; Feb–Dec Tue–Sun 10am–6pm) in **Riihimäki** ㉟, just off route 3, 35km (26 miles) south of Hämeenlinna. The museum is housed in an authentic glassworks from 1914. Exhibits trace the history of glass-making.

Sibelius country

Continuing south from Iittala, route 57 leads to the lake of Hattula and the **Hattulan Church of the Holy Cross**, one of Finland's best-known and oldest churches, built in 1320. Just off the E12, **Aulanko Forest Park**

Worker making an Aalto vase in the Iittala glass factory.

is ideal for a break, overlooking Lake Aulankojärvi. Jean Sibelius, who was born in nearby **Hämeenlinna** ㉘, is said to have commented on Aulanko: "I was thinking of these scenes from my childhood when I composed *Finlandia*."

Hämeenlinna has two claims to fame: first, the early 13th-century **Häme Castle** (tel: 03 675 6820; June–mid-Aug daily 10am–6pm, mid-Aug–Apr Tue–Fri 10am–4pm, Sat–Sun 11am–4pm, May Mon–Fri 10am–4pm, Sat–Sun 11am–4pm), and, second, that Jean Sibelius was born here in December 1865 in the little timberboard house of the town physician, Christian Gustaf Sibelius, now the **Sibelius Childhood Home** (Hallituskatu 11; tel: 03 621 2755; May–Aug Mon–Sun 10am–4pm, Sept–Apr Mon–Sun noon–4pm). The big dining room is used for recitals, and the house is full of memorabilia. In 2015, the town celebrates the 150th anniversary of the composer's birth.

Heading south through Hyvinkää to **Järvenpää** ㉙, you are only 45km (30 miles) from Helsinki. **Lake Tuusula** (Tuusulanjärvi) attracted late 19th-century artists and intellectuals away from their city haunts to build studio-villas on the eastern side. Among them was the portrait painter Eero Järnefelt, noted for his rural and folk scenes, artists Juhani Aho, Pekka Halonen, and Jean Sibelius and his wife Aino.

Ainola ㉚ was the Sibelius home for 53 years (tel: 09 287 322; www.ainola.fi; May–Sept Tue–Sun 10am–5pm). Designed by Lars Sonck in 1904, the original log house in National Romantic style was transformed over the years to accommodate the growing family. It is still furnished as it was in Sibelius's time, with a collection of fine paintings and ceramics by one of the daughters; the drawing room holds the composer's piano. Floral tributes adorn the couple's grave in the garden.

Canoeing the Open Waters

Paddling a canoe on the lakes and rivers of Finland is one of the most pleasurable ways to explore the country.

One of the more challenging annual events on the European canoeing calendar is the Arctic Circle Race, which takes place every summer north of the Arctic Circle from Kilipsjärvi to Tornio along 537km (334 miles) of the border rivers between Finland and Sweden. Another is the six-day 700km (435-mile) Finlandia Canoe Relay each June, usually through the complex Saimaa system.

With 187,888 lakes (at the last count) and innumerable rivers, it's surprising that canoeing has only become popular in Finland in recent years. There is a growing range of packages whereby you can canoe well-tried routes of varying lengths with the option of hiring equipment, camping or staying in farmhouse accommodation.

A particularly well-tried series of routes forms an overall 350km (217-mile) circuit beginning and ending at Heinola. This needs 10–15 days, but can

The best way to explore the lakes.

also be divided into shorter sections. Another, along 320km (200 miles) of the Ounasjoki River in Lapland from Enontekiö to Rovaniemi, features sections of true Arctic wilderness; the rapids are mainly Grade I, but it is possible to portage round the most daunting of these. Yet another follows a 285km (180-mile) lake-and-river route taken by the old tar boats from Kuhmo to Oulu.

If you fancy the idea of pioneering across the lakes, the possibilities are legion. Any country map will be sufficient for general planning, but for more detail opt for the special inland water charts.

It's not until you are in your canoe, however, that navigation problems become clear. From water level one island of rock and pine trees looks like another with few helpful landmarks. You will appreciate those other vital aids to canoeing the Finnish lakes: a GPS and a pair of binoculars. The greatest inconvenience you are likely to encounter is wind. Squalls blow up quickly, and across these great expanses, waters are soon whipped up into turbulence. Head for shelter at the first sign.

Seek permission to camp whenever possible, since the right to pitch your tent anywhere has been abused by some foreigners and is no longer permitted. Often, of course, there is no one to ask. It is one of the joys of canoeing in Finland that you may travel for days without any sign of humanity, bar a tugboat hauling timber, or a fisherman.

FINLAND'S WEST COAST

The beautiful Bothnian coastline preserves its rich maritime heritage and its blend of Finnish-Swedish culture in the islands and towns along the road to Lapland.

The west coast of Finland is a fascinating mixture of past and present: stately churches and old wooden houses, museums and modern industry. With its close proximity to Sweden, Swedish remains the first language for many communities, and some towns have both Swedish and Finnish names.

North of Turku

The first main town north of **Turku** on route 8 is **Uusikaupunki ❶** (Nystad). The **Museum of Culture History** (tel: 044 3515 447; June–Aug Mon–Fri 10am–5pm, Sat–Sun noon–3pm, the rest of the year Tue–Fri noon–5pm) is in the house of F.W. Wahlberg, a former shipowner and tobacco manufacturer. **Myllymäki Windmill Park** is a reminder that many retired sailors became millers and the countryside was once dotted with windmills.

Rauma ❷ is the largest medieval town in Scandinavia, listed as a Unesco World Heritage site with 600 or so wooden buildings painted in traditional pastel shades. Although the dwellings and shops are 18th- and 19th-century buildings, the narrow streets date back to the 16th century.

Pori ❸, some 47km (37 miles) north of Rauma, was founded by Duke Johan of Sweden in 1558. With a population of 140,000 in the region, it is one of Finland's chief export harbours and hosts a popular jazz festival every July

Boats near Vaasa.

(http://porijazz.fi). The **City Hall** was built in the style of a Venetian Palace, and more offbeat is the **Jusélius Mausoleum** (May–Aug daily 11am–4pm, Sept–Apr Sun noon–2pm; free) at Käppärä Cemetery, built by a Pori businessman in memory of his young daughter.

Satakunta Museum (tel: 02 621 1078; Tue–Sun 11am–6pm, Wed until 8pm), is the largest cultural history museum in Finland. The **Pori Art Museum** (Eteläranta; tel: 02 621 1080; www.poriartmuseum.fi; Tue–Sun 11am–6pm, Wed until 8pm; free on Wed after

Main Attractions
Rauma
Brage Open-Air Museum, Vaasa
Jakobstad's Old Town
Koskikeskus Rapids Centre, Oulu
"Cruise" on the Sampo icebreaker

West Coast

0 — 50 km
0 — 50 miles

6pm), housed in a converted customs warehouse, features contemporary art.

The peninsula leading from Pori to **Reposaari** is one of Finland's best beach resorts. **Kristinestad** ❹ (Kristiinankaupunki), 95km (59 miles) to the north, was founded by the Swedish governor Count Per Brahe in 1649. A master of diplomacy, he gave the town the name of both his wife and Queen Kristina of Sweden-Finland.

Vaasa to Oulu

Vaasa ❺ (Vasa), established in the 14th century, devastated by wars and fire in the past, is today a handsome town with wide, attractively laid-out streets and a large market square. Notable buildings include the Orthodox church, the Court of Appeal (1862) and the Town Hall (1883). Vaasa has many museums: the **Ostrobothnian Museum** (Museokatu 3; tel: 06 325 3800; www.pohjanmaanmuseo.fi; Tue–Thur 11am–6pm and Fri–Sun 11am–4pm) covers local history and art, the **Terranova–Kvarken Nature Centre** invites visitors to experience the sights and sounds of nature and the **Brage Open-Air Museum** (tel: 044 012 7166; http://vasabrage.fi; late June–early Aug Wed–Sun 11am–4pm) features nine original houses furnished to depict 19th-century peasant tradition. Ala-Härmä has an amusement park with a wooden rollercoaster and a karting circuit named after the Formula 1 driver Mika Salo, who also helped to plan it (signposted from Route 19).

Jakobstad ❻ (Pietarsaari), a reputed shipbuilding centre, produced vessels that opened new trade routes around the world. One of the town's best-known sailing ships, *Jakobstads Wapen*, a replica of a 1767 galleon, makes cruises. Some 300 or so restored wooden houses may be seen in the old part of town.

From Jakobstad to **Kokkola** ❼, take the attractive route called the "road of seven bridges", which runs from island to island across the archipelago. Kokkola's Town Hall was designed by Carl Ludwig Engel, and there is an English park and boathouse commemorating an episode in the Crimean War with the British fleet. On the 230km (140-mile) road north between Kokkola and Oulu, the town of **Kalajoki** ❽ is a popular spot for fishing and sailing.

Oulu ❾ is the largest city in northern Finland, with a population of 190,000 (www.visitoulu.fi). **Turkansaari Open-Air Museum** (tel: 044 703 7190; mid-May–mid-Aug daily 10am–6pm, mid-Aug–mid-Sept 10am–4pm, Wed 11am–3pm demonstration of old working techniques) can be found on a small island in the Oulujoki, 14km (8 miles) east of Oulu. It has an interesting collection of Ostrobothnian buildings, including a church, farm buildings and windmills. In town, the **Tietomaa Science Centre** (Nahkatehtaankatu 6; tel: 08 5584 1340; www.tietomaa.fi; daily 10am–5pm, Sat–Sun and summer until 6pm) has a wealth of hands-on exhibits, 3D cinema and a planetarium. The **Oulu Art Museum** (tel: 044 703 7471; Sat–Thur 10am–5pm, Fri noon–7pm; Fri free after 5pm), in the old industrial district, has exhibitions of contemporary art. Visit **Koskikeskus** (Rapids Centre)

on the mouth of the Oulujoki, with a power station, driven by the rapids, and 12 fountains designed by Alvar Aalto.

To the Swedish border

Kemi ❿ is known as the seaport of Lapland, and in winter you can take an excursion on the 1961 icebreaker *Sampo* (www.sampotours.com) – a 4-hour journey through the icefields of the Gulf of Bothnia.

On the border a short distance west is **Tornio** ⓫, near the mouth of the Tornionjoki. The **Aine Art Museum** (tel: 05 0594 6868; Tue–Thur 11am–6pm, Fri–Sun until 3pm) houses a fine collection of Finnish art. For a great view, visit the **Vesitorni** water tower (daily June–mid-Aug 11am–6pm). At the **Green Zone Golf Course** (tel: 016 431 711; www.torniogolf.fi; June–Oct) on the Finnish–Swedish border, you can play nine holes in Sweden and nine in Finland. It is a rare delight to play a night round in summer, thanks to the Midnight Sun.

A 9-mile (15km) drive north of Tornio off Route E78, **Kukkolankoski** ⓬ are the longest free-flowing rapids in Finland at 3,500 metres (11,485ft).

TIP

Lumilinna (tel: 016 258 878; www.visitkemi.fi; late Jan–early Apr daily 10am–6pm) is a sight not to miss. The snow castle, with its dazzling white walls, illuminated towers and ice hotel, is rebuilt every year at Kemi. In January 2015, it celebrated its 20th anniversary.

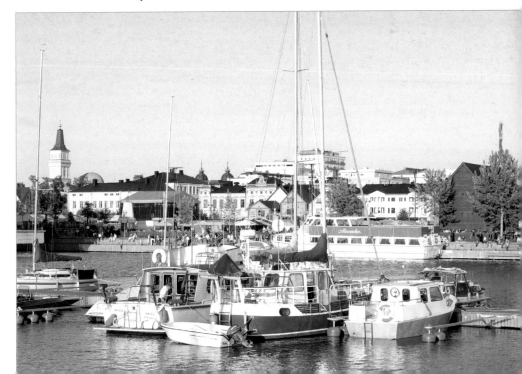

Oulu's marina.

KARELIA AND KUUSAMO

Easterly Karelia with its distinctly Orthodox heritage is the setting for Finland's epic poem Kalevala. Traditions abound, the air is pure and the landscape untouched.

Main Attractions
Joensuu Art Museum
Ruaankoski Rapids
Ferry down Lake Pielinen
  to Kolin National Park
Wilderness walks

Autumn in the Koli Hills lakeland.

Karelia is the general name for the area whose westernmost part is still in Finland and the larger, easternmost part – which was ceded to the Soviet Union as a result of the Treaty of Paris in 1947 – is in Russia. There are many holiday options, including renting a cottage or log cabin by the water or staying in a "working" farmhouse. Depending on the season, one can enjoy a range of water or winter sports, fishing, hiking and berry-picking.

Joensuu ❶, the "capital" of north Karelia, is a lively student town and the starting point for exploration of the surrounding wilderness. The **Careli-cum Cultural and Tourism Centre** (Koskikatu 5; tel: 013 267 5225; Mon–Fri 9am–5pm, Sat–Sun 10am–3pm) by the market square has exhibitions on the history and folk culture of this part of Karelia. The nearby **Art Museum** (Taidemuseo, Kirkkokatu 23; tel: 013 267 5388; Tue–Sun 11am–4pm, Wed until 8pm) occupies an imposing neo-Renaissance building (1894), a former schoolhouse, and contains a diverse collection of art and artefacts from Etruscan pottery, through a fine collection of 19th-century painting to Finnish artworks of the 1950s.

Before turning north, go east to **Ilomantsi ❷**, the oldest inhabited area of north Karelia and a stronghold of the Orthodox Church. Easter is the most impressive festival here, but other colourful events are held throughout the summer. Ilomantsi was one of the main battlegrounds in the war of 1939–45, and the **Fighter's House** on Hattuvaara Hill has exhibitions about that period. Nearby in the village of **Runokylä,** visit **Runonlaulajan Pirtti** (the Singers' Lodge; tel: 050 3758 787; June–Aug daily 10am–4pm, July until 6pm) on Parppeinvaara Hill. A cultural centre in a traditional Karelian log building, where the ancient folk poems of the *Kalevala* are sung by women in traditional costume (accompanied by the *kantele*, a zither-like instrument). The **Parppeinpirtti** restaurant (tel: 10 239 9950; www.parppeinpirtti.fi) on the hill serves traditional Karelian dishes such as *vendace* (tiny fish), cold smoked whitefish, hearty meat casseroles and pies, *pirakka* pastries, and baked cheese with cloudberry jam.

Gateway to the wilderness

Heading north from Joensuu, take route 6 and the eastward fork to route 73 to **Lieksa ❸**, where the **Ruuankoski** (Rapids) must be seen, and possibly experienced, under the supervision of a guide. Lieksa, one of the many forest centres in Finland, is only about 20 years old and has a population of 12,100 in an area larger than London. The **Pielisen Museo** (Pielinen Open-Air Museum; Pappilantie 2; tel: 040 1044 151; mid-May–mid-Sept daily 10am–6pm, mid-Sept–mid-May Tue–Fri 10am–3pm; winter Wed free) has 70 buildings, some dating to the 17th century, which document local settlement.

At **Vuonisjärvi ❹**, 29km (18 miles) from the centre, is **Paateri** (tel: 050 434 6665; mid-May–mid-Sept daily 10am–6pm), the former studio of Eeva Ryynänen (1915–2001), a wood sculptor noted for her spectacular Wilderness Church (adjacent).

Lieksa is the gateway to Finland's wilderness. "Never go hiking on your own"

TIP

Mountain biking is a popular way to explore Karelia. Hire a bike locally, or join a guided trail bike expedition (www.pyoraillensuomessa.fi).

Decorated window at Bomba House.

KARELIA: SOUL AND SAUNA

If Finland has a soul, that soul lives on in Karelia. When Finns have gone to war, it has concerned Karelia. A Karelian theme runs through the music of Sibelius, and his *Karelian Suite* reaches sublime heights of patriotism.

The Karelians were one of the earliest of the Finnish communities; they are evident in Bronze and Iron Age discoveries. The *Kalevala*, the great epic saga of ancient life in the far north, is really about Karelians. The poem, which in the 18th and 19th centuries became the cornerstone of the struggle for national culture, recounts everyday events and rituals and finally the heroes' joy as they celebrate in song the salvation of the land of Kalevala from its enemies.

True Karelia exists only as a fragment of its former self. The greater part of the region lies east of the Russian border, lost to Finland after the Winter War (1939–40). As a result 400,000 Karelians had to be resettled in the 1940s. Since then, people of Karelian origin can be found in all parts of Finland. They tend to be lively and talkative, in contrast with the more taciturn nature of other Finns.

It is they who are responsible for the sauna. Early Karelians cleared woodland to grow crops and used steam heat to dry their grain. The therapeutic benefits of this heat were later realised, and so the sauna was born in Finland.

is the warning motto of this region, whose dense forests are inhabited by bears, wolves, elk and reindeer.

From Lieksa, route 73 leads to the beautiful town of **Nurmes ❺**, its existence first documented in 1556. **Bomba House** (Suojärvenkatu 1; tel: 013 687 2501) is a traditional Karelian log house at Ritoniemi, about 2km (1.25 miles) from the town, surrounded by a "Karelian village" which provides visitors not only with comfortable accommodation, but also with delicious meals of local specialities.

Nurmes is the place to leave the car and take a scenic ride on Finland's largest inland waterway ferry down Lake Pielinen to **Kolin Kansallispuisto ❻** (Kolin National Park; www.koli.fi). You will be captivated by the same views that inspired some of Finland's greatest painters, as well as the composer Sibelius.

Before reaching the Oulu area, if you opt for route 6 north you could detour to the remote national park **Tiilikka-järven Kansallispuisto ❼**, near Rautavaara. It was established to conserve the uninhabited area of Lake Tiilikka and the surrounding bogs.

Another national park, **Hiidenportin Kansallispuisto ❽**, is southeast of Sotkamo and also best reached from route 6. This is a rugged area with the narrow Hiidenporti Gorge, its rift walls dropping 20 metres (70ft) to the floor. There are well-marked trails and campsites in the park.

Both in and outside the parks you may encounter reindeer. These animals are the main source of income for many people living in the region, and it is very important to take special care on roads when reindeer are around, especially at dusk.

The Finnish frontier

Kuhmo ❾ is a frontier town surrounded by dense forests in the wilderness area of Kainuu. It is known for its annual Kuhmo Chamber Music Festival. A recreated **Kalevala Village** lies in a wooded park on the outskirts of Kuhmo. Its Visitor Centre (tel: 040

825 6060, mid-June–mid-Aug daily 9am–5pm, May–mid-June and mid-Aug–Oct Mon–Fri 9am–4pm) displays an array of local folk traditions, to give modern-day visitors an idea of Finnish culture as it was immortalised in Finland's epic poem *Kalevala*. The **Hotel Kalevala** specialises in regional cuisine (tel: 086 554 100).

A long straight road through some of Finland's darkest forests leads west out of Kuhmo to Sotkamo and then onwards to **Kajaani** ⓾, the area's main town, on the eastern edge of Oulujärvi (Lake). Kajaani still has the ruins of the 1604 castle, and its town hall was designed by Carl Ludwig Engel, who was responsible for so much of early Helsinki. The road from Kajaani towards **Oulu** hugs the shores of Oulujärvi, plunging first into thickly wooded hill country. Before entering Oulu, the route goes through **Muhos**, which has the second-oldest church in Finland, dating from 1634.

Kuusamo

The only other main centre in this scantily populated area is **Kuusamo** ⓫, sharing 123km (76 miles) of borderline with Russia. The Kuusamo region is marvellous wilderness country, ideal for canoeing and fishing. This is also berry country, with several varieties growing in great profusion on the Arctic tundra. The only snag is the number of mosquitoes: take plenty of protection.

Karhuntassu Tourist Centre (tel: 040 732 5614; www.outdoors.fi/kuusamo customerservice) provides information on activities, accommodation and most other aspects of the region. It also houses a nature photography centre (www.hannuhautala.fi). In winter, the area is excellent for skiing and snowmobiling. There are two national parks: the larger, **Oulangan Kansallispuisto** ⓬, to the north, covers a largely untouched region bordering the Oulanka River. **Karhunkierros**, the most famous walking route in Finland, stretches some 100km (60 miles) through the Oulanka canyon to the **Rukatunturi Fells** ⓭. A smaller national park, **Riisitunturi**, lies to the southwest of Oulanka. Moving further north approaching Lapland, the landscape and culture change from the traditions of Karelia to the ancient ways of the Sami people.

Inquisitive brown bears in Kuhmo.

FINNISH LAPLAND

For some travellers, Lapland is the land of the Midnight Sun, a haven for fell-walkers and anglers. For others, it's the land of Father Christmas, reindeer-racing and dog-sledging.

Helsinki

Whatever the season, Lapland offers a variety of interesting natural phenomena and cultures, from the mysterious Northern Lights and the dark Kaamos (polar night) skies, to the magical contrast of the Midnight Sun and *Ruska* – Lapland's glorious blaze of autumn colour. However you choose to arrive – by air, sea, train or car – be prepared to experience Lapland and the Arctic Circle on foot, whether reindeer-spotting, cross-country skiing, snowmobiling, salmon-fishing, discovering the Sami culture, or simply hiking the rich swampland in search of cloudberries. These activities will only whet your appetite for the delicious Lappish cuisine.

Two main roads bore their way northwards through the province of Lapland (Lappi). Route 4 (E75), sometimes called the Arctic Highway, links Kemi (coming from Oulu) with Rovaniemi before continuing northeastwards into Norway at Utsjoki. The other is Route 21 (E8), which follows the Tornio Valley upstream from Tornio, continuing beside various tributaries that form the border with Sweden, eventually to cross into Norway near Kilpisjärvi.

When exploring this region, the need for proper clothing and equipment cannot be overstressed. Always inform someone where you are heading and when you expect to return: climatic changes are rapid and, for all its magnificence,

the Arctic wilderness can be a ruthless place. In summer take plenty of mosquito repellent, ideally bought from a local *apteekki* (pharmacy).

Rovaniemi, Lapland's capital

From Kemi, route 4 follows the valley of the Kemijoki for 115km (70 miles) to **Rovaniemi** ❶ (www.visitrovaniemi.fi). The administrative capital of Lapland, on the cusp of the Arctic Circle, is the launching point for most trips into the province. The town has been

Main Attractions

Midnight Sun, Kaamos, Northern Lights and Ruska
Lappia House, the Arctic Centre
Santa Claus's Workshop Village
Hiking in the Pyhä-Luosto and Urho Kekkonen national parks
Tankavaara Gold Village
Siida Sami Village, Inari
Sevettijärvi, Skolt Sami culture
Western Lapland fell country

Reindeer in Kilpisjärvi.

Lapland

0 ___ 50 km
0 ___ 50 miles

completely rebuilt since World War II, following a reconstruction plan drawn up by Alvar Aalto, who also designed the fine **Lappia House** complex on Hallituskatu, containing a theatre, library and congress facilities.

Half underground, the eye-catching **Arktikum** (Pohjoisranta 4; tel: 016 322 3260; www.arktikum.fi; June–Aug daily 9am–6pm, Sept–Nov and mid-Jan–May Tue–Sun 10am–6pm, first half Jan and Dec daily 10am–6pm) houses the Arctic Centre and the Provincial Museum of Lapland, which provide a good introduction to Lapland's nature, Sami traditions and Rovaniemi's history. In 2011, the **Rovaniemi Art Museum** (Lapinkävijäntie 4; tel: 016 322 2822; www.korundi.fi; daily 11am–6pm) reopened within the newly established **Korundi House of Culture**, a former mail-truck depot, and now a state-of-the-art auditorium and home of the Lapland Chamber Orchestra. The Art Museum features contemporary Finnish art.

Two open-air museums in scenic Pöykkölä, 3km (2 miles) south of Rovaniemi, give an insight into 19th-century Lapland life and its logging and farming traditions: the **Forestry Museum of Lapland** (tel: 040 536 0080; June–Aug Thur–Sun noon–6pm) has a number of authentic logging cabins, and nearby **Rovaniemi Local History Museum** (Poykkolantie 4; tel: 050 325 2017; June–Aug Tue–Sun noon–6pm) has more than a dozen original buildings to explore.

Rising up from the confluence of the Ounasjoki and Kemijoki to the south of Rovaniemi are the wooded slopes of **Ounasvaara**, a well-developed skiing area and the site of annual international winter games.

Santa Claus land

About 8km (5 miles) from the town on route 4, soon after the turnoff for Rovaniemi airport, **Joulupukin Pajakylä** ❷ (Santa Claus's Workshop Village; tel: 016 356 2096; www.santa clausvillage.info; June–Aug daily 9am–6pm, Sept–May 10am–5pm, Dec–early Jan 9am–7pm; free) straddles the Arctic Circle. Its post office annually handles thousands of letters from children. There are shops, a puppet theatre, art exhibitions, a glass factory, a few reindeer and, of course, Santa Claus.

Dashing through the snow...

SLEDGING

The easiest way to get across Lapland's vast, icy and largely flat landscape has always been on skis or sledges, the latter less exhausting for longer distances. There are many types of sledging, but the most popular and readily associated with northern Finland is the dog sledge. Four or six husky dogs, hardy beasts naturally acclimatised to snow and ice, are harnessed to the front of the sledge, with passengers standing on the back runners. Unlike horses, the huskies are not readily controllable, so keeping the sledge stationary is done with a hook wedged deep in the snow. Once the hook is withdrawn, the dogs lurch forward.

Reindeer-sledging, as epitomised by images of Santa and his sleigh at Christmas, is another method of getting around the icy wilderness, with the advantage that these animals can cover longer and more snowy distances, although they travel more slowly than dogs.

Many centres in Lapland now offer the chance of sledging excursions. Operating near Kuusamo, Spirit of Adventure, for example, offers exhilarating husky safaris or a combination of dog-sledge and snowmobile safaris along the Russian frontier (www.spirit-of-adventure. com). For details of other operators, contact tourist offices in the main towns. Remember, the right equipment is essential: thermals, waterproofs, hats and goggles are necessary to combat the dampness and brightness of the snow.

You can have a go at gold panning in Gold Village, Lapland.

At Syväsenvaara, 5km (3 miles) from Rovaniemi, **Santapark** (tel: 0600 301 203; www.santapark.com; mid-June–mid-Aug Mon–Sat 10am–6pm, late Nov and Dec daily 10am–6pm) has fun rides and attractions for children.

As you travel further north, the predominantly forested landscapes become progressively emptier. However, there are reindeer aplenty and the occasional elk, so do drive slowly; keep your eyes open and your camera handy – they say white reindeer bring good luck.

Sodankylä and the national parks

One of the best fell areas east of route 4 is centred on **Pyhätunturi,** about 135km (84 miles) northeast of Rovaniemi in the Pyhä-Luosto National Park, which has 102km (63 miles) of marked hiking trails through pine-forested valleys and deep ravines, past lakes and waterfalls. It is a perfect area for short hikes and day trips. The starting point for most trails is the **Pyhä-Luosto Visitor Centre** (Luontotie 1; tel: 020 564 7302) – signposted on route 4 between Rovaniemi and Sodankylä.

Santa Claus is Lapland's most famous export.

The small town of **Sodankylä ❸**, 130km (80 miles) from Rovaniemi, is a stop-off point en route to the north. It is home of the Midnight Sun Film Festival held each June (www.msfilmfestival.fi).

Northwards, there's little to detain you for the next 100km (60 miles) or so until, a few miles beyond Vuotso, you reach **Tankavaara ❹**. Gold panning has been practised in Lapland for well over a century, and at **Tankavaara Gold Village** (tel: 016 626 158; www.tankavaara.fi) you can pan for gold for a modest fee. There are cabins where you may lodge, and a simple restaurant.

About 40km (25 miles) further north there is more self-catering accommodation, together with modern hotels, centred on the resort town of **Saariselkä ❺**, a popular winter sports centre with good facilities. It is also the base for hiking in the spectacular **Urho-Kekkosnen National Park**, which offers gentle trails on its western side, and more demanding treks in its eastern wilderness areas by the Russian border.

Ivalo and Inari

Another 23km (14 miles) north is the turning for Ivalo airport, Finland's northernmost. **Ivalo ❻** is the largest community in northern Lapland. There is an attractive wooden Orthodox church tucked away in the woods, serving the Skolt Sami, a branch of the Sami people who formerly lived in territory ceded to the Soviet Union in 1944. Ivalo's Lutheran church stands near the bridge which carries route 4 over the Ivalojoki; then it's a further 39km (27 miles) to **Inari ❼**, much of it a delightful route along the shores of Inarijärvi. Inari village is an excellent base for wilderness exploration; you can lodge at the traditional Hotel Inarin Kultahovi (tel: 016 511 7100; www.hotelkultahovi.fi). Though smaller than Ivalo, Inari is the administrative centre for a vast if sparsely populated area, and a traditional meeting place for colourfully costumed Sami people, especially during the Easter church festivals. If you have a chance to attend a traditional Sami Joik concert, do so.

Inarijärvi is Finland's third-largest lake, covering 1,300 sq km (500 sq miles) and is dotted with 3,000 islands, some of them considered sacred according to Sami tradition. Boat trips and sightseeing flights are available during the summer to the holy **Ukko Island**.

Inari's excellent **Siida Sami Museum** (Saamelaismuseo; tel: 0400 898 212; www.siida.fi; June–mid-Sept daily 9am–7pm, mid-Sept–May Tue–Sun 10am–5pm) comprises a modern museum building and an open-air section *(skansen)* with old buildings and equipment illustrating the traditionally nomadic way of life. The Siida building also houses the **Customer Service of Metsähallitus at the Nature Centre Siida**, which assists in hiking plans for those wishing to explore the wilderness. Be sure to leave time to shop at Inari's many fine handicraft shops.

Towards Norway

Route 955 from Inari leads 40km (25 miles) southwest to **Menesjärvi ❽**, a Sami settlement from which one can continue by road then riverboat or on foot up the wild and beautiful **Lemmenjoki Valley** ("river of love") to a remote gold prospectors' camp. From Menesjärvi, route 955 continues across Lapland to join route 79 at Kittilä. Around Inari and north of it, the road passes a number of attractive holiday centres, mostly of the self-catering variety. After 26km (16 miles) you come to Kaamanen, from which a minor road branches northeast 100km (60 miles) to **Sevettijärvi ❾**, the modern main settlement for the Skolt Sami. While there, visit the Sami graveyard, with its unusual turf-covered graves.

A couple of kilometres north of Kaamanen, take the minor road to **Utsjoki ❿**, 94km (58 miles) away on the border with Norway, passing a series of beautiful lakes close to the eastern fringes of the **Kevo Nature Park**. Utsjoki is an important Sami community close to Finland's northernmost point. Its church (1860) is one of the few pre-World War II churches still standing.

The village and road follow the Utsjoki downstream to join with the Tenojoki, a renowned salmon river. As you approach the Norwegian border at **Kirkenes**, the landscape changes dramatically. You can connect with a variety of routes, returning into western Lapland at Kilpisjärvi or Enontekiö.

Western Lapland

Your route through western Lapland is likely to begin at **Tornio,** about 80km (50 miles) south of the Arctic Circle. The earlier stretches of the **Way of the Four Winds** (E8) present a very different face of Lapland from the Arctic Road, for the lower section of the Tornio Valley is much more populated, and served by Finland's northernmost railway branch to Kolari. In its southern stages the road passes through a string of small communities mainly based on agriculture and dairy farming. The Tornionjoki is a good salmon river. Perch, whitefish, grayling, trout and even Arctic char can be found in Lapland's waters. Local travel agencies will organise guided fishing trips complete with gear and permits.

TIP

Ranua, south of Rovaniemi, is the cloudberry capital of Finland. These unusual berries grow on peat bogs and pine marshes and are ripe for picking in July. Taste them at Ranua's cloudberry markets in early August.

The Northern Lights.

At **Kukkola** ⑪ look out for the **Kukkolankoski Rapids**.

About 70km (43 miles) north of Tornio, beyond Ylitornio, is the 242-metre (794ft) high **Aavasaksa Hill** ⑫, the most southerly point from which the Midnight Sun can be seen, attracting considerable throngs for Midsummer Eve festivities. A few miles nearer Juoksenki, you cross the Arctic Circle.

Fell country

About 10km (6 miles) north of Kolari, a detour by Route 940 leads to **Akäslompolo** ⑬. This well-equipped tourist resort and skiing centre, on the shores of a small lake, is set among magnificent forested hills and bare-topped fells; the highest is **Ylläs**, at 718 metres (2,355ft), served by chair lifts. A marked trail follows the chain of fells stretching northwards from here, eventually leading in about 150km (90 miles) to the **Pallastunturi** ⑭ fell group. It's a glorious trail, with overnight shelter available in wilderness huts.

From Akäslompolo you can continue north along minor roads and in 31km (19 miles) turn left onto route 79. This is the main road from Rovaniemi, providing an alternative approach to western Lapland. Route 957 to the right is recommended as the best approach to Enontekiö. A further branch left off this route leads to the lonely hotel complex of **Pallastunturi,** magnificently cradled in the lap of five of the 14 fells which make up the Pallastunturi group. From here the choice of fell walks includes the long-distance trail north to Enontekiö.

Enontekiö ⑮, also known as Hetta, sprawls along the northern shore of Ounasjärvi (Lake), looking across to the great rounded shoulders of the Ounastunturi fells. Drop by the pretty wooden church, which has an altar mosaic depicting Sami people.

Soaring mountains

From **Palojoensuu**, route 21 proceeds northwest along the Muonionjoki and Könkämäeno valleys, the scenery becoming even wilder and more barren. At **Järämä** ⑯, 10km (6 miles) further from the tiny settlement of Markkina, German soldiers built fortifications during a standstill in the Lapland War of 1944. Many of these bunkers have been restored and are now open to the public.

South and north of **Ropinsalmi**, the mountains reach ever greater heights; the highest, **Halti**, soars to 1,328 metres (4,357ft) on the Norwegian border at Finland's northwesternmost point. More accessible and distinctive is Saana, at 1,029 metres (3,376ft), above the village and resort of **Kilpisjärvi** ⑰. Kilpisjärvi is an excellent base for wilderness enthusiasts. The western shore of its lake forms the border with Sweden, and a trail which takes about a day leads to the boundary stone marking the triple junction of Finland, Sweden and Norway. Motor boats take visitors to the **Mallan Luonnonpuisto**, a nature reserve to the north of the lake (entry permit required, details from **Kilpisjärvi Hiking Centre;** tel: 016 537 771). Within the reserve, there is a pleasant 15km (9-mile) trek. The rest of these immense, empty, rugged acres are as free to all as the elements – and as unpredictable.

Lapland's fell country.

INSIGHT GUIDES TRAVEL TIPS
SCANDINAVIA

DENMARK A–Z

A HANDY SUMMARY OF PRACTICAL INFORMATION

A

Accommodation

Danish hotels are not cheap, but have first-class facilities and are very much business-orientated. Around 500 of the country's larger hotels are classified by one to five stars by HORESTA (Danish Hotel, Restaurant and Tourist Employers' Association).

Greenland

In Greenland hotels come into the expensive category and there is not a wide selection of alternatives. Confirm your booking before you go.
Greenland Tourism
Tel: +299 34 28 20
www.greenland.com

Faroe Islands

Apart from a few good-quality hotels in Torshavn, modern facilities are not plentiful. Private houses and youth hostels provide an alternative.
Faroe Islands Tourist Board
Tel: +298 20 61 00
www.visitfaroeislands.com

Information and Reservations

Danish Hotels, www.allhotels indenmark.com, have a very comprehensive list of hotels and other places to stay. You can also browse through listings of recommended hotels on www. visitcopenhagen.com.

Camping/caravanning

You can hire stationary caravans or huts on many campsites (all high standard), or take your own tent. You will need a Camping Card Scandinavia, which you can buy at the first campsite you stay at, or online

before travelling. For a list of sites, ask Visit Denmark or contact:
Camping Rådet (Danish Camping Board)
Tel: 39 27 88 44
www.campingraadet.dk

Farm Holidays

For details contact:
Landboferie i Danmark
www.bondegaardsferie.dk

Youth Hostels

Denmark has around 100 youth hostels (vandrerhjem). Visit www. danhostel.dk for a list of sites.

Activities

Cycling

Cycling is easy and safe in Denmark, with flat terrain, beautiful scenery, plenty of dedicated cycle lanes and a high awareness of cyclists by car drivers. There are 11 long-distance national cycle routes, covering over 4,000km (2,500 miles), and good-quality cycles are available to rent across the country for around DKK45/300 per day/week.

Bornholm is the most popular place for cycling holidays. For cycling in Copenhagen, see page 362.

Fishing

Anglers must have fishing permits, which can be obtained at any post office or tourist office, or online at www.fisketegn.dk. Fishing rights in lakes and streams are usually privately owned, but permits can often be hired from the local tourist office.

Golf

There are more than 140 golf courses in Denmark. Guests are welcomed at

Danish golf clubs on presentation of a valid membership card from their home club. For more information, contact:
Danish Golf Union
Brøndby Station 20, Brøndby
Tel: 43 26 2700; www.danskgolfunion.dk

Hiking

There are many beautiful places for hiking in Denmark. Local tourist offices have maps of tested walks and will help you to plan routes. Try walking from Rødvig (just an hour south of Copenhagen) along the lovely wooded chalk cliffs of Stevns to Bøgeskov harbour (22km/13 miles). For more ideas on hiking and walking holidays, maps and guides, go to www.visitdenmark.com.

Sailing

Boats and yachts are available for hire on a weekly basis. Visitors should ask to see a certificate from the Shipping Inspection Office before hiring a boat. Contact the main tourist office of the region you will be visiting to obtain lists of local boat-hire companies.

Swimming

Aside from Denmark's excellent sandy beaches, there are swimming facilities in most Danish towns as well as several funparks with water slides for children, etc. Tourist offices have details. Copenhagen has a superb swimming-pool complex with six pools:
Vandkulturhuset, DGI-byen, Tietgensgade 65, near the Central Station. Tel: 33 29 81 40; www.dgi-byen.com.

Admission Charges

Admission to Denmark's museums and galleries ranges from around

Riding high in Tivoli Gardens.

DKK25 to DKK95. Many museums in Copenhagen offer free entrance on Wednesdays. For free entry to museums outside the capital, contact the local tourist office.

C

Children

Denmark is a peaceful, safe country with many suitable attractions, such as amusement parks, playgrounds, parks and children's theatres. Many museums have opened children's sections, and music festivals are often arranged so kids can take part. Highlights include:

Copenhagen

Experimentarium (Science Centre)
Trangravsvej 12, Christiansholm
Tel: 39 27 33 33
www.experimentarium.dk
A hands-on science museum where you can try more than 300 experiments with sound, light, water, currents and more. With short demonstrations and special exhibits. Daily 10am–4pm.
Marionetteatret
Tel: 33 12 12 29
www.marionetteatret.dk
From June to August there are free puppet shows for small children in Kongens Have (the Royal Gardens) near Rosenborg Palace. At 2pm and 3pm, Tue–Sun.
Tivoli
Vesterbrogade 3
Tel: 33 15 10 01
www.tivoli.dk
The amusement park, Tivoli, just across from Central Station, is a delight, with a variety of rides, parades and summer pantomimes. Mid-Apr–late Sept Sun–Thur 11am–11pm, Fri and Sat 11am–midnight, also open for Halloween and Christmas (mid-Nov–early Jan).
Zoologisk Have (Zoo)
Roskildevej 38
Tel: 72 20 02 00

www.zoo.dk
There is a special children's zoo here, where children are allowed to pet the animals, watch chickens peck their way out of eggs and ride on ponies. Daily 10am–4pm, Apr, May, Sept–Oct until 5pm, June, Aug until 6pm, July until 8pm.

Outside Copenhagen

Bakken
A traditional amusement park in the beautiful Dyrehaven area near Klampenborg. This is also a perfect place for a walk in the countryside. Daily Apr–late Aug, times vary. Tel: 39 63 35 44; www.bakken.dk.
Benneweis Circus
The largest touring circus in Northern Europe. Contact the circus for tour dates. Tel: 40 40 20 20; email: info@benneweis.dk; www.benneweis.dk.
Legoland
The original Legoland, built out of 59 million bricks, with rides and a water playground. Daily Apr–end Oct. Tel: 75 33 13 33; www.legoland.dk.
Land of Legends (Sagnlandet Lejre)
Historical-archaeological centre in Zealand with a reconstructed Iron Age village. Children can grind flour, chop wood, paddle log canoes and make Viking bread. May–mid-Sept, 3rd week in Oct and Christmas. Tel: 46 48 08 78; www.sagnlandet.dk.

Climate

Denmark's temperate marine climate keeps the weather mild, with the North Atlantic Drift, part of the Gulf Stream, providing a warming influence. Average rainfall is 610mm (24in) a year. Be prepared for a variable climate. You are most likely to encounter good weather in mid-May to mid-June.

What to Bring

Even if Denmark is experiencing a fine summer, you should still prepare for some cold and rainy days. Bring a swimsuit for those sandy beaches... but bring a sweater and rainwear too.

Danes dress casually: when going out for the evening, men rarely have to put on a suit and tie.

Culture

BILLETnet is an information network where you can reserve tickets and get details on entertainment events. Tel: 70 15 65 65; www.billetnet.dk.

Festivals

CPH:PIX – Denmark's biggest international film festival, held in Copenhagen (April); www.cphpix.dk
Roskilde Festival – one of Europe's biggest rock festivals (July); www.roskilde-festival.dk
Arhus International Jazz Festival – (July); www.jazzfest.dk
Hamlet Summer – Shakespeare performances, staged in Hamlet's castle at Helsingør (August); www.hamletscenen.dk
European Medieval Festival – Middle Ages fun and games in Horsens (August); www.middelalderfestival.dk
Culture Night – Copenhageners stay up late to participate in cultural events (October); www.kulturnatten.dk

Theatre

Most theatre is in Danish, even though the piece may have been written in another language.
Det Kongelige Teater – Skuespilhuset
Royal Danish Playhouse
Tel: 33 69 69 69
http://kglteater.dk
The new national playhouse, opened in 2008, stages major plays, ballets and symphonies. Some performances still take place at the 18th-century Old Stage on Kongens Nytorv.
The London Toast Theatre
Kochsvej 18
Tel: 33 22 86 86

CLIMATE CHART

Copenhagen

Legend:
- Maximum temperature
- Minimum temperature
- Rainfall

www.londontoast.dk
The only English-language theatre in Copenhagen, showing plays of a high standard. It is most famous for its annual Christmas show, the "Crazy Christmas Cabaret", held in Tivoli Gardens.
The Opera House
Ekvipagemestervej 10
Tel: 33 69 69 69
http://kglteater.dk
The impressive new Opera House on the south bank of the river holds major operas.
Wallmans
The Circus Building, Jernbanegade 8
Tel: 33 16 37 00.
www.wallmans.dk
A very popular international dinner show.

Live Music

Copenhagen
Copenhagen Jazz House
Niels Hemmingsensgade 10
Tel: 33 15 47 00
www.jazzhouse.dk
The place for jazz.
Mojo Blues Bar
Løngangstræde 21C
Tel: 33 11 64 53
www.mojo.dk
Live blues every night.
Rust
Guldbergsgade 8
Tel: 35 24 52 00
www.rust.dk
With three floors, this venue hosts upcoming indie bands, and is popular with students.
Vega
Enghavevej 40
Tel: 33 25 70 11
www.vega.dk
Housed in a large 1950s trade union building, this is one of the most popular venues in Copenhagen.

Odense
Jazzhus Dexter
Vindegade 65
Tel: 63 11 27 28
www.dexter.dk
Live jazz. This is Denmark's biggest jazz club.
Odense Symphony Orchestra
Claus Berg Gade 9
Tel: 63 75 00 50
www.odensesymfoni.dk
Classical music.
Odense Theatre
Jernbanegade 21
Tel: 66 12 00 52
www.odenseteater.dk
Theatre and opera performances.
Posten
Østre Stationsvej 35

Tel: 66 13 60 20
www.postenlive.dk
Occasional blues/rock/metal gigs.

Århus
Århus is one of the best places in Denmark for a night out, with a multitude of good restaurants and performance venues. Nightlife is centred around Skolegade.
Fatter Eskil
Skolegade 25
Tel: 86 19 44 11
www.fattereskil.dk
Jazz and blues music, Tuesday to Saturday.
Musikhus Århus
Thomas Jensens Allé
Tel: 89 40 40 40
www.musikhusetaarhus.dk
The city's main concert hall, with theatre, dance and music performances.
Radar
Skovgaardsgade 3
Tel: 86 76 03 44
www.radarlive.dk
Rock, blues, soul, electronica, folk: music of all kinds.
Train
Toldbodgade 6
Tel: 86 13 47 22
www.train.dk
Concert venue and nightclub, hosting several home-grown/international bands each week.

Cinema

All foreign films are shown with their original soundtrack. Local newspapers have the details of what's on where.

Customs Regulations

Danish customs formalities are usually painless and baggage is rarely opened, but it's sensible to observe the duty-free limits and other rules.
  Cigarettes, spirits, perfume, cameras and other luxury items are relatively expensive in Denmark. The rules about how much one can bring into Denmark depend on whether or not you are coming from an EU country. Most EU citizens can now carry almost any amount across EU borders, so long as it is for "personal use". If you are coming from outside the EU, you can bring only 1 litre of spirits or 2 litres of wine; 200 cigarettes or 50 cigars or 250g of tobacco; 500g of coffee; 100g of tea; 50g of perfume; 250ml of eau de toilette; and goods/gifts not exceeding DKK1,350 in value. It is wise to check with your local Danish consul if in doubt. The Danish customs and tax authority website is: www.skat.dk.

D

Disabled Travellers

In Denmark as a whole, a lot of thought is given to the comfort and unhindered access to all parts of society for those with disabilities, including on public transport. For further information contact:
Danske Handicaporganisationer,
Blekinge Boulevard 2, Taastrup
Tel: 36 75 17 17
www.handicap.dk
  The Danish Accessibility Association has a growing online database where you can check the accessibility of specific restaurants, museums and tourist attractions (www.godadgang.dk).
  Local tourist information offices can provide specific information about facilities in their area.

E

Embassies and Consulates

The following embassies and consulates are in Copenhagen.
Canada
Kristen Bernikowsgade 1
Tel: 33 48 32 00
www.denmark.gc.ca
Germany
Stockholmsgade 57
Tel: 35 45 99 00
www.kopenhagen.diplo.de
Ireland
Østbanegade 21
Tel: 35 47 32 00
www.embassyofireland.dk
UK
Kastelsvej 36-40
Tel: 35 44 52 00
http://ukindenmark.fco.gov.uk
US
Daghammarskjölds Allé 24
Tel: 33 41 71 00
http://denmark.usembassy.gov

Emergencies

Police, ambulance, fire 112
International collect calls 80 30 40 00

G

Gay and Lesbian Travellers

Denmark is one of the most liberal and gay-friendly countries in the world. It has had anti-discrimination laws since 1987, and in 1989 was the first nation to recognise same-sex marriages, which it legalised in 2012. The age of consent for homosexuals is 15, the same as for heterosexuals. Contact LGBT Denmark for general information: Nygade 7, Copenhagen; tel: 33 13 19 48; www.lgbt.dk.

Copenhagen is a very welcoming city for gay people and has been for years. Its first gay bar, Centralhjørnet, opened over 80 years ago and is still open today (www.centralhjornet. dk). There are smaller gay scenes in towns such as Aalborg, Århus and Odense.

Tourist offices in Copenhagen will provide a list of the latest venues and events, or visit the comprehensive website www. copenhagen-gay-life.dk. In mid-August Copenhagen has an annual gay pride parade, **Copenhagen Pride** (www.copenhagenpride.dk), and every October hosts **MIX Copenhagen,** a gay and lesbian film festival (http:// mixcopenhagen.dk).

Some of the most popular gay venues include:
Cosy Bar
Studiestræde 24; tel: 33 12 74 27; http://cosybar.dk
Masken Bar
Studiestræde 33; tel: 33 91 09 37; www.maskenbar.dk
Oscar Bar café
Rådhuspladsen 77; tel: 33 12 09 99; www.oscarbarcafe.dk

For more information see www.out-and-about.dk.

H

Health and Medical Care

Standards of hygiene in Scandinavia are among the highest in the world. There are no major health hazards and the tap water is safe to drink.

The Danish medical system will assist anyone in an emergency; however, you should take out travel insurance before you leave. British nationals should take a European Health Insurance Card (EHIC), which you can apply for online (www.ehic. org.uk), by phone (0845 606 2030), or by post (form available from any post office in the UK). You will be charged for doctors' and dentists' consultations and prescriptions, but not hospital treatment. To get a refund, take the receipts and your EHIC and passport to the local council. Citizens of other non-EU countries should ensure that they take out private health insurance before departing for Denmark.

Medical Services

Health care is generally free in Denmark. Acute illnesses or accidents will be treated at the casualty department of the nearest hospital. To contact a doctor outside normal business hours: In Copenhagen tel: 70 13 00 41; Zealand tel: 70 15 07 00; north Jutland tel: 70 15 03 00; mid-Jutland tel: 70 11 31 31; south Jutland tel: 70 11 07 07.

Pharmacies

There is a 24-hour pharmacy in every region, the name and address of which is posted on the door of every pharmacy. In Copenhagen: Steno Apotek, Vesterbrogade 6c; tel: 33 14 82 66.

Dental Services

Dental care is by appointment only. Check the listings under Tandlæger in the Yellow Pages. **Tandlægevagten**, Oslo Plads 14, Copenhagen, tel: 35 38 02 51, www.tandlægevagten.dk, is open for personal callers on an emergency basis daily 8–9.30pm, plus weekends and holidays 10am–noon.

L

Language

Pronunciation

The old joke says that Danish is not so much a language as a disease of the throat, and so it sometimes seems. Danish has three extra letters – æ, ø, and å – plus unpronounceable sub-glottal stops, and myriad dialects and accents. Here are a few simple rules of thumb for pronouncing vowels:
a = a, as in bar
å = aw, as in paw
æ = e, as in pear
e = e, as in bed
i = ee, as in sleep
ø = u, as in fur

General

yes/no ja/nej
big/little stor(t)/lille
good/bad god(t)/dårlig(t)
hot/cold varm/kold
much/little meget/lidt
many/few mange/få
and/or og/eller
please/thank you vær så venlig/tak
I jeg
you (formal) du (De)
he/she han/hun
it den/det

we vi
you (plural, formal) I (De)
they de

Medical

pharmacy (et) apotek
hospital (et) hospital
casualty (en) skadestue
doctor (en) læge

Food and Drink

breakfast morgenmad
lunch (break) frokost (pause)
dinner middag
tea te
coffee kaffe
beer (bottle/draught) øl/fadøl

Getting Around

left venstre
right højre
street (en) gade/vej
bicycle (path) (en) cykel (sti)
car (en) bil
bus/coach (en) bus
train (et) tog
ferry (en) færge
bridge (en) bro
traffic light (et) trafiklys
square (et) torv
north nord
south syd
east øst
west vest

Buying a Ticket

ticket billet
adult voksen
child barn
single enkelt
return retur

Money

How much is it? Hvad koster det?
Can I pay with... Må jeg betale med...
Please may I have...? Må jeg få...?
the bill regningen
May I have a...? Må jeg få en...?
receipt kvittering
exchange veksle
open åben
closed lukket
value-added tax (VAT) MOMS

Time

good morning godmorgen
good day/evening goddag
goodnight godaften/godnat
today i dag
tomorrow i morgen
yesterday i går
morning formiddag
noon middag
afternoon eftermiddag
evening aften
night nat
What time is it? Hvad er klokken?

Days of the Week
Monday *mandag*
Tuesday *tirsdag*
Wednesday *onsdag*
Thursday *torsdag*
Friday *fredag*
Saturday *lørdag*
Sunday *søndag*

Numbers
0 *nul*
1 *en/et*
2 *to*
3 *tre*
4 *fire*
5 *fem*
6 *seks*
7 *syv*
8 *otte*
9 *ni*
10 *ti*
11 *elleve*
12 *tolv*
13 *tretten*
14 *fjorten*
15 *femten*
16 *seksten*
17 *sytten*
18 *atten*
19 *nitten*
20 *tyve*
30 *tredive*
40 *fyrre*
50 *halvtreds*
60 *tres*
70 *halvfjerds*
80 *firs*
90 *halvfems*
100 *hundrede*

M

Media

Newspapers and Magazines
English-language newspapers are widely available at all main train stations and kiosks. Read them free at the Central Library, Krystalgade

Music Festivals

These are just a few of the music festivals taking place in Denmark every year.
Copenhagen Jazz Festival
For 10 days in July the streets of Copenhagen are filled with the sound of jazz. One of the world's best jazz festivals (http://jazz.dk).
Skanderborg Festival
"Denmark's most beautiful festival", featuring Danish and international acts, is held in August in a beechwood (www.smukfest.dk).

15 (https://bibliotek.kk.dk), or Café Europa 1989, Amagertorv 1 (http://europa1989.dk), Copenhagen.
The English-language weekly *The Copenhagen Post* (www.cphpost.dk) has news, entertainment and restaurant guides (from tourist offices and newsstands).

Books
Many public libraries have books in English, and Copenhagen has bookshops that specialise in foreign literature (see Shopping below).

Television
Most hotels have satellite/cable channels featuring CNN, BBC and MTV in English. In addition, there are often movies in English on the national channels DR1, DR2 and TV2.

Money

Currency and Exchange
Danish krone (crown); plural kroner; marked kr in shops or DKK internationally; split into 100 øre. Notes come in 50, 100, 200, 500 and 1,000 denominations. There is a 50 øre coin (copper-coloured), 1 krone, 2 krone, 5 krone (silver-coloured with a hole in the centre), and 10 and 20 krone (solid gold-coloured coins that are similar-looking, except the 20 krone piece is a little bigger than the 10 krone).
Exchanges are open outside normal business hours at the Copenhagen Central Railway Station, and in the city centre. Forex is open daily 8am–9pm. There are several 24-hour machines near Copenhagen City Hall.

How to Pay
Visa is the most widely accepted credit card, and you can usually pay by MasterCard and American Express in hotels, restaurants and shops. Note that some places will charge a fee if you pay with a foreign credit

Roskilde Festival
Late June/early July near Roskilde on Zealand. The largest music festival in Denmark and one of the biggest in Europe, featuring major acts from around the world (www.roskilde-festival.dk).
Skagen Festival
In early July at the northernmost tip of Denmark – beautiful windswept Skagen. One of Denmark's largest folk music festivals (http://skagenfestival.dk).

card. Diners Club is accepted in many restaurants.

Banks and ATMs
Most banks have 24-hour cash machines (ATMs) – look for the word *Kontanten*. The smallest amount you can draw out is DKK100, the maximum depends on the bank who owns the cash machine and varies from DKK2000 to DKK6000. Check with your bank for your daily limits and ATM fees.

Tipping
Service is included in all bills, but in restaurants it is a friendly gesture to pick up the notes but leave the coins. Taxi drivers appreciate it if the fare is rounded up to the nearest DKK5 or 10.

N

Nightlife

The best clubs are found in Copenhagen, Århus and Odense. Check the local newspapers or call tourist information offices for current listings. See also Culture, page 355.

O

Opening Hours

Offices: 8/9am–4/5pm.
Shops: Mon–Thur 9.30am/10am–5.30pm, Fri until 7pm (8pm in Copenhagen), Sat 9am–noon or 1pm (5pm in Copenhagen). All are closed on Sunday except for bakeries and kiosks, some of which are open around the clock.
Pharmacies: as shops, except Steno Apotek in Copenhagen (across the street from the train station) which opens all hours.
Supermarkets: until 7/8pm, at least in Copenhagen. The one at the railway station opens all hours.
Banks: Mon–Fri 10am–4pm, some Thur until 6pm.
Post offices: Mon–Fri 9am–5pm, Sat 9am–noon.

P

Postal Services

The Danish postal service is fast and efficient (www.postdanmark.dk). A letter to the UK/US costs DKK11.50/14.50 economy, DKK14/16 priority. Post offices are generally open 9am–5pm on weekdays, and 9am–noon (smaller branches closed) on Saturday. In

Illums Bolighus features the best in Danish design.

Copenhagen, the most central **post office**, at the main railway station, opens Mon–Fri 8am–9pm, Sat–Sun 10am–4pm.

Money orders can be collected or dispatched at all post offices during normal business hours.

Public Holidays

1 January New Year's Day
March/April Maundy Thursday, Good Friday, Easter Day and Easter Monday
May/June Whit Monday, Ascension Day
5 June Constitution Day
24–26 Dec Christmas
31 Dec New Year's Eve
A floating holiday is **Prayer Day** (*Store Bededag*), which falls on the fourth Friday after Easter. All shops close during holidays.

R

Religious Services

The official Church is the Evangelical Lutheran Church of Denmark. Church attendance is low, and many Danes are agnostic or atheist. For details of church services, ask at the tourist office.

S

Shopping

What to Buy

Danish design is famous all over the world, especially in kitchenware, furniture and stereo equipment.

Beautiful amber necklaces are to be found in all jewellery stores, along with exquisite replicas of ancient Viking jewellery in silver and gold.

Ceramics and glassware are a tradition in Denmark and, in addition to Royal Copenhagen Porcelain, there are many small ceramic studios scattered throughout the country.

Danish furs are very popular among tourists, and countless shops specialise in traditional and modern knitwear.

Lego bricks originated in Denmark, but most Danish children's toys are made of strong, durable wood with designs and functions that are based on educational principles.

Feather bedding is a Danish speciality, and many stores sell down duvets, eiderdowns, quilts and pillows, and can arrange shipment of bulky items.

Danish pipe makers carve wood and meerschaum pipes with excellent craftsmanship.

Tax-Free Shopping

Part of the reason for the high prices is a value-added tax (called MOMS) of 25 percent, added to all sales and services.

Non-EU residents can avoid making this contribution to the Danish state by having their purchases shipped home directly. They can also get a tax refund by shopping in stores that offer a tax-free service – minimum spend is DKK300. See www.globalblue.com for details. (See Customs, page 356, for further details.)

Shopping in Copenhagen

The main shopping in Copenhagen is along the "walking street" Strøget, which is actually four streets that stretch from the Rådhuspladsen for about 1km (0.75 mile) to Kongens Nytorv. Unfortunately, in the last couple of years or so rising rents have forced out many of the characterful small stores and they have been replaced, mainly, by large chain stores. But small stores still remain in the streets parallel to and to the side of Strøget, particularly the interesting Strædet.

Amber

Copenhagen is the capital of amber, and in recent years the **House of Amber** (www.houseofamber.com) has consolidated its position as the leading retailer in the city and now has three stores in Copenhagen, with the most prominent being at

Kongens Nytorv 2 – which also includes the Amber Museum, tel: 33 11 67 00; Nygade 6, tel: 39 55 14 00; Frederiksberggade 34, Vesterbrogade 1A, tel: 33 11 35 30.

Books

The following shops all have good selections of foreign-language literature:
Arnold Busck
Købmagergade 49
Tel: 33 73 35 00
www.arnoldbusck.dk
Atheneum Academic Books
Norregade 6
Tel: 33 12 69 70
www.academicbooks.dk/atheneum
The Book Trader
Skindergade 23
Tel: 33 12 06 69
www.booktrader.dk
Second-hand humanities books.
Politikens Boghallen
Rådhuspladsen 37
Tel: 33 67 28 06
www.boghallen.dk
Two floors of books, with an excellent English-language selection.

Danish Design
Bodum
Østergade 10 (Strøget)
Tel: 33 36 40 80
www.bodum.com
Bodum has lots of outlets in the city, but this is its flagship store.
DZOO, Designer Zoo
Vesterbrogade 137
Tel: 33 24 94 93
www.dzoo.dk
In this part of now fashionable Vesterbrogade, you will find an innovative and interesting collection of clothing, jewellery and houseware.
Illums Bolighus
Amagertorv 10
Tel: 33 14 19 41
www.illumsbolighus.dk
Mouthwatering collections of homeware (if design is your thing), from shining teaspoons to curvy chairs and sofas.

Department Stores
Magasin du Nord
Kongens Nytorv 13
Tel: 33 11 44 33
www.magasin.dk
Once the Hotel du Nord and facing the famous Kongens Nytorv, this is Denmark's most famous department store and has branches in other cities in the country.

Fashion
Kronprinsensgade is a good place to start looking for designer clothing.

By Malene Birger
Antonigade 10
Tel: 35 43 22 33
www.bymalenebirger.com
Winner of the Best Danish Designer
award in 2009, Malene Birger makes
contemporary women's clothing and
accessories.
Bruuns Bazaar Women Store
Kronprinsensgade 8 & 9
Tel: 33 32 19 99
www.bruunsbazaar.dk
A leading men's and women's fashion
design shop, with other branches
around Europe and in North America.
Munthe
Grønnegade 10
Tel: 33 32 03 12
http://dk.munthe.com
A highly fashionable women's store,
with other branches at Østergade 52
and in Århus.

Handicrafts
Danish Crafts
Kongens Nytorv 1E
Tel: 33 12 61 62
An information centre for Danish
handicrafts, which organises
exhibitions to promote the country's
craftsmen and women.
Workshop Copenhagen
Thorshavnsgade 22
Tel: 28 87 65 64
www.workshop-cph.dk
Unique, handmade designs by a
collective of Danish artists.

Outdoor Wear
Guns & Gents
Skindergade 31
Tel: 33 91 24 24
www.gunsandgents.dk
Although primarily a hunting shop,
this also has the best collection
of waterproof and windproof
Barbour jackets – often needed in
Copenhagen even in summer.

Porcelain
Royal Copenhagen Porcelain
Amagertorv 6

Copenhagen Card

We suggest you buy a Copenhagen
Card (CPHCARD; www.copenhagen
card.com) at your hotel, the Central
Railway Station or the Copenhagen
tourist information office. The
card gives you free entry to 72
attractions across Copenhagen
and north Zealand, free bus/train/
metro rides in the same area, and
an informative guide. The card is
available for periods of 24, 48, 72
and 120 hours.

Tel: 33 13 71 81
www.royalcopenhagen.com
Located in a beautiful building on
Strøget, this company has been going
for over 235 years. This flagship
store contains a museum and mini-
production line.

Silverwear
Georg Jensen
Amagertorv 4
Tel: 33 11 40 80
www.georgjensen.com
Look no farther than here, on Strøget,
for all kinds of beautifully designed
silver jewellery.

Stereo Equipment
Bang & Olufsen
Østergade 18
Tel: 33 11 14 15
www.bang-olufsen.com
The company's flagship shore, where
you can admire their full range of top-
quality stereo equipment.

T

Telephones

Most phone boxes take prepaid
telephone cards, available from
newsagents, supermarkets, petrol
stations, etc.
Danish mobile phones operate
on the 900/1800 MHz GSM
network – most European phones
are compatible, although your phone
must be unlocked in order to link up
with the network. US phones work on
a slightly different frequency, so US
visitors will only be able to use their
mobile in Denmark if it is a tri-band
phone that can switch bands (most
smartphones are tri-band).
If you are likely to be making a lot
of phone calls in Denmark, it's worth
buying a Danish pre-paid phone SIM
card, available from mobile phone
shops; buy top-ups from newsagents
and supermarkets. Danish mobile
phone operators include Telenor
(www.telenor.dk), Telia (http://telia.dk)
and TDC (http://tdc.dk).
To call abroad, dial 00 followed by the
country code (44 for the UK, 1 for the US
and Canada, 353 for Ireland), then dial
the number, omitting any initial 0.
Denmark's country code is 45.
There are no area codes.

Tourist Information

The Danish tourist board can provide
helpful information and brochures
before you travel:
UK VisitDenmark, 55 Sloane Street,

London SW1X 9SY; email: london@visit
denmark.com; www.visitdenmark.com.
US VisitDenmark, 655 Third Avenue,
Ste. 1810, NY 10017, New York;
tel: 212-885 9700; email: usa@visit
denmark.com; www.visitdenmark.com.
There is a tourist office in almost
every city, with knowledgeable and
friendly staff. They can assist in
planning a trip, make reservations, or
provide directions and leaflets. Some
of the main tourist bureaus are:
Copenhagen
Vesterbrogade 4A (across from the
Tivoli main entrance)
Tel: 70 22 24 42
Email: touristinfo@woco.dk
www.visitcopenhagen.com
North Zealand
Havnepladsen 3, 3000 Helsingør
Tel: 49 21 13 33. Email: info@
visitnordsjaelland.dk
www.visitnordsjaelland.com
Southwest Zealand
Stændertorvet 1, 4000 Roskilde
Tel: 46 31 65 65
Email: visit@roskilde.dk
www.visitroskilde.com
Bornholms Velkomstcenter
Ndr. Kystvej 3, 3700 Rønne
Tel: 56 95 95 00
Email: info@bornholm.info
www.bornholm.info
Funen
Vestergade 2, 5000 Odense C
Tel: 63 75 75 20
Email: otb@visitodense.com
www.visitodense.com
East Jutland
Pakhus 13, Nordhavnsgade 4, 8000
Århus C
Tel: 87 31 50 10
Email: info@visitaarhus.com
www.visitaarhus.com
North Jutland
Kjellerups Torv 5, Kedelhallen, 9000
Ålborg
Tel: 99 31 75 00
www.visitaalborg.com
West Jutland
Tingvej 2A, 8800 Viborg
Tel: 87 87 88 88
Email: info@visitviborg.dk
www.visitviborg.dk
South Jutland
Torvet 3, 6760 Ribe
Tel: 75 42 15 00
Email: info@visitribe.dk
www.visitribe.dk
Greenland
Greenland Tourism, Hans Egedesvej
29, 3900 Nuuk
Tel: +299 34 28 20
Email: info@greenland.com
www.greenland.com
The Faroe Islands
í Gongini 9, 110 Tórshavn
Tel: +298 20 61 00

Email: info@visitfaroeislands.com
www.visitfaroeislands.com

Useful Copenhagen Websites
www.aok.dk: all about Copenhagen.
www.visitcopenhagen.dk: the Tourist
Board site.
www.out-and-about.dk: gay life.

Tour Operators

Copenhagen
To hire an authorised guide to the city,
contact:
The Association of Authorised Tourist
Guides
Nørregade 41
Tel: 033 113 310
www.guides.dk

Transport

Getting There

By Air
Main international airports: Copen-
hagen airport (at Kastrup, 8km/5
miles from central Copenhagen; www.
cph.dk) and Billund airport in Jutland
(www.bll.dk).
Denmark's national airline is SAS
AB (Scandinavian Airlines).From the
UK, British Airways flies daily from
London Heathrow. Low-cost operators
Norwegian, and easyJet fly daily from
London airports to Copenhagen or
Billund; easyJet flies five to seven
times per week from Manchester, it
also operates flights from Glasgow and
Bristol. Ryanair flies from Stansted
to Århus and Billund. Norwegian also
flies from Edinburgh to Billund and
Copenhagen, but less frequently.
From the US, SAS, Delta, KLM and
Condorfly direct to Copenhagen.
From the UK
British Airways, tel: 0844 493 0787;
www.ba.com
easyJet, tel: 0871 244 2366;
www.easyjet.com
Norwegian, tel: 0330 828 0854;
www.norwegian.com
Ryanair, tel: 0871 246 000
SAS, tel: 0871 521 6000; www.flysas.
com
From the US
Several airlines fly direct to
Copenhagen. An interesting alternative
is to fly **Icelandair** (tel: 1-800-223-
5500; www.icelandair.com), with a free
stopover in Reykjavik, Iceland, before
continuing to Copenhagen or other
European destinations.
Condor, tel: 1-866 960 7915;
www.condor.com
Delta Airlines, tel: 1-800 241 4141;

www.delta.com
KLM, tel: 1-800 618 0104; www.klm.
com
SAS, tel: 1-800 221 2350;
www.flysas.com

By Sea
From Germany
From Germany, Scandlines (www.scand
lines.dk) ferries connect Puttgarden
and Rødby (Lolland), and Rostock
and Gedser. From April to October,
Bornholm Ferries (www.bornholmer
faergen.dk) have a route between
Sassnitz and Rønne (Bornholm).
From Sweden
HH Ferries (www.hhferries.se) and
Scandlines (www.scandlines.dk) both
operate ferries on the busy crossing
between Helsingborg and Helsingør
(north Zealand). Stena Line (www.
stenaline.dk) operates two routes,
from Varberg to Grenå (east Jutland),
and from Göteborg to Frederikshavn
(north Jutland). Bornholm Ferries sail
between Rønne (Bornholm) and Ystad.
From Norway
DFDS Seaways (www.dfdsseaways.dk)
run from Oslo to Copenhagen. Stena
Lines run from Oslo to Frederikshavn
(north Jutland). Colour Line (www.
colorline.dk) run, from both Larvik
and Kristiansand to Hirtshals (north
Jutland). Fjord Line (http://fjordline.
dk) has express boats between
Kristiansand and Hirtshals, and a
normal-speed service from both
Bergen and Stavanger to Hirtshals.

By Rail
Trains arrive daily from Germany, Britain
(via Eurostar to Brussels) and Sweden.
For trains from Britain:
Tel: 0844 848 5848
www.raileurope.co.uk
For train information in Denmark:
Tel: 70 13 14 15
www.rejseplanen.dk

By Coach
Eurolines (www.eurolines-travel.com)
is the leading operator of scheduled
coach services, with coaches from
Denmark to various European
countries. Their Scandinavian
routes run between Oslo, Göteborg,
Malmö and Copenhagen, and from
Stockholm to Copenhagen.
Nettbuss express (www.nettbuss.se)
and Swebus (http://swebusexpress.
com) run similar routes through
Scandinavia.

Getting Around

On Arrival
Almost all international flights
arrive and depart from Copenhagen

Airport, 8km (5 miles) outside the
city in Kastrup. Trains run six times
an hour directly from Terminal 3, the
international terminal, to Central
Station and take 12 minutes.
Intercity express trains run from
the airport direct to Helsingør and
Bornholm. Trains run between the
airport and many major Swedish cities.
The Øresund bridge connects
Denmark and Sweden. Starting
near Copenhagen airport, you can
reach the Swedish city of Malmö
in 20–30 minutes, Stockholm in
5 hrs and Gothenburg in 3 hrs 20
minutes. There is a taxi stand next to
Terminal 3.

By Air
If you fly you can be on the other side
of Denmark in less than an hour.
Domestic flights are operated by SAS.

By Metro
Copenhagen's tiny metro system
(www.m.dk) was extended out to
Copenhagen airport in 2007 and
now has two lines, M1 and M2.
Trains run to the city centre every
4–6 minutes from 5am–midnight
Sunday to Wednesday, with a less
frequent (every 15–20 minutes)
round-the-clock service from
Thursday to Saturday.

By Coach (Long-Distance Bus)
Denmark is not a big country,
and its local bus network covers
most of the country. For details of
local buses on Zealand, contact
Movia Customer Service; tel: 36
13 14 15; www.moviatrafik.dk;
Mon–Fri 7am–9.30pm, Sat–Sun
8am–9.30pm.
Abildskou (http://abildskou.dk)
runs "long-distance" coaches from
Copenhagen to Jutland. Thinggaard
(www.ekspresbus.dk) runs from
Frederikshavn to Esbjerg.
The website www.rejseplanen.dk
allows you to plan journeys by bus
and train.

By Train
There is a very efficient train service
linking all major cities and some of
the smaller towns.
There is a boat-train link from
Copenhagen to Rønne, Bornholm.
For train information, contact the
DSB Customer Centre
Tel: 70 13 14 15; www.dsb.dk

By Car
Rules of the Road. Drive on the right,
and always give way at pedestrian
crossings and look out for bicycles
when turning right. Look over your

left shoulder every time you open the doors on the driver's side – bicycles are everywhere. Overtake on the left only.

Drivers and passengers must wear seat belts, and dipped head-lights are required. Using a mobile phone while driving is illegal at all times. Strict drink-driving laws set the legal limit for blood-alcohol content at 0.05 percent – one drink may put you over.
Speed limits. These are standard speed limits, which are enforced:
Built-up areas. 50kph (30mph)
Main roads. 80kph (50mph)
Motorways. 130kph (80mph) or 110kph (70mph)
For a car with a trailer, the limits are 50kph (30mph), 70kph (40mph) and 80kph (50mph) respectively.
Roadside Assistance. In the event of a breakdown, contact your car rental company or your own private insurer.
Car Rental. It pays to shop around. Ask travel agents about special offers, or try the *Yellow Pages*. **Avis** (www. avis.dk), **Europcar** (www.europcar.dk), **Budget Rent A Car** (www.budget.dk), **Hertz** (www.hertzdk.dk), and **Sixt Rent A Car** (www.sixt.com) all have offices all around the country. You need a valid driving licence and must be at least 20–25 years old.

By Taxi

Taxis are available at airports, central train and bus stations and in city centres. Pick them up at taxi ranks or flag them down in the street.
Århus Taxi. Tel: 89 48 48 48, www.aarhustaxa.dk
Copenhagen Taxi. Tel: 35 35 35 35, www.taxa.dk

On Your Bike

The best way to enjoy the Danish landscape is on a bicycle. You would do best to bring your own bike if you want to tour the country, but for getting around the city, a rented one will do. The local tourist information office can tell you where to pick one up.

For information on routes and practical advice, contact:
Dansk Cyklistforbund (Danish Association of Cyclists)
Rømersgade 7, 1362 Copenhagen K
Tel: 33 32 31 21; www. cyklistforbundet.dk
Mon–Fri 10am–5.30pm, Sat 10am–2pm.
City Bikes (Bycyklen)
Tel: 88 82 64 98; www.bycyklen.dk
In the centre of Copenhagen you can borrow bikes under a scheme operated by GoBike. You pay DKK25 an hour, or you can get a monthly

Odense Mini-Taxi. Tel: 66 12 27 12, http://odenseminitaxi.dk

V

Visas and Passports

A valid passport entitles you to a stay of up to three months. Visas are not required for EU citizens, or those from Canada and the US. Denmark is a member of the Schengen Agreement, whereby citizens of other member states don't need passports to enter Denmark. Other nationalities may need to obtain a visa before arriving. If in doubt, ask at the nearest Danish Embassy or Consulate.

If you arrive from another Scandinavian country, you will often find that passports aren't checked at all. If you intend to stay longer than three months you will have to obtain a resident's permit.

W

What to Read

Complete Hans Christian Andersen Fairy Tales (Gramercy Books). The classic collection of children's tales by Denmark's master storyteller.
A Conspiracy of Decency by Emmy Werner (Westview Press). The story of how Denmark's Jews were saved from the Nazis, based partly on living eyewitness accounts.
Culture Shock! Denmark by M. Strange (Kuperard). A short guide to

subscription for DKK70, and ride for the first half hour free, while every consecutive hour will cost you DKK6. Prior to rental you should create a user account on www.bycyklen.dk. You will need a credit card to register. There are 20 docking stations throughout the city, and more are opening in 2015.
In addition, there are plenty of places to rent bikes at reasonable prices. Contact:
Københavns Cyklebørs
157 Gothersgade
Tel: 33 14 07 17
www.cykelborsen.dk
Cycle tours of Copenhagen are also available, for example with:
Copenhagen Tours
Vodroffsvej 55
Tel: 35 43 01 22
www.copenhagen-tours.dk

Harbour Tours

One of the best ways of seeing Copenhagen is on a boat cruising the main harbour and the canals around Slotsholmen and Christianshavn.
Strömma Canal Tours
Tel: 32 96 30 00; www.canaltours. com
60-minute guided tours are the most popular. Prices are DKK75. They also offer dinner cruises that last two hours and cost about 499DKK.
The Netto Boats
Tel: 32 54 41 02
www.nettobaadene.dk
The open-top Netto Boats also make a 60-minute guided tour of the harbour and the canals, but cost less at DKK40 (DKK15 for children).

Denmark's customs and culture.
How to Be Danish: A Journey to the Cultural Heart of Denmark by Patrick Kingsley (Atria Books/Marble Arch Press). A witty introduction to contemporary Danish culture.
Miss Smilla's Feeling for Snow by Peter Høeg (Flamingo). A worldwide best-selling novel that spawned a mediocre film.
The Name of This Book is Dogme 95 by Richard Kelly (Faber). Was Denmark's most famous cinematic innovation a genuine breakthrough or just a clever marketing ploy? Includes interviews with all the key figures, including Lars von Trier.
A Piece of Danish Happiness: One Woman finds the secrets of the happiest people in the world by Sharmi Albrechtsen (CreateSpace Independent Publishing Platform). An entertaining memoir loaded with facts and anecdotes.
Seven Gothic Tales by Isak Dinesen, aka Karen Blixen (Penguin Classics). Dark, dreamy fairytales for adults from one of Denmark's most enigmatic 20th-century authors.
The Sixth Floor by Robin Reilly (Cassell). Dramatic account of the Danish Resistance in World War II and the tragic consequences of the British RAF raid on the Gestapo's Copenhagen headquarters.
Society without God: What the Least Religious Nations Can Tell Us About Contentment by Phil Zuckerman (NYU Press). A sociologist's observation of life in two least religious countries in the world: Denmark and Sweden.
Other Insight Guides
Explore Copenhagen provides a series of detailed routes throughout the Danish capital.

DENMARK EATING OUT

RESTAURANTS AND CAFES

WHAT TO EAT

Within the past couple of decades the Danish kitchen has gone through a quiet revolution, and a new pride in Scandinavian cuisine has taken root. Traditional dishes such as pork and beef are still appreciated, but have been transformed into lighter delicacies for a modern palate. World-class restaurants serving distinctly Scandinavian dishes have popped up all over Copenhagen.

However, the food that is most strongly associated with Denmark has not suffered from this New Nordic wave: open sandwiches (*smørrebrød*) are still the most popular choice at lunchtime. *Smorgåsbord* is a lunch buffet of cold dishes, where you can pick and choose from a range of Danish specialities. Do take advantage of the varieties of fish from the Baltic and North seas. Fowl and game are common, especially in autumn.

Many restaurants offer "a two-course meal of good, Danish food". This is where one finds roast pork, minced beef, meat or fish balls, and other traditional dishes.

RESTAURANT LISTINGS

Restaurants are grouped by area, starting with Copenhagen. Within each city or region they are listed in alphabetical order.

COPENHAGEN

Michelin-Starred

As of 2014 Copenhagen has 15 Michelin-starred restaurants, including the following:

Era Ora
Overgaden Neden, Vandet 33B
Tel: 32 54 06 93
www.era-ora.dk
Considered to be the best Italian restaurant in Northern Europe, it also has a wine cellar containing over 75,000 bottles and 700 labels. The cellar can be visited by those so interested. **$$$**

Formel B
Vesterbrogade 182
Tel: 33 25 10 66
www.formel-b.dk
Stylish and modern, this restaurant is famous for its French/Danish cuisine. Its six-course menu is one of the country's finest. **$$$**

Geranium
Per Henrik Lings Allé 4, 8.
Tel: 69 96 00 20
http://geranium.dk
Run by renowned chef Rasmus Kofoed, Geranium was once ranked 42nd best restaurant in the world.

$$$

Noma
Strandgade 93
Tel: 32 96 32 97
www.noma.dk
People come to Denmark just to eat here – bookings taken three months prior to dining. Renowned for its "New Nordic" cuisine and innovative presentation. Voted World's Best Restaurant in 2010, 2011, 2012 and 2014. **$$$**

Other Restaurants

Aamanns
Øster Farimagsgade 10
Tel: 35 55 33 44
www.aamanns.dk
Copenhagen folk swear by Aamanns deli/takeaway, where traditional Danish *smørrebrød* are given a contemporary touch. (Aamanns also have a fine-dining restaurant next door). **$**

Famo
Saxogade 3
Tel: 33 23 22 50
www.famo.dk
Cheerful Italian restaurant with a set four-course seasonal menu. The antipasti in particular are full of rich, authentic flavours. **$$$**

Restaurant Cofoco
Abel Cathrines Gade 7
Tel: 33 13 60 60
www.cofoco.dk
Top-quality French/Danish cuisine at an excellent price. Eat at private tables, or turn it into a shared dining experience and join the sociable long table. **$$**

Restaurant Godt
Gothersgade 38
Tel: 33 15 21 22
www.restaurant-godt.dk
This tiny, cosy family-run restaurant (seats 20) serves finely balanced seasonal menus. Reservations are advised. **$$–$$$**

Restaurant Puk
Vandkunsten 8
Tel: 33 11 14 17
www.restaurantpuk.dk
This basement restaurant serves up perfectly cooked traditional/ Bornholm dishes – *plankebøf*, Danish hash, roast pork – in a homey atmosphere. **$$**

Shellfish are always on the menu.

Restaurationen
Møntergade 19
Tel: 33 14 94 95
www.restaurationen.com
With its one fixed Danish-style menu
of five courses (changed weekly), this
is a Copenhagen favourite. **$$$**

Riz Raz
Store Kannikestræde 19
Tel: 33 32 33 45
Kompagnistræde 20
Tel: 33 15 05 75
www.rizraz.dk
With two locations in Copenhagen,
Riz Raz is famed for its ultra-good-
value vegetarian buffet, bursting with
Mediterranean flavours. Very popular
with locals. **$**

Spiseloppen
43 Bådsmandsstræde, Christiania
Tel: 32 57 95 58
www.spiseloppen.dk
Featuring an international menu
prepared by chefs from around
the globe, Spiseloppen is an ever-
surprising restaurant at the heart of
Christiania. **$$**

Cafés

Bang & Jensen
Istedgade 130, 1650 V

Tel: 33 25 53 18
Popular with the young. Tasty
brunches. **$**

Café Dan Turell
Store Regnegade 3, 1110 K
Tel: 33 14 10 47
www.cafedanturell.dkArtists frequent
this café. **$**

Café Katz
Frederiksholms Kanal 1
Tel: 33 93 33 87
www.katz.dk
Great waterside location. **$**

Park Café
Østerbrogade 79, 2100 Ø
Tel: 70 333 222
www.parkcafe.dk
Often has live contemporary music. **$**

Zirup
Læderstræde 32
Tel: 33 13 50 60
www.zirup.dk
Perfect place for people-watching.
$$

ZEALAND

Helsingør

Café Hyacint
Bjerggade 4a
Tel: 49 21 69 70
www.cafehyacint.n.nu
Stop here for mid-morning coffee, or
indulge in one of the excellent Danish
lunch platters. **$**

Madam Sprunck
Bramstræde 5Tel: 49 26 48 49
www.madamsprunck.dk

A varied international menu awaits
at this atmospheric courtyard
restaurant. A popular brunch is also
served here. **$$–$$$**

Hillerød

Spisestedet Leonora
Frederiksborg Slot, 3400
Tel: 48 26 75 16
www.leonora.dk
A good lunch choice, particularly on

sunny days when the terrace opens.
$$

Kongens Lyngby

Brede Spisehus
I.C. Modewegsvej
Tel: 45 85 54 57
www.bredespisehus.dk
Danish/French cuisine in wonderful
natural setting in a small village just
outside Copenhagen. **$$–$$$**

BORNHOLM

Gudhjem

Café Provianten
Ejnar Mikkelsensvej 28
Tel: 40 76 81 96
A cosy café in a superb location
serving tasty sandwiches and
cocktails. **$**

Rønne

Arnager Rogeri and Restaurant

Arnagervej 4
Tel: 56 97 22 00
www.arnager-rogeri.dk
A family-owned restaurant and
smokery. Excellent fish dishes. **$**

Di 5 Ståuerna
Strandvejen 116
Tel: 56 90 44 44
www.radissonblu.com/hotel-bornholm
The Radisson Hotel's excellent

restaurant with a perfect sea view. **$$$**

Svaneke

Rogeriet I Svaneke
Fiskergade 12
Tel: 56 49 63 24
http://roegerietsvaneke.dk
Wash down smoked eel, salmon and
Baltic herring with home-brewed
beer. **$$**

FUNEN

Odense

Den Gamle Kro
Overgade 23
Tel: 66 12 14 33
www.dengamlekro.eu
Traditional Danish and French
cuisine in a higgledy-piggledy
building (1683): in sunny weather,

head for the leafy courtyard.
$$–$$$

Olivia Brasserie
Vintapperstræde 37
Tel: 66 17 87 44
www.cafeolivia.dk
This smart, welcoming brasserie
serves epic brunches, light lunches

and a "rustic" evening menu. **$$**

Restaurant under Lindetræet
Ramsherred 2
Tel: 66 12 92 86
www.underlindetraet.dk
This lovely old inn serves up
mouthwatering Danish/French
dishes. Odense's finest. **$$**

JUTLAND

Aabenraa

Krusmølle
Krusmøllevej 10, Feldstedskov
Tel: 74 68 61 72
www.krusmoelle.dk
Linger over coffee and cake or a light lunch at this café, which shares an old mill building with glass and ceramics workshops. **$$**

Ålborg

Mortens Kro
Mølleå 2-6
Tel: 98 12 48 60
www.mortenskro.com
Super-swish gourmet restaurant, with its own champagne bar. **$$$**

Arden

Rold Gammel Kro
Hobrovej 11
Tel: 98 56 17 00
www.roldkro.dk
Small lunchtime selection of smørrebrød and meat/fish/cheese platters, with meaty Danish dishes (boar, beef, pork) at night. **$$$**

Århus

L'Estragon
Klostergade 6
Tel: 86 12 40 66
www.lestragon.dk
Top-class Danish/French food served in an intimate setting. **$$$**
Klassisk 65

Jægergårdsgade 65
Tel: 86 13 12 21
www.klassiskbistro.dk
This bistro/wine bar offers fabulously tasty food in a cosy atmosphere. Excellent service. Recommended Sunday brunch. **$$**
Mefisto
Volden 28
Tel: 86 13 18 13
www.mefisto.dk
A smashing little café/restaurant in the Latin quarter, Mefisto is open for coffee, brunch, lunch and dinner. On Tuesdays there's a gourmet fish menu, created from whatever the fishermen bring in. **$$–$$$**
Miro
Marstrandsgade 2
Tel: 86 13 87 00
www.restaurant-miro.dk
Visit this city-centre restaurant for an unforgettable gourmet experience and an amazing selection of wines that enhance the dishes' flavour. **$$$**
Pind's Café
Skolegade 11
Tel: 86 12 20 60
www.pindscafe.dk
An Århus institution serving traditional Danish fare. **$**

Esbjerg

Café Energien
Frodesgade 175
Tel: 50 59 84 86

Dining out in Copenhagen.

http://cafeenergien.dk
Healthy seasonal food in a great ambience. Danish and Spanish cuisine. **$**

Skagen

Brøndums Hotel
Anchersvej 3
Tel: 98 44 10 55
www.broendums-hotel.dk
Established in 1840. Good-quality wine and traditional Danish cuisine. Book ahead. **$$$**

Viborg

Kafé & Restaurant Arthur
Vestergade 4
Tel: 86 62 21 26
www.restaurant-arthur.dk
An excellent choice: part of the slow food movement, Arthur serves classy, flavour-packed modern Danish cuisine at reasonable prices. **$$–$$$**

GREENLAND

Nuuk

Restaurant Charoen Porn
Aqqusinersuaq 3
Tel: +299 32 57 59
http://charoenporn.gl
Cuisine as far away from the

icebergs as it's possible to get – here you'll find spicy flavours from the Far East at a genuine Thai restaurant. **$–$$**
Restaurant Sarfalik
Hotel Hans Egede, 3900

Tel: +299 32 42 22
On the fifth floor of Hotel Hans Egede, this is another top-class restaurant serving traditional Greenland dishes. With fine views. **$$$**

THE FAROE ISLANDS

Tórshavn

Áarstova
Gongin 1
Tel: +298 33 30 00
www.aarstova.fo
Tórshavn's gourmet choice, with top-quality Faroese and New Nordic cuisine, with an emphasis on fish dishes, served in a wooden house near the harbour. **$$$**
Koks at Hotel Føroyar
Oyggjarvegur 45
Tel: +298 333 999; www.koks.fo

An upmarket choice with fine views over Tórshavn, Koks offers classic dishes from a seasonal menu. **$$$**
Marco Polo
Sverrisgøta 12
Tel: 298 31 34 30
www.marcopolo.fo
A well-priced family restaurant, serving pizzas, burgers, steaks and fish mains. **$–$$**
Toscana
Nólsoyar Pálsgøta 13
Tel: 298 21 11 09

www.toscana.fo
Exceedingly pleasant Italian restaurant, with rich dishes of venison, seafood, meat and pasta. **$$–$$$**

PRICE CATEGORIES

Price categories are per person for an average two-course meal, excluding drinks but with tax:
$ = under DKK150
$$ = DKK150–300
$$$ = over DKK300

DENMARK

NORWAY

SWEDEN

FINLAND

NORWAY A–Z

A HANDY SUMMARY OF PRACTICAL INFORMATION

A

Accommodation

When it comes to places to stay, Norway has something to suit every requirement. The range covers hotels from the luxurious to the simple, to bed and breakfasts, guesthouses, cosy self-catering cottages, seaside cabins, mountain lodges, youth hostels and campsites.

Children often go free, provided the child stays in the parents' room. Guesthouses *(pensjonat)* offer lower rates and may have shared baths (the bathroom may be down the hall). A breakfast buffet is almost always included in the room rate.

Norwegian hotels reduce their rates during the outdoor summer holiday period, and often at weekends, when business decreases. This makes May to September attractive when compared with standard rates. Hotel taxes are included in the quoted rates.

The state-run visitors' site, www. visitnorway.com, can be a good starting point for tracking down accommodation.

Hotel Chains

Some of the major hotel chains are well represented in Norway's cities (Best Western, Choice, Norlandia, Rica, Scandic, Thon, Radisson Blu). Together with several local chains, they offer passes and discount schemes to help reduce the cost of accommodation. These passes, available for sale at participating hotels, usually involve a modest one-time fee (around NOK100) and then entitle the holder to discounted rates, mostly in the summer and at weekends. Some passes also offer a free night of accommodation after the pass holder has logged several nights on the programme.

Chalets (Hytte)

There are abundant holiday hytte (cabins or chalets) available for rent. These are often situated in more remote locations by the sea or in the heart of the forest, ideal for those in search of nature and tranquillity. They usually house four to six people. If you want to spend just one night in a chalet and then move on, you can stay in one on a campsite without booking ahead. See accommodation guides at www. visitnorway.com.

Fishermen's Cabins (Rorbuer)

In the Lofoten Islands in northern Norway, and at numerous places elsewhere along the coast, you can rent a traditional former fisherman's cabin, or *rorbu*. Most of them have been modernised, and some have their own shower and toilet.

Destination Lofoten Tourist Office
Tel: 76 06 98 00; www.lofoten.info.

Camping

Norway has more than 1,000 campsites, classified by 1–5 stars, depending on the standard and facilities available. The fixed charge per plot is usually NOK80–160, with additional charges per person.

With the Norwegian camping card (Norsk Campingkort) you receive a faster checking-in service along with special discount deals. The card is available from participating campsites.

Many campsites have cabins that may be booked in advance. Some are small and basic, but others are large and well equipped. Both close to Oslo, Ekeberg Camping (tel: 22 19 85 68; www.ekebergcamping.no) and Bogstad Camping (tel: 22 51 08 00; http://bogstadcamping.no) – the largest campsite in Norway – also have cabins.

For further information visit www. camping.no.

Bed and Breakfasts

British-style bed and breakfasts are catching on in Norway, and they are all of a high standard. You can book online, at local tourist offices or at Oslo's Central Railway Station, or look out for signs for Rom or Husrom outside houses as you drive.

Youth and Family Hostels

There are approximately 100 youth hostels in Norway, all of a relatively high standard. A night's accommodation costs from NOK200, breakfast NOK60–75. Reserving space during the high season is essential.

Norske Vandrerhjem
(Hostelling International Norway)
Tel: 23 12 45 10
www.hihostels.no
Hotels vary in price seasonally and some offer special weekend rates, so be sure to double check the exact price when you book. Breakfast is almost always included in Norwegian hotels.

Activities

Outdoor Sports

If Norwegians can contrive a sport as an excuse to be outdoors, they'll do it.

For a full listing of the range of sports and sports facilities in the Oslo region, visit www.visitoslo.com or see the outdoor activities pages of the annual Oslo Guide from tourist offices (also available online).

Canoeing
Some of the best canoeing and kayaking lakes and rivers are in the Femund area, Østfold, Aust and Vest Agder, Telemark and suburban Oslo. Contact the local tourist office for details.

Cycling
Cycling in Norway is safe and pleasurable, as there is relatively little traffic on many minor roads. But although there are a few cycle routes, it is not an integrated system, so you should still ride with caution. Helmets are advised. Cycling is a particularly good way of exploring the area outside Oslo: bicycles are allowed on most trains and buses for a small charge. Note that cyclists are not permitted to travel through the longer tunnels (because of car fumes).

Fishing
The fishing is excellent in Norway, whether you're at sea or on a fjord, lake or river. You need a local fishing permit to fish sea char, salmon or sea trout and a national fishing licence for inland fishing in Norway. You can buy a fishing permit at or near to your holiday spot. See the tourist board's Angling in Norway for full details.

Glacier Hiking
Glacier hiking is an exhilarating experience, but should be attempted only with an experienced local guide. Several Norwegian tour companies offer guided glacier walks *(breer)*, particularly in the following areas:
Fjord Norway: Hardangerjøkulen, Folgefonna, Buarbre, Bondhusbre, Smørstabbre, Fannaråkbre and Nigardsbre.
Norland Reiseliv: Svartisen and Engenbreen.
Oppland: Styggebre.
Sognefjord: Jostedalsbreen and Fjæland.
For details, contact Glacier Information Centres in western Norway at Jostedalsbreen National Park Centre at Oppstryn (tel: 57 87 72 00, 47 915 80 078; http://jostedalsbreenadventure. com), Tourist Office Fjærland (tel: 57 69 32 33; www.fjaerland.org) and Breheimsenteret Jostedal (tel: 57 68 32 50; http://jostedal.com).

Golf
Norwegian golf courses are by and large difficult and challenging. Most require either a Green Card or a handicap under 20. Green fees are in line with most European golf courses. Some nine-hole courses offer day fees.
In the Oslo region professional competitions are held at Bogstad, Larvik, Borre and Vestfold golf clubs, but by far the most beautifully situated is the Tyrifjord golf links. For information, contact:
Norges Golfforbund (Golf Federation)
Sognsveien 75 A1, Ullevål Stadion, 0840 Oslo; tel: 21 02 91 50; www.golfforbundet.no.

Hiking
The country's extensive mountain ranges and high plains make ideal walking terrain. The most popular areas include the Jotunheim, Rondane and Dovrefjell mountains, the Hardangervidda plateau in the Trollheimen district, and the Finnmarksvidda plain. Mountain cabins are open from the end of June until mid-September, plus over the Easter holiday.
The Norwegian Mountain Touring Association (DNT) runs about 300 guided hikes in summer, and glacier walks in winter. Membership includes hut (hytte) access. For details:
Norwegian Trekking Association (Den Norske Turistforening)
Youngstorget 1, 0181 Oslo; tel: 4000 1868; email: info@turistforeningen.no; www.turistforeningen.no.
(See also Norway on Foot, page 379.)

Horse Riding
There are riding centres and hotels all over Norway where you can hire a horse for organised trekking or take lessons. For further details contact tourist offices, or:
Norges Rytterforbund (Riding Federation)
Tel: 21 02 96 50; email: nryf@rytter.no; www.rytter.no.

Husky Safaris
The most thrilling way to explore the northeastern Finnmark region, the heart of the Sami country. Choose from a variety of adventures: drive your own dog team, join a dog-sledge safari, observe the Sami reindeer migration, or enjoy a horse safari. Lodge in authentic log cabins and enjoy the rugged northern landscape.
Sven Engholm's Husky Lodge (B&B), tel: 91 58 66 25; www.engholm.no.
Direct Adventures, tel: +44 (0)207 381 5385; www.directadventures. co.uk.

Skiing
Even in summer Norwegians take to the slopes (as a rule from June to September), and the sight of people skiing in bikinis and trunks is something to behold.
The main ski resorts are at Lillehammer, Trysil, Geilo, Hemsedal, Voss, Norefjell (the nearest to Oslo) and of course Tryvann, Oslo's Winter Park; all tourist offices can advise on local ski facilities for cross-country and slalom. Also check the Norwegian ski guide on www.skiinfo.no, or www.skiforbundet.no.

Sailing
There are sailing and boating clubs and associations throughout Norway.

Dog-sledging is one of Norway's winter attractions.

DENMARK

NORWAY

SWEDEN

FINLAND

The spectacular Northern Lights.

Without your own boat, sailing of any sort can be expensive, and the closest you may get is a small catamaran or even a windsurfer. In Oslo you can hire equipment from:

SrfSnoSk8
Munkedamsveien 20; tel: 22 83 78 73; email: oslo@srfsnosk8.no; http://www.srfsnosk8.no.

Norges Seilforbund (Sailing Federation)
Serviceboks 1, Ullevål Stadion, 0840 Oslo; tel: 21 02 90 00; www.seiling.no.

Swimming
Temperatures along the coast and inland reach 25°C (77°F) in summer, and even in the north it can be warm enough to swim. Nude beaches are to be found in Oslo, Moss, Halden, Tønsberg, Larvik, Molde, Ålesund, Bergen, Trondheim and Salten. Most larger hotels have pools, and there are numerous leisure centres throughout Norway.

Watersports
There are several possibilities for waterskiing and windsurfing along the coast, as well as on Norway's numerous lakes.

White-water rafting is available on the following rivers: Sjoaelva in Oppland, Trysilelva in Hedmark and Driva in Sør-Trøndelag.

The Norwegian coast offers good conditions for diving. There are several diving centres along the west coast, particularly in the counties of Møre and Romsdal, and in north Norway.

Norges Dykkeforbund (Diving Federation)
Sognsveien 73, Ullevål Stadion, 0480 Oslo; tel: 21 02 97 42; www.ndf.no.
Sjoa Raftingsenter
Varphaugen Gård, 2670 Otta; Tel: 47 66 06 80; email: rafting@sjoaraftingsenter.no; www.sjoarafting senter.no.

Whale Safaris
In northern Norway between May and September, massive sperm whales can be found in the area around the Lofoten Islands. There are also minkes and orcas, and on some of these "safaris", seals, and various seabirds – puffins and gullemots – can be observed. Despite propaganda that cameras are replacing harpoons, the area remains a prime hunting ground for Norway's still prevalent whaling industry.

Arctic Whale Tours, in Andenes; tel: 47 38 46 21; www.arcticwhaletours. com.

Hvalsafari in Stø; tel: 76 11 56 00; www.whalesafari.com.

C

Children

With its wide open spaces, beaches within easy reach of the city centre and attractions on the Bygdoy peninsula, Oslo is a particularly family-friendly city. Here is a small selection of the many family attractions Norway has to offer:

In and around Oslo
International Museum of Children's Art
Lille Frøens vei 4; tel: 22 46 85 73; www.barnekunst.no; July–Aug Tue–Thur, Sun 11am–4pm, Sept–mid-Dec and mid-Jan–June Tue–Thur 9.30am–2pm, Sun 11am–4pm.
A unique museum exhibiting children's art from 150 countries. Ekeberg Minigolf Park near Ekeberghallen, tel: 22 68 26 69; www.minigolf.no (summer only).

Puppet Theatre
Torshovgata 33; tel: 22 34 86 80; http://oslonye.no.
High-quality performances for children aged 4 and above.
Tusenfryd Amusement Park Ås,

see Specialist Tour Operators on page 375

Winter Norway

Norway is often dubbed the "Cradle of Skiing"; but skiing is just one of Norway's winter attractions. There are snowmobile trips to the North Cape, reindeer safaris and dog-sledge races over the plain of Finnmarksvidda.

You can go on horse-drawn sleigh rides, or try your hand at sledging, ice fishing, snow-boarding or ice skating. For details of tour operators who specialise in winter holidays in Norway, see Specialist Tour Operators on page 375, or contact the Norwegian Tourist Board, which has a list of holiday agents offering packages.

Østfold; tel: 64 97 64 97 www.tusenfryd.no.
Attractions include: rollercoaster, waterpark, flume ride, carousel and magic carpet. Transport by the TusenFryd Bus from Oslo bus station, every half-hour. June–Aug (May and Sept Sat–Sun).

Youth Information in Oslo
Møllergata 3, Oslo; tel: 24 14 98 20 www.unginfo.oslo.no.
Provides information on all subjects for young people. Mon–Fri 11am–5pm, Sat 12pm–5pm, July–Aug 10am–6pm, Sat 12pm–5pm.

Around Norway
The Troll Family Park
Near Lillehammer; tel: 61 27 55 30; www.hunderfossen.no
Main attractions are: river rafting, the fairytale castle, the world's largest troll, fairytale cave, racing-car track, high-wire forest course, raft ride and Wax Museum. Mid-June–late August.

Kongeparken
Near Stavanger; tel: 815 22 673; www.kongeparken.no.
Over 40 attractions, including "life-sized" model of the Giant Gulliver (85 x 7.5 metres/279 x 25ft), riding tracks, bob track, farm, car track, Wild West City, birds and funfair. Apr–mid-Oct.

Telemark Sommarland
Bø in Telemark; tel: 35 06 16 00; www.sommarland.no
Norway's biggest water park with various wet and dry attractions, including many waterslides and Magasuget, a 26-metre (80ft) high water chute, Flow Rider, said to be the world's biggest surf wave, and a floating river. Plus live entertainment, pony rides, Wild West City and

CLIMATE CHART

Oslo

- ▭ Maximum temperature
- ▭ Minimum temperature
- — Rainfall

children's playground. Early June–mid-August.

Kristiansand Dyrepark
Tel: 38 04 97 00; www.dyreparken.no. Norway's largest wildlife park and most visited tourist attraction. The park has a wide range of other attractions: amusement park, water-park, show and entertainment park. Open all year, times vary.

Climate

Oslo is one of the warmest places in Norway during winter; in January the average 24-hour high is −2°C (28°F) and the low is −7°C (19°F). Bergen is slightly warmer but wetter, and snow rarely lies for long. Up north, sub-zero temperatures reign for months and a good number of roads shut over winter due to long-term snow. February and March are the best skiing months. March, April and early May are the late spring months, when roads are buckled due to thaws and refreezes; through this period the temperature slowly lifts from about 4°C (39°F) to 16°C (61°F).

Come summertime and the season of the Midnight Sun, Oslo enjoys average temperatures in the low to mid-20s°C (70s°F), while the sunlight-bathed north has a perfect hiking temperature, around 20°C (68°F). October is the time for autumn rains as temperatures dip below 10°C (50°F), then continue their slide towards zero. The first snow arrives mid-October.

What to Bring

You're in for a pleasant surprise if travelling to Norway in summer. As it is influenced by the Gulf Stream, it can get even warmer than some of its southern neighbours. In the south, temperatures above 25°C (77°F) are not unusual. The average temperature for the country as a whole in July, including the far north, is about 16°C (60°F), 22°C (71°F) in Oslo. Bring swimming gear, as the water in most fjords, except northern Norway, is 20°C (68°F) in midsummer.

A first-aid kit is recommended for those who plan to make any trips to remoter parts. And be sure to include medicines for preventing and treating mosquito bites, as from midsummer into early autumn biting insects are rife, especially in Finnmark. If you plan to visit Bergen, pack an umbrella – it may be one of Norway's warmest cities, but it is also its wettest.

Culture

Music and Opera

In summer the arts take to the outdoors in Norway, and classical music and opera are no exception. For Oslo dates, pick up the annual Oslo guide. The very active Oslo Philharmonic, founded by Edvard Grieg, is conducted by Vasily Eduardovich Petrenko at the Konserthus, with frequent visits by acclaimed guest conductors and soloists. Den Norske Opera & Ballett (National Opera) stages big productions in its magnificent new waterfront location just east of Akershus.

Akershus Fortress and the Henie Onstad Art Centre (Høvikodden) are two other fine settings for summer concerts, and there are several outdoor jazz, folk, rock, and pop festivals from June to August.

Whether the performers are Norwegian or foreign, the season winter or summer, Norway has a rich and varied musical and operatic life.

Den Norske Opera & Ballett
Kirsten Flagstads pl. 1

Night Skies

Midnight Sun In the north of Norway the sun does not sink below the horizon for several weeks in the summer. The best time to see the "Midnight Sun" is mid-May to late July. Longyearbyen on Svalbard has the longest period of Midnight Suns, from about 20 April to 20 August.

Aurora borealis The Northern Lights, or aurora borealis, are best seen from November to February. You need to go north of the Arctic Circle, which cuts through Norway just south of Bodø on the Nordland coast. There is, unfortunately, no guarantee they will not be obscured by clouds.

Tel: 21 42 21 21
www.operaen.no
Oslo Konserthus
Munkedamsveien 14
Tel: 23 11 31 00
www.oslokonserthus.no

Festivals

Norwegians love a festival, and there are far too many to list them all (consult area guides for festival schedules local to your destination or visit www.visitnorway.com). Here is a small selection:
Holmenkollen Ski Festival – ski-jumping competitions, cross-country races and other events (March).
Sami Easter Festival – a seven-day celebration of Sami culture, from films and concerts to reindeer racing (Easter); www.samieasterfestival.com.
Bergen International Festival – a 15-day arts festival in Norway's culture capital, devoted to music, theatre, dance, opera and visual arts (May/June); www.fib.no.
Norwegian Wood Festival – Norway's top rock festival brings big-name international artists to the stage, Oslo (June); http://norwegianwood.no.
Molde International Jazz Festival – attracts some of the best jazz artists in the world (July); www.moldejazz.no.
National Day (17 May) and Midsummer's Eve (around 21 June, the longest day) are both celebrated throughout the country with parades, music, feasting and bonfires.

Theatre and Dance

Theatre is booming in Norway, but performances are in Norwegian. Some plays are held in English at Oslo's National Theatre during the International Ibsen Festival, which

A night out at the theatre.

is held every other year (Sept; next edition in 2016).

Dance has also come into its own. Classical ballet is performed at the Oslo Opera House. Traditional folk dances can be seen in many towns on National Day (17 May).

National Theatret Oslo
Stortingsgate 15
Tel: 22 00 14 73
www.nationaltheatret.no

Cinema

The Norwegians love films, hence the vast number of cinemas; Oslo has around 40 screens, including the impressive wide-screen cinema at the Colosseum in Frogner. First-run and repertory films are always shown in the original language, with Norwegian subtitles. Kiosks, newspapers and local city guides have listings. Booking tickets is recommended for Fridays and Saturdays.

Customs Regulations

The following can be brought into Norway by visitors:
Money Notes and coins (Norwegian and foreign) up to NOK25,000 or equivalent. If you intend to import more, you must fill in a form (available at all entry and exit points) for the Customs Office.
Alcohol Permitted imports for people aged 20 and over include 1 litre of spirits (up to 60 percent vol.) plus 1.5 litre of fortified wine (up to 22 percent vol.) or 3 litres of wine (if no spirits) and 2 litres of beer, or 5 litres of beer. If you don't bring any tobacco, you may import additional 1.5 litre of beer or wine (up to 4.7 percent vol.).
Tobacco European residents over the age of 18 may bring 200 cigarettes or 250g of other tobacco goods.
Sweets 1kg (2.25 pounds) duty-free chocolate and sweets.
Meat and dairy products Meat, meat products, cheese and foodstuffs except dog and cat food, totalling 10kg (22 pounds) altogether from EEA (European Economic Area) countries. From countries outside the EEA, it is prohibited to bring meat, meat products, milk and milk products with you in your luggage.
Sundries All goods (excluding articles for personal use, but including alcohol and tobacco, etc.) may be brought in duty-free up to a value of NOK6,000.
Prohibited goods Narcotics, medicines (except for personal use), poisons, firearms, ammunition and explosives. Note: the mild narcotic leaf khat is illegal in Norway.
Agricultural produce This comes

under strict surveillance. If it concerns you, get specific details beforehand. For more information visit www.toll.no.

D

Disabled Travellers

Visitors in need of assistance should contact Norges handikapforbund, Schweigaards gate 12, 0134 Oslo; tel: 24 10 24 00; www.nhf.no.

The Terra Nova Scandinavia, at Grenseveien 82, 0663 Oslo, offers brochures on coach tours around Norway especially for wheelchair users. They also provide hotel bookings and hire cars; tel: 22 94 13 50; www.euroterranova.no.

The Society for Accessible Travel and Hospitality (SATH) provides information and advice for travellers with disabilities. Their website is: www.sath.org.

E

Electricity

220 volts AC, 50 cycles. Plugs have two small round pins, so you may need an adaptor for appliances you bring with you.

Embassies

In Oslo

Canada
Wergelandsveien 7
Tel: 22 99 53 00

Enjoying the water.

UK
Thomas Heftyes gate 8
Tel: 23 13 27 00
USA
Henrik Ibsens gate 48
Tel: 21 30 85 40
www.usa.no

Emergencies

Fire 110
Police 112, non-emergency calls 02 800
Ambulance 113
Emergency at sea 120
Medical problems for emergency medical treatment in Oslo (legevakt) Tel: 22 93 22 93

G

Gay and Lesbian Travellers

In common with the rest of Scandinavia, Norway has a very relaxed attitude to homosexuality. There is very little open hostility to gays and lesbians in general society and, partly as a result, the commercial gay scene is relatively small. Tourist offices (see page 374) carry details of the main places and events, including the Oslo Gay Pride, known as "Skeive Dager" in Norwegian.

H

Health and Medical Care

There are no major health hazards in Norway. No vaccinations are necessary to enter Norway and the tap water is (generally) good. A degree of common sense is required when travelling in remote areas, especially during the winter. When hiking/skiing in the mountains, always let someone know of your travel intentions, and use guides wherever possible.

Norway has reciprocal treatment agreements with the UK and many other European countries; your own National Insurance should cover you to receive free treatment at public hospitals. EU citizens should obtain the relevant documentation to entitle them to this (for British citizens an EHIC, European Health Insurance Card, is available from post offices or online at www.ehic.org.uk). EHIC entitles you to the treatment on the same terms as permanent residents of Norway, which means for example that in order to see a GP you will have to pay a small fee (so called patient contribution). People from countries without such agreements, and those without an EHIC card, will have to pay a full fee. If you are concerned whether you need extra cover, check in your own country before you go. The EHIC card only covers the basics and does not include the cost of medicine, so it is advisable to take out additional medical insurance. You will need to take out extra cover if you are going skiing or considering any other possibly dangerous sports.

Medical Services

If you are ill or have an accident while you are in Norway and you need to see a doctor, visit the Accident and Emergency (Legevakt) department of the hospital. A full list of doctors can be found in the Yellow Pages, or ask the hotel for an English-speaking doctor.
Oslo Emergency Medical Centre (Oslo Legevakt)
Storgata 40, Oslo Tel: 22 93 22 93; www.oslolegevakt.no
Bergen Emergency Hospital (Bergen Legevakt)
Vestre Strømskaien 19, Bergen Tel: 55 56 87 60

Pharmacies

For minor problems, head for a pharmacy, or Apotek. Most larger cities have all-night or late-night pharmacies. In other cities enquire at your hotel, or try the emergency number in the phone book under Legevakt (doctor on duty). Where there is a rota of 24-hour pharmacies in a city, a list will usually be posted on

the door of each one.
Oslo
Vitusapotek Jernbanetorget, across from Central Station, Jernbanetorget 4B. Tel: 23 35 81 00. 24 hours.
Bergen
Vitusapotek Nordstjernen, at Storsenter, Strøm gate 8. Tel: 55 21 83 84. Mon–Sat 8am–11pm, Sun 1–11pm.
Stavanger
Vitusapotek Løven, Olav V gate 11. Tel: 51 91 08 80. Daily until 11pm, Mon–Fri from 8.30am, Sat from 9am, Sun from 10am.
Trondheim
Ditt Apotek Solsiden, Beddingen 4. Tel: 73 88 37 37. Mon–Sat 8.30am–midnight, Sun 10am–midnight.

Dental Services

Emergency dental treatment in Oslo and Bergen, outside regular dentists' office hours, is available from:
Oslo Kommunale Tannlegevakt, Schweigaards gate 6c, 3rd floor (near the Central Railway Station). Tel: 22 67 30 00. Mon–Fri 7–10pm, Sat–Sun and holidays 11am–2pm, 7–10pm.
Bergen Tannlegevakt, Vestre Strømkai 19; Tel: 55 56 87 17. Mon–Fri 6–8.30pm, Sat–Sun 3.30–8.30pm.

I

Internet

Besides most hotels, free internet access is available at public libraries in Norway. Screen time is limited, and you may need to book a slot in advance. Oslo internet cafés include Riverside (Grønland 1; tel: 023 43 14 65; www.riverside.no). Free wireless internet is available at the airports, hotels and restaurants, onboard most NSB's regional trains and on some buses.

L

Language

Introduction

Germanic in origin, Norwegian is one of the three Scandinavian languages, and is closely related to Danish and Swedish. There are two official forms of Norwegian, bokmål and nynorsk. The former reflects Norway's 400 years of Danish domination, while nynorsk is built on native Norwegian dialects. The Sami population in north Norway speak

a version of Samic, a Uralic language. English is widely understood.

Getting By

Yes Ja
No Nei
Good morning God morgen
Good afternoon God eftermiddag
Good evening God kveld
Today I dag
Tomorrow I morgen
Yesterday I går
Hello Hei
How do you do? Står det til?
Goodbye Adjø/Ha det bra/Hadet
Thank you Takk
How do I get to...? Hvordan kommer jeg til...?
Where is...? Hvor er...?
What time is it? Hvor mye er klokken?
It is (The time is...) Den er (Klokken er...)
When? Når
Where? Hvor?
Could I have your name please? Hva er navnet?
My name is... Mitt navn er...
Do you have English newspapers? Har du engelske aviser?
Do you speak English? Snakker du engelsk?
I only speak English Jeg snakker bare engelsk
May I help you? Kan jeg hjelpe deg?
I do not understand Jeg forstår ikke
I do not know Jeg vet ikke
It has disappeared Den har forsvunnet
aircraft flymaskin
car bil
train tog
ticket billet
single/return en vei/tur-retur
To rent Leie
Free Ledig
Room to rent Rom til leie
chalet hytte
Can we camp here? Kan vi campe her?
No camping Camping forbudt

Signs and Sights

Right Høyre
To the right Til høyre
Left Venstre
To the left Til venstre
Straight on Rett frem
phrasebook parlør
dictionary ordbok
money penger
chemist apotek
hospital sykehus
doctor lege
police station politistasjon
parking parkering
department store hus/stormagasin
toilet toalett/WC
Gentlemen Herrer

DENMARK

NORWAY

SWEDEN

FINLAND

Ladies *Damer*
Vacant *Ledig*
Engaged *Opptatt*
Entrance *Inngang*
Exit *Utgang*
No entry *Ingen adgang*
Open *Åpent*
Closed *Stengt*
Push *Skyv*
Pull *Trekk*
No smoking *Røyking* forbudt
breakfast *frokost*
lunch *lunsj*
dinner *middag*
Can I order please? *Kan jeg få bestille?*
Could I have the bill please? *Kan jeg få regningen?*
eat *spise*
drink *drikke*
Cheers! *Skål!*
hot *varm*
cold *kald*

Shopping

grocery store (in countryside) *landhandel*
shop *butikk*
food *mat/kost*
to buy *kjøpe*
sauna *badstue*
off licence/liquor store *vinmonopol*
How much is this? *Hvor mye koster det?*
It costs *Det koster...*
clothes *klær*
overcoat *frakk*
jacket *jakke*
suit *dress*
shoes *sko*
skirt *skjørt*
blouse *bluse*
jersey *genser*

Days of the Week

Sunday *søndag*
Monday *mondag*
Tuesday *tirsdag*
Wednesday *onsdag*
Thursday *torsdag*
Friday *fredag*
Saturday *lørdag*

Numbers

1 *en*
2 *to*
3 *tre*
4 *fire*
5 *fem*
6 *seks*
7 *sju*
8 *åtte*
9 *ni*
10 *ti*
11 *elleve*
12 *tolv*
13 *tretten*
14 *fjorten*
15 *femten*
16 *seksten*
17 *sytten*
18 *åtten*
19 *nitten*
20 *tjue*
40 *forti*
60 *seksti*
80 *åtti*
100 *hundre*
200 *to hundre*
1,000 *tusen*

M

Media

Newspapers

Most larger kiosks (like the Narvesen chain) and some bookshops sell English-language newspapers. Norway's main newspaper is Aftenposten: www.aftenposten.no. Norwegian news in English can be found on the following websites: www. norwaypost.no, www.thelocal.no and www.newsinenglish.no.

Deichmanske Bibliotek, the main public library, is at Arne Garborgs plass 4 in Oslo; you'll find a selection of international papers and periodicals in its reading rooms, as well as free internet access. Mon–Fri 9am–7pm, Sat 10am–4pm; www.deichman.no.

Bookshops

There are several bookshops in Oslo with English-language sections, including:
Tronsmo
Kristian Augusts gate 19
Tel: 22 99 03 99
www.tronsmo.no
A classic indie shop by the university with a great selection of fiction, politics, gay and lesbian literature, and comics.
Litteraturhuset
Wergelandsveien 29
Tel: 22 95 55 30
www.litteraturhuset.no
Plus **Tanum** (www.tanum.no) and **Norli (**www.norli.no) are quality book chains with many locations.

Radio

On Sundays, Radio Norway (93 FM) broadcasts the news from Norway in English, daily at 5pm. During the winter months BBC radios 1, 2, 3 and 4 can sometimes be received on AM, but reception is often distorted.

Television

The Norwegian government is the leading broadcaster in Norway which owns and operates the NRK stations. Cable TV is common here and allows you to pick up a variety of channels, including BBC World, CNN, Swedish STV1 and STV2, Discovery, MTV, French TV5, Eurosport, TV3 and so on, depending on the distributor. Most hotels have pay channels in addition to the above. English films on Norwegian television are subtitled, not dubbed.

Money

The Norwegian krone (NOK) is divided into 100 øre. Notes come in denominations of NOK50, 100, 200, 500 and 1,000, and coins are 50 øre and NOK1, 5, 10 and 20.

You can change currency at post offices, the Oslo S train station, international airports, some hotels and commercial banks. The forex offices have good rates and no fees. It is always useful to carry a certain amount of cash with you in case of emergency.

Credit Cards

Use of credit cards is widespread in Norway, with Visa, MasterCard and American Express the most common. Check with your own credit card company about acceptability and other services.

In most banks you can generally get cash on a debit card or a Visa or MasterCard.

Tipping

Tipping is quite straightforward in Norway. Hotels include a service charge and tipping is generally not expected. Restaurants usually have the service charge included, in which case it's your choice to add anything (5–10 percent is customary). The same applies to taxis. Table service in bars (particularly outdoor tables) requires tipping. With hairdressers a tip isn't quite as customary, but again 5–10 percent would be appropriate. Cloakrooms usually have a fixed fee of about NOK5–10; if not, leave a few krone for the attendant.

N

Nightlife

Oslo is now vying with Stockholm and Copenhagen to be Scandinavia's nightlife capital. For up-to-date venue listings check the official free Oslo Guide or www.visitoslo.com. In Bergen, Stavanger, Trondheim and Tromsø nightlife exists to a much lesser extent. But you can guarantee that most large hotels have nightclubs and bars. In small towns, you may be out of luck altogether.

International rock, folk and jazz musicians often include Oslo on European tours.

There are only two things you need to be warned about before a night out: the high cost of drinking, and age restrictions: some clubs have minimum ages as high as 26 (although 21 and 23 are more common).

O

Opening Hours

Offices 8 or 9am–4pm; lunch is taken early, 11.30am–12.30pm, or noon–2pm at a restaurant.
Shops Mon–Fri 9am–5pm, Thur until 8pm, Sat from 9am until 1, or until 3pm.
Shopping centres 10am–9pm on weekdays, 9am–6pm on Sat.
Banks Mon–Wed and Fri 8.30am–3.30pm, summer until 3pm, Thur until 5pm.
Pharmacies Mon–Fri 9am–5pm, Saturday mornings and on a rota basis in larger cities.

P

Postal Services

Post offices in Oslo open Mon–Fri 9am–5pm and Sat 9am–3pm.

Letters and postcards cost the same price to send to the UK and Continental Europe, slightly more to send outside Europe. Post takes 2–3 days to Europe and 7–10 days to North America. For more information, see www.posten.no.

Public Holidays

1 January New Year's Day
March/April Easter: Thursday to Monday inclusive
1 May Labour Day
17 May National Independence Day
May/June Ascension Day
May/June Whit Monday
25 December Christmas Day
26 December 2nd Christmas Day

R

Religious Services

The Lutheran Church is Norway's state Church, with around 83 percent of the population registered as Lutherans. Oslo has many Lutheran places of worship, including the American Lutheran Congregation (Fritzners gate 15; tel: 22 44 35 84; www.alcoslo.org).

Services are held in English at the American Lutheran church and the Anglican/Episcopalian church (St Edmund's, Møllergate 30; tel: 22 69 22 14; www.osloanglicans.no).

The Protestant Oslo Cathedral (Oslo Domkirke; Karl Johans gate 11; tel: 23 62 90 1031; daily 10am–4pm; www.oslodomkirke.no) reopened in 2010 after being closed for renovations; concerts are often held Wednesdays.

S

Shopping

In Oslo, Karl Johans gate, Grensen and Bogstadveien are all major shopping streets. With the exception of Oslo, most Norwegian towns are so compact that your best bet is to window-shop and go into the places that look most appealing.

Look out for lavpris (low-price) shops offering discounts. The first Saturday of each month is "Super Saturday" (Super lørdag), when shops in Oslo open longer and offer special discounts.

What to Buy

Popular souvenirs include knitted jumpers, cardigans, gloves and mittens, pewter, silver jewellery and cutlery, hand-painted wooden objects (like bowls with rose designs), trolls and fjord horses carved out of wood, goat and reindeer skin, enamel jewellery, woven wall designs, furs, handicrafts, glassware and pottery – to name just a few.

Department Stores

The major department stores are Glasmagasinet (Stortorvet 9; www.glasmagasinet.no) and Steen & Strøm (Nedre Slottsgate 8; www.steenogstrommagasin.no), both of which have a good selection of most of the above items. House of Oslo (Ruseløkkveien 26; www.houseofoslo.no) specialises in design.

Art

Anyone interested in buying Norwegian art will have ample prospects – from south to north, Norway abounds in galleries, and museum shops are often a good source for interesting items. The reputed Kaare Berntsen used to be the largest dealer and art gallery in Northern Europe, for modern works as well as fine Norwegian classics, including Munch. Recently, the company has been taken over by Sofie Berntsen (www.kaareberntsenantikviteter.no).

Tax-Free Shopping

Norway is the only Scandinavian country in which visitors from the British Isles can claim VAT refunds. All residents outside Scandinavia will get the Norwegian Value Added Tax (MOMS) refunded at the airport when leaving the country. Pick up a brochure at the tourist information office, or contact Global Blue (www.globalblue.com)for details.

In the shop, you pay in full (the amount must be over NOK315 for ordinary goods and NOK290 for food items) and collect a "cheque" for the amount. The tax portion is refunded on the way out of the country from special refund offices (not customs offices) at airports, ports and frontiers.

T

Telephones

International dialling code: +47
When calling from Norway to foreign countries, always dial 00 first. Cheapest calling times are outside business hours: 5pm–8am. Calls abroad can be made from hotels – with a hefty surcharge – or from phone booths or the main telegraph office at Kongens gate 21 (entrance Prinsensgate), Oslo.

Colourful glassware for sale.

Fjord Tours

Whether you are planning a short break or a long holiday, many companies offer tours of the fjord, coastal and mountain scenery. Two of the main ones are:
Fjord Tours
Møllendalsveien 1A5009 Bergen
Tel: +47 55 55 76 60
www.fjordtours.comFjord **Travel Norway**
Østre Nesttunvei 4–6
5221 Nesttun, Bergen
Tel: +47 55 13 13 10
http://fjordtravel.no

Norwegian payphones take 1, 5, 10 and 20 kroner pieces. Phonecards, which can be used in the green phone booths, can be bought in Narvesen kiosks and at post offices. Credit cards are accepted in card phones. Telephone directories have a page of instructions in English in the index. When looking up names, remember the vowels æ, ø, and å come at the end of the alphabet, in that order.

Some US phone companies have their own international access numbers, to allow US citizens cheaper calls, check with AT&T, Sprint or WorldPhone.

Mobile phones

Norway is well covered with mobile network, however you may experience problems in mountainous areas and off the coast. Charges for mobile phone roaming can be high for visitors outside of the European Union. For longer stays consider buying a pre-paid phone card. Local mobile phone companies include Djuice (www.djuice.no), Lyca Mobile (www.lyca-mobile.no), Netcom (https://netcom.no), Network Norway (www.networknorway.no) and OneCall (www.onecall.no). SIM cards can be bought online, in 7-Eleven shops, the Narvesen kiosks, petrol stations, etc. Another option to save on calls is renting a Norwegian mobile phone. Check with CelloMobile (www.cellomobile.com) and RangeRoamer (www.rangeroamer.com).

Time Zone

Central European Time, 1 hour ahead of Greenwich Mean Time, 6 hours ahead of Eastern Standard Time. The clock is set forward an hour to summer time at the end of March, and back an hour at the end of September.

Tourist Information

Before You Go

The Norwegian tourist board can provide helpful information and brochures before you travel, which can be posted or downloaded from the VisitNorway website:

UK
Innovation Norway
(no walk-in service)
InfoUK@innovationnorway.no
www.visitnorway.com

USA/Canada
Innovation Norway
655 Third Avenue, Suite 1810, New York NY 10017
Tel: 212-885 9700
www.visitnorway.com

Tourist Offices in Norway

There are about 350 local tourist offices around Norway, as well as a number of regional tourist offices. For general information, including for hotel bookings in Oslo, contact:
Oslo Visitor Centre Centre
Jernbanetorget 1 (outside Oslo Central Station), Oslo
Tel: 815 30 555
www.visitoslo.com

Regional Information

Regional tourist offices are experts in the county they represent. They are not usually open to personal callers, with the exception of the VisitOslo offices, but will supply advice and information in writing or over the phone.

East Norway
Fjell og Fjord Ferie
Gamlevegen 6, 3550 Gol
Tel: 32 02 99 26
www.fjellandfjord.comwww.golinfo.no
Hedmark Reiseliv BA
Grønnegata 11, 2317 Hamar
Tel: 62 55 33 20
www.visit-hedmark.no

South Norway
Arendal Turist Kontor
Sam Eydes Plass, Postboks 780 Stoa, 4809 Arendal
Tel: 37 00 55 44
www.arendal.com
Kristiansand Tourist Information Office
Rådhusgata 6, 4611 Kristiansand
Tel: 38 12 13 14
www.visitsorlandet.com
Telemarkreiser
Uniongata 18, Kunnskapsverkstedet, 3732 Skien

Tel: 35 90 00 20
www.visittelemark.com

Fjord Norway
Bergen
Slottsgaten 3, 3rd floor, 5835 Bergen
Tel: 55 55 20 00
www.visitbergen.com
Fjord Norge AS
www.fjordnorway.com
Møre og Romsdal Reiselivsråd
Fylkeshuset, 6404 Molde
Tel: 71 24 50 80
www.visitmr.com

Central Norway
Trøndelag Reiseliv AS
Nordre gate 11, 7011Trondheim
Tel: 73 84 24 50
www.trondelag.com

Northern Norway
Northern Norway Tourist Board
Tollbugata 13, Bodø
Tel: 901 77 500
www.nordnorge.no
Visit Svalbard AS Vei 221-1
9171 Longyearbyen
Tel: 79 02 55 50
www.svalbard.net
Tromsø Tourist Information
Kirkegata 2, 9008 Tromsø
Tel: 77 61 00 00
www.visittromso.no

Transport

Getting There

By Air
Norway is exceptionally well served by domestic airlines, with about 50 airports and airfields throughout the country. The main international airport is Oslo airport, Gardermoen, 45km (28 miles) northeast of Oslo (www.osl.no). The main domestic airlines are SAS, Widerøe and Norwegian Air Shuttle. Each offers discount travel passes.

Transport Information

For tickets, routes, times and all other queries about public transport in Oslo and Akershus, information and booking service, visit the Ruter's Customer Service Centre (Trafikanten) by the Oslo Sentralstasjon (Jernbanetorget 1); Mon–Fri 7am–8pm, Sat–Sun 8am–6pm, or call 177 or 815 00 176 (when in Norway), Mon–Fri 7am–10pm, Sat–Sun 8am–10pm, or visit https://ruter.no.

Scandinavian Airlines (SAS) offers daily flights from London Heathrow to Oslo and Stavanger (www.flysas.com). There are also direct daily flights to Oslo Gardermoen and Oslo Torp from Aberdeen, Dublin, and Manchester.

SAS also offers special cheap tickets for flights within Norway, such as Oslo to Bergen for around NOK400 one way.

British Airways (tel: 0844 493 0787 from the UK; www.britishairways.com) runs around five flights daily from London (Heathrow) to Oslo.

Wideroe (tel: +47 671 20 551 or 81 00 12 00; www.wideroe.no) flies to 44 destinations within Norway and has flights to Aberdeen, Newcastle, Copenhagen, and Gothenburg. It is based at Oslo Torp airport in Sandefjord (www.torp.no), 130km (80 miles) south of Oslo.

Norwegian Air Shuttle (tel: 47 214 90015 (outside of Norway); 0330 828 0854 (from the UK); 815 21 815 (within Norway); www.norwegian.com) operates on a daily basis from eight major airports in Norway, in addition to daily flights from Oslo, Bergen and Trondheim to London Gatwick, Southern Europe and regional routes in northern Norway.

Ryanair operates bargain flights from London Gatwick, Luton or Stansted, Edinburgh, Dublin, Manchester and Liverpool to Oslo Rygge airport at Moss (www.ryg.no) or Oslo Torp airport at Sandefjord (www.torp.no). Buses transport visitors into Oslo (for an extra charge). For details tel: 0871 246 0000 (from the UK) or visit www.ryanair.com.

For budget travel to Norway it may be easier to book online. Try these booking agents: www.cheapflights.com offers online

bookings from the US. www.lastminute.com has flights from the UK to Norway. www.priceline.com allows you to pick your own flights and times or name your own price. Price reductions of up to 30 percent on fares. US only. www.opodo.co.uk. A fast search engine with instant access to cheap flights from over 400 airlines around the world, as well as accommodation, car hire and holidays.

Specialist Tour Operators in the UK

Activity Holidays
Inntravel
Whitewell Grange, Nr Castle Howard, York YO60 7JU
Tel: 01653 617 001
www.inntravel.co.uk

Arctic Voyages/Dog-sledging/ Whale-Watching
Arctic Experience and Discover the World
8 Bolters Lane, Banstead, Surrey SM7 2AR
Tel: 01737 214 250
www.arctic-experience.co.uk
Arcturus Expeditions
Ninestone, South Zeal, Devon EX20 2PZ
Tel: 01837 840 640
www.arcturusexpeditions.co.uk

Norway Specialists
Norsc Holidays
The Court, The Street, Charmouth DT6 6PE
Tel: 01297 560 033
www.norsc.co.uk
Taber Holidays
Tofts House, Tofts Road, Cleckheaton, West Yorkshire BD19 3WX

Tel: 01274 875 199
www.taberhols.co.uk

Skiing/Walking
Crystal Holidays
DST House, St. Mark's Hill, Surbiton, Surrey KT6 4BHTel: 020 8939 0726, 020 8939 0739
www.crystalholidays.co.uk
Exodus Travel
Grange Mills, Weir Road, London SW12 0NE
Tel: 0845 287 3629
www.exodus.co.uk

Tours
Explore Worldwide
55 Victoria Road, Farnborough, Hampshire GU14 7PA
Tel: 01252 883 859
www.explore.co.uk
ScanMeridian (Nordic Experience)
39 Crouch Street, Colchester, Essex CO3 3EN
Tel: 01206 708 888
www.nordicexperience.co.uk
Great Rail Journeys
Saviour House, 9 St Saviourgate, York YO1 8NL
Tel: 01904 521 936, 0800 140 4444
www.greatrail.com

By Sea
There is currently no ferry service between the UK and Norway. Color Line is the main ferry service linking Oslo to the Continent, with big cruise ferries sailing to Kiel in Germany, and services to the northern tip of Denmark (Hirtshals) from Kristiansand and Larvik. Color Line, tel: 81 00 08 11, +49 40 381096 9113; www.colorline.com. However, you may travel as a passenger on the DFDS freight line between Immingham and Brevik. For details contact: tel: +44 1469 55 26 98, http://freight.dfdsseaways.com.

By Rail
Numerous rail services link Norway with the rest of Scandinavia and Europe. From mainland Europe, express trains operate to Copenhagen, where inter-Scandinavian trains connect to Oslo. There are frequent connections from Copenhagen, Stockholm and Götenborg to Oslo. You can also get to northern Norway from Stockholm, with Trondheim and Narvik the principal destinations.

International arrivals and departures are located at

The Lærdal tunnel, the longest in the world, links Oslo with Bergen.

Norway in a Nutshell

One of the most pleasurable ways of seeing western Norway is to take a Norway in a Nutshell journey (see page 209). The trip uses various forms of public transport and takes you from Myrdal to Flåm, Gudvangen and Voss through some of the country's most beautiful scenery. A selection of packages is on offer. Tel: 55 55 76 60; www. norwaynutshell.com.

The railway line from Myrdal to Flåm is a masterpiece of engineering. When you have made the 850-metre (2,800ft) descent you are at the head of one of the longest fjords in the world,

Sognefjord, and on the brink of another scenic high.

The trips can be made in either direction and from any of the stations between Oslo and Bergen.

Norway in a Nutshell round trip: train from Oslo to Myrdal/ Flåm, boat to Gudvangen, bus to Voss, train to Oslo.

Norway in a Nutshell one way: train from Oslo to Myrdal/Flåm, boat to Gudvangen, bus to Voss, train to Bergen.

Tickets are sold at the railway stations in Oslo and Bergen or from travel agencies. See www.norway nutshell.com for more details.

speed services.

Rail passes make travelling in Norway cheaper. The Norwegian State Railway (NSB) is part of the InterRail, EuroDomino, Eurailpass and Eurail Youthpass system, which offers various discount tickets (including to students). If you live in Europe, the InterRail Norway Pass gives 3, 4, 6 or 8 days' unlimited 1st- or 2nd-class travel within a one-month period. It also offers discounts on some ferry services. See www.interrail.eu for details. If you live outside Europe, the Eurail Scandinavia Pass entitles you to unlimited second-class travel across Scandinavia, for 4, 5, 6, 8 or 10 days within a two-month period. Eurail Norway Pass is also available. Buy the pass before you travel from www.scandinavianrail.com.

Norwegian State Railways
Tel: 81 50 08 88
www.nsb.no
NSB provides train information and also operates as a travel bureau across Norway. For information about timetables, ticket prices and bookings in Oslo and Akershus, contact Ruter's Customer Service Centre (Trafikanten), Jernbanetorvet 1, by Oslo S, tel: 81 50 01 76 or 177, https://ruter.no. A similar website for all of Norway is being developed, check rutebok.no.

Sentralstasjon (Oslo-S).

Getting Around

There is an excellent network of domestic transport services – a necessity in a country so large and often impassable by land. You may have to use more than one means (for example, train and bus or plane and bus), but if you're travelling beyond Oslo you'll find these services indispensable.

Although covering great distances can be expensive, Norway offers transport bargains through special tourist cards like the Fjord Pass, the Bonus Pass (which covers the whole of Scandinavia), plus some of the pan-European programmes like InterRail and Eurail. Within larger cities, tourist passes cover urban transport and give free entry to many museums.

On Arrival

Gardermoen airport is 45km (28 miles) north of Oslo. It is served by the Airport Express Train/Flytoget to Oslo S (the Central Station) every 10–20 minutes and takes 19–22 minutes. Details at www.flytoget. no; tel: 815 00 777. For about half the price, regional and local trains also connect Oslo and the airport and take about 37 minutes; there is normally a train at least every hour. Note that rail passes are not valid on the Airport Express. See also www. nsb.no.

The airport bus departs six times an hour to and from the Radisson Blu Scandinavia Hotel via Oslo Busterminal/Clarion Royal Christiania Hotel, Helsfyr and Furuset. It takes 45 minutes. There are also regular buses 855, 811, 818 and 344 (SAS bus; from the Radisson Blu

Scandinavia Hotel via Oslo S; three departures an hour; 50 minutes). For details check https://ruter.no or call tel: 177. The Flybussekspressen is another option, departing from 120 places around Oslo. Tel: 815 44 444; www.flybussen.no.

If you arrive from London Stansted at Torp airport at Sandefjord on the southwest side of the fjord, buses and trains will take up to 2.5 hours to reach the capital, depending on traffic conditions.

Bergen Flesland airport is 19km (12 miles) south of the city. The airport bus goes to the Radisson Blu Royal at Bryggen, via Radisson Blu Hotel Norge and the bus station. There are around four buses per hour and the journey takes between 35 and 45 minutes, depending on traffic. Check www.flybussen.no or call 177. You may also take one of local buses: 23, 56 or 57. For schedules visit www.skyss.no.

A taxi to/from the city is around NOK700 before 5pm, when it increases to around NOK800. Local taxi companies: www.bergentaxi.no, www.bryggentaxi.no, www.02365.no, www.norgestaxi.no, www.taxi1.no.

By Train

Most of Norwegian State Railways (NSB) lines run through tourist country, presenting continuous panoramas of unspoilt scenic beauty. The Oslo–Bergen line is hailed as one of the world's most spectacular for its scenery.

There are fast train connections from Oslo to other cities in Norway, with sleeper coaches on all of the overnight expresses. Seat reservations are required on all night and long-distance day trains, as well as on express and high-

By Road

Most major shipping lines to Norway allow passengers to bring cars. But coming by car increases sea travel costs, and petrol is expensive in Norway.

Norges Automobil Forbund
(NAF or Norwegian Automobile Association)
Østensjøveien 14, 0609 Oslo
In Norway tel: 08 505
From abroad tel: +47 926 08505
www.naf.no

Kongelig Norsk Automobilklub
(KNA or Royal Norwegian Automobile Club)
Cort Adelers Gate 16, 0201 Oslo
Tel: 21 60 49 00
Emergency tel: 800 31 660 (in Norway, members only)
http://kna.no

By Bus

Where the rail network stops, the bus goes further: you can get to practically anywhere you want by bus on an ever-growing number of bus lines. Time Express is a popular one (see www.nettbuss.no). Usually it is not necessary to book in advance; just pay the driver on boarding. Nor-way Bussekspress (bus pass) guarantees a seat for all passengers. Children up to the age of 4 travel free, while 4 to 16 years pay 75 percent of the adult price.

Nor-way Bussekspress AS, Karl Johans Gate 2, 0154 Oslo; tel: 81 54 44 44; www.nor-way.no.

Water Ferries

Ferries are an invaluable means of transport that allow short cuts across fjords to eliminate long road journeys; in built-up areas they are crucial to commuters, like the Horten-Moss ferry across Oslofjord between Vestfold and Østfold. Ferries to the fjord islands around Oslo leave from the Vippetangen quay near Akershus Castle.

The following company operates the ferries which run between the centre of Oslo and the Bygdøy peninsula:

Bygdøfærgene Skibs
Rådhusbrygge 3, Oslo
Tel: 23 35 68 90
www.boatsightseeing.com

Long-Distance Ships
Hurtigruten, the Norwegian Coastal Express service, is a vital means of water transport for Norwegians, but also a superb way for visitors to see Norway's dramatic coast. In summer, boats leave daily, travelling between Bergen and Kirkenes in 11 days and putting in at 34 ports.

The Oslo Pass

The Oslo Pass, issued for 24, 48 or 72 hours, with half-price for children, is your ticket to unlimited public transport (including city ferries) and free entry to 33 museums and attractions. If you want a card for travel only, there are all kinds of passes available, including a Dagskortet (valid for 24 hours) and Flexikort (eight rides at a discount), plus passes appropriate for longer stays.

The Oslo Pass may be purchased at the Tourist Information Centre outside the Central Railway Station (Oslo S), Ruter's Customer Service Centre (Trafikanten), as well as all Narvesen kiosks and hotels, camp sites and tourist offices.

Other cities offer similar tourist travel cards: for example, the Bergen Card, a 24-hour or 48-hour pass available from tourist information offices, hotels and campsites.

Children (between 4 and 15 years old) pay a child's fare. The steamers take cars, and should be booked well in advance. Contact:

Hurtigruten
Tel: 81 00 30 30, +44 208 846 2666
www.hurtigruten.com

Getting around in Oslo

Public Buses and Trams

Oslo's bus and tram system is comprehensive and punctual; there are detailed timetables at every stop. Ruter's Customer Service Centre (Trafikanten) (177 or 815 00 176; https://ruter.no) can suggest bus or tram routes to get you where you wish to go. There are night buses on some routes and very early morning buses (starting at 4am), so that public transport is available virtually around the clock. Bergen and Trondheim also have tram systems.

Underground
Oslo's underground is called the T-bane (see map on inside back cover) and is simple to use (www. tbanen.no). There are six lines that converge under the centre of Oslo. A circle line linking the station of Storo with Carl Berners plass was completed in 2006. You can catch any train to any of the far-flung suburbs from any of the stations between Tøyen and Majorstuen. Station entrances are marked with a "T". The most scenic route is T-bane 1 up to Frognerseteren. From there enjoy panoramic views back down to Oslo.

Taxis
Taxis are widely available, even in many suburban and rural areas, so you need never risk drink-driving (for which penalties are severe).

No matter where you are in Oslo, telephone 023 23 and your call will be transferred to the nearest taxi rank. Minibuses and taxis (for up to 16 people) can also be booked on tel: 22 38 80 70. Otherwise, you can take a taxi from one of the many taxi ranks scattered around the city or simply hail one.

In Oslo, taxis are more expensive at night or if ordered by phone. At night there are two things to watch out for: when everyone leaves the bars and restaurants late, long queues build up at taxi ranks. This can be extremely uncomfortable in the winter if you are not dressed appropriately. The problem has given rise to a second difficulty: "pirate" taxis. These either cruise up out of

the blue or a "dummy" comes and asks you if you want a taxi without queuing. Pirate taxis are a risk, but if you do use one, make sure you agree a price beforehand. They tend to gather at Stortorget, opposite GlassMagasin.

Private By Car
Norway's roads are extremely good, particularly in view of the treacherous weather conditions encountered in winter. Be prepared for tunnels, though, as some routes have long lengths of road underground. For information on toll roads visit www.autopass.no.

EU and EEA driving licences are valid in Norway, but visitors from other countries can use their driving licences for up to three months after their arrival in Norway. Drive on the right.

Traffic regulations are strictly enforced. For more information on driving in Norway check www.vegvesen.no.

Winter Driving
With Norway's winters, you should never assume all roads are passable. Small roads in the north are often closed so the authorities can put all manpower into keeping main roads safe, and even the E6 highway from Oslo to Trondheim has been known to close. If you intend to travel on minor roads, seek a local's advice or phone the 24-hour Road-User Information Centre (tel: 175 in Norway; tel: 08 15 48 991 from abroad; www.vegvesen.no) and go prepared for anything. Your car must be equipped with winter tyres.

Snow-Tyre Hire
If you're driving in Norway in winter you can hire the appropriate tyres and snow chains by the week. Ask in any petrol station. In the UK contact:

Snowchains Europroducts
Tel: 01732 884 408
www.snowchains.co.uk

Breakdown and Accidents
The AA and RAC are affiliated to the AIT (Alliance Internationale de Tourisme), so members receive free assistance (with journey planning as well as backup in case of breakdown or accident) from Norway's NAF (Norges Automobilforbund). More comprehensive repairs can be carried out at NAF-contracted garages (for which you will have to pay). NAF also patrols Norway's main roads and mountain passes from mid-June to mid-August. They have emergency phones along the mountain passes.

Hiking is a great way to explore.

NAF

Østensjøveien 14, 0609 Oslo
Tel: 08 505
www.naf.no
24-hour emergency service (for members of AIT clubs), tel: 22 34 16 00.

If you are involved in an accident where there are no injuries, telephone **Falck Rescue Service** at 02222 (www.falck.no) or **Viking Redningstjeneste AS** at 06000 (www.vikingredning.no). Their offices provide a 24-hour service for all Norway.

It is not necessary to call the police for minor accidents, but drivers must exchange names and addresses; leaving the scene without doing so is a crime.

Only call the **police** (on **112**) or an **ambulance** (on **113**) if it's a real emergency.

Rules of the Road

It is essential for visitors to Norway to be aware of Norwegian driving regulations, some of which vary significantly from those in the UK and on the continent. Here are a few tips to help you drive safely, but for further guidance it's worth downloading a copy of Norwegian traffic rules from www.vegvesen.no (available in English).

Speed limits The maximum speed limit is usually 80kph (50mph), though 100kph (62mph) is permitted on some roads (mainly motorways). The limit is reduced to 40kph (24mph) in built-up areas, and even 30kph (18mph) on certain residential roads. On-the-spot fines are given for drivers found speeding (this may be as much as NOK3,500). Speed cameras and radar traps are both used.

Giving way Roads marked at intervals by yellow diamond signs indicate that you have priority. On all other roads you are required to give way to traffic entering from the right. On roundabouts, priority is from the left. Always give way to trams, buses and taxis. Many roads have a right-hand lane exclusively for buses and taxis.

Drinking and driving You are strongly advised not to drink at all if you anticipate driving within at least eight hours. The current permissible limit is 0.02 per ml, and penalties are severe (imprisonment, a high fine and loss of licence are automatic).

Documentation and equipment You must always have the following with you in your car: driving licence, car registration documents, European accident statement form, insurance policy and a reflective warning triangle. A snow shovel and tow rope are also useful in winter. For regularly updated information in the UK, call the AA: tel: 0870 600 0371; www.theaa.com.

Lights It is obligatory to drive with dipped headlights on during the daytime, even on the brightest summer day. This rule applies to all vehicles, including motorcycles and mopeds. We recommend you carry spare bulbs. Do not forget that right-hand drive cars require black adhesive triangles (often supplied by ferry companies), or clip-on beam deflectors, so you don't dazzle oncoming drivers.

Seat belts must be worn, both front and back (again, there are on-the-spot fines for failing to comply). Motorcycle and moped drivers and their passengers must wear helmets.

Tyres In winter, the tread depth must be at least 3mm. Winter tyres should be used from 15 November to 31 March, and they are obligatory in this period for vehicles over 3,500 kg. Studded tyres and snow chains are not permitted from the second Monday after Easter Sunday until 31 October, and in Nordland, Troms and Finnmark between 1 May and 15 October.

Car Hire

Hiring a car in Norway can be expensive, but may be worthwhile if shared between several people. Otherwise, watch for special weekend and summer prices. Most agencies have offices at Gardermoen international airport.

Avis Bilutleie-RAC Norway AS
Drengsrudbekken 12
1383 Asker
Tel: 66 77 11 00
www.avis.no
Europcar
2060 GardermoenTel: 64 81 05 60, 815 51 800
www.europcar.no
Hertz Bilutleie
Holbergs gate 30
Tel: 22 21 0000
www.hertz.no

Cycling

Norway has a series of national cycle routes. Though the terrain can be challenging, the scenery makes the effort worthwhile. If you're tempted to embark on some pedal-powered exploration, there are plenty of bike rental companies around. Cycling is also a good way of exploring many towns and cities. Trondheim is a particularly bike-friendly city – it was the first place to introduce the bicycle lift (Trampe), to help cyclists uphill (http://trampe.no).

Most ferries will carry bikes free of charge. Buses vary – not all will carry bikes, and of those that do, some charge a nominal fee. NSB trains charge a fee of around 10 percent of the price of your ticket. Note that special cycle trains are laid on during the summer.

Sykkelturisme i Norge

Strandgaten 59, 5004 Bergen
Email: post@cyclingnorway.no
www.cyclingnorway.no
Sykkelturisme i Norge – the Institute for Cycle Tourism – was set up in conjunction with the Norwegian Tourist Board to help promote cycling in Norway. It gives details of marked cycle paths

throughout the country including the Bergen–Voss, the Rallarvegen and the Lofoten Isles cycle routes, and suggest routes for a variety of skill levels, from gentle rides on relatively easy terrain to challenging expeditions on tough terrain. Its website is full of practical information and inspiration.

Syklistens Landsforening
Østensjøveien 29, 06610slo
Tel: 22 47 30 30
Email:post@syklistene.no
www.syklistene.noSyklistens Landsforening – the Norwegian Cycling Association – can help plan tours and cycling holidays. They also have a good range of guides (some translated into English) and maps of cycle routes.

Cycle Rental
In Oslo and Bergen, bikes can be hired from hotels, campsites, local tourist offices or sports shops, as well as small cycle-hire shops.
The City Bike campaign is a cycling initiative for short and medium-range transport. It is currently available in three Norwegian cities: Oslo, Trondheim and Drammen (www.bysykler.no). To access one of the army of bikes parked at stands throughout the city centres, you need to buy an electronic smartcard from the tourist office. Armed with the card, you can pick up a bike and deposit it back at any one of the many bike stations (over 100 in Oslo) in and around the city centre. Bicycles are available from April/May until October/November.

Norway on Foot

Norway is a nation of devout walkers, and walking is one of the most popular outdoor activities at weekends. The law of access to the natural environment, known as "everyman's right", allows you to walk wherever you want in the wilderness such as seashore, forests, mountains and in other non-cultivated regions. This should be done with consideration. Use paths and roads when walking in

Weights and Measures

Metric. Distances are given in kilometres (km), but Norwegians often refer to a mil, which is 10km (thus 10 mil = 100km). When talking about land area you will often hear the word mål. This old measure of 984.34 sq metres has been rounded up to 1,000 sq metres (or 1 decare).

agricultural and populated areas.
With a network of well-marked trails and welcoming mountain cabins set in magnificent mountain scenery, Norway's national parks (there are 34 national parks on the Norwegian mainland) draw hikers in their thousands (see page 367).
Campers are advised to make use of campsites, though you can, by rights, pitch a tent anywhere in the wilderness, so long as it is situated at least 150 metres/yds from the nearest house or hut. Open fires are prohibited from 15 April to 15 September.
The Norwegian Tourist Board publishes a handbook, Mountain Hiking in Norway, which gives suggested itineraries for mountain walks and details of chalets and where to stay.

Den Norske Turistforening
(Norwegian Trekking Association) Tour Information Centre Storgata 3, 0101 Oslo
Tel: 22 82 28 22
www.turistforeningen.no.
Detailed maps are available from the Norwegian Trekking Association (DNT). Membership gives you rights to use the association's huts. The map and guidebook selection is excellent.

V

Visas and Passports

A valid passport is all that is necessary for citizens of most countries to enter Norway. Visas are not required. Norway is a member of the Schengen Agreement, allowing citizens of other Schengen countries to enter without passports. If you enter from another Nordic country (Denmark, Finland, Iceland, or Sweden), you won't get an entry stamp. Tourists are generally limited to a three-month visit; it is possible to stay longer, but you must apply for a visa after the initial three months (Scandinavian passport holders are exempt from this requirement), or if you plan to work in Norway.

Animals

Dogs, cats and ferrets from all EU countries except Sweden must have pet passports, ID marking, a valid rabies vaccination and valid blood-test documentation (this does not apply to ferrets). Dogs and cats must also be given approved tapeworm treatment during the week before

and the week after they have been brought into the country.

W

What to Read

History and society

Heimskringla by Snorri Sturluson (University of Texas Press). History of the Kings of Norway.
In Cod We Trust: Living the Norwegian Dream by Eric Dregni (University of Minnesota Press). A journey to the country of author's great-grandfather.
King Harald's Saga by Snorri Sturluson (Penguin Classics). An excerpt from the Heimskringla.
One of Us: The Story of Anders Breivik and the Massacre in Norway by Asne Seierstad (Farrar, Straus and Giroux). A detailed account of Norway's worst massacre.
The Real Heroes of Telemark: the True Story of the Secret Mission to Stop Hitler's Atomic Bomb by Ray Mears (Coronet).

Art and Literature

Knut Hamsun: Hunger, Mysteries, Victoria, The Growth of the Soil, Wayfarers, are excellent novels and available in Penguin Classics, Oxford Classics, Condor Books and other imprints.
Knut Hamsun, Dreamer and Dissenter by Ingar Sletten Kolloen (Yale University Press).
Henrik Ibsen: A Doll's House, Peer Gynt, The Master Builder, Hedda Gabler, The Wild Duck, among other works available in Oxford World's Classics and other imprints.
Edvard Munch: Behind the Scream by Sue Prideaux (Yale University Press).
Kristin Lavransdatter by Sigrid Undset (Penguin Classics). Historical epic by Nobel laureate Sigrid Undset.

Arctic Explorers

Scott and Amundsen: Last Place on Earth by Roland Huntford (Abacus).
The South Pole: An Account of the Norwegian Antarctic Exploration in the Fram, 1910–12, by Roald Amundsen (Cooper Square Press).
Kon Tiki: across the Pacific by Raft by Thor Heyerdahl (Simon and Schuster Press).
Kon Tiki Expedition by Thor Heyerdahl (Flamingo).

NORWAY EATING OUT

RESTAURANTS AND CAFES

WHAT TO EAT

Norwegians eat hearty breakfasts, but light lunches; the size of the evening meal (middag) depends on the day of the week and the occasion.

With the abundant supply of seafood and what can be gleaned from forest and field, the Norwegian diet has traditionally been healthy and appetising. For those who relish game, the hunting season (early autumn) offers some irresistible temptations: pheasant, grouse, elk and reindeer steaks served with peppercorns and rich wild mushroom sauces. It is also a good time of year to make the most of seafood (with cod considered best in months with an r in them).

Frokost (breakfast) is more or less a variation of the lunch Kaldtbord, a spread including breads (try grovbrød and knekkebrød), sausage, cheese – Norway's national cheese is geitost, a caramel-brown goat's-milk cheese (try the piquant Gudbrandalsost variety) – eggs, herrings, gravlax (marinated salmon), and coffee and tea.

The lunch version has hot dishes, such as sliced roast meats, meatballs or fish. Øllebrød (beef marinated in beer and served inside pitta bread with salad) makes a hearty, inexpensive lunch; an open-faced shrimp or ham sandwich is another staple.

Dinner in a city restaurant can be anything you wish, and many of the new, modern restaurants in Oslo or Bergen could just as easily be found in London or Los Angeles. When dining in more remote places, the menus will invariably be limited by availability. A more traditional menu might include mutton stew or a fish ragout, and boiled potatoes with dill

or parsley will often accompany a hot main course.

For dessert, ice cream is a favourite, as is apple pie. In summer there are all kinds of puddings based on the fresh berries that grow profusely in the Norwegian woods.

Outside main meals there are many coffee breaks, often accompanied with fresh pastries, including bolle (raisin buns) and wienerbrød (lighter pastries laced with fruit or nuts). Smørbrød is a snack (called aftens when eaten late at night), usually of bread or crackers with butter, cheese and salami or ham.

For more on classic Norwegian food, see page 94.

WHERE TO EAT

There has been a significant increase in what's on offer when you choose to eat out in Norway. Pizza is very popular, and the cynic may even describe it as the Norwegian national dish. Asian food has also become a local favourite, although Indian restaurants tend to tone down the spices to suit the more delicate Norwegian palate. Continental European dishes have always played a role in Norwegian cuisine (such as Viennese- and French-style dishes), but pride in native foods and an interest in "New Scandinavian" cuisine is prevalent.

At lunchtime many restaurants offer special fixed-price menus. Reasonably priced snacks and simple meals can be enjoyed in museum cafés and such informal establishments as stovas, kros and gjæstgiveris, which may sell alcohol as well as coffee and soft drinks. For

an even more casual meal, buy a hot dog (pølse), kebab or a waffle from a kiosk; these stay open late to catch pub-crawlers.

RESTAURANT LISTINGS

Restaurants are grouped by area starting with Oslo. They are listed alphabetically.

DRINKING NOTES

No one talks about a trip to Norway without complaining of the high cost of alcohol. For those who can afford the prices, serving hours are long; in Oslo you can drink spirits until midnight and wine or beer until 3am. Outside Oslo, times are less predictable; a conservative Lutheran culture holds sway in many west-coast areas, rendering some counties virtually dry. But there are exceptions to this: in Oslo, for example, there are some no-alcohol hotel/restaurants and in the "dry" counties it is always possible to find a hotel/restaurant that serves some form of alcohol.

The Vinmonopolet (state off licences/liquor stores; www.vinmono polet.no) in cities are open Mon–Fri 10am–6pm and Sat 9am–2pm; they are closed on election days, holidays and the preceding day of a holiday.

Most Norwegians drink beer and/ or wine. Traditional akevitt, similar in taste to schnapps, is derived from potato and caraway seeds, and is also a favourite. It can be sipped neat in small glasses at room temperature, or served cold with beer to accompany salty, spicy or pungent dishes.

OSLO

Norwegian: Classic and Modern

De Fem Stuer
Holmenkollen Park Hotel, Kongeveien 26
Tel: 22 92 20 00
www.holmenkollenparkhotel.no
Elegant dining inside the historic timbered salons of this fairytale-like hotel overlooking the city and fjord. Booking recommended. **$$$**

Det Gamle Raadhus
Nedre Slottsgate 1
Tel: 22 42 01 07
www.gamleraadhus.no
Housed in the capital's old City Hall from the 1600s, now best known for its lutefisk (a pungent Scandinavian speciality of cod marinated in lye) in the months leading up to Christmas. **$$**

DS Louise
Stranden 3
Tel: 22 83 00 60
www.restaurantlouise.no
Roomy waterfront restaurant in a former mechanical workshop, decorated with ship and shipyard paraphernalia, offering both informal and fine dining. There's an outdoor terrace with great views over Aker Brygge. **$$$**

Restaurant Eik
Universitetsgata 11
Tel: 22 36 07 10
www.restauranteik.no
Arguably the best of Oslo's "menu-based" restaurants, where you select how many courses you want from a carefully planned multi-course meal. Next to Oslo's National Gallery. **$$**

Ekeberg Restaurant
Kongsveien 15
Tel: 23 24 23 00
www.ekebergrestauranten.com
Take the No. 18–19 tram to Sjømannsskolen and walk up the hill to this restored gem. Knockout view over the city and fjord, with a large outdoor terrace complementing the

restaurant inside. **$$**

Feinschmecker
Balchens gate 5
Tel: 22 12 93 80
www.feinschmecker.no
The chef of this long-established Michelin-star restaurant favours seasonal specialities like crayfish or cod. The dessert menu is an absolute must. Old-school fine dining, in the upmarket Frogner area. Closed Sunday. **$$$**

Fru Hagen
Thorvald Meyers gate 40
Tel: 45 49 19 04
www.fruhagen.no
A lively bistro/bakery where the young and the hip come for Thai wok specialities, pastas or burgers. **$–$$**

Grand Café
Karl Johans gate 31
Tel: 23 21 20 00
www.grand.no
Henrik Ibsen's former haunt, known for its murals and stylish surroundings just across from the Parliament. **$$**

Kaffistova
Rosenkrantz gate 8
Tel: 23 21 42 10
www.kaffistova.com
Cafeteria-style place dishing up authentic rural Norwegian food. Fast and filling. **$**

Lille Herbern
Herbernveien, Lille Herbern
Tel: 22 44 97 00
www.lilleherbern.no
One of Oslo's most romantic summer destinations for seafood, drinks and all-round ambience. Accessible only by ferry – a 25-minute ride from the Herbern Marina near Aker Brygge. **$$–$$$**

Solsiden
Akershusstranda 13, Skur 34 Tel: 22 33 36 30
www.solsiden.no

One of the best seafood restaurants in Oslo, situated right on the harbour under the historic Akershus Fortress. Try the shellfish platter or catch of the day. Summer only. **$$$**

Statholdergaarden
Rådhusgata 11
Tel: 22 41 88 00
http://statholdergaarden.no
Danish chef Bent Stiansen's inventive dishes are impeccably served in the elegant upstairs restaurant of this fine 17th-century townhouse. **$$$**

Sult
Maridalsveien 91 Tel: 67 10 99 70
www.sult.no
Named after Knut Hamsun's novel Hunger, this was one of the first restaurants to pop up in the lively Grünerløkka district. Simple, fresh food dubbed "neo-Norsk". **$$**

Theatercafeen
Stortingsgaten 24–26
Tel: 22 82 40 50
www.theatercafeen.no
Famed Vienna-style café; classic dishes served with flair, live violin music. A place to see and be seen in Oslo. **$$**

Euro/Asian

Bistro Brocante
Thorvald Meyers gate 40
Tel: 22 35 68 71
www.bistrobrocante.no
A friendly French bistro specialising in seasonal French fare for lunch and dinner. In summers, the terrace is "le happening" spot. **$$**

Curry & Ketchup
Kirkveien 51
Tel: 22 69 05 22
Inexpensive curries and South Asian vegetarian dishes in the unpretentious Majorstua quarter. **$**

Sake Aker Brygge
Aker Brygge Bryggetorget 7
Tel: 22 83 63 51
A good value for money sushi-restaurant located in a pretty neighbourhood. Delicious food. **$$**

Ruffino Ristorante Italiano
Arbinsgate 1
Tel: 22 55 32 80
Excellent Italian food, from antipasti to full-course meals, located just under the Ibsen Museum. **$–$$**

There is always an abundance of fresh ingredients.

PRICE CATEGORIES

Price categories are per person for an average three-course meal, excluding wine:
$ = under NOK280
$$ = NOK280–560
$$$ = over NOK560

STAVANGER

Charlottenlund
Kongsgaten 45
Tel: 51 91 76 00
www.charlottenlund.no
Graceful, Norwegian- and French-inspired cuisine served in a former private mansion on the lake in the heart of town. **$$**

Gaffel & Karaffel
Øvre Holmgate 20
Tel: 51 86 41 58
http://gaffelogkaraffel.no
This excellent, unpretentious restaurant offers a seasonal menu, featuring wild salmon and reindeer among other succulent offerings. Champagne bar. **$$**

N.B. Sørensens

Dampskibsexpedition
Skagen 26
Tel: 51 84 38 20
One of the most traditional restaurants in Stavanger, at the marina. The international menu makes full use of fresh Norwegian ingredients. **$$**

Ostehuset
Hospitalgaten 6
Tel: 51 86 40 10
www.ostehuset.no
Fresh and health-conscious ingredients are a speciality of this "cheese house", which dishes up salads, sandwiches and unique pizzas. **$–$$**

Renaa
Breitorget 6

Tel: 51 55 11 11
www.restaurantrenaa.no
The two restaurants (Craig's Kjøkken and Jan's Mat og Vinhus) that occupied this two-storey building were a tough act to follow, but in less than a year, nationally reputed chef Sven Erik Renaa created his own following for two restaurants of his own: The Matbaren bistro upstairs and the gourmet dining room below. **$$–$$$**

Tango Bar & Kjøkken
Nedre Strandgate 25
Tel: 51 50 12 30
www.tango-bk.no
Fresh ingredients and excellent preparation have made this jewel by the harbour a real success story. **$$$**

BERGEN

Boha
Vaskerelven
Tel: 55 31 31 60
www.boha.no
Proprietors Arve Haga and Per Trygve Bolstad are committed to translating their passion to the fresh, seasonal food they serve. The "pavement" restaurant for alfresco dining is a recent innovation, and the ground-floor Onkel Lauritz bar is a popular meeting place. **$$–$$$**

Bryggeloftet & Stuene
Bryggen 11
Tel: 55 30 20 70
www.bryggeloftet.no
A favourite with tourists, this typical Norwegian restaurant features

Fresh prawns are a favourite.

traditional meals, such as reindeer, fillet of wolf fish, cod, and holiday specialities such as pinnekjøtt (salted mutton) and lutefisk, the traditional fishy Christmas dish. **$$$**

Café Opera
Engen 18
Tel: 55 23 03 15
www.cafeopera.org
Hang out for the hip crowd serving salads, snacks, sandwiches and light traditional Norwegian dishes. Open daily for lunch and dinner. It also operates as a bar and popular club. **$$**

Dr. Livingstone Bar and Amore Restaurant (Three Lions Pub)
Kong Oscars gate 12
Tel: 55 56 03 12
In an old Bergen homestead dating back to 1702, this is a laidback gastro pub spread across two floors, with an outside dining area. It is centrally situated at the beginning of Bergen's most cosmopolitan street. **$–$$**

Finnegaardstuene
Rosenkrantz gate 6
Tel: 55 55 03 00
Fresh seasonal ingredients – from halibut to venison – are presented in a (13th- century) former Hanseatic warehouse by an inspired culinary team in four separate dining rooms. **$$$**

Fløien Folkerestaurant
Top of Fløien funicular
Tel: 55 33 69 99
www.bellevue-restauranter.no
Good, reasonably priced food with an intoxicating view. Work up an appetite by walking there. **$$**

Nama Sushi & Noodles
Lodin Lepps gate 2B

Tel: 55 32 20 10
www.namasushi.no
East meets North with top-quality Norwegian seafood prepared Japanese style – sushi, noodles, raw fish, halibut, oysters. **$$–$$$**

Pasta Sentral
Vestre Torggaten 5
Tel: 55 96 00 37
www.pastasentral.no
A well-priced oasis for pasta, pizza and other Italian specialities, which makes it very popular with students, families and visitors. Try the daily special – for around NOK70 you can get bread, a drink and your main course. Cash only. **$**

Potetkjellern
Kong Oscars gate 1A
Tel: 55 32 00 70
www.potetkjelleren.no
Located in an old potato cellar with a comfortable atmosphere, it specialises in seasonal specialities from halibut and cod to lamb and reindeer. Excellent wine list. **$$–$$$**

Restaurant 1877
Vetrlidsallmenningen 2
Tel: 09 28 71 877
www.restaurant1877.no
Opened in 2013 in a 1877 building, this popular restaurant serves impressive gourmet food. $$$

Wesselstuen
Ole Bulls plass 6
Tel: 55 55 49 49
www.wesselstuen.no
Traditional Norwegian fish and stews are served to a loyal local crowd. Good atmosphere. **$$**

Yang Tse Kiang
Torget 3

Tel: 55 31 66 66
www.yangtsekiang.no
A simple, pleasant Chinese restaurant that offers good-value lunch specials, including classics such as sweet and sour chicken and beef in black-bean sauce, from around NOK90. **$**

Zupperia
Vaskerelven 12
Vågsallmenningen 1
Torget 13
Tel: 55 55 81 14
http://zupperia.no
A popular "soup kitchen" (even dessert soups are available) with several branchesthroughout the city. Long opening hours (11am until 11pm or midnight). Sandwiches and salads are also on the menu. **$**

Norwegian treats.

TRONDHEIM

Bari Café and Bar
Munkegata 25
Tel: 73 60 60 24
www.bari.no
Bari has an Italian-influenced menu with dishes ranging from lunchtime burgers to more sophisticated fish and meat evening mains. **$$**

Credo Restaurant and Bar
Ørjaveita 4A
Tel: 73 53 03 88
www.restaurantcredo.no
An unconventional gourmet restaurant with no fixed menu, which instead offers a different fish and a meat special each day. The wine cellar is one of Norway's best. **$$**

Eld
Kongens gate 30
Tel: 47 93 10 10
www.eldrestaurant.no
Eld is an old Norwegian word for flame or fire, which is the theme of this spacious restaurant with open kitchen, fireplace and the largest grill in Scandinavia. Launched in 2011, their entrecôte is already legendary. Look out for the daily 3-course special. **$$–$$$**

Emilies
Erling Skaktes gate 45
Tel: 73 92 96 41
www.emilies.no
At this intimate, modern restaurant, you can dine on tapas or from a three-course menu with matching wine. **$$**

Grenaderen
Kongsgårdsgata 1
Tel: 73 51 66 80
www.grenaderen.no
In an old 16th-century forge with a large terrace. Choose from a traditional menu including fish and reindeer, or go on one of the special buffet days that focus on salads and warm dishes. **$$**

Havfruen Fiskerestaurant
Kjøpmannsgata 7
Tel: 73 87 40 70
www.havfruen.no
Some of the finest Norwegian fish and seafood, plus meat, in a converted riverside warehouse. Trendy bar. **$$**

Palmehaven Restaurant
Dronningensgate 5
Tel: 73 80 08 00
Situated in the stylish Brittania Hotel with Moorish-style garden, this has been a traditional haunt among locals for fine dining and festive occasions since 1918. **$$**

To Rom og Kjøkken
Carl Johansgate 5
Tel: 73 56 89 00
www.toromogkjokken.no
Opened in 2005 by two gentleman with a passionate commitment to food and wine. The focus is on using the freshest local ingredients and giving them a Mediterranean twist. **$$$**

TROMSØ

Emmas Drømmekjøkken
Kirkegata 8
Tel: 77 63 77 30
http://emmasdrommekjokken.no
Emma's Dream Kitchen delivers high-quality Norwegian fish, seafood, duck and lamb dishes, pepped with ginger, enriched by truffle sauces, and generally turned into culinary triumphs. The service is excellent and the ambience warm. Just across the street from the cathedral. Reservations advised. **$$$**

Fiskekompaniet
Killengrens Gate
Tel: 77 68 76 00
http://fiskekompani.no
Just fish and seafood served in a modern, Scandic environment, taken straight from the harbour and prepared in a variety of styles, from traditional to "New Scandinavian". On the town's main shopping street. **$$$**

Vertshuset Skarven
Strandtorget 1
Tel: 77 60 07 20
http://skarven.no
Skarven is made up of two adjacent restaurants which attract loyal customers. The old brick building, Arctandria, specialises in fresh fish and shellfish. Smoked and salted seal meat is a speciality. The yellow wood building, BiffHuset, serves several varieties of steak alongside other well-prepared meat dishes. Good value and a cheerful atmosphere. **$$**

PRICE CATEGORIES

Price categories are per person for an average three-course meal, excluding wine:
$ = under NOK280
$$ = NOK280–560
$$$ = over NOK560

DENMARK

NORWAY

SWEDEN

FINLAND

SWEDEN A–Z

A HANDY SUMMARY OF PRACTICAL INFORMATION

A

Accommodation

Choosing a Hotel

Swedish hotels are of a uniformly high standard, and can be expensive. However, hotel rates do come down on weekdays in high summer when the expense-account business travellers are on holiday. Big international hotel chains have made little impact. Accommodation is dominated by Scandinavian chains such as Scandic or Sweden Hotels. Away from the big cities, there are plenty of privately owned hotels with the individuality lacking in chains. Visit www.hotelsinsweden.net for details on hotels in most towns and cities.

You can book accommodation in Stockholm online through the tourist information office website www.visit stockholm.com.

Discounts

All the hotel groups run discount schemes during summer. Stockholm, Göteborg and Malmö also offer special discount packages at weekends year-round and daily in summer. These often include free public transport and free admission to visitor attractions.

Bed and Breakfasts

The bed and breakfast system is becoming more popular. Look for the Rum sign (it means "room" and does not include breakfast). Ask at local tourist offices if any rum accommodation is available. Prices are very reasonable. There are also many working farms across Sweden offering self-catering and B&B accommodation (www.bopalantgard.org).

Youth Hostels

Sweden has 400 inexpensive youth hostels (vandrarhem), from mansion houses and castles to renovated ships like the 100-year-old af Chapman in Stockholm harbour, and modern purpose-built hostels. These are mainly in southern and central Sweden. There are also plenty of youth hostels in the Stockholm archipelago. Most have two- and four-bed rooms or family rooms. Hostels have self-catering facilities, but meals or snacks are provided in some. There is often use of a washing machine. Most hostels will charge extra for bed linen, so bring your own sheets and towels. Always book ahead in the summer. For details contact Svenska Turistföreningen (STF), tel: 08 463 21 00, www.stfturist.se.

Camping

There are more than 1,000 campsites in Sweden, many in pretty locations and generally of a high standard. Most open from early June to the end of August. You can also rent camping chalets and cottages, cabins and mountain huts, caravans and motor homes. Popular Camping Card Scandinavia has been replaced by Camping Key Europe, which enables a fast check-in at the affiliated campsites, entitles holders to discounts and includes an insurance. For details visit www.campingkey.com. Another useful site is www.camping.se.

Activities

Outdoor Sports

Sweden is a health-conscious nation, offering copious sports facilities nationwide. Visitors who wish to

centre their holiday around sport can order the brochures Outdoor Activities, Summer Activities and Winter Activities from VisitSweden (www.visitsweden.com).

Cycling

There are some pleasant bike trails in Sweden, and bikes are available to rent around the country. Gotland is a cyclists' favourite, as is the scenic towpath alongside the Göta Kanal. For more information contact:
Svenska Cykelförbundet
Idrottens Hus, Fiskartorpsvägen 15A, 114 73 Stockholm
Tel: 08 699 60 00
Email: kansli@scf.se
www.scf.se

Fishing

You can fish in the sea with rod and line free of charge around the Swedish coastline. Fishing is also free from the shores of the five largest lakes: Vänern, Vättern, Mälaren, Hjälmaren and Storsjön; elsewhere a permit is required, available from local tourist information offices. For special conditions regarding permitted equipment, close seasons, minimum size and catch limits, check with tourist offices. Poaching is severely punished. For further information:
Swedish Angling Federation
Svartviksslingan 28, 16739 Bromma
Tel: 08 410 80 600
Email: info@sportfiskarna.se
www.sportfiskarna.se

Golf

Golf is played at more than 300 courses. The best are located in the south, but you can even play a round in the light of the Midnight Sun at several courses inside the Arctic

Having fun at Astrid Lindgren's World in Småland.

Circle: the world's most northerly golf course is at Bjorkliden. The more popular golf courses can be extremely busy in the summer, so booking is advisable. For information contact:

Svenska Golfförbundet
182 11 Danderyd
Tel: 08 622 15 00
Email: info@sgf.golf.se
www.golf.se

Hiking

In the countryside, serious walkers will find plenty of long-distance paths, including the *Kungsleden* (King's Trail), which traverses the high peaks of Lapland. The Swedish Tourist Federation *(Svenska Turistföreningen)* maintains a network of cabins for overnight accommodation and also operates Sweden's youth hostels. For more details contact:

Svenska Turistföreningen
Tel: 08 463 21 00
Email: info@stfturist.se
www.svenskaturistforeningen.se

Sweden's National Parks
Valhallavägen 195,
106 48 Stockholm
Tel: 010 698 10 00
www.naturvardsverket.se

Horse Riding

Almost every town has riding stables or a riding school, and more experienced riders can enjoy a pony-trekking safari in the Kebnekaise mountain range. For further information contact:

Svenska Ridsport Förbundet
Ridsportenshus, 734 94
Strömsholm
Tel: 0220 456 00
Email: kansliet@ridsport.se
www.ridsport.se

Husky Safaris

Winter tourism is really taking off in Sweden, and one of the most popular icy activities is a husky safari. Long

and short trips are available from mid-November to late April; the weather is generally best towards the end of the season.

Sailing

Right on the city's doorstep lie 24,000 islets and skerries which provide some of the most sheltered waters in Europe. No wonder, then, that the Swedes are such keen sailors. Opportunities for sailing adventures abound, with many charter companies running day cruises, or longer, to picturesque islands. Stockholm Adventures operate day sails in a historic schooner or luxury yacht (www.stockholmadventures.se).

Skiing

Swedes learn to ski when they are toddlers, so there are plenty of facilities for both downhill and cross-country enthusiasts. The best-known resorts are Åre and Sälen in the province of Dalarna. The skiing season in Riksgränsen in the far north of the country extends into the summer: pistes open from February until late May, and over the Midsummer holiday in June. For more information:

Svenska Skidförbundet
Riksskidstadion
Lugnetvägen 16, 791 19 Falun
Tel: 010 708 69 00
www.skidor.com

Tennis

The country's tennis facilities are excellent. There is a wide range of both indoor and outdoor courts for public use throughout Sweden, and tennis is not at all considered an exclusive sport.

Svenska Tennisförbundet (Tennis)
Lidingövägen 75, 115 41 Stockholm
Tel: 08 450 43 10
Email: info@tennis.se
www.tennis.se

Watersports

With almost 100,000 lakes and thousands of kilometres of waterways, Sweden has a lot to offer to watersports devotees, including waterskiing, windsurfing, canoeing and white-water rafting. Dalsland and Värmland are good areas for canoe safaris.

Spectator Sports

Göteborg is probably the most sport-focused town in Sweden, and its Scandinavium (www.scandinavium. se) is the venue for major tennis, ice hockey and table tennis events. The Ullevi Stadium stages international tournaments in football, athletics and speedway.
Tennis is a favourite spectator sport: the Swedish Open (www.swedishopen. org) is held at Båstad, on the southwest coast, in mid-July and the Stockholm Open in October.
Horse-racing and trotting are popular in Sweden, with the best-known courses at Stockholm (Täby and Solvalla), Göteborg (Åby) and Malmö (Jägersro). Another important annual international horse show is held at the Göteborg Scandinavium in April.

Admission Charges

Admission to museums, galleries and palaces varies enormously, from free to around 120 kronor. Stockholm and Göteborg both offer superb tourist cards giving free admission to heaps of attractions and free public transport.

C

Children

Sweden is child-friendly, and Swedes are good at devising excellent attractions for the whole family, like amusement parks such as **Liseberg** (www.liseberg.se) in Göteborg and **Gröna Lund Tivoli** (www.gronalund. com) in Stockholm.

Astrid Lindgren Fantasies

The famous author Astrid Lindgren is a master at creating fantasy characters that appeal to children. Pippi Longstocking, Emil and Karlsson on the Roof are just some of the attractions at Junibacken, a wonderful fairytale house in Stockholm, where characters from many favourite children's books come to life and kids can play, discover and learn. All activities are indoors, and there's

DENMARK

NORWAY

SWEDEN

FINLAND

also a restaurant and a bookshop with Sweden's largest selection of children's books.

Junibacken, Galärvarvsvägen, close to Gröna Lund Tivoli, Stockholm
Tel: 08 587 230 00
Email: info@junibacken.se
www.junibacken.se

The author was born in Vimmerby in the province of Småland, where you can also visit Astrid Lindgren's World, another fairytale land with living characters from her books. It is open daily from mid-May until the end of August, plus weekends in September.

Astrid Lindgren's World
Tel: 0492 798 00
Email: info@alv.se
www.alv.se

Skara Sommarland

Scandinavia's largest waterpark is Skara Sommarland at Skara, northeast of Göteborg. As well as water slides, flumes and wave pools, other attractions include a grand prix race track, fairground rides, a railway and three boating lakes. Tel: 010 708 8000; www.sommarland.se.

Zoos

The best-known zoo/safari park is at Kolmården (tel: 010 708 7000; www.kolmarden.com) near Norrköping. It has lions, giraffes, elephants and so on, as well as Sweden's only dolphinarium. Other zoos of note are Borås zoo (www.boraszoo.se), Ölands Djur & Nöjespark near Kalmar (www.olandsdjurpark.com), Parken Zoo at Eskilstuna (http://parkenzoo. se), Furuvik zoo (www.furuvik. se) and Skansen in Stockholm (www.skansen.se).

In a park in Grönklitt (tel: 0250 462 00; www.orsabjornpark.se), Dalarna, brown bears live in their natural forest habitat. This park offers a great opportunity to see them and their cubs up close.

Göteborg Opera House.

Santaworld

Not far from Orsa is Tomteland (Santaworld; tel: 0250 287 70; www.santaworld.se), where children can explore Santa's house, workshop and animals, the elf village, the Snow Queen's Palace... and place orders for Christmas.

Vintage Railways

Sweden has a number of vintage railways, some of which still operate steam locomotives. The longest preserved railway is the 32km (20-mile) narrow-gauge line Lennakatten (www.lennakatten.se), running from Uppsala to Länna in high summer.

Cowboy Capers

An unusual visitor attraction in Småland is **High Chaparral** (tel: 0370 827 00; www.highchaparral.se), a mock Wild West town, complete with cowboys, Indians, bandits and sheriffs.

Climate

In summer Sweden's weather is similar to that in Britain – and just as unpredictable – although in a good year some remarkably high temperatures can be recorded in the Arctic regions. The area round Piteå on the Gulf of Bothnia is known as the Northern Riviera because of its warmth. But in the north, autumn and winter arrive early and spring comes in late May.

Winter can be cold; even in Stockholm, maximum temperatures in the day are likely to remain below freezing in January and February.

What to Bring

Sweden's weather is unpredictable, so plan for any eventuality. In summer, even in the Arctic north, you could have hot sunny days that call for shorts and T-shirts, or it could

CLIMATE CHART

Stockholm

	Maximum temperature
	Minimum temperature
—	Rainfall

be one of those summers when the sun never appears and sweaters and rainwear are needed. Winters can be very cold, but this is "dry" cold. Still, you should take a heavy coat and warm headgear, as well as sturdy footwear for the slushy streets.

Culture

Festivals

Kiruna Snow Festival – a celebration of Sami traditions and snow-sculpting (January).

Vasaloppet – the exalted cross-country ski race, held between Sälen and Mora (March); www.vasaloppet.se.

Walpurgis Night – across Sweden, parades, singing and bonfires mark the beginning of spring (30 April).

Midsummer's Eve – Sweden's biggest celebration, with more bonfires, plus maypoles, drinking and dancing (June).

Music vid Siljan – folk and jazz in venues around Lake Siljan (July); www.musikvidsiljan.se.

Medieval Week – parades, plays and performances with a medieval feel, held in Visby (August); www.medeltidsveckan.se.

Nobel Prize Day – the prestigious prizes are given out at a ceremony in Stockholm (10 December).

Music

The musical scene in Sweden is busiest in the autumn, winter and spring, but there is still a lot going on in summer. In Dalarna, for example, several communities organise traditional music festivals. The town of Borlänge in Dalarna also hosts Sweden's biggest pop and rock festival, Peace & Love, held in late June/early July.

Stockholm, Göteborg and Malmö all have highly regarded orchestras based in the cities' main Konserthus.

Each city also has a dedicated modern opera house, offering varied programmes of opera, ballet and musicals. Most concert halls are closed in the month of July.

Theatre

Sweden has a lively theatrical scene in the major cities, but many theatres close during the peak summer months. Performances are usually in Swedish.

Stockholm

The most prestigious theatre is the Royal Dramatic Theatre (Dramaten; www.dramaten.se) on Nybroplan, which contains eight stages. The most unusual one is the Drottningholms Slottsteater (www.dtm.se) at Drottningholms Palace, founded by King Gustav III in 1766. More than 30 sets from then are still in use today. In summer it stages 17th- and 18th-century operas, attracting music-lovers from around the world.

There is a booth on Norrmalmstorg Square, Biljett Direkt, where you can buy last-minute theatre seats.

Göteborg

The two main theatres are Stadsteatern (www.stadsteatern. goteborg.se) and Folkteatern (www.folk teatern.se); both open from September to May. In summer, the Liseberg amusement park hosts many famous artists (http://liseberg.se).

Malmö

The Stadsteater (www.malmo stadsteater.se) is a modern building with three stages. Plays are in Swedish, but you can often catch an opera or musical performance.

Traditional Plays

Several places in Sweden stage traditional plays in summer. For example, Rune Lindström's play Himlaspelet (The Road to Heaven) has been performed in Leksand in mid-July since 1949. In Visby, on the island of Gotland, the atmospheric Medieval Week (Medeltidsveckan; www.medeltidsveckan.se) in early August features lively parades and theatrical performances.

Cinema

Virtually all foreign films are shown with their original soundtracks and Swedish subtitles (rather than being dubbed). Local newspapers have full details of programmes and times. In Stockholm, cinemas showing first-run international films include Filmstaden Sergel, Filmstaden Söder, Rigoletto and Filmstaden Kista.

The film company SF has a website where you can book your ticket for any cinema around the country; www.sf.se.

Customs Regulations

There are no restrictions on importing/exporting goods for people travelling between Sweden and other EU countries, as long as the goods are for personal use or your family's use and not for resale; it is up to the individual customs officer to decide whether quantities of imported alcohol and tobacco products are for personal use or should be considered commercial imports. Visitors travelling to/from non-EU countries can import duty-free 200 cigarettes/100 cigarillos/50 cigars or 250g tobacco, 1 litre of spirits or 2 litres of dessert wine (maximum 22 percent alcohol by volume), 4 litres of wine plus 16 litres of beer. In order to import alcohol you need to be at least 20 years old.

D

Disabled Travellers

In line with its enlightened social attitudes, Sweden has long been a pioneer in accommodating travellers with disabilities. Many hotel rooms and facilities are adapted for the needs of people with mobility problems. New public buildings are all accessible to people with disabilities, and toilets with the handicap symbol can be found almost everywhere. In Stockholm, most buses are designed for easy access for people with wheelchairs and pushchairs. Mainline and underground trains have elevators or ramps.

For general information contact:
DHR De Handikappades Riksförbund
Storforsplan 44, 123 21 Farsta
Tel: 08 685 80 00
Email: info@dhr.se
www.dhr.se
For wheelchair rental contact:
Contact Hjälpmedelsinstitutet
Tel: 072 544 01 20
Email: registrator@hi.se
www.hi.se

E

Embassies and Consulates

Canada
Klarabergsgatan 23, 6th floor, 103 23 Stockholm
Tel: 08 453 30 00

Dance Boats

A popular outing – among young and old as well as conference parties – is to take the boat from Stockholm to Finland for a day's visit to Helsinki or Åbo (Turku). The round trip takes about 40 hours and includes one or two nights on the boat and one day in Helsinki or Åbo. The boats have several dance floors, bars and a restaurant to entertain the captive audience. Contact Tallink Silja (tel: 08 22 21 40; www.tallinksilja.com) or Viking Line (tel: 08 452 40 00; www.viking line.se) for information.

www.sweden.gc.calreland
Hovslagargatan 5, 100 55 Stockholm
Tel: 08 545 04 040
www.embassyofireland.se
UK
Skarpögatan 6–8, 115 93 Stockholm
Tel: 08 671 30 00
http://ukinsweden.fco.gov.uk/en
US
Dag Hammarskjölds Väg 31
Tel: 08 783 53 00, 115 89 Stockholm
www.usemb.se

Emergencies

Police, fire, ambulance 112 (calls are free)

G

Gay and Lesbian Travellers

Sweden is renowned for its liberal attitudes to sex, and its age of consent is 15 for heterosexuals and gays. Same-sex marriages have been legal in Sweden since 2009. But there is nevertheless little open affection between gay couples, and the gay scene is less apparent in Stockholm than in other capitals, with few places for gays only. Södermalm is the most relaxed, gay-friendly area of the city.

QX is a gay/lesbian magazine that offers information about clubs, restaurants, bars and shops mainly in Stockholm, Göteborg, Malmö and Copenhagen (www.qx.se).

H

Health and Medical Care

Precautions

Standards of hygiene in Sweden are among the highest in the world. No

DAGENS RÄTT
KL. 11⁰⁰ ~ 15⁰⁰
* BAKAD POTATIS
m. SKAGEN RÖRA
* HEMLAGAD
LASAGNE
* PAJER 59:-
INKL. SMÖR, BRÖD, SALLAD
OCH DRYCK
VÄLKOMNA!

Lunch is served.

inoculations are needed, and tap water is safe to drink.

In the far north of Sweden in high summer, precautions need to be taken against the vicious mosquitoes. In forested areas, wear long socks and use insect repellent to guard against ticks.

Medical Treatment

Sweden has reciprocal agreements with the UK and other countries, under which visitors are entitled to the same medical treatment as Swedes. To qualify, EU nationals must obtain an European Health Insurance Card (EHIC; available in the UK through post offices and online at www.ehic.org.uk). To see a doctor, take the EHIC and your passport to the nearest hospital clinic ("Akutmottagning" or "Vårdcentral"). With the EHIC, visitors pay a small fee (the same as Swedes); without it, visitors must pay for the actual cost of the treatment. For hospital treatment, inpatient care is usually free, with just a small daily rate payable.

Visitors from outside the EU pay higher clinic consultation fees, although these are modest compared with those charged in North America. Non-EU visitors also pay in full for hospital treatment, so it is important to take out adequate medical insurance coverage before your visit so that you can reclaim the money on your return.

Pharmacies

The larger cities all have a 24-hour pharmacy *(apotek)*. In Stockholm, it is located opposite the Central Railway Station: Apoteket C.W. Scheele, Klarabergsgatan 64; tel: 0771 450 450 (it's also the number for general pharmacy information in Sweden).

Internet

Most hotels offer WiFi internet access; cybercafés are easy to find in towns and cities. Ask at the local tourist office for details.

Language

The Alphabet

The Swedish alphabet has 29 letters; the additional three are å, ä and ö, and come after the letter z. To find Mr Åkerblad in the phone book, therefore, look at the end of the listings.

Useful Words and Phrases

Yes *Ja*
No *Nej*
Hello *Hej*
Goodbye *Hejdå*
Thank you *Tack*
Please *Tack/Var så god*
Do you speak English? *Talar du engelska?*
I only speak English *Jag talar bara engelska*
Good morning *God morgon*
Good afternoon *God eftermiddag*
Good evening *God kväll*
Today *Idag*
Tomorrow *I morgon*
Yesterday *Igår*
How do you do *Goddag*
What time is it? *Hur mycket är klockan?*
It is (the time is) *Den är (klockan är)*
Could I have your name please? *Hur var namnet?*
My name is *Jag heter*
Can I help you? *Kan jag hjälpa till?*
I do not understand *Jag förstår inte*
I do not know *Jag vet inte*

Eating and Drinking

breakfast *frukost*
lunch *lunch*
dinner *middag*
eat *äta*
drink *dricka*
Cheers *Skål!*
off-licence *Systembolaget*
Can I order please? *Får jag beställa?*
Could I have the bill please? *Kan jag få notan?*

Getting Around

aircraft *flygplan*
bus/coach *buss*
car *bil*
parking *parkering, garage*

train *tåg*
How do I get to ...? *Hur kommer jag till ...?*
Where is ...? *Var finns ...?*
Right *Höger*
To the right *Till höger*
Left *Vänster*
To the left *Till vänster*
Straight on *Rakt fram*

Shopping

to buy *att köpa*
department store *varuhus*
food *mat*
grocery store (in countryside) *lanthandel*
handicraft *hemslöjd*
money *pengar*
shop *affär*
clothes *kläder*
overcoat *kappa, överrock*
jacket *jacka*
suit *kostym*
shoes *skor*
skirt *kjol*
jersey *tröja, jumper*
How much is this? *Vad kostar det?*
It costs ... *Det kostar ...*
Do you have English newspapers? *Har du engelska tidningar?*

Health and Security

chemist *apotek*
accident and emergency clinic *akutmottagning/vårdcentral*
hospital *sjukhus*
doctor *doktor*
police station *polisstation*

Miscellaneous

Toilet *Toalett*
Gentlemen *Herrar*
Ladies *Damer*
Vacant *Ledigt*
Engaged *Upptagen*
No smoking *Rökning förbjuden*
Entrance *Ingång*
Exit *Utgång*
No entry *Ingen ingång*
Open *Öppen/Öppet*
Closed *Stängt*

Days of the Week

Monday *måndag*
Tuesday *tisdag*
Wednesday *onsdag*
Thursday *torsdag*
Friday *fredag*
Saturday *lördag*
Sunday *söndag*

Numbers

0 *noll*
1 *en/ett*
2 *två*
3 *tre*
4 *fyra*
5 *fem*

6 *sex*
7 *sju*
8 *åtta*
9 *nio*
10 *tio*
11 *elva*
12 *tolv*
13 *tretton*
14 *fjorton*
15 *femton*
16 *sexton*
17 *sjutton*
18 *arton*
19 *nitton*
20 *tjugo*
21 *tjugoen*
22 *tjugotvå*
30 *trettio*
40 *fyrtio*
50 *femtio*
60 *sextio*
70 *sjuttio*
80 *åttio*
90 *nittio* .
100 *hundra*
200 *två hundra*
1,000 *tusen*

M

Media

Newspapers and Magazines

English-language newspapers are widely available at kiosks in larger cities, usually on the day of publication. Kulturhus (the cultural centre) in Stockholm at Sergels Torg has a good selection of English newspapers and magazines that can be read for free, as does the City Library in Göteborg on the main square, Götaplatsen. For a wide selection of English-language magazines try a Press Stop Store (in Stockholm there's one in the central Gallerian shopping centre, on Hamngatan; www.pressbyran.se).

Books

English-language books are widely available. In Stockholm, excellent bookshops include:
Akademibokhandeln, Mäster Samuelsgaten 28 (Scandinavia's largest bookshop); www.akademibokhandeln.se.
Hedengrens Bokhandel, Stureplan 4; www.hedengrens.se.
For maps and guides, try **Kartbutiken**, Mäster Samuelsgatan 54; www.kartbutiken.se.

Television

Sweden's state-run STV1 and STV2 show a film most evenings. The commercial channels TV3, TV4, TV6, Kanal 5 and Kanal 9 run American chat shows, movies, and comedy and drama series. Plus there are many satellite/cable channels, featuring CNN, BBC and MTV, broadcast in English with subtitles.

Radio

Radio Sweden has a 30-minute English-language Monday-to-Friday broadcast with news and information about Sweden on the P2 network at 3pm and in the Stockholm area on the P6 FM 89.6 MHz network at 3pm and 8.30pm. You can also listen to it online at http://sverigesradio.se.
BBC World Service programmes are also available on channel 89.6 FM.

Money

There is no limit on the import of either Swedish or foreign currency.
Travellers' cheques can be exchanged without difficulty at banks all over Sweden. A foreign exchange service is also provided by post offices with the "PK Exchange" sign. Forex and X-change, bureaux de change with branches in most major towns and airports, usually have better exchange rates than the banks and post offices and don't charge any commission.
Leading credit cards (although some restrictions may apply to American Express) are accepted by most hotels, restaurants and shops throughout the country, and you can also take out cash on these cards at foreign exchange offices and banks.

Currency

Swedish krona (plural kronor), marked ":-" or "kr" or "Skr" in shops, or SEK internationally, and split into 100 öre. The 50-öre coin is no longer legal tender. Valid coins are 1-krona, 5- and 10-krona. Lighter copper-coloured 1-, 2- and gold-coloured 5-krona coins will be introduced late 2016, which will also see the arrival of newly designed 100- and 500-krona banknotes. Current notes are 20-, 50-, 100-, 500- and 1,000-kronor. New 20-, 50-, 200- and 1,000-krona banknotes will be introduced late 2015. Old 20-, 50- and 1000-krona banknotes will be discontinued after 30 June 2016. A year later, on 30 June 2017, the 100-krona and 500-krona banknotes and 1-, 2- and 5-krona coins will become invalid. Novel banknotes will be equipped with state-of-the-art security features and will depict Swedish prominent 20th-century figures, for example the 200-krona note will feature Ingmar Bergman. You should also be aware that since the end of 2013 the old no-foil-strip versions of 50- and 1000-krona banknotes are invalid. For more information, visit the website of Sweden's central bank: www.riksbank.se.

Tipping

In hotels and restaurants a service charge is included in the bill and a further tip is not generally expected, although it's usual to round up the bill to the nearest SEK10 or 20 for an evening meal.
Taxi drivers are usually tipped. Cloakrooms at restaurants and clubs charge about SEK15–20.
Tipping for special services provided by hotel staff is fine but not expected.

N

Nightlife

Where to Go

There is an active nightlife in the larger cities, but nothing particularly hectic in the smaller communities. Many hotels have bars, nightclubs and sometimes even live dance music. University cities like Uppsala, Lund, Linköping and Umeå have a busy nightlife, at least for the students.
Skiing resorts like Åre and Sälen are also good for nightlife from December to April, with après-ski bands playing covers of well-known tunes to packed crowds.
Out in the countryside and in smaller towns *dansband* music is popular – Swedish-style country music to which people dance foxtrot and a kind of jive. If you like dancing this could be a fun thing to try and a chance to meet the locals. Dancing may not begin until midnight.
The cost of drinking has fallen a little in recent years, but a night out on the town can still be expensive. The best value is probably at a jazz club, or at one of the piano bars, which offer a quieter and more relaxing environment for a late-night drink.

Nightclubs, Bars and Live Music

Opening Hours
Nightclubs and discos usually close around 3am (sometimes 5am in Stockholm). Unfortunately, numerous nightclubs have long queues outside after 9 or 10pm, even if it's not full inside – an

DENMARK

NORWAY

SWEDEN

FINLAND

irritating way of showing that the club is popular. Avoid the queue by getting there early, or booking a table and having dinner there (Swedes often combine dining and drinking on a night out), which also means you avoid paying the nightclub entrance fee.

Age Limits
If you're in your early 20s or younger, you may not be able to get into some clubs. Some have remarkably high minimum age limits: the more upmarket night-clubs impose a minimum age of up to 26 for men and 24 for women.

Stockholm
For the most happening clubs and bars, check out www.visitstockholm.com.

Absolut Ice Bar
Vasaplan 4
Tel: 08 505 635 20
www.nordicseahotel.se
A little gimmicky! Nevertheless, you may want to sip a quick cocktail at the world's first permanent ice bar. Its −5°C (23°F) interior is entirely sculpted from Lapland ice – including the glasses. Reservations required.

Akkurat
Hornsgatan 18
Tel: 08 644 00 15
www.akkurat.se
Popular Söder hangout for those who enjoy listening to good blues, rock and soul, played here on Sunday nights. Also has a wide selection of whiskies and beers.

Berns
Berzelli Park 6
Tel: 08 566 322 00
www.berns.se
This entertainment palace at Berzelli Park has been in existence since 1863, but it has never been in better form since Sir Terence Conran redesigned it a few years ago. It now

has several stylish bars, including the Berns Bar under crystal chandeliers, the cocktail bar in a sober glass veranda and a cellar bar that attracts the trendy crowd. Its 2.35:1 nightclub opens until 5am on Fridays and Saturdays.

Café Opera
Operahus, Karl XII:s torg
Tel: 08 676 58 07
www.cafeopera.se
Expensive but ever-popular bar, restaurant and club (which starts around midnight) with a mix of younger people and older regulars. There is an impressive classical architectural interior. Minimum age is 23.

Debaser Medis
Medborgarplatsen 8Tel: 08 694 79 00
www.debaser.se
Great live metal and rock gigs. Debaser Medis, in Södermalm, is a newer venue hosting everything from world music and hip hop to rock and pop. Wednesday to Sunday.

Fasching
Kungsgatan 63
Tel: 0771 47 70 70www.fasching.se
This is Stockholm's largest and most popular jazz club, with restaurant and nightclub.

Glenn Miller Café
Brunnsgatan 21A
Tel: 08 10 03 22
www.glennmillercafe.com
Small bar and restaurant with nightly jazz from 8pm.

La Habana
Sveavägen 108
Tel: 08 16 64 65
www.lahabana.se
Rum, cigars and salsa are the order of the day at this fun, rough-and-ready Cuban place, with live music from Tuesday to Saturday.

Nada
Åsögatan 140
Tel: 076 309 95 78

Pleasant, cosy bar with DJs spinning indie-pop tunes.

Och Himlen Därtill
Götgatan 78
Tel: 08 660 60 68
www.restauranghimlen.se
This super-chic skybar is the place to sip cocktails and admire spectacular views of Stockholm from the 26th floor.

Patricia
Söder Mälarstrand, Kajplats 19
Tel: 08 743 05 70
www.patricia.st
The steamship M/S Patricia is now a party boat, with three floors of bars and dancing and a great mix of people. Gay club night on Sundays.

Spy Bar
Birger Jarlsgatan 20
Tel: 08 545 076 55
One of Stockholm's most legendary nightclubs, Spy Bar is popular with an intellectual, media-savvy crowd.

Stampen
Stora Nygatan 5
Tel: 08 20 57 93
www.stampen.se
Lively, well-known jazz pub in the Old Town, with live music from 8pm until late.

Sturecompagniet
Sturegatan 4
Tel: 08 545 076 01
www.sturecompagniet.se
This massive club, with its dramatic ballroom entrance, sprawls across three floors in the city centre, packed with bars and dance floors.

Göteborg
For the latest on Göteborg's nightlife, see www.goteborg.com.

Excet
Vasagatan 52
Tel: 031 711 99 11
http://excet.se
One of Göteborg's biggest, this three-storey nightclub attracts a mixed crowd with its two dance floors, DJs and a summer terrace.

Jazzhuset
Erik Dahlbergsgatan 3
Tel: 031 13 35 44
www.jazzhuset.se
There's always live music here. Various club nights feature different sounds, from pure jazz to electronica.

Lou lou
Magasinsgatan 3
Tel: 031 13 85 55
http://loulougbg.comThis steakhouse slides into clubland as evening becomes night on Friday and Saturday, with DJs and dancing until late. Perfect cocktails.

Lounge(s)
Kungsportsavenyen 5

Taking part in Midsummer festivities.

Tel: 031 711 15 41
www.lounges.se
Stylish club with themed lounges,
resident DJs and a very sleek casino.
Nefertiti Jazz Club
Hvidfeldtsplatsen 6
Tel: 031 711 40 76
www.nefertiti.se
Running for over 30 years, this
popular place bursts at the seams
on club nights, when happy revellers
dance to jazz, blues, soul, electronic
and world music.
Park Lane
Kungsportsavenyn 36–38
Tel: 031 20 60 58
www.parklane.se
An upmarket nightclub with an
international atmosphere and
clientele of all ages and orientation.
There are three bars, a restaurant, a
casino and live performances.
Push
Kungsportsavenyn 11
www.push.se
One of Göteborg's newest
nightclubs, set up by Stockholm's
Sturecompagniet crew. The fabulous
interior (Scandinavian-minimalism
with retro-future touches) throbs to
the sounds of mainstream house.
Rooftop terrace.
Trädgår'n
Nya Allén
Tel: 031 10 20 80
http://tradgarn.se
Restaurant in the centre of the city's
botanical garden, with outdoor dining,
live performances and weekend
nightclub.

Malmö
Lilla Torg (Small Square) is a buzzing
area where new restaurants and bars
open up all the time.
Etage
Stortorget 6
Tel: 040 23 20 60
http://etagegruppen.se
Popular place with young people.
Gamla Brogatan
Brogatan 12
Tel: 04062 00 301
www.gamlabrogatan.se
The place to be seen, this is a popular
bar among Malmö's celebrities.
At summer weekends there is a
nightclub until 3am.
Harry's
Södergatan 14
Tel: 040 12 34 90
www.harrys.se/malmo
Bar and disco with a friendly and
relaxed atmosphere.
Hipp
Kalendegatan 12
Tel: 040 97 40 30
www.hipp.se

Beautiful, late 19th-century-style
restaurant and bar with club
arrangements every Saturday.
Kulturbolaget
Bergsgatan 18
Tel: 040 30 20 11
http://kulturbolaget.se
This big rock-music venue becomes
a club on Fridays and Saturdays,
featuring rock/pop music and
sometimes disco.
Swing Inn
Malmborgsgatan 7
Tel: 040 12 22 21
Popular among 30-somethings.
Several dance floors, 70s and 80s
music on Saturday. Minimum age
limit between 25 and 35 depending
on the day.

O

Opening Hours

Shops on the whole open
9.30am–6pm on weekdays and until
between 1 and 4pm on Saturdays. In
larger cities many shops are open on
Sundays as well, usually noon–4pm.
Shops generally close early the day
before a public holiday.
Department stores may remain open
until 8pm or 9pm and possibly also
on Sundays.
Banks Monday–Friday 10am–3pm
(6pm in some larger cities), but
closed on Saturdays. SEB Exchange
at Stockholm Arlanda airport's
Terminal 5 arrival hall is open daily
5am–11pm.

P

Postal Services

Post offices have been phased out
and franchise postal services are
now run by supermarkets, grocery
stores and petrol stations. Stamps
(frimärken) are also on sale at
Pressbyrån newsstands, bookstalls
and stationers' shops. Mailboxes
are blue for local letters and yellow
for all other destinations. For more
information visit www.posten.se.

R

Religious Services

The Swedish State Church is in the
Lutheran tradition and has churches
throughout the country.
    Stockholm has the widest range of
places of worship, including Catholic

Public Holidays

Sweden has several official
holidays:
1 January New Year's Day
6 January Epiphany
March/April Good Friday and
Easter Monday
1 May Labour Day
May Ascension (usually second
part of the month); Pentecost (10
days after Ascension)
6 June National Day
June Midsummer's Day
(around the 24th)
November All Saints' Day (usually
at start of the month)
25 and 26 December Christmas
31 December New Year's Eve

churches, a Greek Orthodox church,
several synagogues and a mosque.
    Protestant services in English are
usually held once a week in major
cities. Enquire at your hotel for more
information.

S

Shopping

Where to Shop
Sweden is famous the world over for
its elegant design, and you will find
plenty of good buys in glassware,
stainless steel, silver, pottery,
ceramics, textiles and leather goods.
Department stores such as NK (www.
nk.se) and Åhléns (www.ahlens.
se) are noted for their high-quality,
inexpensive kitchenware.
Glass The best bargains are found
in "Glass Country" – Småland, in
the southeast – where there are 13
glassworks. Most of the glassworks,
including Orrefors (www.orrefors.se),
Kosta-Boda (www.kostaboda.com),
SEA and Skruf, have shops adjoining
their factories where you can buy
everything from one-off sculptures
to cheap factory seconds. Visitors to
Stockholm can buy Swedish glass
from department stores like NK, or
dedicated glass shops such as Crystal
Art Centre (www.cac.se), Nordiska
Kristall (www.nordiskakristall.se) or
Orrefors Kosta Boda.
Porcelain and Ceramics Sweden
is also renowned for its high-quality
porcelain, and bargains can be found
at the Gustavsberg factory outside
Stockholm (www.gustavsberg.com) and
at the Rörstrand factory in Lidköping
(www.rorstrand.com). Höganäs
in Skåne has a strong history of

ceramics: a factory outlet there sells quality Swedish brands.

Fashion For cheap clothing, try Hennes & Mauritz (H&M), Lindex, JC and KappAhl. The best shopping area is probably Borås, near Göteborg, which is the centre of the *Tygriket* (Weavers' Country). Knalleland (/www.knalleland.se) is a large shopping centre in Borås where you can get bargains from the leading direct-mail companies.

The centre of the fur business is Tranås in the province of Småland, where you can usually find bargains.

Tax-Free Shopping

Visitors from outside the EU are entitled to a tax refund of up to 19 percent on purchases of over 200 euro in shops displaying the Tax Free Shopping sign. For further details, see www.globalblue.com.

Markets

Stockholm has markets at Hötorget, Östermalmstorg and Medborgarplatsen, which are worth a visit, while Göteborg has its "Fish Church", a thriving fish market built in an ecclesiastical style. Göteborg also has a fascinating food market *(Saluhallen)*.

Stockholm's suburbs contain what is claimed to be Northern Europe's largest flea market at Vårberg, 30 minutes on the underground from the city centre. It's open daily, but Saturday and Sunday are the best days to go (a small admission charge applies at weekends).

Factory Outlets

Below are factory outlets selling Swedish and international brand names:

Abecita
Borås, Herrljungagatan 17
Tel: 033 23 76 05
www.abecita.com

Glassware is a popular gift.

Ladies' underwear, swimsuits, dressing gowns.

Freeport Kungsbacka Designer Outlet Village
Kungsparksvägen 80, Kungsbacka
Tel: 0300 57 00 00
www.freeport.se
Designer clothes, toys, home furnishings in 50 shops.

Ge-Kås
Danska vägen 13, Ullared
Tel: 0346 375 00
www.gekas.se
Clothes, kitchenware, food.

Stockholm Quality Outlet
Flyginfarten 4, Järfälla
www.qualityoutlet.com
Outside Stockholm, 50 brand-name shops.

Visko
Maskingatan 2, Skene
Tel: 0320 322 90
www.visko.se
Shoes and more near Göteborg.

Local Crafts

All over Sweden you can see crafts-people at work and buy their work at low prices. In the countryside, look out for *hemslöjd, or* handicraft centres. Women's and children's clothes are especially good buys, as well as furs and needlework.

Below is a selection of outlets in Stockholm and Göteborg. The *Yellow Pages* website (www.gulasidorna.se; in Swedish) lists shops in Sweden: search for *hemslöjd, slöjd or konsthantverk*.

Bäx Krukmakeri
Kronhusbodarna, Postgatan 8, Göteborg
Tel: 031 13 18 00
www.baxkrukmakeri.com
Handicraft centre with glass and ceramic workshops.

Svensk Hemslöjd
Norrlandsgatan 20, Stockholm
Tel: 08 23 21 15
www.svenskhemslojd.com

Svensk Slöjd
Nybrogatan 23, Stockholm
Tel: 08 663 66 50
www.svenskslojd.se

Design

For contemporary Swedish (and international) design, several shops in Stockholm are worth visiting:

Blås & Knåda
Hornsgatan 26a
Tel: 08 642 77 67
www.blasknada.se
Co-operative selling modern ceramic and glass items.

Design House Stockholm
NK Hamngatan 18-20
Tel: 08 762 81 19
www.designhousestockholm.com
Acts as a "publisher" for new talent – classics in the making, from candlesticks and clothing to chests of drawers.

DesignTorget
Kungsgatan 52 Tel: 08 662 35 15
www.designtorget.se
Homeware and gifts from established and up-and-coming designers. With seven other outlets in Stockholm, including at Arlanda airport.

G.A.D.
Tegnérgatan 4
Tel: 08 545 480 08
www.gad.se
Homeware and clean-lined furniture manufactured in Sweden.

Nordiska Galleriet
Nybrogatan 11
Tel: 08 442 83 60
www.nordiskagalleriet.se
Established in 1913, this is one of the city's leading interior design stores.

Norrgavel
Birger Jarlsgatan 27
Tel: 08 545 220 50
www.norrgavel.se
Two floors of furniture, ceramics, glass and textiles.

Malmstenbutiken
Strandvägen 5B
Tel: 08 23 33 80
www.malmsten.se
Selling furniture-maker Carl Malmsten's designs, alongside work by designers inspired by him.

R.O.O.M.
Täby Torg 4 Plan 1
Tel: 08 692 50 00
www.room.se

Svenskt Tenn
Strandvägen 5
Tel: 08 670 16 00
www.svenskttenn.se
Tiny glass vases, jewellery, bright fabrics, furniture and more.

IKEA
After exhorting people the world over to "chuck out the chintz",

the Swedish behemoth IKEA will probably need no introduction to readers. The company's creative headquarters is based in Älmhult, in Småland – fans can stay in town at the Värdshuset IKEA hotel (www.vardshuset.nu). IKEA stores are found across Sweden, usually on the outskirts of towns.

T

Telephones

Mobile phones are widely used across Sweden, although you can still find payphones on the street, at petrol stations and post offices. Most payphones no longer take coins – they operate only with credit cards (signposted CCC) or a telephone card (telia telefonkort). Telephone cards are widely available in Pressbyrån, kiosks, bookstalls, grocery stores and stationers' shops. As elsewhere, it is expensive to phone from hotel rooms. The telephone directory enquiry service is also expensive.

To call abroad, dial 00 followed by the country code (44 for the UK, 1 for the US and Canada, 353 for Ireland, 61 for Australia and 64 for New Zealand), then dial the number, omitting any initial 0.

Swedish mobile phones operate on the 900/1800 MHz GSM network – most European phones are compatible, although your phone must be unlocked in order to link up with the network. US phones work on a slightly different frequency, so US visitors should check with their phone company first regarding usability. The cheapest way to use your own mobile phone in is to buy a Swedish SIM card from a newsagent – ask for a startpaket. Local mobile network operators include Tele2 (www.tele2.se), Telenor (www.telenor.se), Telia (www.telia.se) and 3 (www.tre.se).

To make a call from your mobile phone, dial the area code (e.g. 08 for Stockholm) followed by the number. To ring a friend's (foreign) mobile phone in Sweden you have to dial 00 followed by your friend's country code and area code (omitting the 0), plus the number.

Useful Numbers

Swedish directory enquiries 118 118
International directory enquiries 118 119
International dialling code: +46

Tourist Information

A good starting point for national tourist information is:
VisitSweden
Sveavägen 21, StockholmEmail: reception@visitsweden.com
www.visitsweden.com

Local Offices

Sweden has a country-wide network of tourist information offices, or Turistbyrå, in more than 300 cities and towns, which can be identified by the international "I" sign. They have multilingual staff, and can supply information about local sightseeing and sporting activities. Some are open during the summer only. About half of the tourist information offices sport a blue-and-yellow (rather than a green) "I" sign: these provide a more comprehensive service, with local and national information, and hotel booking systems (rumsförmedling or hotellcentral) that cover the whole country.

The main tourist offices are:
Stockholm Vistor Centre
Sergels Torg 3
Tel: 08 508 285 08
Email: touristinfo@stockholm.se
www.visitstockholm.com
This is the country's busiest tourist office. Run by the Stockholm Visitors Board, it can book tickets, tours and accommodation for you. It also publishes a guide to what is happening around the capital.
Göteborg
Kungsportsplatsen 2, 411 10 Göteborg
Tel: 031 368 42 00
www.goteborg.com
Gotland
Donnerska huset, Donners plats 1, Visby
Tel: 0498 20 17 00
Email: info@gotland.info
www.gotland.info
Lapland
Lars Janssonsgatan 17, 981 31 Kiruna
Tel: 0980 188 80
www.kirunalapland.se
Skåne and Malmö
Börshuset, Skeppsbron 2, 211 20Malmö
Tel: 040 34 12 00
http://visitskane.comwww.malmotown.com
Småland
Email: info@destinationsmaland.se
www.visitsmaland.se

Tour Operators

The brochures which list tour operators offering holidays in Sweden

are available to order or to download from www.visitsweden.com.

A selection of tour operators with interests in Sweden includes:

UK
Best Served Scandinavia
Tel: 020 7838 5956
Email: sales@best-served.co.uk
www.best-served.co.uk
Large range of packages, including city breaks, Göta Kanal cruises, cycling holidays and winter safaris.
Discover the World
Arctic House, 8 Bolters Lane, Banstead, Surrey SM7 2AR
Tel: 01737 214 250
Email: travel@discover-the-world.co.uk
www.discover-the-world.co.uk
Specialist in activity holidays, plus self-drive summer holidays and winter breaks to Lapland.
Nordic Experience
39 Crouch Street, Colchester, Essex CO3 3EN
Tel: 01206 708 888
Email: reservations@nordicexperience.co.uk
www.nordicexperience.co.uk
Offers Stockholm breaks, Ice Hotel packages, husky mushing and winter holidays.
Simply Sweden
The Poplars, Bridge Street, Brigg, Lincolnshire DN20 8NQ
Tel: 01427 700115
Email: info@simplysweden.co.uk
www.simplysweden.co.uk
Offers tailor-made Swedish holidays including Ice Hotel, city breaks, log cabins, rafting, etc.

US and Canada
There are numerous tour operators in the US, a complete list of which can be obtained from the Scandinavian Tourist Board in New York (see www.goscandinavia.com). The following is just a selection:
Five Stars of Scandinavia
Tel: 1-800 722 41 26
http://5stars-scandinavia.com
Nelson's Scandinavia
Tel: 1-800 542 16 89
www.nelsonsscandinavia.com
Nordic Saga Tours
Tel: 1-800 848 64 49
www.nordicsaga.com

Unique Holidays
Vildmark I Värmland
Tel: 0560-140 40
www.vildmark.se
One-, two-, five- and eight-day cruises on the Klarälven River. Not just any cruise, though: they assist you in building a log raft and provide camping equipment for your journey.

DENMARK

NORWAY

SWEDEN

FINLAND

Be prepared for all weathers.

Transport

Getting There

By Air
From the UK and Ireland
Scandinavian Airlines (SAS), Finnair and British Airways operate direct daily flights from London Heathrow to Stockholm Arlanda, and Norwegian Air fly there from London Gatwick. SAS also flies direct to Stockholm from Manchester, and Norwegian Air from Edinburgh. Ryanair also operates flights from London Stansted to Stockholm's Vasterås and Skavsta airports, both about an hour and 20 minutes' drive from the capital (to the northwest and southwest respectively), and also from London Gatwick to Skavsta. From London, SAS and British Airways fly daily to Göteborg (Gothenburg), as does Ryanair. Travelling time from the UK is around 2.5 hours.

From the US
Services between Stockholm and North America are operated by SAS, Finnair, Iceland Air, and by the US airlines Delta and American.

Airline offices in the UK and Ireland
British Airways, tel: 0844 493 0787; www.ba.com.
Finnair, tel: 0208 0 010101; www.finnair.com.
Norwegian Air, tel: 0330 828 0854; www.norwegian.com.
Ryanair, UK, tel: 0871 246 0000; www.ryanair.com.
Dublin, tel: 0818 30 30 30
SAS, tel: 0871 521 6000; www.flysas.com.

Airline offices in the US
Finnair, tel: 1-800 950 50 00; www.finnair.com.

Icelandair, tel: 1-800 223 55 00; www.icelandair.com.
SAS, tel: 1-800 221 23 50; www.flysas.com.

By Sea
There are no longer any ferries from the UK to Sweden. There are many ferry links from Denmark and Germany to Sweden, as well as from Sweden to Finland. However, you may travel as a passenger on the DFDS freight line between Immingham and Göteborg. For details contact: tel: +44 1469 55 26 16, http://freight.dfdsseaways.com.

By Train
The fastest rail route from the UK to Sweden is via the Eurostar service, through the Channel Tunnel from London St Pancras to Brussels, with onward trains to Copenhagen and then connecting services to Sweden.
For further information call and see:
Eurostar, tel: 03432 186 186; www.eurostar.com.
InterRail; www.interrail.eu.

By Car
With the 16km (10-mile) Öresund bridge connecting Copenhagen with Malmö, you can drive all the way to Sweden from Denmark. The drive from Copenhagen airport to Malmö takes about 45 minutes. For more information visit http://uk.oresundsbron.com.Getting Around

On Arrival
All three of Sweden's major international airports – Stockholm (Arlanda; www.arlanda.se), Göteborg (Landvetter; www.swedavia.se/landvetter) and Malmö (Sturup; www.sturup.se – have excellent links to their respective city centres. From Arlanda, passengers can use the Arlanda Express high-speed train which operates four times an hour to Stockholm Central Station in only 20 minutes (www.arlandaexpress.com). There are also frequent bus services from Arlanda's international and domestic terminals to the City Terminal at Klarabergsgatan above Central Station. In Göteborg and Malmö, coaches operate from the airport to the cities' Central Stations.
A connecting bus meets all Ryanair flights at Vasterås and Skavsta airports and goes directly to the Cityterminalen bus terminal in central Stockholm, taking around 1 hour and 20 minutes from both.
Taxis are always available. Get a price

for your destination before getting into the taxi – you are not obliged to take the cab at the head of the taxi rank. At Arlanda airport, the larger taxi companies – Taxi 020 (www.taxi020.se), Taxi Kurir (www.taxikurir.se) or Taxi Stockholm (www.taxistockholm.se) – offer fixed fares for rides into the city centre: these are usually cheaper than a metered taxi ride, particularly during rush hour.

By Air
Air travel is part of everyday life in a country as large as Sweden, and all major cities and towns are linked by an efficient network of services operated mainly by SAS. Stockholm alone has flights to almost 40 places within Sweden.
Cheap flights are available on selected domestic services all year, as well as standby flights for under-25s and special fares for senior citizens. But many of the best deals are during the summer peak season in July, when few business executives are travelling.
Air Passes, sold in conjunction with an international fare, allow up to six flights within Scandinavia at affordable prices. For more information call:
Malmö Aviation, www.malmoaviation.se
SAS, www.flysas.com

By Train
Swedish State Railways, or SJ (tel: 0771 75 75 75; www.sj.se), operate an efficient electrified network covering the entire country. The route from Trelleborg in the south to Riksgränsen in the far north is reckoned to be the longest continuous stretch of electrified rail line in the world.
Swedish trains run at a high frequency, particularly on the main trunk route linking Stockholm with Göteborg, on which there is an hourly service. The high-speed train X2000 travels at up to 200kph (125mph) and is a good choice if you want to travel long distances; the journey from Göteborg to Stockholm, for example, takes only three hours.

Rail Passes
Swedish State Railways offer a wide range of fares for both business and leisure travellers. Conditions and prices may depend on whether you buy your ticket in Sweden or abroad. A number of discount fares are available, including the following, which must be purchased outside Sweden:

InterRail Sweden Passes offer travellers who live in Europe but outside Sweden unlimited rail travel within Sweden. Check www. interrailnet.com for details.

Eurail Sweden (or Eurail Scandinavia) Passes offer travellers who live outside Europe unlimited rail travel within Sweden (or Scandinavia). Check www.eurail.com for details.

Resplus If you want to combine rail, bus and boat in one ticket, the best way is probably to buy a *Resplus* ticket that enables you to reach over 3,500 destinations within Sweden. For more information, see www.resplus.se.

To get a *förköpsbiljett* (reduced-rate ticket) in Sweden, you must book 7 days in advance. For more information, prices and bookings call: 0771 75 75 75.

Scenic Train Route
One very beautiful journey to take by train is the *Inlandsbanan* (Inland Railway), which runs for more than 1,300km (800 miles) down the spine of Sweden from Gällivare, north of the Arctic Circle, to Kristinehamn in the south. You can explore stretches of the route with point-to-point tickets; or purchase the Inlandsbane Kort, a card that is valid for 14 days, allowing you to stop and continue wherever you please within the time limit.

More information is available from Inlandsbanan, tel: 0771 53 53 53, www.inlandsbanan.se.

By Underground
Stockholm is justifiably proud of its underground railway, known as T-banan (the "T" stands for "tunnel" – all stations are identified by the "T" sign; http://sl.se). The T-banan is spotless, with 100 stations covering 108km (67 miles). Work on new extensions are to start in 2016.

The commuter trains *(pendeltåg)* take you very quickly to the suburbs of Stockholm as well as down to Nynäshamn, where you can board the ferry to the island of Gotland.

By Bus
Travelling by bus is usually cheap compared to rail, but travelling time is longer. There are weekend-only services on a number of key routes.

An efficient network of express bus services links all major towns and cities, operated mainly by:
Svenska Buss, tel: 0771 67 67 67; www.svenskabuss.se.
Swebus Express, tel: 0771 21 82 18; www.swebus.se.
Stockholm
Stockholm Transit Authority (www.sl.se) is the umbrella organisation that oversees the city's integrated transport system. The same travel tickets are used on the bus, the train and the underground systems. Tickets are used according to which of Stockholm's three transport zones you are travelling in – most visitors to the city will travel within Zone A. You are allowed to travel freely within one zone on the bus, train and underground for an hour on the same ticket.

It is no longer possible to buy tickets on the bus. Most bus stops have ticket machines that take cards and cash. The bus driver stamps your ticket when you board the bus and start your journey.

If you are intending to make several journeys within the city, it is cheaper to buy a set of 10 tickets, a one-, three- or seven-day travel card or the worthwhile *Stockholmskortet* tourist card, which gives free public transport in the Greater Stockholm area for a period of one, two, three or five days.

Göteborg
Göteborg has a superior tram system, as well as a good network of bus routes.

By Boat or Ferry
For a country that boasts about its 96,000 lakes and countless rivers and canals, water transport plays a surprisingly small part in Sweden's public transport system. The main ferry links the Baltic island of Gotland and has services from Nynäshamn and Oskarshamn. For more information check with the local tourist office or call Destination Gotland, tel: 0771 22 33 00; www.destinationgotland.se.

There are also innumerable commuter services in the Stockholm archipelago operated by the famous white boats of the Waxholm Steamship Company. In the summer, visitors can buy a range of discounted tickets which give unlimited travel on the Waxholm boats. For information call: 08 679 58 30; www.waxholmsbolaget.se.

Strömma Kanalbolaget runs cruises in the Stockholm archipelago: www.stromma.se.

By Taxi
Swedish taxis are usually efficient, but rely more on the telephone than being flagged down. In larger cities, a computer system gives instructions to drivers to indicate where the next person is to be picked up.

Fares are steep. There is a minimum charge, and the meter goes on as soon as the taxi arrives at your address. If you are late, the meter starts at the time you ordered the taxi – even a five-minute delay can be costly. The bigger firms accept credit cards. In Stockholm, some companies have a maximum fare for rides within the centre. This is good value when crossing the city or if there are traffic jams.

By Bicycle
Many of Sweden's towns are ideal for exploring by bike, with good cycle lanes. Stockholm has a public bike scheme operating between April and October from 6am until 10pm. You can rent and drop off bikes at some 100 stands throughout the city (tel: 077 444 24 24; www.citybikes.se). There is a similar bicycle rental system in Göteborg with 50 stations, and bikes are available from March until 31 December (tel: 031 227 227; www.goteborgbikes.se).

Cycling holidays are also popular in Sweden. The Sweden Trail *(Sverigeleden)* is the largest network of cycle paths, linking a great number of tourist centres and ports. Cykelspåret follows the entire Swedish coastline. And a particularly

The Øresund bridge links Denmark and Sweden.

DENMARK

NORWAY

SWEDEN

FINLAND

scenic and popular ride for cyclists is alongside the Göta Kanal.

Bikes can be hired in most places; just enquire at the local tourist office. Costs are per day or per week.

On Foot
Sightseeing
All three of Sweden's largest cities, Stockholm, Malmö and Göteborg, are compact enough to sightsee on foot. They are pedestrian-friendly and motorists always observe traffic lights; conversely, Swedish pedestrians are disciplined, and respect red lights even when there is not a car in sight.
Hitchhiking
This is officially discouraged, and in any case finding a lift can be difficult in the holiday season, when every Swedish car seems to be packed with children, baggage and camping gear.

Driving
Main Routes
Sweden's roads are uncrowded, with toll-free motorways covering more than 1,400km (870 miles), trunk roads some 80,500km (50,000 miles), and then there are thousands of kilometres of often picturesque byroads. The Öresund Bridge, Svinesund Bridge and Sundsvall Bridge have tolls. There are also congestion taxes in place in Stockholm and Göteborg; foreign-registered vehicles are exempt for now, but there are plans to tax foreign visitors too.
Rules of the Road
Traffic gives way to approaching traffic from the right, unless signs indicate otherwise, and gives way to traffic already on a roundabout.
Everyone must wear seat belts.
Headlights are obligatory both day and night.
Drivers are not required to call the police after accidents but must exchange names and addresses. If you do not stop at all you may be liable to a fine or imprisonment.
Sweden's drink-drive laws are strictly enforced, with spot checks, heavy fines, loss of licences and even prison sentences imposed. The blood/alcohol limit is 0.02, which equates to less than a can of beer.
Drivers must stop at pedestrian crossings when a person is crossing or indicates an intention to cross. Swedes often forget to indicate when changing lanes, so be careful.
Speed Limits
Motorways 110kph (70mph)
Dual carriageways 90kph (55mph)
Unsigned roads 70kph (43mph)
Built-up areas 50kph (31mph), or

30kph (19mph) around school areas.
Over the last few years, municipalities have been given more freedom to set new speed limits to suit local road conditions better, so you may also see speed-limit signs for 30, 40, 60, 80, 100 and 120kph.
Car Hire
All the major companies have desks at the airports.
Stockholm
Avis; tel: 0770 82 00 82; www.avis.se.
Budget; tel: 0770 11 00 12; www. budget.se.
Europcar; tel: 08 462 48 00; www. europcar.se.
Hertz; tel: 0771 21 12 12; www. hertz.se.

V

Visas and Passports

A valid passport entitles EU and North American visitors to stay for up to three months, and visas are not normally required. Sweden is part of the Schengen Area, and citizens of other Schengen countries are allowed to enter without passports. Immigration rarely causes problems in Sweden. If you arrive from another Scandinavian country, passports aren't usually checked at all. If you intend to stay longer than three months you will need to obtain a resident's permit, which you can do once you are in Sweden.

W

What to Read

Good books on Sweden are few and far between, but the best source of information on publications in English is the Swedish Institute, which itself publishes a good range of guides, available through its website.
Svenska Institutet
Slottsbacken 10, 103 91 Stockholm.
Tel: 08 453 78 00
www.si.se (also search under Sweden bookshop; www.swedenbookshop.com)

History
A History of the Swedish People by Vilhelm Moberg Vols I & II (University of Minnesota Press). Iconoclastic view of Sweden's history by one of the country's greatest authors.
Sweden: The Nation's History by Franklin D. Scott (Southern Illinois University Press). Swedish history from its beginnings.
Swedish History in Outline by Jörgen

Welbull (Swedish Institute).
The Vikings, Lords of the Seas by Yves Cohat (Thames & Hudson). History of the Vikings, with excellent colour photography.

Architecture
The Complete Guide to Architecture in Stockholm (Arkitektur Forlag AB). A guide to over 400 of the city's buildings, plus detailed maps.
Great Royal Palaces of Sweden by Göran Alm (M.T. Train/Scala Books). A dozen castles, palaces and pavilions belonging to Swedish royalty over the past 500 years.

See also the bookshop on the Swedish architecture website www. arkitektur.se.

Art and Design
Carl and Karin Larsson: Creators of the Swedish Style by Michael Snodin and Elisabet Stavenow-Hidemark (eds). A profile of two of Sweden's most influential designers.
A History of Swedish Art by Mereth Lindgren, Louise Lyberg, Birgitta Sandström and Anna Greta Wahlberg (Bokförlaget Signum). A bird's-eye view of Swedish painting, sculpture and architecture.
The Swedish Room by Lars Sjöberg and Ursula Sjöberg (Frances Lincoln Limited). Some of Sweden's most classic interiors.

Food
The Swedish Kitchen: a Culinary Journey by Lennart Hagerfors (Norstedts). A cookbook by one of the best-known chefs in Sweden, with 198 modern Swedish recipes.
The Swedish Table by Helene Henderson (University of Minnesota Press). A native Swede updates traditional dishes to suit a more modern palate.

Fiction
The Girl with the Dragon Tattoo, *The Girl Who Played with Fire* and *The Girl Who Kicked the Hornets' Nest* by Stieg Larsson. Larsson's best-selling Millennium trilogy is currently taking the world by storm, and Hollywood film versions are out. A sequel to the trilogy from Swedish writer David Lagercrantz called *That Which Does Not Kill* is due to hit the shelves in August 2015.
The Wonderful Adventures of Nils and *The Further Adventures of Nils* by Selma Lagerlöv. Captivating stories about a boy who flies around Sweden on a goose, have made Lagerlöv one of the nation's most popular children's authors.

SWEDEN EATING OUT

RESTAURANTS AND CAFES

CHOOSING A RESTAURANT

Sweden, once known as the land of *husmanskost* (homely fare), is currently enjoying a culinary renaissance, thanks to a new generation of chefs who know how to give a sophisticated twist to classic Swedish dishes such as reindeer, elk, lingonberries, salmon and herring.

Eating out has become increasingly popular, but can seem expensive, particularly if you drink a lot of wine or beer. Stockholm has more than 700 restaurants covering at least 30 national cuisines: eight of them flaunt Michelin stars. Göteborg is particularly good for seafood, and with four Michelin-starred restaurants, is another of Europe's top culinary destinations. Malmö claims to have more restaurants per head than any other Swedish city.

For the latest top-notch restaurants, consult The White Guide (www.whiteguide.se; in Swedish only),

the bible to fine dining in Sweden.

For travellers on a tight budget there is no shortage of inexpensive places to eat. Look for the *dagens rätt* (dish of the day), a lunch that usually includes bread, a simple salad and a soft drink for around 75Skr. And fast-food outlets are everywhere. The ubiquitous *korvkiosk* sells grilled chicken, sausages, hamburgers and *tunnbrödsrulle* (a parcel of mashed potato, sausage and ketchup or mustard wrapped in soft bread).

The Swedes generally eat early. Restaurants start serving lunch at about 11am, and some small hotels, particularly in country areas, serve evening meals around 6pm. In the cities you can eat much later. Many of the top restaurants in Stockholm close in July for staff holidays.

RESTAURANT LISTINGS

Below is a selection of restaurants around the country. Restaurants are

grouped by area with Stockholm first, and are listed alphabetically.

WHAT TO DRINK

There is no difficulty in ordering a drink with your meal, although the stronger Class III beer (*starköl*) may not be available in restaurants and bars until noon. However, alcohol is expensive in Sweden due to high taxes.

You can buy strong alcohol only through branches of the State-controlled monopoly Systembolaget (www.systembolaget.se), generally open Mon–Fri 10am–6pm and Sat 10am–1pm (closes early the day before a public holiday).

The minimum age for buying alcohol is 20; you may be asked for proof of your age if you are in your early 20s.

Some bars and cafés advertise a reduced-price happy hour. This may be at any time of the day, but is worth finding as it can bring the cost of half a litre of lager down to half the price charged in nightclubs.

STOCKHOLM

Den Gyldene Freden
Österlånggatan 51
Tel: 08 24 97 60
www.gyldenefreden.se
Dating from 1722, and with an atmosphere almost unchanged since then, this is the classical restaurant in Stockholm where you'll combine excellent cuisine with a historical environment. **$$$**
Eriks Bakfickan
Fredrikshovsgatan 4
Tel: 08 66 01 599
www.eriks.se

A longstanding and reliable restaurant, Bakfickan serves traditional Swedish dishes.
$$$
Esperanto
Kungstensgatan 2
Tel: 08 696 23 23
www.esperantorestaurant.se
Another of Stockholm's fabulous restaurants, Esperanto gained its first Michelin star in 2007, and tables have been among the city's most wanted ever since. Two tasting menus are on offer. **$$$**

Gondolen
Stadsgården 6
Tel: 08 641 70 90
www.eriks.se
Highly recommended. Eating here is a real Stockholm experience. Offers excellent traditional Swedish cuisine with a great view over the city. Those on a tighter budget can enjoy the same view at the bar. A Stockholm institution. **$$$**
Hermans
Fjällgatan 23B
Tel: 08 643 94 80
www.hermans.se

One for vegetarian visitors – and those who love beautiful views. There's no menu here: Hermans serves all-you-can-eat organic veggie buffets at lunchtime and in the evening. Come hungry. Garden for eating alfresco in summer. **$**

Indian Garden
Västgötagatan 18Tel: 08 849 498
Warm, cosy and welcoming, and with an ever-present crowd that testifies to the quality of its curries and baltis. **$$**

Mathias Dahlgren
Grand Hotel, Södra Blasieholmshamnen 6
Tel: 08 679 35 84
www.mathiasdahlgren.com
The eponymous masterchef uses the best Swedish ingredients to create elegant, unusual, melt-in-the-mouth dishes in his two restaurants at the Grand Hotel. Matbaren has one Michelin star; Matsalen has two. Superb. **$$$**

Operakällaren
Operan (Royal Opera House), Karl XII:s Torg
Tel: 08 676 58 01
www.operakallaren.se
Arguably Stockholm's best-known restaurant and worth visiting for the fantastic decor alone. The lovely Opera Bar also serves food, in a slightly more low-key setting. **$$$**

Pelikan
Blekingegatan 40
Tel: 08 556 09 090
www.pelikan.se
A Stockholm institution, this bar-restaurant has been going for well over a century. Food is traditional Swedish (meatballs, veal schnitzel, and classic appetiser "SOS" or "smör, ost, sill" – butter, cheese and herring), all served in a high-ceilinged hall. **$$**

Pontus
Brunnsgatan 1Tel: 08 545 273 00
www.pontusfrithiof.com
A highly-praised restaurant with high-concept cuisine and a chic, cosmopolitan décor. Spread out over

three floors, there is an oyster bar, a cocktail bar and a dining room. Dishes also come in three sizes. Many vegetarian options. **$$$**

Sturehof
Stureplan 2
Tel: 08 440 57 30
www.sturehof.com
Super-trendy spot serving stylish Swedish food, with the emphasis on seafood. Has a popular bar and live music. **$$–$$$**

Cafés

Café Blå Porten
Djurgårdsvägen 64
Tel: 08 663 87 59
www.blaporten.com
Unpretentious café with good cakes and a light food menu.

Café String
Nytorgsgatan 38
Tel: 08 714 85 14
http://cafestring.se
Café with hip 1950s and 60s decor that is all for sale.

Chokladkoppen
Stortorget 20
Tel: 08 20 31 70
www.chokladkoppen.se
A small and cosy café, with outdoor seating in one of the best people-watching spots in Stockholm.

Fåfängan
Klockestapelsbacken 3
Tel: 08 642 99 00
http://fafangan.se/
A visit here is essential in the summer if you can manage the long, steep walk up – the view over Stockholm is fantastic.

Flickorna Helin Voltaire
Rosendalsvägen 14, Djurgården
Tel: 08 664 51 08
www.helinvoltaire.com
Housed in a twisty, fairytale-castle building on Djurgården, this is the place for coffee and delicious cake after a visit to the Vasa Museum.

Konditori Sturekatten

Riddargatan 4
Tel: 08 611 16 12
www.sturekatten.se
Classic, cosy café, worth a visit for the old-fashioned decor alone. Home-baked bread and pastries are on offer.

Rosendals Trädgård
Rosendalsterassen 12
Tel: 08 545 812 70
www.rosendalstradgard.se
This café within the garden by Rosendal Palace, on Djurgården, attracts hordes of visitors in fine weather for its home-baked goodies, fresh from the bakery's wood-fired oven.

Taxinge Slottscafé
Näsby 52, Nykvarn
Tel: 0159 701 14
www.taxingeslott.se/slottscafe
Located a 45-minute drive south of Stockholm (or a four-hour weekend steamboat ride for the more romantically inclined), this beautiful castle's café features a buffet of around 60 different cakes and buns.

Around Stockholm

Mariefred
Gripsholms Värdshus & Hotel
Kyrkoplan 1
Tel: 0159 347 50
www.gripsholms-vardshus.se
Sweden's oldest inn has a first-class restaurant that specialises in local produce, international cooking as well as fine wines. **$$–$$$**

Norrköping
Fiskmagasinet
Skolgatan 1b
Tel: 011 13 45 60
www.fiskmagasinet.se
This stylish place, with rustic wooden floors and creamy seating, specialises in melt-in-the-mouth fish dishes – everything from pickled herring to fresh lobster. **$$–$$$**

SOUTHERN SWEDEN

Helsingborg

Pålsjö Matbar
Drottninggatan 151
Tel: 042 149 730
http://palsjomatbar.seFor beautifully presented Swedish dishes. **$$**

Kalmar

HK Hamnkrogen
Skeppsbrogatan 30
Tel: 0480 41 10 20
http://hkhamnkrogen.se
Gourmet restaurant with a sea view. **$$**

Malmö

Gamla Brogatan
Brogatan 12
Tel: 040 62 00 301
www.gamlabrogatan.se
Popular among the famous. Organic Swedish food and live music. **$$–$$$**

Restaurang Johan P
Hjulhamnsgatan 5Tel: 040 97 18 18
www.johanp.nu
A rather stark, white-tiled setting, but Johan P is considered the best place in Malmö for fish dishes. **$$**

Salt & Brygga

Sundspromenaden 7
Tel: 040 611 59 40
www.saltobrygga.se
A little way out of the centre, close to the Turning Torso, this eco-conscious restaurant uses local organic produce wherever possible in its deeply tasty dishes. **$$–$$$**

Skeppsbron 2
Börshuset
Tel: 040 30 62 02
www.skeppsbron2.com
Modern and inventive cuisine in a building overlooking the sea. **$$**

Visby

Bakfickan
Stora Torget 1
Tel: 0498 27 18 07
www.bakfickan-visby.nu
Seafood restaurant serving excellent
dishes. Warm, cosy atmosphere. **$–$$**

Donners Brunn
Donners Plats
Tel: 0498 27 10 90
www.donnersbrunn.nu
Friendly gourmet restaurant with the
"Best Lamb Chef" in Sweden. **$$$**

Isola Bella
Södra Kyrkogatan 20
Tel: 0498 21 87 87; www.isolabella.se
An airy Italian restaurant with a long
pizza menu. Friendly service. **$$**

Värdshuset Lindgården
Strandgatan 26
Tel: 0498 21 87 00
www.lindgarden.com
A particularly charming restaurant
for a summer evening, thanks to the
lovely garden. The gourmet Gotland
menu features regional specialities,
such as roast lamb. **$$$**

WEST COAST

Göteborg

Café Husaren
Haga Nygata 28
Tel: 031 136 378
www.cafehusaren.se
A classic café with a beautiful
19th-century glass roof. Serves the
world's largest cinnamon buns! **$**

La Cucina Italiana
Skånegatan 33
Tel: 031 16 63 07
www.lacucinaitaliana.nu
A high-end Italian restaurant with an
underlying gourmet concept. **$$–$$$**

Fiskekrogen
Lilla Torget 1
Tel: 031 10 10 05
www.fiskekrogen.com
Best fish restaurant in town; exciting
wines at good prices. **$$$**

Heaven 23
Hotel Gothia Towers, Mässans Gata 24
Tel: 031 75 08 805
www.heaven23.se
Excellent food, with city views to
match. The king-size shrimp sandwich
is their best-seller. **$$–$$$**

M2 – Magnus & Magnus
Magasinsgatan 8
Tel: 031 13 30 00
www.magnusmagnus.se
An intimate restaurant: the candlelit
courtyard is a favourite summer
eating place. Good value for such
high-quality food. **$$–$$$**

Trädgår'n
Nya Allén 11
Tel: 031 10 20 80
www.tradgarn.se
Exotic award-winning international
restaurant. Also has live music
performances. **$$$**

Tvåkanten
Kungsportsavenyn 27
Tel: 031 18 21 15
www.tvakanten.se
Traditional Swedish dishes are given
the contemporary treatment at this
classy restaurant. The Sunday roast
dinner is particularly good value. **$$$**

Halmstad

Pio & Company
Storgatan 37
Tel: 035 21 06 69
www.pio.se
Italian dishes and traditional Swedish
food, planked steak a classic. **$$**

Tanumshede

Tanums Gestgifveri
Apoteksvägen 7
Tel: 0525 290 10
www.hoteltanum.se
Traditional Swedish food. Fish and
oysters feature high on the menu. **$$$**

GREAT LAKES AND DALARNA

Dalarna

Värdshuset Dala Floda
Badvägen 6, Dala Floda (40km/25 miles
from Borlänge)
Tel: 0241 220 50
www.dalafloda-vardshus.se
Excellent, well-known inn/restaurant,
serving perfect summer meals
using home-grown ingredients. Best
experienced as part of a half- or full-
board package. **$$–$$$**

Two-Michelin-star Matsalen.

Falun

Banken Två Rum & Kök
Stadshusgränd 2
Tel: 023 260 25
www.bankenfalun.se
This elegant, award-winning
restaurant with Art Nouveau interior,
close to the main square, is Falun's
best. Serves traditional Swedish and
gourmet food. Impeccable service.
$$–$$$

Jönköping

Mäster Gudmunds Källare
Kapellgatan 2
Tel: 036 10 06 40
www.mastergudmund.se
Atmospheric medieval cellar-
restaurant, focusing on simple home
cooking at a decent price.
$$

Restaurang Hemma
Smedjegatan 36
Tel: 036 10 01 15
www.restauranghemma.se
Jönköping's best restaurant,
serving well-rounded, high-class
meals without being overly fussy.
Vegetarians are well catered for.
$$–$$$

PRICE CATEGORIES

Price categories are per person for
an average three-course meal,
excluding drinks but with tax:
$ = under 300Skr
$$ = 300–500Skr
$$$ = over 500Skr

Karlstad

Lilla Martina Bar & Bistro
Hamngatan 22
Tel: 054 18 65 00
www.lillamartina.se
A tiny restaurant with a short-but-sweet menu that shows off the kitchen's French-inspired dishes.
$$–$$$

Tiffanys
Västra Torggatan 19
Tel: 054 15 33 83
www.tiffanys.se
Stylish restaurant specialising in local fish and game. **$$–$$$**

Leksand

Åkerblads Hotell & Gästgiveri
Sjögattu 2, Tällberg (13km/8 miles from Leksand)
Tel: 0247 508 00
www.akerblads.se
Romantic lakeside hotel serving everything from morning coffee and cakes to a seven-course tasting menu. Traditional Swedish fare (with the odd surprise!) and a good-value weekend smörgåsbord. **$$–$$$**

Söderköping

Romantik Hotel Söderköpings Brunn
Skönbergagatan 35
Tel: 0121 109 00
www.soderkopingsbrunn.se
Fine Swedish cooking, serving very traditional dishes – pea soup, meatballs, venison. **$$$**

Vadstena

Restaurang Munkklostret
Lasarettsgatan 5
Tel: 0143 315 30
www.klosterhotel.se
Part of a medieval monastery, set into green parkland close to Lake Vättern. The atmospheric hotel restaurant serves gourmet meals made from local organic produce. With a lovely summer terrace. **$$$**

Vadstena Valven
Storgatan 18
Tel: 0143 123 40
www.valven.se
In a medieval vaulted cellar, Valven serves excellent food using local ingredients. **$$**

CENTRAL SWEDEN

Åre

Villa Tottebo
Parkvägen 1
Tel: 0647 506 20
www.villatottebo.se
Pleasant restaurant serving mostly local products, with succulent reindeer a speciality. **$$$**

Östersund

Brunkullans Brasserie
Postgränd 5
Tel: 063 10 14 54
http://brunkullanbrasserie.se
A beguiling little bar-restaurant with some good traditional dishes.
$$

Innefickan Restaurant and Bar
Postgränd 11
Tel: 063 12 90 99
www.innefickan.se
Former warehouse, now turned into a successful bar and restaurant serving Swedish and Mediterranean-influenced food. **$$–$$$**

Mikado
Infanterig. 12
Tel: 063 209 08
www.mikadosweden.com
Beautifully presented Japanese food created by chef Tsukasa Takeuchi.
$$–$$$

Sundsvall

7 Kryddor
Trädgårdsgatan 25
Tel: 060 61 50 80
www.7kryddor.com
For a touch of spice, head to this Turkish restaurant. The barbecued meat dishes are recommended; also good for vegetarian meze. **$$**

Saffran
Nybrogatan 25
Tel: 060 17 11 07
www.saffran.nu
Small, cosy Spanish restaurant with tapas bar. Very reasonable prices and a varied menu. **$–$$**

NORTHERN SWEDEN

Jukkasjärvi

Icehotel Restaurant
Marknadsvägen 63
Tel: 0980 668 00
www.icehotel.com
The excellent Ice hotel restaurant specialises in local produce such as reindeer, grouse, char and cloudberries. The cheaper Homestead restaurant is just down the road. **$$$**

Kiruna

Arctic Thai & Grill
Foraregatan 18
Tel: 0980 681 58
http://arcticthai.se
Fresh Thai food at reasonable prices, so the place is usually very busy. **$**

Luleå

Cafe Tallkotten
Luleå Stadshotel, Storgatan 15
Tel: 0920 27 40 20
www.tallkotten.se
Busy hotel restaurant with an Italian menu. **$$$**

Tärnaby

Sånninggården Restaurang & Pensionat
Dearna Klippen, Hemavan (25km/15 miles from Tärnaby)
Tel: 0954 330 00
www.sanninggarden.com
Beautifully located restaurant, specialising in local game and poultry. The special wild menu (featuring elk, grouse, beaver, boar and reindeer) must be booked three days ahead.
$$–$$$

Umeå

Rex Bar & Grill
Rådhustorget
Tel: 090 70 60 50
www.rexbar.com
Trendy, stylish bar and restaurant mixing local produce with inspiration from the Med. Inside the Town Hall.
$–$$$

Restaurant Sävargården
Gammlia
Tel: 090 77 02 22
www.savargarden.se
Patronised by royalty, Sävargården is open at lunchtimes only, when you can choose between a grand buffet spread or several set menus.
$–$$

Sjöbris
Kajen 10
Tel: 090 77 71 23
www.sjobris.nu
Enjoy the sjöbris (sea breeze) on board this summer fishing-boat restaurant, and a light meal or buffet spread. Live blues on Thursdays.
$–$$

FINLAND A-Z

A HANDY SUMMARY OF PRACTICAL INFORMATION

A

Acommodation

Choosing a Hotel

Hotels throughout Finland are clean and well equipped, though expensive. One can find bargains at the chain hotels (generally up to 60 percent of standard prices) at weekends, and in summer when they lose their business and conference trade. A generous buffet breakfast is often included in the rate. There are also elegant historic villas which now operate as hostelries.

Budget accommodation includes youth and family hostels, farmhouses, guesthouses, family villages, camping and various forms of self-catering. During the summer holidays, some student residences become Summer Hotels, opening on 1 June.

Local tourist offices and booking centres will provide up-to-date prices, including details of weekend and summer discounts. General information on accommodation is available from the Finnish Tourist Board in your home country, or from the head office in Helsinki. For more information see www.visithelsinki.fi. For details of youth hostels:
Hostelling International Finland
Yrjönkatu 38B 15
Tel: 09 565 7150
www.hihostels.fi

Hotel Chains

Finland has many large hotel chains of its own, as well as foreign ones. Scandic (www.scandichotels. fi), Sokos (www.sokos.fi) and Cumulus (www.cumulus.fi) offer fairly comfortable standard services in most big towns.

Activities

Outdoor Sports

Finland is known as a sporting nation, and has won more Olympic medals per head than any other country. Devotion to training is constant; it is not unusual on a hot summer's day to see squadrons of muscular youths out on roller-skis to make sure they do not lose their touch for the coming winter.

Canoeing

Canoeing is popular in the Lakelands region. Canoe and kayak rental (in the Vuosaari district, near Helsinki) is possible from:
Natura Viva/Vuosaari Paddling Centre
Conference Hotel Rantapuisto, Ramsinniementie 14, 00980 Helsinki.
Tel: 010 292 4030
www.seakayakfinland.com

Cycling

Bicycling is big in Finland. The countryside is ideal for cyclists, dead flat on the west coast leading to gently rolling hill areas. For more information on cycling in Finland, routes and maps visit www.pyoraillensuomessa.fi.

Hiking

Thanks to its pristine forests and lakes, and freedom to roam policy, Finland offers wonderful hiking and backpacking opportunities. Finland's national parks are all designated hiking areas. For more information on destinations and facilities visit www.outdoors.fi.

Husky Safaris

Explore Lapland's wilderness in traditional style on a husky-drawn sled, or a reindeer sleigh, or opt for the more contemporary mode of transport and explore on a snowmobile. For more information and suggestions for winter adventures, visit www.onlyinlapland. com/winter-fun.

Sailing

With its tens of thousands of lakes, and 4,830km (3,000 miles) of coastline, summer sailing opportunities abound in Finland, though the season is short. The most important sailing area is the Åland archipelago, the largest island group in the Baltic. Most harbours have guest marinas where one can dock for reasonable overnight fees.

Skiing

Finns are particularly famous as cross-country runners and skiers, as well as ski-jumpers. You'll find facilities for any of these sports excellent; in most major urban areas there are maps of the non-auto paths set aside for such pastimes. Ask for the Ulkoilukartta (outdoor map) from tourist boards.

One can ski cross-country anywhere in Finland, but Lapland is a favourite spot for this very Nordic sport, as well as for downhill skiing (try to avoid school holiday weeks). Unlike Norway and even Sweden, Finland has very little in the way of mountains, except in the far north, where the Lappish hills, the highest over 1,400 metres (4,000ft), are called tunturi.

There are many participant cross-country ski events as well; information is available from **Finnish Ski Trek**

Association (Suomen Latu), Radiokatu 20, 00240 Helsinki; tel: 044 722 6300; www.suomenlatu.fi. Another useful site is www.ski.fi.

Other Sports
For information on any sport in Finland, contact the **Finnish Sports Federation (Suomen Urheilu ja Liikunta)**, Radiokatu 20, 7th floor, 00240 Helsinki; tel: 09 3481 21; www.slu.fi.

Spectator Sports
There is a near endless list of spectator sports in Finland, but a shortlist of the most popular must include ski-jumping, regatta sailing and ice hockey.

Summer
One of the biggest sailing events of the year is the Hanko Regatta, which takes place in early July off Finland's south coast. Kotka also sponsors a yearly Tall Ships event. The biggest inland sailing regatta is on Lake Päijänne, also in July. Details are available from the **Finnish Sailing Federation**, Westendinkatu 7, Espoo; tel: 020 796 4200; www.spv.fi.
Before mid-June is the annual **Finlandia Canoe Relay**, held in the large Lakeland region – the venue changes annually, and it is geared for exercise and good fun rather than competition. It lasts six days and covers over 545km (350 miles), with day and night action. See www.suomimeloo.fi for details.

Winter
Lahti, about 105km (65 miles) north of Helsinki, is the best place to watch ski-jumping.
For winter spectator sports, the **Finlandia Ski Race** (Hiihto)

Welcome to Moomin World.

in mid-February is one of the top events. This 60km (37-mile) event attracts the best Finnish skiers and has ample spectator opportunities: www.finlandiahiihto.fi.

C

Children

Attractions
Heureka, the Finnish Science Centre (in Tikkurila, 15 minutes by train from downtown Helsinki), has exhibitions, a planetarium/cinema and hands-on experiments, and opens daily year-round. Tel: 09 85799; www.heureka.fi.
Moomin World, theme park based on the popular Moomin characters created by Tove Jansson. Situated 16km (10 miles) from Turku; daily year-round. Tel: 02 511 1111; www.muumimaailma.fi.
There are several good spots in the Lakeland region:
The Snow Centre, Messilä, in Hollola near Lahti, features many supervised activities, including pony riding and (in winter) skiing. Tel: 03 860 11; www.messila.fi.
The Musta and Valkea Ratsu Dollshouse and Puppet Theatre is north from Hollola, Onkiniementie 222, 19230 Onkiniemi. Tel: 03 718 6959; www.mustavalkearatsu.fi.
Santa Claus's Village, Rovaniemi, near the Arctic Circle. Rumour has it Santa stops off here when travelling from his secret hideaway. Daily year-round. www.santaclausvillage.info.
In Finland, almost every hotel has a list of English-speaking babysitters who can look after children.

Climate

Finland has cold winters and fairly warm summers. In July, the south has similar temperatures to southern England, with less rain and more sunshine. The hottest months are July–Aug, when temperatures average 18°C (65°F); the coldest are Jan–Feb, averaging –4°C (25°F). In south and central Finland snow settles at the start of Dec and melts mid–late Apr (or May in the forests). In the north snow comes about five weeks earlier and ends about three weeks later.

What to Bring
The best advice on packing for Finland is to bring layers of clothes, no matter what the season. While it is famous for icy winters – when gloves, long underwear, hats, woollen

CLIMATE CHART

Helsinki

■ Maximum temperature
□ Minimum temperature
— Rainfall

tights and socks, and several layers of cotton topped by wool and something waterproof are recommended – Finland is less known for its very sunny temperate summers. As a result, sun block and a sunhat are as essential at these times as warm clothes are in the winter. When travelling to northern Finland in summer, bring a strong mosquito repellent, although local brands seem to work better.

Culture

Museums
Art and design dominate the museum scene, with the greatest variety of venues in Helsinki. Most museums close on Monday. Be prepared that many museums also close for public holidays.

Classical Music and Opera
Most larger cities have a steady itinerary of concerts throughout the year, but music festivals abound in Finland in summer, and many of these are staged in stunning settings. The most famous of these are held in July: the Savonlinna Opera Festival at Olavinlinna Castle in eastern Finland (www.operafestival.fi), and the Kuhmo Chamber Music Festival, also in eastern Finland (www.kuhmofestival.fi).
In 2011, the brand new Helsinki Music Centre (Musiikkitalo) opened its impressive new residence for the Helsinki Radio Symphony and Helsinki Philharmonic orchestras, and the Sibelius Academy (www.musiikkitalo.fi). The National Opera House (Oopera and ballet) is also nearby (www.opera.fi).

Helsinki Events
The Helsinki Festival (Juhlaviikot) begins at the end of August and

The Pori Jazz Festival at Tampere.

extends into the first week of September. It features broad-ranging programmes with artists from Finland and abroad, set at different venues around the city. It is kicked off (around 26 Aug) with the city-wide Night of the Arts, which goes on late into the morning around town at all sorts of venues, from museums and art galleries to nightclubs and parks. Information from: Festival Office (at Lasipalatsi), Mannerheimintie 22–24, tel: 09 6126 5100; www.helsingin juhlaviikot.fi.

Try the weekday evening series of concerts at the unique Church in the Rock (Temppeliaukio) in Töölö, Helsinki.

Turku Events

Turku is a lively musical city, and 2011 was even more exceptional when it reigned as European Capital of Culture, jointly with Tallinn. One can enjoy performances by the Turku City Orchestra, a weekly concert series in the Sibelius Museum, as well as events in the cathedral and the castle.

The **Turku Music Festival** (Konserttitalo; Aninkaistenkatu 9; tel: 02 262 0812; www.tmj.fi), held in mid-August, is the oldest in Finland. It hosts world premiere performances of operas, traditional symphonies and chamber music events, as well as more intimate jazz programmes with top international artists.

Tampere Events

Tampere has always had its share of music. Since 1975 the city has held an international Vocal Music Festival each year. The Tampere Biennale (Tullikamarinaukio 2; tel: 03 5656 6172), started in 1986, is a festival of new Finnish music, arranged in cooperation with the Association of Finnish Composers. The city also hosts the Tampere Jazz Happening; for more

information on Tampere festivals see http://tamperemusicfestivals.fi.

Since the opening of the grand Tampere Hall and Congress Centre in 1990 (www.tamperehall.com), attendance has soared, as well as its reputation for excellent acoustics and world-class musical events. Tampere holds numerous concerts in its cathedral, churches and halls.

Jazz, Rock and Folk

The most famous of Finland's jazz festivals is **PoriJazz** (www.porijazz.fi).

In Tampere there is an annual jazz festival called Jazz Happening (see above Tampere events).

Joensuu, once known for its annual song festival, now hosts Ilosaari, a 3-day rock concert event in mid-July that attracts top Finnish and international bands, and around 25,000 delirious fans: www.ilosaarirock.fi.

There is also Ruisrock on the island of Ruissalo in Turku (www.ruisrock.fi), Finland's oldest and highly popular rock festival.

Traditional music remains popular, and the Kaustinen Folk Music Festival in western Finland is one the oldest and largest of Nordic festivals, held mid-July (http://kaustinen.net).

Theatre

Helsinki

The Savoy Theatre has been a fixture in Helsinki since 1937 (www.savoyteatteri.fi). Situated in a stately Functionalist building that seats 700, it was once Finland's largest cinema, until it was converted to a concert hall in 1987. These days you can see top international artists in music, dance and theatre performances. Finnish National Theatre (www.kansallis teatteri.fi) and Svenska Teatern (www.svenskateatern.fi) in Helsinki both enjoy long traditions of performance in, respectively,

Finnish and Swedish. The buildings themselves are worth peeking into, or at least enjoy the outdoor terrace of the Svenska Teatern where Esplanadi meets Mannerheimintie.

Tampere

Tampere rivals Helsinki for year-round theatrical events but, again, the difficulty for a visitor is language. At the Pyynikki Summer Theatre (reservations essential; tel: 0600 900 900; www.pyynikinkesateatteri.fi) you can see original and imaginative plays from mid-June to mid-August, with synopses in English. This is particularly worthwhile if you want to enjoy the setting at the edge of Lake Pyhäjärvi and its amazing revolving auditorium which turns 360 degrees. The Tampere Theatre Festival (tel: 03 222 8536; www.teatterikesa.fi) in August includes many international companies which produce plays in their own languages. A fringe festival called Off Tampere takes place at the same time, with its own offbeat programme.

Turku

Plays performed are of a high standard but rarely in languages other than Finnish or Swedish. In winter, there is the Turku City Theatre on the bank of the River Aura and the Swedish Theatre on the corner of the market place – the oldest theatre in Finland still in use. Summer festivals sometimes offer an English-speaking production.

Cinema

Finns do not dub foreign films, and you can enjoy as good a selection of movies here as in any other European city of moderate size.

Helsinki has two big cinema complexes, the 10-screen Kinopalatsi at Kaisaniemenkatu 2 and the 14-screen Tennispalatsi at Salomonkatu 15, both belong to the Finnkino chain (www.finnkino. fi). These feature mainly Finnish films with some US blockbusters and attract a younger, noisy crowd who like to use their phones during the film. There are several smaller art-house cinemas around the city centre, which show a wider range of independent and quality mainstream titles. Film director Aki Kaurismaki owns Kino-Andorra (Eerikinkatu 11; http://andorra.fi), which attracts an eclectic group of film buffs who come for new and old classics. Next door at No. 15 is Orion, which operates as both film archive and cinema.

Film showings begin early and run until 9pm (and up to 11pm). Seats are reserved at the time you buy the tickets, and box offices usually open 30–45 minutes before show time but at some cinemas may be purchased even earlier.

Tampere has a cinema centre, Finnkino Plevna, in the Finlayson area (Itäinen katu 4).

In Turku, Kinopalatsi is opposite the Market Square at Kauppiaskatu 11 and usually has something in English. There is a multi-screen theatre in the Hansa Shopping Centre on Eerikinkatu.

Customs Regulations

The following items may be brought into Finland.

Cigarettes/Tobacco

Visitors over 17 years of age from non-EU countries may bring in 200 cigarettes, 50 cigars or 250g (1–2lb) of tobacco products duty-free.

Alcohol

Visitors from non-EU countries aged 20 or over can bring in 16 litres of beer, 2 litres of other mild alcohol (drinks containing not more than 22 percent by volume of alcohol) and 1 litre of strong alcohol (spirits). For visitors of 18–19 years of age, the quantity limit is the same, but must not include strong alcohol. EU residents are allowed to bring into Finland any amounts of cigarettes and alcohol as long as they are for personal use.

D

Disabled Travellers

For disabled people, travelling should not pose tremendous problems in Finland. Most newer buildings have access for disabled people, in terms of ramps and lifts. With careful planning, transport should also go smoothly; when ordering a taxi, specify your needs (wheelchair is pyörätuoli). The Helsinki metro is accessible for wheelchair users, but other forms of public transport may be a bit more problematic, although some city buses "kneel", making it easier to board.

E

Embassies and Consulates

Australian Consulate
Aurorankatu 11A 4, Helsinki

Tel: 010 42 04 492
Canada
Pohjoisesplanadi 25B, Helsinki
Tel: 09 228 530
Irish
Erottajankatu 7A, Helsinki
Tel: 09 682 4240
www.embassyofireland.fi
UK
Itäinen Puistotie 17, Helsinki
Tel: 09 2286 5100
US
Itäinen Puistotie 14A, Helsinki
Tel: 09 616 250

Emergencies

**Ambulance, rescue services, fire department and police: 112
Police: 10022**

G

Gay and Lesbian Travellers

Finns have a tolerant attitude to gay and lesbian travellers, and the image of the notorious fetish artist Tom of Finland has become internationally iconic. Helsinki's scene has picked up in recent years, and there was even a leather convention held a few years ago. Same-sex marriages are to be legalised in 2017. For general information, contact SETA, a non-governmental gay rights organisation. Pasilanraitio 5; www.seta.fi.

(See listings for bars and nightclubs under Helsinki.)

H

Health and Medical Care

You'll have little to worry about healthwise in Finland. However, you may have an uncomfortable time with the mosquitoes in northern and central parts in July and August. Ask your GP about appropriate mosquito treatment before you go and enquire at chemists in Finland about the most effective repellent.

Finland's medical facilities have an excellent reputation worldwide. The country has reciprocal health arrangements with other EU members, so visitors are entitled to the same treatment as Finns (this means you may have to pay some fees). British nationals should take a European Health Insurance Card (EHIC), which you can apply for online (www.ehic.org.uk), by phone (0845 606 2030) or by post (form available from any post office in the UK).

Hospitals

If you need medical treatment, almost any health clinic (terveysasema) or hospital (sairaala) will treat you for a nominal fee or will bill your insurance firm. All doctors speak English. Casualty is generally called Ensiapu. Visitors needing hospital care in Helsinki should contact the following.
For surgery and medicine:
Meilahti Hospital, Haartmaninkatu 4, Helsinki. Tel: 09 4711 for all emergencies, or the 24-medical advice hotline 09 310 10023.
For serious accidents:
Töölö Hospital, Topeliuksenkatu 5, Helsinki. Tel: 09 471 87383.
For 24-hour private medical care:
Mehiläinen, 3rd floor, Runeberginkatu 47a, Helsinki. Tel: 010 414 0200; www.mehilainen.fi.

Pharmacies

A pharmacy is called apteekki. There is at least one open late at night in larger towns. In Helsinki, the Yliopiston Apteekki at Mannerheimintie 96 is open 24 hours a day (www.yliopistonapteekki.fi).

Dentists

Haartman Hospital treats dental emergencies 24 hours a day. Haartmaninkatu 4, Bldg 12. Tel: 09 310 4999. Emergencies in working hours: Dentarium, Mikaelsgatan 8 Helsinki. Tel: 09 622 1533.
Out-of-hours emergencies:
Oral, 2nd Floor, Erottajankatu 5A, Helsinki. Tel: 010 400 3400; http://www.oral.fi.

I

Internet

Finland is one of the most "wired" countries in the world. In 2010 the government introduced a law guaranteeing broadband access to every person living in Finland, including those in secluded, sparsely populated regions. Service is very reliable. Wireless internet hotspots are widespread. There is free Wi-Fi in Helsinki for both locals and tourists to use. No password is required, just find "Helsinki City Open WLAN" and log in. Most cafés provide free access to the web. Internet cafés, where you can also use printing facilities, include mbar (Mannerheimintie 22–24 http://mbar.fi/netcafe) and Netcup Cafés, located in Stockmann department stores throughout Finland and at most libraries.

The Hartwall Arena in Helsinki.

Language

Getting By

Good morning *Hyvää huomenta*
Good day *Hyvää päivää*
Good evening *Hyvää iltaa*
Today *Tänään*
Tomorrow *Huomenna*
Yesterday *Eilen*
Hello *Terve or hei*
How do you do? *Kuinka voit*
Goodbye *Näkemiin or hei hei*
Yes *Kyllä or joo*
No *Ei*
Thank you *Kiitos*
How much does this cost? *Paljonko tämä maksaa?*
It costs... *Se maksaa...*
How do I get to..? *Miten pääsen..?*
Where is...? *Missä on...?*
Right *Oikealla*
To the right *Oikealle*
Left *Vasemmalla*
To the left *Vasemmalle*
Straight on *Suoraan*
What time is it? *Paljonko kello on?*
It is (the time is) *Kello on*
Could I have your name? *Saisinko nimesi?*
My name is... *Nimeni on...*
Do you speak English? *Puhutko englantia?*
I only speak English *Puhun vain englantia*
Can I help you? *Voinko auttaa sinua?*
I do not understand *En ymmärrä*
I do not know *En tiedä*
breakfast *aamiainen*
lunch *lounas*
dinner *illallinen*
eat *syödä*
drink *juoda*
I would like to order... *Haluaisin tilata*
Could I have the bill? *Saisko laskun?*
Could I have the key? *Saisko avaimen?*
Toilet *Vessa*

Gentlemen *Miehet (Swedish: Herrar)*
Ladies *Naiset (Swedish: Damer)*
Vacant *Vapaa*
Engaged *Varattu*
Entrance *Sisäänkäynti*
Exit *Uloskäaynti*
No entry *Pääsy kielletty*
Open *Avoinna, Auki*
Closed *Suljettu, Kiinni*
Push *Työnnä*
Pull *Vedä*

Days of the Week

Monday *Maanantai*
Tuesday *Tiistai*
Wednesday *Keskiviikko*
Thursday *Torstai*
Friday *Perjantai*
Saturday *Launantai*
Sunday *Sunnuntai*

Useful Words

chemist *apteekki*
hospital *sairaala*
doctor *lääkäri*
police station *poliisilaitos*
parking *paikoitus*
phrasebook *turistien sanakirja*
dictionary *sanakirja*
car *auto*
bus, coach *bussi, linja-auto*
train *juna*
aircraft *lentokone*
Cheers *Kippis (Swedish: skål)*
To rent *Vuokrata*
For sale *Myytävänä*
Free, no charge *Ilmainen*
Room to rent *Vuokrattavana huone*

Media

Newspapers and Books

With the exception of the *International Herald Tribune*, which arrives on the afternoon of its publication date, you'll have to wait a day and a half for English-language newspapers to get to Helsinki. Foreign papers are sold at Helsinki Railway Station and Akateeminen Kirjakauppa (Academic Bookstore) at Keskuskatu 1 (tel: 09 1211; www.akateeminen.com), where you can also get books in English, and at the larger hotels in other cities, as well as at main airports.

The *Helsinki Times* (www.helsinki times.fi) is a weekly English-language newspaper, presenting news about Finland, and sold at various news kiosks. *Helsingin Sanomat* is one of the largest daily newspapers in Finland (www.hs.fi); unfortunately it no longer publishes an English edition.

Tourist Publications

Helsinki This Week is an English-language guide to cultural and tourist events in the capital (http://helsinkithisweek.com). *SixDegrees* is a free monthly magazine in English with events, trends and current affairs (www.6d.fi). You can pick up many useful brochures and maps with sightseeing routes from the Helsinki visitor centre at Pohjoisesplanadi 19 or download them on www.visithelsinki.fi.

Radio and Television

The news in English is broadcast daily on YLE Radio 1 (87.9 FM in the Helsinki region) daily at 3.30pm; you can also read news stories and listen to podcasts online on http://yle.fi/uutiset/news.

Money

Finland's unit of currency is the euro. Notes are available in 500, 200, 100, 50, 20, 10 and 5 euros and coins in 2 and 1 euros, 50, 20, 10, 5, 2, and 1 cents. Shops do not have to accept 2 and 1 cent coins.

How to Pay

Credit cards MasterCard, Visa, Diner's Club and American Express are accepted in most establishments in main cities.

ATMs marked "Otto" give local currency if you have an international credit or debit card (Visa, Cirrus, Plus, MasterCard and so on).

Nightlife

Pubs, Bars and Clubs

Pub-crawling remains popular, and there are several clubs that attract the best pop bands. Increasing

DENMARK

NORWAY

SWEDEN

FINLAND

numbers of international stars make a stop at the Hartwall Arena (www.hartwall-areena.com) in Helsinki on their world tours.

The minimum age for drinking alcohol is 18, but some clubs have an age limit of 21. Entrance fees vary.

Helsinki
Ahjo Wine Bar & Night Club
Bulevardi 2/4; tel: 20 770 4711; www.ahjoclub.fi.
Terminally hip and ultra-modern bar and club.
Corona Bar
Eerikinkatu 11; tel: 020 175 1610.
Attracts a young hip crowd who come to talk, drink beer, eat toasted sandwiches and play pool.
Storyville
Museokatu 8; tel: 50 3632664; http://storyville.fi.
A cosy jazz club to have a late drink. In the summer, the terrace is the place to be. Cover charge.
Tavastia
Urho Kekkosenkatu 4; tel: 09 7746 74 20; www.tavastiaklubi.fi.
This university-owned club attracts some of Helsinki's best live music.
Teatteri
Pohjoisesplanadi 2; tel: 09 6128 5000; www.teatteri.fi.
Located in the Swedish Theatre complex, the Klubi nightclub attracts stylish 30- and 40-somethings.
The Tiger
Urho Kekkosenkatu 1A; tel: 020 7759 350; www.thetiger.fi.
Considered the number one nightclub in Helsinki for 20-somethings and their admirers, it is immense and absolutely in tune.
Ateljée
Yrjönkatu 26; tel: 010 7842 080
The exclusive Ateljée bar on the 13th floor is famous for its great views over Helsinki, which are included in the price of the drinks.
Zetor
Mannerheimintie 3–5, Kaivopiha; tel: 010 766 4450; www.zetor.net.
This "tractor-style" pub and restaurant has to be seen to be believed. Experience the surrealism of the Finnish countryside.

Tampere
Nightlife is very evident on the main street, **Hämeenkatu**. Bar-hopping is easy, although more "traditional" pubs are elsewhere, such as **Salhojankadun Pub** on Salhojankatu and **Ohranjyvä** at Näsilinnankatu 15 (www.ohranjyva.fi). Locally brewed beer is available at **Plevna** (Itäinenkatu 8; www.plevna.fi) and **Wanha Posti** (Hämeenkatu 13A; www.wanhaposti.fi).

Turku
Old Bank
Aurakatu 3; tel: 02 274 5711; www.oldbank.fi.
This pub serves more varieties of beer than any other in town.
Panimoravintola Koulu
Eerikinkatu 18; tel: 02 274 5757; www.panimoravintolakoulu.fi.
This former school has a brewery, and the classrooms are now pubs or restaurants.
Uusi Apteekki
Kaskenkatu 1; tel: 02 250 2595; www.uusiapteekki.fi.
Literally "new pharmacy", this pub is set in one from the past.

O
Opening Hours
Shops Generally open from Monday to Saturday, except for small food stores, which are allowed to stay open on Sunday. In larger cities, hours are 9am–5pm, with late-night opening on Thursday. In Helsinki, many open until 9pm on weekdays and 6pm on Saturday. Larger food stores usually open 9am–8pm weekdays and 9am–4pm on Saturday. The only late shops are in the tunnel under the Helsinki Railway Station: open weekdays 10am–10pm and weekends noon–10pm.
Banks Mon–Fri 9.15am–4.15pm; bureaux de change open a bit later. The one at the airport opens daily 6am–10pm.

P
Postal Services
Post offices are usually open 9am–5pm weekdays. Services include stamps, registered mail and poste restante. Helsinki's main post office is at Elielinaukio 2F, tel: 0200 71000, opposite the railway square. Mon–Fri 8am–8pm, Sat–Sun 10am–2pm.

R
Religious Services
The Lutheran Church is the state Church of Finland, with 82 percent of Finns counted as Lutherans. There is a small Greek Orthodox population, and only around 9,000 Catholics in Finland. In Helsinki, services in English are held at the Temppeliaukio church (Church in the Rock) on Lutherinkatu; there are both Lutheran and ecumenical services here. There is also one synagogue and one mosque in Helsinki.

S
Shopping
What to Buy
Finnish Design
Helsinki was named World Design Capital 2012, and you can discover the Design District via a "Design Walk" (www.designdistrict.fi).
Esplanadi is a compact version of the Champs Elysées, and is the mecca for Finnish design on both sides of its tree-lined park that stretches from Mannerheimintie to the harbour. Choose from jewellery, woodwork, clothing, glass or kitchenware.
Aarikka (www.aarikka.) and **Kalevala Koru** (www.kalevalakoru.fi) jewellery are particularly Finnish, the first being a mainly contemporary collection and the second a collection based on designs from the Finnish epic poem Kalevala, rendered in silver, gold and brass. **Aarikka** also supplies some fine woodwork products, including chopping boards, Christmas decorations, toys and wooden jewellery. **Iittala** (www.iittala.com) is known for its stunning glass, dining and cooking utensils, and the most impressive ceramic work is produced by **Arabia** (www.arabia.fi), one of the older Finnish firms. Its factory and museum (Hämeentie 135; tel: 204 39 5357; Tue–Fri noon–6pm, Sat–Sun 10am–4pm) are just a 20-minute tram ride from Helsinki centre. There is an outlet on the premises for Arabia, Pentik, iittala and Finlayson products (outlet hours are Mon–Fri 10am–8pm, Sat–Sun 10am–4pm).

Marimekko (www.marimekko.fi) is the quintessential Finnish clothing designer, with its typical brightly coloured fabrics for men, women and children, as well as more elegant clothing for women and textiles for home use. These popular Finnish brands can be found both in their own stores and department stores in most Finnish towns of any size, including several shops on both the Pohjoisesplanadi and Eteläesplanadi in Helsinki.

Other Finnish designers along the block are **Vuokko**, **Annikki Karvanen** (www.annikkikarvinen.fi) and shoe designer **Pertti Palmroth** (www.palmroth.com). There are also stylish furniture showrooms like **Artek** (www.artek.fi), as well as home furnishing shops. For functional and distinctive souvenirs of contemporary Finnish design – from stylish wool felt hats to candlestick holders – visit the **Design Forum in Helsinki** (Erottajankatu 7; tel: 09 6220810; www.designforum.fi).

Department Stores

The king of department stores in Finland is **Stockmann** (https:// stockmann.com), which is found in most Finnish cities like Helsinki, Turku, Tampere and Rovaniemi. Stockmann also owns **Akateeminen Kirjakauppa** (Academic Bookstore; https://akateeminen.com), Finland's best-known bookstore, which sells international periodicals. Another good department store to look out for throughout Finland is **Sokos** (www.sokos.fi), and like Stockmann, it is known for its excellent food hall.

Shopping Areas

Helsinki

The city centre has several shopping centres like **Kamppi** (www.kamppi.fi), **Aleksi 13** (www.aleksi13.fi), **Forum** (www.forum.fi) and **Galleria Esplanadi** (www. galleriaesplanad.fi): from basic to upmarket. There are also many local and international boutiques in various neighbourhoods, like Ullanlinna along Korkeovuorenkatu or west of Mannerheimintie on Frederikinkatu and Uudenmaankatu. There are several market squares that sell both fresh food and a range of other consumer goods, from second-hand clothes and records to designer jewellery, Sami mittens and fur hats.

Kauppatori (at the harbour) is the main market, followed by **Hietalaniemi Flea Market** (on the west end of Bulevardi) and the indoor **Hakaniemmi market hall** (www.hakaniemenkauppahalli. fi) that is frequented by locals. Markets have extended hours in summer and are open until about 8pm. In the weeks leading up to Christmas, there are many markets and fairs around the city centre selling handicrafts, decorations and seasonal treats.

Turku

In the Turku city centre, at Yliopistonkatu 26, you will find **Pentik** (www.pentik.com), which is famous for ceramics, and **Aarikka** (No. 22, Stockmann), for handmade wooden crafts and decorations. For crafts, look into Sylvi Salonen (www. sylvisalonen.fi), specialising in linens and decorative crafts at Linnankatu 14. Markets are generally open daily except Sunday. Turku's open-air market features flowers, fish, fruit, vegetables and some crafts. The indoor market hall offers all that and more, including bread, cheese, coffee, tea, spices, snacks and many handicrafts.

Tampere

The **Tampere Market Hall**, at Hämeenkatu 19, is open Mon– Fri 8am–6pm, Sat 8am–4pm. **Koskikeskus** is a big shopping centre situated in the very centre (www.koskikeskus.fi).

T

Telephones

International dialling code: 358 Finland is a world leader in telecommunications, with a highly sophisticated, deregulated phone system. The best way to call overseas cheaply is at certain internet cafés in main cities. Hotels usually add a surcharge for calls made from your room.

Callers from outside Finland should dial the international code, then the country code (358) followed by the area code, omitting the initial zero (0).

Mobile Phones

Finland is the home of Nokia and has one of the world's highest ownership of mobile (cell) phones – 5.5 million Finns own over 9.3 million phones. The country also boasts 100 percent mobile network coverage. Charges for mobile phone roaming can be high for visitors outside of the European Union. For longer stays it's worth buying a Finnish prepaid phone SIM card. There are several operators, which include DNA (www.dna.fi), Elisa (http://elisa.fi) and Sonera (www.sonera.fi). You can also get a prepaid starter pack at any R-Kioski convenience store.

Before You Go

Australia
Embassy (supplies tourist information)
12 Darwin Avenue, Yarralumla, ACT 2600
Tel: 02 6273 3800
www.finland.org.au
UK/Ireland
Finnish Tourist Board
PO Box 33213, London W6 8JX
Tel: 020 7365 2512
www.visitfinland.com/uk
US/Canada
Finnish Tourist Board/Scandinavian Tourist Boards
655 Third Avenue, Suite 1810, New York, NY 10017 Tel: 212 885 9700
www.goscandinavia.com

In Finland

Finland has over 50 main tourist information offices, marked with an "i", as well as many summer tourist offices. The following are the main tourist offices, but a full list can be obtained at www.visitfinland.com:
Helsinki City Tourist Office
Pohjoisesplanadi 19, 00100
Helsinki; tel: 09 3101 3300;
www.visithelsinki.fi.
Rovaniemi Tourist Information
Sampo Shopping Centre,
Maakuntakatu 29–31, 96200
Rovaniemi; tel: 016 346 270;
www.visitrovaniemi.fi.
Tampere City Tourist Office
Hämeenkatu 14B, 33100
Tampere; tel: 03 56 56 6800;
http://visittampere.fi.
Turku Touring
Aurakatu 4, 20100 Turku; tel: 02 262 7444; www.visitturku.fi.

Transport

Getting There

By Air
Finnair is the national carrier of Finland and operates international and national routes. Both Finnair (www.finnair.com) and British Airways (www.ba.com) connect London and Helsinki with daily flights. Finnair (and many other airlines, including Lufthansa and SAS Scandinavian Airlines) fly

direct between Helsinki and most European capitals.

Finnair also links with several North American cities, including New York. You may be able to find value-for-money package fares and charter flights from New York or London, but they are rare.

From Helsinki, Finnair flies numerous domestic routes to more than 20 cities, including several to north Finland airports, and have cross-country flights between some of them. Budget airline Ryanair (www.ryanair.com) flies between Tampere and London, Frankfurt and several Spanish and Italian airports. Flights to Mariehamn from Helsinki or Stockholm are operated by Next Jet; www.nextjet.se.

Finnair also operates flights to Tallinn and Tartu in Estonia.

By Sea
You can travel to Finland by boat from Sweden, Estonia and Germany. **Tallink Line** and **Viking Line** have daily routes between Stockholm and Helsinki, which are very popular with locals for the duty-free shopping on Åland Islands. These ferries are luxurious with restaurants, saunas, swimming pools, tax-free shops and children's playrooms.

There are plenty of services to choose from for a trip between Helsinki and Tallinn. For a fast trip Tallink operates a year-round Shuttle Star service to Tallinn which takes only two hours; there are restaurants, a business lounge with Wi-Fi connections and television, and duty-free shopping. **Eckerö Lines'** M/S Finlandia makes the trip in three hours. **Linda Line**'s hydrofoil is running catamaran voyages from Helsinki to Tallinn, in 1.5 hours during the ice-free period. These fast boats are dependent on weather conditions, whereas the bigger boats also manage in rough weather.

Finland is perfect cycling country.

It's less expensive to travel by ferry from Stockholm to , and then overland to Helsinki rather than by direct ship to Helsinki. Viking provides very cheap bus tickets for the overland trip; the ferry ticket is also cheaper as the voyage is shorter. One can also travel to Finland's Åland Islands by boat from Stockholm or Turku – Viking has a daily service to Mariehamn.

Eckerö Line (West Terminal)
Tel: +358 6000 4300 (€€1.75 per call + operator's charges)
www.eckeroline.fi

Linda Line (South Terminal)
Tel: 0600 066 8970 (€€1.64 per call + operator's charges)
www.lindaline.fi

Tallink Line (West Terminal)
Tel: 0600 157 00
www.tallink.com

Viking Line (Katajanokka Terminal)
Tel: 0600 41577
www.vikingline.fi

By Rail
It's a long haul to Finland from just about anywhere by rail, because you inevitably finish the long rail trip north with a 15-hour journey by boat and train from Stockholm to Helsinki. From Britain, the handiest route is from Harwich to the Hook of Holland, overland to Copenhagen, then the connecting train to Stockholm and boat/boat and train to Helsinki. Total travel time is about 45 hours. This is cheaper than a flight only if you get a special fare rail ticket, for example InterRail.

Getting Around

On Arrival
Finland's main international airport, Helsinki-Vantaa (www.helsinki-vantaa.fi), is connected by Finnair City Bus or the Yellow Line shared taxi (fixed fares to any destination within Helsinki city centre; www.airporttaxi.

fi); fares are less on the Finnair bus, which leaves every 20 minutes with connections to Helsinki Railway Station.

By Air
Finnair operates domestic flight services. Fares are relatively inexpensive; in July, fares are very cheap. It is a good idea to fly if, for example, you want to get to Lapland from the south without spending days on the road. Discounts are available for groups, families and senior citizens.

By Rail
The Finnish rail network is limited, but service is adequate in most cases and very good between major points like Turku and Helsinki. Rail travel to north Finland requires completion by bus as Finnish rail lines only run as far as Rovaniemi and Kemijärvi (in winter to Kolari). Rail passes are available for 3 days, 4 days, 6 days and 8 days within one month (for European citizens; www.interrail.eu). There are also season passes worth considering. For more information on family tickets, group tickets and other types of discount contact:

VR Ltd (Finnish Railways)
Tel: 0600 41 900
www.vr.fi

Water Transport
Ferries and passenger boats in Finland play a strong role where international destinations are concerned, but there are some lakeland ferry routes worth pursuing. There are the Silverline and Poet's Way, which begin in Tampere and cover much of the western lakelands, tours in the Päijänne region and over Finland's largest lake, Saimaa, in the east. Many other operators run trips on the lakes; for more information, contact the central or regional tourist boards.

Helsinki's only real commuter island is Suomenlinna, with ferries travelling back and forth roughly every half-hour (schedule depends on season). Most of these ferries are part of the public transport network of Helsinki. Other Helsinki islands closer to the coast are connected by road.

Lake Päijänne Cruises
Tel: 010 320 8820
www.paijanne-risteilythilden.fi
Roll Risteilyt
Tel: 017 266 2466
www.roll.fi
Silverline and Poet's Way
Tel: 010 422 5600
www.runoilijantie.fi

Bus and Coach

Finland is greatly dependent on buses for transporting the bulk of its passenger traffic. There are coach services on 90 percent of Finland's public roads (40,000 long-distance departures a day) which also cover the areas that trains don't, particularly in the north and in smaller places throughout the country. Long-distance bus timetables can be checked at www. matkahuolto.fi. ExpressBus offers journeys run by 15 Finnish bus companies (tel: 200 4000; www. expressbus.fi). There is no penalty for buying a ticket on the coach, but you cannot get group discounts (for three adults or more on trips over 80km/50 miles) from the coach ticket seller. Senior citizens and full-time students (university and lower) are also eligible for discounts, but must purchase, for €5, a coach card entitling them to this discount – at least 30 percent. Bring a photo, ID and international ISIC student card. Accompanied children under four travel free.

Driving

Finland's roads are not too plagued by traffic, although they do get very busy between the capital and the countryside on Fridays and Sundays during the summer. There are few multi-lane motorways. Most are two-lane only. Pay attention to road signs showing elk and reindeer zones. Collisions with these animals are usually serious. Use caution at all hours, but especially at dusk when elk are most active. For winter driving, studded tyres should ideally be used from November to March and are strongly recommended throughout December at all times.

Rules of the Road

Drive on the right, overtake on the left. All cars must use their lights outside built-up areas. Elsewhere, lights must be used at dusk or at night or in bad weather (UK cars must sweep their lights right). Wearing of seat belts is also compulsory.

Traffic coming from the right has right of way. Exceptions are on roads marked by a triangle sign; if this is facing you, you must give right of way; similarly, if you are on a very major thoroughfare it is likely that the feed-in streets will have triangles, giving you the right of way. On roundabouts (rotaries), the first vehicle to reach the roundabout has right of way.

Speed limits are signposted, and range from 30kmph (18mph) in school zones to 120kmph (74mph) on motorways.

Taxis

Finnish taxis run throughout the country, with fares starting at around €4.50. Helsinki city centre and the centres of other large cities, as well as most major airports, bus and railway stations, have taxi stands. Otherwise local telephone books list the number of the nearest dispatcher (under Taksi in the White Pages). Finding the closest one is worthwhile, especially in Helsinki, as taxis charge from embarkation point (plus an order fee). You can also hail a cab on the street, but this is a rarer way of getting a taxi in Finland than those mentioned above.

Bicycles

Finland is a good cycling country with its well-engineered cycle paths and gently rolling landscape. The Helsinki free summer bike scheme has been suspended, contact the tourist office for the latest information. In the meantime, try Greenbike rental shop (Bulevardi 32; tel: 050 550 1020; www.greenbike.fi). You can rent bikes from the harbours of Mariehamn in the Åland Islands (a popular summer cycling destination). Visit the website run by the Network of Finnish Cycling Municipalities, www.pyorailensuomessa.fi, for more information on cycling in Finland.

Hitchhiking

Thumbing is still a time-honoured way to get a cheap ride in Finland, but you may have to wait a long time to get picked up, particularly at weekends and in the furthest reaches of Lapland where traffic can be pretty thin. Hitchhiking is prohibited on motorways; the smaller secondary routes are a better bet. As with any country in the world, however, safety can never be guaranteed on the road, and this mode of transport is not recommended.

V

Visas and Passports

Citizens belonging to Schengen member states can enter Finland simply with a valid ID card. Most other Western countries, including Ireland, the UK, the US, Canada, Australia and New Zealand, do not need visas to travel to Finland – a passport will suffice, as long as it has been issued within the last 10 years and will remain valid for three months after leaving Finland. Citizens of South Africa do need to obtain a visa before travel from the Embassy of Finland in Pretoria (P.O. Box 443, Pretoria 0001, Republic of South Africa, tel: +27-12-343 0275; www.finland.org.za), and must also have a valid passport, as above.

If you are in any doubt, check the visa requirements on the website of the Ministry for Foreign Affairs in Finland (Ulkoasiainministeriö; http://formin.finland.fi).

W

What to Read

The Almost Nearly Perfect People: Behind the Myth of the Scandinavian Utopia by Michael Booth (Picador). Journalist Michael Booth demystifies the Scandinavian dream in a witty travelogue. *Finnish Design: A Concise History* by Pekka Korvenmaa (Victoria & Albert Museum). *The Lighter Side of Finland* by Russel Snyder (Klaava Media). Informative and entertaining book on what makes Finns tick.

Send Us Your Thoughts

We do our best to ensure the information in our books is as accurate and up-to-date as possible. The books are updated on a regular basis using local contacts, who painstakingly add, amend and correct as required. However, some details (such as telephone numbers and opening times) are liable to change, and we are ultimately reliant on our readers to put us in the picture.

We welcome your feedback, especially your experience of using the book "on the road". Maybe we recommended a hotel that you liked (or another that you didn't), or you came across a great bar or new attraction we missed.

We will acknowledge all contributions, and we'll offer an Insight Guide to the best letters received.

Please write to us at:
Insight Guides
PO Box 7910
London SE1 1WE
Or email us at:
hello@insightguides.com

DENMARK

NORWAY

SWEDEN

FINLAND

FINLAND EATING OUT

RESTAURANTS AND CAFES

WHAT TO EAT

Finnish cuisine has broadened and improved enormously in recent years. Tradition was that Finns would eat a large hot lunch, then a smaller cold meal in the evening. Only businessmen dined out, and it was usually white fish, boiled potatoes and mushrooms. Happily that has radically changed in the last decade, as Helsinki has become more cosmopolitan and now boasts a myriad of gourmet establishments and cosmopolitan restaurants, from Turkish to Thai. The best Russian cuisine outside of Russia continues to be found in Helsinki. Enjoy the seasonal cuisine: crayfish in summer, game (reindeer and elk) in autumn. For more on eating and drinking in Finland, see Food and Drink chapter.

WHERE TO EAT

In the past, it was difficult to get a really cheap meal in Finland, but you can find places where you will definitely get value for money. Fixed-price lunches are often very good deals and are usually advertised on boards outside restaurants. Many serve an extensive buffet including tea or coffee for a low price.

The Sokos and Stockmann department stores have excellent food halls; otherwise, for snacks there are more and more cafés sprouting up that supply sandwiches, quiche, soups and salads at reasonable prices. In Helsinki, the Market Square (Kauppatori) has all kinds of delicious cheap eats. Museum cafés are usually reliable places to go for delicious, reasonably priced fare.

DRINKING NOTES

Alcohol remains expensive in Finland due to high taxes.
Beer The Finnish tuoppi is slightly smaller than the British pint. If you do not specify, you will usually be served a keskiolut (3.5 percent alcohol). The strongest beer is number 4 (nelosolut, 4.5 percent) and the weakest number 1 (ykkösolut, just over 1 percent). **Wine** is imported and very costly. Alko, the state alcohol monopoly, continues to keep prices high and opening hours still limited at its outlets.

RESTAURANT LISTINGS

Restaurants are listed in alphabetical order by region, with the most expensive first.

HELSINKI

Bellevue
Rahapajankatu 3
Tel: 09 179 560
www.restaurantbellevue.com
Superb cuisine in Helsinki's oldest (established in 1917) and most refined Russian restaurant, in the shadow of the Uspenski Orthodox Cathedral. Try the blinis with herring caviar or the borscht, then move on to the filet of beef with barley or a classic chicken Kiev. **€€€**
G.W. Sundmans
Eteläranta 16
Tel: 09 6128 5400
www.sundmans.fi
Situated in a 19th-century Empire-style building designed by Engel,

this elegant restaurant serves light, seasonal dishes, and the extensive wine list includes some surprisingly inexpensive wines. For a more casual atmosphere and less pricy menu, dine at the Sundmans Krog, a gastro pub on the ground floor of the same premises. Close to Market Square. **€€–€€€**
Juuri
Korkeavuorenkatu 27
Tel: 09 635 732
http://juuri.fi
This intimate bistro opened in 2009 and is constantly packed, so book ahead. They serve an assortment of sapas (Finnish tapas!), and the fish of the day is a good choice. **€€**

Karljohan
Yrjönkatu 21
Tel: 09 612 1121
www.ravintolakarljohan.fi
Traditional Finnish dishes at good prices which attract locals who come for their daily lunch specials. Fish of the day a good choice here too. **€–€€**
Kellarikrouvi & Fabian
Pohkoinen Makasiinikatu 6
Tel: 09 6128 5100
www.kellarikrouvi.fi
Savvy locals come to dine in this unpretentious vaulted cellar for reasonably priced, seasonal Finnish food. Upstairs the weekly lunch buffet is very popular. **€–€€**

Brunch in Helsinki.

Lappi
Annankatu 22
Tel: 09 645 550
www.lappires.com
An authentic Lapland experience is a bonus when sampling anything made of reindeer, tasty fish, salted fungi and exotic berries. Try the Lappish plate to savour a full range of northern specialities. €€

Restaurant Klippan
Luoto Island
Tel: 09 633 408
The red roof of this distinguished wooden villa is easily reached on the island of Luoto, in the South Harbour. It is a summer restaurant, only open from May to September. The chef is a passionate fisherman and a fanatic for seasonal ingredients. Lunch on Sunday. The shuttle boat leaves from Olympia terminaali by the Peace statue. €€

Sandeep
Lönnrotinkatu 22
Tel: 09 685 6206
Tandoori and vegetarian Indian dishes in a cosy ambience. €€

Savoy
Eteläesplanadi 14
Tel: 09 6128 5300
www.ravintolasavoy.fi
The ultimate Finnish dining experience since 1937, with a timeless interior by Alvar Aalto. It was a favourite of Marshall Mannerheim, whose vorsch-mack (a spicy meat dish) remains on the menu. Reserve a table on the terrace for a drop-dead view. €€€

THE SOUTH

Turku

Summer in Turku is not complete without a session in one of the dozen boat restaurants on the River Aurajoki, but proceed carefully, as the food doesn't always live up to the surroundings.

Blanko
Aurakatu 1
Tel: 02 233 3966
www.blanko.net
This oasis of cool serves simple fusion cooking in a unique vaulted environment. It has a disco on Friday and Saturday evenings. €€€

Fontana
Aurakatu 1
Tel: 02 250 1444
www.fontanacafe.fi
An Art Nouveau café in a prime location serving up simple fare that attracts students, young mums, hip grannies and amorous couples. Lunch buffet for € 9.70. €

Pinella
Vanha Suurtori 2,
Tel: 02 445 6500
www.pinella.fi
Finland's oldest restaurant reopened in 2011 after restoration of its historic premises. Enjoy contemporary cuisine in a classic ambience or on the riverside terrace in summer. Start with an aperitif at the new cocktail and champagne bar. €€€

Pizzeria Dennis
Linnankatu 17
Tel: 02 469 1191
www.dennis.fi
Tasty and authentic pizzas, good toppings. €

Tinta
Läntinen Rantakatu 9
Tel: 02 230 7023
www.tinta.fi
A cosy and relaxed restaurant by the river, one of the best in Turku. Menu includes teriyaki-glazed salmon, elk goulash soup as well as pizzas, all served with rucola and roasted pine nuts. €€

Viking Restaurant Harald
Auragatan 3
Tel: 044 766 8204
www.ravintolaharald.fi
A themed restaurant that serves up hearty game, fish and vegetarian fare on rustic earthenware. Start with the salmon or red beet soup, then let your costumed server advise you. €€

LAKELAND

Kuopio

Musta Lammas
Satamakatu 4
Tel: 017 5810 458
http://mustalammas.ravintolamestarit.net
This pleasant restaurant specialises in fresh seasonal dishes like pike perch, reindeer, and the lamb you will see in its logo. Start off with blinis and salmon roe as an appetiser. €€

Muikkuravintola Sampo
Kauppakatu 13
Tel: 017 261 4677
Informal atmosphere, serving excellent fish. €€

Wanha Satama
Matkustajasatama

PRICE CATEGORIES

Price categories are per person for an average three-course meal, excluding drinks but with tax:
€€ = under €€20
€€ = €€20–40
€€€ = over €40

Smoked fish is a Baltic delicacy.

Tel: 010 762 9723
www.wanhasatama.net
Rustic and lively; located by the
passenger harbour. Serves tasty

muikku (whitefish) with garlic and
mashed potatoes. €

Savonlinna

Savonlinna market (kauppatori) is
a busy and popular place to indulge
in a snack from one of the many
tempting food stalls. Prices are
steep during the Opera Festival,
but the market is also at its liveliest
then.
Majakka
Satamakatu 11
Tel: 015 206 282
A popular place near the market,
serving fish and hearty Finnish
dishes. $$
Olutravintola Sillansuu
Verkkosaarenkatu 1
Tel: 015 531 451
Popular pub near Market Bridge. €€

Tampere

Astor
Aleksis Kivenkatu 26
Tel: 010 321 1600

www.ravintola-astor.fi
Live piano music every night. Try the
fillets of Baltic herring in mustard
sauce. €€€
Eetvartti
Sumeliuksenkatu 16
Tel: 020 123 4630
www.eetvartti.fi
Run by the Pirkanmaa Hotel and
Restaurant School. High-quality food
cooked by the students. €€€
Näsinneula
Särkänniemi AdventurePark & Tower
Tel: 0207 130 234
Revolving restaurant high in the
Näsinneula Observation Tower, where
you dine 168 metres (635ft) above
the scenic landscape of Tampere.
€€€
Plevna
Itäinenkatu 8
Tel: 03 260 1200
www.plevna.fi
Lively pub/café specialising in steaks
and sausages. Beers are brewed on
the premises. €€

WEST COAST

Oulu

Pannu
Kauppurienkatu 12
Tel: 020 792 8 200
www.ravintolapannu.com
Located next to the Stockmann
department store, this popular,
well-priced pit stop is busy for lunch
and dinner. There's a large pizza
selection, but standard Finnish
specialities such as wild boar and
fresh fish also appear on the menu.
€
Toripolliisi Rantakatu 6
Tel: 08 333 013
www.toripolliisi.fi
Oulu's gastro pub located on the

shoreline at Market Square.
Start off with the blinis with salmon
roe. Main courses include fresh fish
and game in season. There are
also sandwiches and salads.
€€–€€€

Pori

Raatihuoneen Kellari
Hallituskatu 9
Tel: 02 633 4804
www.raatihuoneenkellari.fi
First-class establishment serving
Finnish-style meat and fish
dishes. Located in the basement
of the old Town Hall. €
€€

Vaasa

Gustav Wasa
Rådhusgatan 24
Tel: 050 466 3208
www.gustavwasa.com
Cellar restaurant serving excellent
meat portions and some fish. The
rustic dining hall used to be a coal-
storing cellar. €€€
Strampen
Rantakatu 6
Tel: 041 451 4512
www.strampen.com
A summer-only pavilion restaurant,
with a fine terrace for people-
watching. Good selection of evening
dishes and lighter lunches. €€–€€€

LAPLAND

Rovaniemi

Fransmanni
Sokos Vaakuna Hotel, Koskikatu 4
Tel: 016 3322 515
Rather pricey, but excellent food. A
good place to try Lappish specialities,
such as reindeer filet and cloudberry
liqueur. If you are on a budget or
travelling with children, try the other
in-house restaurant, Amarillo, known
for tasty Tex-Mex dining, as well as
pastas and salads. €€€€
Nili
Valtakatu 20
Tel: 0400 369 669

www.nili.fi
Nili is a snug place, decorated with
Lappish woodcarvings and furs.
It offers traditional Lapp food –
Arctic char, pike perch, reindeer
and bear, served with seasonal
accompaniments. €€€
Sky Ounasvaara
Juhannuskalliontie 2
Tel: 016 323 400
For startling beautiful views, head
for this panoramic restaurant 3km
(2 miles) outside town in the Hotel
Sky Ounasvaara. There's a selection
of classy international dishes, or try

local treats from the Lapp menu.
€€€

Saariselkä

Ravintola Pirkon Pirtti
Honkapolku 2
Tel: 016 668 050
www.pirkonpirtti.fi
Popular restaurant serving reindeer
and game dishes, and pizzas for the
less adventurous. Also on the menu
is braised lamb neck, and "glow-fried"
arctic salmon. Round off the meal
with Arctic cloudberry sorbet. Closes
in summer. €€–€€€

CREDITS

Insight Guide Credits

Distribution
UK
Dorling Kindersley Ltd
A Penguin Group company
80 Strand, London, WC2R 0RL
sales@uk.dk.com

United States
Ingram Publisher Services
1 Ingram Boulevard, PO Box 3006,
La Vergne, TN 37086-1986
ips@ingramcontent.com

Australia and New Zealand
Woodslane
10 Apollo St, Warriewood,
NSW 2102, Australia
info@woodslane.com.au

Worldwide
Apa Publications GmbH & Co. Verlag
KG (Singapore branch)
7030 Ang Mo Kio Avenue 5
08-65 Northstar @ AMK
Singapore 569880
apasin@singnet.com.sg

Printing
CTPS-China
© 2015 Apa Publications (UK) Ltd
All Rights Reserved
First Edition 2001
Third Edition 2015

www.insightguides.com

Project Editor
Carine Tracanelli
Authors
Fran Parnell, Joan Gannij and
Katarzyna Marcinkowska
Picture Editor
Tom Smyth
Map Production
Original cartography Gar Bowes
Design and Geodata, updated by
Carte
Update Production
AM Services
Production
Rebeka Davies

Legend

City maps

Freeway/Highway/Motorway
Divided Highway
Main Roads
Minor Roads
Pedestrian Roads
Steps
Footpath
Railway
Funicular Railway
Cable Car
Tunnel
City Wall
Important Building
Built Up Area
Other Land
Transport Hub
Park
Pedestrian Area
Bus Station
Tourist Information
Main Post Office
Cathedral/Church
Mosque
Synagogue
Statue/Monument
Beach
Airport

Regional maps

Freeway/Highway/Motorway (with junction)
Freeway/Highway/Motorway (under construction)
Divided Highway
Main Road
Secondary Road
Minor Road
Track
Footpath
International Boundary
State/Province Boundary
National Park/Reserve
Marine Park
Ferry Route
Marshland/Swamp
Glacier   Salt Lake
Airport/Airfield
Ancient Site
Border Control
Cable Car
Castle/Castle Ruins
Cave
Chateau/Stately Home
Church/Church Ruins
Crater
Lighthouse
Mountain Peak
Place of Interest
Viewpoint

Contributors

Insight Guide: Scandinavia was commissioned by **Carine Tracanelli** and updated by **Katarzyna Marcinkowska**, an editor, writer and photographer who enjoys contemporary art museums as much as the great outdoors, particularly hiking and yachting. She will never forget sailing to Bornholm on a 9-metre long yacht.

The book builds on the solid foundations laid by **Fran Parnell** (Denmark and Sweden) and **Joan**

Gannij (Finland and Norway). Fran Parnell's passion for Scandinavia began while studying Anglo-Saxon, Norse and Celtic at Cambridge University. Since then, she has travelled regularly in the region, writing travel guides to Iceland, Sweden, Denmark and Scandinavia, between climbing glaciers and cross-country skiing. Joan Gannij relocated to Amsterdam from the US and has been travelling to all Scandinavian countries ever since.

About Insight Guides

Insight Guides have more than 40 years' experience of publishing high-quality, visual travel guides. We produce 400 full-colour titles, in both print and digital form, covering more than 200 destinations across the globe, in a variety of formats to meet your different needs.

Insight Guides are written by local authors who use their on-the-ground experience to provide the

very latest information; their local expertise is evident in the extensive historical and cultural background features. All the reviews in **Insight Guides** are independent; we strive to maintain an impartial view. Our reviews are carefully selected to guide you to the best places to eat, go out and shop, so you can be confident that when we say a place is special, we really mean it.

INDEX

Main references are in bold type

INSIGHT GUIDES

INSPIRING YOUR NEXT ADVENTURE

Insight Guides offers you a range of travel guides
to match your needs. Whether you are looking for
inspiration for planning a trip, cultural information,
walks and tours, great listings, or practical advice, we
have a product to suit you.

Helsinki Metro

MELLUNMÄKI
MELLUNGSBACKA

Myllypuro
Kvambäcken

Kontula
Gårdsbacka

Sörnäinen
Skrnäs

Kaisaniemi
Fiskhamnen

Herttoniemi
Hertonäs

Kalasatama

Kaisaniemi
Kajsaniemi

Hakaniemi
Hagnäs

Kulosaari
Brändö

Siilitie
Igelkottsvägen

Itäkeskus
Östra centrum

Puotila
Botby gård

Rastila
Rastböle

VUOSAARI
NORDSJÖ

Kamppi
Kampen

Rautatientori
Järnvägstorget

RUOHOLAHTI
GRÄSVIKEN

Copenhagen

Copenhagen M

Vanløse
Flintholm
Lindevang
Fasanvej
Solbjerg
Frederiksberg
Forum
Nørreport
Kongens Nytorv
Christianshavn
Amagerbro
Lergravsparken
Øresund
Amager Strand
Femøren
Kastrup
Lufthavnen
Copenhagen Airport

Islands Brygge
DR Byen
Universitetet
Sundby
Bella Center
Ørestad
Vestamager
M1

M2

Copenhagen S-tog (S-train)

A Hillerød
Allerød
Birkerød
Holte
Virum
Sorgenfri
Lyngby
Jægersborg
Gentofte
Bernstorffsvej

C
Klampenborg
Ordrup
Charlottenlund

Hellerup
Svanemøllen
Nordhavn
Østerport
Nørreport
Vesterport
København H
Copenhagen
Central
Station

H B Farum
Værløse
Hareskov
Skovbrynet
Bagsværd
Stengården
Buddinge
Kildebakke
Vangede
Dyssegård
Emdrup
Ryparken

C H
Frederikssund
Ølstykke
Gl. Toftgrad
Stenløse
Veksø
Kildedal
Måløv
Ballerup
Malmparken
Skovlunde
Herlev
Husum
Islev
Jyllingevej
Vanløse
Flintholm
KB Hallen
Ålholm

Bispebjerg
Nørrebro
Fuglebakken
Grøndal
Peter Bangs Vej
Langgade
Valby
Enghave
Dybbølsbro

Bx

Bx
B
Høje Taastrup
Taastrup
Albertslund
Glostrup
Brøndbyøster
Rødovre
Hvidovre
Danshøj
Vigerslev Allé

Sydhavn
Sjælør
Ny Ellebjerg
Amarken
Friheden
Avedøre
Brøndby Strand
Vallensbæk
Ishøj
Hundige
Greve
Karlslunde
A Solrød Strand
Jersie
Ølby
Køge

- Interchange Station
- **A** (Solrød Strand) – Hundige – København H – Hillerød
- **B** Høje Taastrup – København H – Farum
- **Bx** Høje Taastrup – København H – Østerport
- **C** (Frederikssund) – Ballerup – København H – Klampenborg
- **E** Køge – København H – Holte
- **F** Ny Ellebjerg – Flintholm – Hellerup
- **H** Frederikssund – København H – Østerport – (Farum)

Stockholm Transport